Racism and Philosophy

RACISM AND PHILOSOPHY

EDITED BY
SUSAN E. BABBITT AND
SUE CAMPBELL

Cornell University Press

Ithaca and London

Permission has been granted to reprint the following essays:

Lucius T. Outlaw Jr. "On Race and Philosophy." From *On Race and Philosophy*,
by Dr. Lucius Outlaw. Reproduced by permission of Routledge, Inc. Copyright © 1996. An
earlier version of the essay appeared in vol. 18, no. 2, of the *Graduate Philosophy Journal*.

Charles W. Mills, "The Racial Polity." From *Blackness Visible: Essays on Philosophy and
Race*, by Charles W. Mills. Copyright © 1998 by Cornell University.

First published 1999 by Cornell University Press
First printing, Cornell Paperbacks, 1999

Printed in the United States of America

Library of Congress Cataloging-in-Publication Data

Racism and philosophy / edited by Susan E. Babbitt and Sue Campbell.
p.   cm.
Includes bibliographical references.
ISBN 0-8014-3502-1 (cloth : alk. paper). — ISBN 0-8014-8504-5 (paper : alk. paper)
1. Racism.   2. Philosophy.   I. Babbitt, Susan E.   II. Campbell, Sue.
HT1523.R255   1999
305.8—dc21   99-13358

Cloth printing   10   9   8   7   6   5   4   3   2   1
Paperback printing   10   9   8   7   6   5   4   3   2   1

Contents

III. Morality, Identities, and "Race"

Acknowledgments

Plans for *Racism and Philosophy* emerged out of a small, workshop-type conference in February 1996, at Queen's University at Kingston, Ontario, supported entirely by the John Milton Scott fund and the Philosophy Department at Queen's. We are grateful to the participants for making the journey and contributing to an intellectually and socially invigorating weekend. We would also like to thank those who traveled from Toronto, Ottawa, and Montreal for the conference, and to the faculty and students from across the campus who demonstrated their interest in the issues. Special thanks are in order to Haideh Moghissi for the inspiration for the event and for her important role in the discussions. The contributors to the volume, both those who attended the conference and those who submitted papers later, have been encouraging of the volume and patient with our inquiries, and we are very indebted to them for their hard work. We also thank Alison Shonkwiler and the editorial staff at Cornell University Press, especially Teresa Jesionowski and freelance editor Annie Barva. Maxine Wilson cheerfully helped us with formatting and printing the final version. Jan Sutherland and Jane Isaacs-Doyle were invaluable help in preparing the volume. We thank them both for the diligence and good humor with which they undertook bibliographic, editorial, and organizational work, and the grace with which they responded to eleventh-hour requests.

S. C.
S. E. B.

Introduction

> The ideological dependence on racialism is intact and, like its metaphysical
> existence, offers in historical, political and literary discourse a safe route
> into meditations on morality and ethics; a way of examining the mind-body
> dichotomy; a way of thinking about justice; a way of contemplating the
> modern world.
>
> —Toni Morrison, *Playing in the Dark:*
> *Whiteness and the Literary Imagination*

Racism must be of concern to all philosophers in all areas of philosophy. Racism is not just a topic for ethics and political philosophy. The existence of systemic racism—its consequences for the structures of the societies in which philosophy is done, as well as for how philosophy has been done and by whom—has deep implications for epistemology, metaphysics, philosophy of mind, and philosophical methodology.

The contributors to this volume attempt to identify and clarify important structures of meaning through which Western philosophy has both evaded acknowledgment of racism and has, at the same time, offered influential conceptual schemas that have helped produce the destructive racializations of contemporary society. In rethinking the implications of philosophical accounts of the social contract; the great chain of being; the idea of history; the liberal analysis of harm, of persons, and of rationality, this volume suggests that acknowledging the importance of racism can effectively inform the development of questions in all areas of philosophy.

There is an urgency to this task. Although Olufemi Taiwo and Nkiru Nzegwu point out that it is a mistake to understand racism uniquely in terms of a U.S. model, the racial situation of the United States has a particular significance for philosophy. One consequence of U.S. economic, military, and ideological power is that it is increasingly assumed that one philosophical world view has triumphed. Not only must philosophers understand the varied forms and expressions of racism, we must also come to grips with particular racial contexts in which certain philosophical understandings of human well-being, freedom, justice, authority, and individualism have arisen.

A second motivation for this volume is the idea that unless philosophy is taken seriously in interdisciplinary debates, important abstractions necessarily involved and presupposed in drawing political conclusions are left unexamined and will negatively affect those conclusions. It is frustrating to hear the complaint that philosophy is too abstract even though the arguments of those who reject philosophy draw uncritically on questionable philosophical assumptions about such important notions as objectivity, rationality, individualism, agency, contingency, truth, and essential properties. It has become almost trendy in the more politically motivated debates in a number of disciplines to reject and even mock abstract conceptual analyses although important conclusions are drawn precisely by presupposing some (unexamined) understanding of the same concepts whose philosophical analysis has been devalued.

Certain issues arising in interdisciplinary debates about racism suggest that philosophy should be taken more seriously: For example, in one popular line of criticism, scholars in the First World inadequately understand the Third World because of Western "knowledge production" (e.g., Chandra Talpade Mohanty, "Under Western Eyes: Feminist Scholarship and Colonial Discourses"). The idea that some accepted ways of dividing up the world distort the interpretation of empirical evidence has been important in feminist, antiracist, and development studies. This view, roughly, claims that research into the lives and experience of other cultures is guided by racist, imperialist categories that distort the reality of Third World people. An important answer to this problem is that analysis must be more particularized; in other words, it must start from alternative standpoints—say, of women. Yet for close to half a century, philosophers within the Anglo-American analytic tradition have been concerned with questions about acquiring understanding when interpretive categories are inadequate. Such questions are fundamental to the philosophy of science following the work of Russell Hanson and Thomas Kuhn, who point out that all observation and interpretation depend on background concepts and beliefs. When we consider the nature of knowledge more generally, it becomes clear that emphasis on particular experience is not in opposition to reliance on general categories. The political consequences of this philosophical insight for worries about dominant racist and imperialist conceptualizations are that more particularized sorts of storytelling must be accompanied by concern about the single story that explains those particular stories and how they are told.

Certainly, philosophers have not been as involved in interdisciplinary debates as they might. Philosophers have neglected the importance of race to discussions in ethics, political philosophy, epistemology, and moral psychology, as well as more broadly in considering the social responsibility of philosophy, its history, and its appropriate methodology. We believe that those who practice and teach philosophy have not been sufficiently committed to using and developing the discipline to advance debates of broad social and theoretical importance. Much contemporary philosophy arising from North American and European traditions has indeed been only narrowly philosophical, either in the sense of ignoring the interdisciplinary nature of race theory or in the deep and pernicious sense of merely attempting to abstract from history and context, including the context of philosophical theorizing.

One of the unifying and distinctive characteristics of the papers solicited for this volume is that the authors draw on empirical, historical, and sociological investigation, and on the work of both activists and theorists, while undertaking the task of identifying and explicating the central philosophical issues involved in or emerging from these investigations. All authors would deplore the too frequent restriction of philosophy to narrow "discipline immanent" debates (Lucius T. Outlaw Jr., *On Race and Philosophy*, 25). The volume also displays the fruitfulness of a variety of approaches in rethinking philosophy's obligations to critical race theory. The contributors not only bring a rich range of oppositional writings to their investigations, but maintain self-critical alliances with a number of philosophical traditions: feminist, Aristotelian, Marxist, analytic, existential, and phenomenological. The idea behind this volume is not to debunk philosophy by showing its complicity in the more dubious aspects of a dominant worldview. What it means to say, as Ruth Ginzberg does, that philosophy is "not a luxury," is to acknowledge philosophy's role in defining moral and human expectations and to try to make that role more explicit and responsible.

The first part of this volume, "Racism and the Practice of Philosophy," addresses questions about the implications of racism for the practice of philosophy. The essays by Charles W. Mills, Lewis R. Gordon and Lucius Outlaw Jr. provide substantive reflections on the intersection of philosophy and race. Each paper attends to the philosophical traditions that, in conjunction with the historical developments of Western modernity, have promoted and accommodated racism, and the authors utilize oppositional traditions to bring the complicity of philosophy into sharp relief.

In "The Racial Polity," Charles W. Mills demands a reconceptualization of political philosophy that acknowledges and theorizes race as the major organizing principle of a global white supremacy. Mills notes that although race has been all but ignored in political philosophy, it has been a central organizing category in global politics. To those who might suggest that philosophy is an abstract and normative enterprise and ought not to concern itself with the descriptions of actual political life, Mills first responds that it is a mistake to separate the descriptive from the normative. Political philosophy is concerned with how nations arise and how people are bound together, and an examination of race as a category that acts to group certain people together to the exclusion of others thus helps us better understand the deep structure of our political theories. Second, Mills argues that race has indeed played a significant role in the normative dimensions of political theory. Social contract theory, for instance, which substantively shapes modern liberalism, reached its full flower at the height of European colonial expansion. The theory contrasted the European man of reason, for whom liberty is the product of a contract between free and equal beings, to non-European savages or subpersons who cannot be a party to the contract, but who remain in a state of nature subject to domination and exploitation. Mills details the existence and structure of a global white supremacy through a comprehensive and energetic use of oppositional traditions in political theory that make evident political philosophy's evasion of race.

In "Fanon, Philosophy, and Racism," Lewis R. Gordon examines the racism of philosophy through a vigorous performative text that invokes Frantz Fanon's writings on the existential phenomenological dimensions of antiblack racism both as an embodiment of the tension between philosophy and antiracism and as an interrogative response. As is brutally evident in the texts of Hegel and Nietzsche, Western philosophers have excluded blacks from humanity, reason, history, and universality. With no "other," there is no grounds for a dialectical recognition of blacks as subjects; Fanon's work challenges and displaces the understanding of racism as a conflict between self and other with an account of the lived reality of antiblack racism. This lived experience is one of "perverse anonymity" in which blacks, as outside humanity and the symbolic order, are treated as a visible absence of human presence. Thus, contends Gordon, blacks are rendered invisible precisely through how they are seen. Moreover, because the black in antiblack racist reality is outside the symbolic order, Gordon maintains that those who are both black and philosophical risk a "performative contradiction." Fanon's pointed establishment of black subjectivity through and in the context of his theorizing must thus be seen as deeply ironical, as a "provocative demonstration by failure" that calls for a revolutionary response. Gordon's own use of irony invites Fanon's presence into this volume.

In "On Race and Philosophy," Lucius Outlaw Jr. critically engages a growing theoretical debate about the role of racial categorization in theory and politics. His essay explores the problem of preserving and valuing positive notions of race and ethnicity without slipping into racism and ethnocentrism. Outlaw thus positions himself against those who would argue that race is a dangerous fiction—scientifically invalid and inevitably pernicious. Drawing on the philosophical anthropology of W. E. B. Du Bois, Outlaw argues that racial and ethnic identities are best thought of as "social-natural" kinds that play a central role in how we define ourselves and in the meanings we attach to our heritage. These identities cannot be delegitimated in our attempts to bring about a just society. But if race and ethnicity are essential features of how we make sense of our lives, and if categories of race and ethnicity have been used to establish the dominators and the dominated, how can we rescue race and ethnicity from the legacy of uses to which they have been put? Outlaw begins this task by sketching the value of racial and ethnic identity, seeing them as processes and structures of meaning built upon some minimal, nonfixed set of biological features. The concept of a shared identity in virtue of race or ethnicity is a construction that serves to transfer meanings, skills, and values across generations, thus shaping identities and preserving life-worlds. Outlaw believes, however, that though different races and ethnies may have different life-worlds, there is no necessary path from difference to dominance. Philosophers have had considerable authority to rationalize and protect legitimated knowledges and in the past have contributed to the "pernicious racializations" that rank populations for exploitation. Outlaw urges us to contribute now to the understanding and valuing of the human processes of racialization and ethnicization and to help integrate that knowledge into the formation of a just polity.

Part 2, "Racism: Paradigms and Perspectives" addresses questions about the nature of both U.S. and colonial systemic racism and about what is involved in understanding and taking responsibility for it. Some claim that only white people can be racist and that antipathy of blacks towards white people is not racism. Others claim that no ethnic or racial group is immune from charges of racism. The essays by Lawrence Blum, Marilyn Friedman, and David Haekwon Kim offer competing views of racism in response to this public debate. The essays by Nkiru Nzegwu and Olufemi Taiwo direct our attention to colonial racism—which, as Nzegwu notes, theorists have failed to examine adequately. They have, instead, taken North American racism, with its emphasis on racial purity and its negrophobia, as standing for racism. Taiwo and Nzegwu call attention to the forms and legacies of colonial racism in West Africa and to the distorted and incomplete understanding of its distinctive character.

In "Moral Asymmetries in Racism," Blum focuses on individual racism and contends that the racial identities of both the target and the perpetrator of racism are factors that either mitigate or aggravate the degree of wrongness of a racist act. Blum rejects the view that only whites can be racist, insisting that any individual can exhibit the racial hatred or scorn that he considers to be the paradigm cases of racist acts. He also rejects the view that racist acts are of equal moral weight (i.e., "all racism is equal") considered independently of the identities of the target and perpetrator. According to Blum's analysis, the moral seriousness of racism against vulnerable groups cannot be established by making it the only type of racism, but it can be made evident if we compare types of racism to generate a more adequate taxonomy of the harms of racist actions. Each racist act against a member of a group vulnerable to a wider social pattern of racism may invoke both that pattern of racism and the historical legacy of oppression against that group. Such acts will tend to produce particular kinds of fear, self-doubt, and shame in their targets, which is often their intent. A comparable type of act in the absence of a wider social pattern of racism will not produce these harms. Blum thus constructs and defends a consequentialist taxonomy of the specific types of harms involved when the perpetrators of racism belong to socially dominant categories.

Marilyn Friedman challenges Blum's account. "Racism: Paradigms and Moral Appraisal (A Response to Blum)" begins by proposing that the wrongness of a racist act depends crucially on the pattern of racism it instantiates. Friedman thus contends that Blum's account relies on the wrong conceptual paradigm of a racist act. Blum holds that the moral seriousness of racist acts are intensified when they are directed at a person who belongs to a group that has a history of being the target of racism. Friedman breaks this view into two parts. First, there is the core moral wrong of racial hatred or scorn, and second, there are three features mentioned by Blum that intensify the moral wrong. Friedman charges that this paradigm isolates the racial hatred or scorn from patterns of racism. Moreover, she suggests that the meaning of racism is decentered by Blum's analysis, arguing that Blum's account gives rise to a standard of racism that doesn't seem bad enough to explain the moral seriousness of racism and that marginalizes the very kinds of racism—antiblack racism in the United States, for example—that for Friedman are paradigmatic. She agrees with much of Blum's contention that there is an asymmetry of harm in racist acts, but her shift in paradigm is meant to recalibrate our perspective. In her view, being vulnerable to dominant racism is an incomplete, less serious form of racism. Friedman then asks whether reactive racism—racial hatred or scorn provoked by being the target of the racist patterns of others—may, on occasion, have positive moral value.

In "Contempt and Ordinary Inequality," David Haekwon Kim's account of personal racism develops the analysis of racial scorn or contempt and offers an interesting contrast to Blum and Friedman's concerns. Kim concentrates directly on the emotional grounds of racist agency. Racism, he argues, is inevitably structured by a contempt matrix. He offers an account of contempt modeled on Aristotle's comprehensive framework for analyzing emotions, which gives equal regard to the phenomenology of emotion, its object directedness, and the evaluative grounds of emotional response. These grounds typically involve perspectives that reflect social norms; thus, emotional responses play a crucial role in configuring social relations. Working through examples, Kim defines *contempt* as a sense of offense toward an object or target in virtue of the perceived baseness of its qualities. Moreover, this baseness is regarded as potentially contagious and thus gives rise to the desire to distance oneself from the contemptible object, a distancing that guarantees both safety and superiority. Kim's analysis both highlights and comments on the informal segregation that persists in North America. Once again, our understanding of racism is redirected: a paradigm racist act, for Kim, is one of contemptuous distancing, and the shift in paradigm has interesting consequences. Acts of benevolence and concern can be structured by a contempt matrix and can therefore be racist, whereas animosity toward whites by those subject to the racism of whites is not any kind of racism.

"Colonial Racism: Sweeping out Africa with Mother Europe's Broom" explicitly contrasts New World racism with colonial racism in West Africa in order to condemn the misunderstandings and distortions of Africans' experience that result from using New World racism as an exemplar. Nkiru Nzegwu argues that New World racism, which operates through negrophobia and negation of the black body, cannot be and should not be used to understand the experience of Africans. In West Africa, Africans remained the source of meaning and value and regarded only white people as colored. Moreover, whiteness did not signify superiority; Africans regarded it as a sign of duplicity. Nevertheless, as Nzegwu demonstrates through a careful historical examination, the Asante did not debase Europeans or assign to them the subhuman status that Europeans assigned to Africans. Colonial racist narratives found their audience not in Africa, but in Europe as a justification for colonial exploitation. Nzegwu characterizes this distinctive racism as an invidious cultural racism that circulates through representing loyalty to Europe as a sign of modernization, but loyalty to Africa as "misguided, heathen, and anachronistic." Finally, she argues that transporting New World constructs of racism to explain Africa and Africans maintains and repeats colonial racism. To illustrate this claim, she engages Kwame Anthony Appiah's highly influential *In My Father's House* and calls to account its de-Africanization of Africa through its demonization and near erasure of African women.

In "Reading the Colonizer's Mind: Lord Lugard and the Philosophical Foundations of British Colonialism," Olufemi Taiwo offers a close analysis of the writings of Lord Lugard, one of the principal architects of British colonialism in West Africa, in order to challenge conventional views about the harm done to African societies by the supposed imposition of Western values. Taiwo argues that modernity was not meant to be an option for West African cultures; to the contrary, colonial administrators such as Lugard practiced and promoted a damaging "sociocryonics" (i.e., "the frozen preservation of outmoded and moribund social forms") antithetical to the principle of liberal modernity. Taiwo illustrates this sociocryonics by referring to Lugard's administrative principles and isolates its justificatory basis in Lugard's philosophical anthropology. Lugard was committed to a hierarchy of races, with Europeans at the top and Africans at the bottom as animals or savages. Lugard reasoned that savages were too far down the chain of being to benefit directly from the laws, justice, or education fit for Europeans, so incorporating these principles into colonial practice would thus be unsuccessful and lead to insolence. Taiwo characterizes the colonial relation between Europeans and Africans as indirect—mediated by outmoded, frozen, and partly contrived structures of native government, law, and education, many of which were already undergoing transformation.

Colonial racism thus did much of its damage in its very decision to leave indigenous populations "untouched."

In the last part, "Morality, Identities, and Race," the essays by Laurence
M. Thomas and Elizabeth V. Spelman involve consideration of how we relate to each other through structures of ethnicized and racialized difference in ways that keeps racism intact. The essays by Sue Campbell and
Susan E. Babbitt pursue the theme of identity raised in Spelman's essay, but
with a specific focus on the development of identities adequate to antiracist
commitments.

In "Split-Level Equality: Mixing Love and Equality," Laurence M.
Thomas challenges the strength of people's avowed commitments to equality. He points out that those who would rule out the relevance of ethnic preferences in the public sphere may privilege ethnicity as a matter of principle
in the private sphere. That is, we might all agree that it would be wrong to
deny someone a job if he or she is of a different race or ethnicity, but we
might all also agree that it is perfectly appropriate not to want to marry
someone of a different race or ethnicity. Like Kim, Thomas scrutinizes action that passes for permissible. He charges that our failure to subject our
private lives to the demands of equality is insupportable. If relations of
friendship and romance constitute some of the most important bonds in our
lives, and if these relations are protected from moral criticism in matters of
equality, then equality only matters to us in the sphere that is less important
to us—the public world. Moreover, our decisions in the public world are
framed through the values that we hold in our private lives. Thomas argues
that unless we seriously interrogate the privileging that we allow in our private lives, we cannot hope to address inequality in the public sphere.

In " 'Race' and the Labor of Identity," Elizabeth V. Spelman contends that
we must understand the construction of racial identity—particularly whiteness—materially and historically as the product of human labor extracted
from blacks and other nonwhite groups. She agrees with Outlaw that contemporary understandings of race as socially constructed are too often
facile. Her own engaged exploration of the meanings of construction locates
and exposes the paradoxical character of "innate white superiority." Drawing on writers such as James Baldwin and Judith Rollins, Spelman notes how
white identity is dependent not only upon commitment to black inferiority,
but also upon black affirmation of white superiority. Blacks are consistently
called upon to act in ways that attest to the inferiority of blacks to whites.
Spelman sees the work blacks are required to do as a kind of labor in a racial
economy, but it is labor that cannot be acknowledged, for to notice this labor and, moreover, to notice it as labor that is constantly demanded would
undermine the very idea of innate white superiority that the labor is meant
to support. Spelman characterizes the work required to maintain the fabric
of inequality as socially reproductive "shadow work"—work that must be
done, but that remains invisible. Conceiving of the network of social rela-

tions in economic terms reveals to us how wholly exploitative the racial economy is, for it requires blacks to work in order to prop up the value of white currency. Spelman's analysis also highlights the unstable and vulnerable value of white currency, as well as the bizarre, delusional existence of a supposedly innate superiority that requires constant affirmation by those very groups whites take to be innately inferior.

In "Dominant Identities and Settled Expectations," Sue Campbell examines the writing of southern author and activist Minnie Bruce Pratt to argue that in order to become antiracist, those groups with dominant social identities explicitly need to challenge the complex psychic/social nature of settled expectations of privilege. Recent constructivist theories present people as socially situated knowers who can undertake radical and politically liberatory kinds of self-change by altering the ways in which they are situated in the social world. Theorists such as Sandra Harding and Maria Lugones have offered models of political identity transformation based on the experiences of multiplicity and fragmentation common to "outsiders" to the dominant Western culture. Campbell argues that such models are not appropriate to those with dominant identities, who instead must find a way to transform the uniform and restricted perspective formed by settled expectations of privilege. As psychic habits, settled expectations are a perceptual map of dominance—determining what is attended to and what is excluded, as well as structuring and sustaining racist action. As social structures, settled expectations confer dominance through rights, properties, and entitlements that privilege whites and exclude others. Campbell concludes that those with dominant identities must take responsibility for both levels of exclusion and unsettle the expectations that structure dominance. As a deep shift in the self, this unsettling is an alternative model of identity transformation.

In "Moral Risk and Dark Waters," Susan E. Babbitt approaches identity change from an epistemic perspective, investigating the risks involved for those who take responsibility for their identities in circumstances of systemic injustice. Drawing on Claudia Card's work on moral risk, Babbitt explores Card's suggestion that to take responsibility for an identity is to commit oneself to creating new and adequate meanings for that identity. Babbitt argues that the person who undertakes such a project bears a complex burden of explanation that has three dimensions. First, one must reject not only the expectations of others about who one should be, but also the burden of explaining to others who one is or is trying to become. Second, to challenge and reject oppressive explanatory frameworks, one must often proceed without being able to fully articulate one's new understandings and reasons for acting. Babbitt draws on studies of theory construction in philosophy of science to show how metaphorical resources can support the perspectives necessary to new projects. Finally, there is the risk of becoming unintelligible if new meaning does not secure uptake, but Babbitt insists that new meaning emerges only through a committed and single-minded engagement with a certain direction of development, just as in science a commitment to a hypothesis tailors avenues of investigation, which yield new knowledge if successful. There is real moral danger, though, in the case of self-understanding: if the new direction of development will not yield adequate understanding, we do not have the option of comfortably returning to who we once were. Babbitt illustrates the necessary daring of pursuing an adequate identity through a reading of *Between Two Worlds (Muriel at Metropolitan)*, Miriam Tlali's novel of apartheid South Africa.

In his introduction to *The Mismeasure of Man*, Stephen Jay Gould refers to Socrates' suggestion that a stable society requires that its members be divided into social classes and that they be persuaded that such divisions are natural. Gould suggests that the difference between Socrates' tale of inherited biological differences and much intellectual racism of today is that Socrates knew that he was telling a lie. We hope that this volume shows, first, that philosophy can and must help to identify the lie and what it consists of; philosophy can and must examine what racism means and what is involved is resisting the lie. But we also hope to clarify philosophy's special role—which is, arguably, to explain how it is that we might not know we are telling such a lie and what this implies for who we are as human beings and how we get along. Philosophy can look at the more general views—of knowledge, of human nature, of justice—that might make it so difficult to see that there is a lie or that we can be unwittingly involved in promoting it. Some of this work has been done outside philosophy, admittedly, but we hope that this volume helps to invite respect for and interest in the more abstract philosophical work in epistemology, metaphysics, and philosophy of mind upon which many crucial political and ethical conclusions importantly depend.[1]

I RACISM AND THE PRACTICE OF PHILOSOPHY

I   *The Racial Polity*

CHARLES W. MILLS

A new paradigm is beginning to emerge across a variety of subjects, a paradigm that takes race, normative whiteness, and white supremacy
to be central to U.S. and indeed recent global history.[1] The rate of emergence
is by no means uniform—far advanced in cultural studies, retarded in other
areas such as political philosophy (unsurprisingly, considering that philosophy is one of the very "whitest" of the humanities)[2]—nor are the theoretical presuppositions always the same. If the latter feature is a prerequisite for
paradigmhood, therefore, one might want to speak more cautiously of an
"orientation" or a "perspective" instead.[3] Some authors draw on decon-
struction and discourse theory, on Derrida and Foucault. Others seek to
modify and update old-fashioned Marxist frameworks to give race an autonomy—and perhaps even a "material" status—not usually conceded to it
in more class-reductivist accounts. Still others would consider themselves
traditional liberals, though with a nontraditional appreciation of how racialized actual liberalism has been. And a few view themselves as working toward new theorizations that do not readily fit into any of the standard
metatheoretical taxonomies. What they all have in common, however, is that
they see race as central (though not foundational) and as sociopolitically
"constructed," thus distinguishing themselves from earlier theorists of race,
who usually took race to be a transhistorical biological essence and whose
assumptions were in fact often simply racist. A term originally associated
specifically with minority viewpoints in legal studies is now being used more
generally by some writers to refer to this new paradigm: *critical race theory.*[4]

For racial minorities and Third World scholars long interested in the theorization of race and Western domination, critical race theory is a welcome
development that provides them with a recognized academic space for work
previously regarded as marginal. The perspective holds out the prospect
of mounting a challenge to the conceptualizations of orthodox theory, a

States: Adressly Backwardness

challenge that will parallel the impressive achievements of several decades of feminist scholarship. My particular interest here is in that unfortunate area of backwardness, political philosophy. How does ostensibly raceless, but actually white First World political philosophy need to be rethought and transformed so as to formally incorporate race into its anatomies of the body politic—instead of, as at present, tacitly taking the white body as normative?

Comparison of Gender and Race Theory

White Western moral and political philosophers have had relatively little to say about race, even though race has constituted a central line of moral and political demarcation, of privilege and subordination in the global polity for hundreds of years. As Robert Blauner pointed out many years ago in his pioneering work on race and racism: "The colonial order in the modern world has been based on the dominance of white Westerners over non-Western people of color; racial oppression and the racial conflict to which it gives rise are endemic to it. . . . [I]n the United States, as elsewhere, it was a colonial experience that generated the lineup of ethnic and racial division. . . . [T]he colonial system brought into being races, from an array of distinct tribes and ethnic peoples" (*Racial Oppression in America*, 12–13). Yet First World political philosophy has not shown much interest in critically analyzing this historic system of domination or its contemporary legacy. A flurry of articles and books specifically about affirmative action were published in the 1970s and 1980s. In work essentially focused on other themes, there were and continue to be general declarations about the evils of discrimination. In philosophy, however, race remains conceptually and theoretically residual. The historic contradictions between European liberalism at home and conquest, slavery, and imperialism abroad, as well as the inconsistencies of a color-coded white egalitarianism in the United States that rests on nonwhite subordination, have received little systematic exploration in the discipline.

Historically little focus on race

Where gender is concerned, the picture is much brighter. In recent decades, there has been such a burgeoning of feminist scholarship in philosophy—articles, books, special journal issues, anthologies, series—that it now merits its own category, whereas scholarship on race (as against routine condemnations of racism) has yet to arrive. Thus, to cite one current reference work, Robert Goodin and Philip Pettit's nearly seven-hundred-page Blackwell *Companion to Contemporary Political Philosophy* (1993) has feminism as one of the six entries in the "major ideologies" section (along with anarchism, conservatism, liberalism, Marxism, socialism), but no entry on black nationalism or Pan-Africanism, for example.[5] Nor do such subjects or the related topics of race, racism, and white supremacy appear in the subsequent list of twenty-eight "special topics," though this list extends to such nontra-

Comparison of history Between gender - Race

ditional political topics as environmentalism and sociobiology. W. E. B. Du Bois and Frantz Fanon do not even make the index.

Thus, even though feminism is by no means completely respectable yet, it clearly represents a comparative success story in contrast to the silence about race. The revisionary feminist cartography—the redrawing of the map of the political so that what was formerly taken to be natural, personal, and unchanging becomes the object of political discourse—has shifted the terms of the debate. It has become possible to see male domination as political, and to categorize Plato and Aristotle, Hobbes and Rousseau, Locke and Marx, Rawls and Nozick as *male* theorists in a sense deeper than their mere possession of one kind of genitalia.

What I want to suggest is that feminist challenges to mainstream political philosophy may provide a useful model to follow in theorizing race, so let us examine the evolution of these challenges as they developed out of the "second wave" of feminism.[6] It is possible to distinguish at least three separate aspects of feminist theory—though in practice, of course, they are often found together.

First, there is the discovery, analysis, and critique of the sexism of the major figures of the canon. The aim is not muckraking for its own sake (though muckraking is not without its peculiar pleasures), but a demonstration of how deeply embedded in the tradition are assumptions of the naturalness and rightness of male domination. This discovery can be seen as a kind of cognitive awakening, the initially hesitant and then increasingly self-confident perception that this supposedly universalist tradition is not really speaking for "you." The problem is not that these canonical figures just happen to be male, but that their maleness enters into and seminally penetrates their theories, a conceptual DNA that reproduces a template of particular concerns, foci, values, and perspectives.

Second, there is the parallel enterprise of the excavation and rediscovery of oppositional political texts or fragments by women: Olympe de Gouges's "Declaration of the Rights of Woman and Citizen," Mary Wollstonecraft's *Vindication of the Rights of Woman*, Simone de Beauvoir's *Second Sex*. The aim is to demonstrate the existence of a tradition of resistance, a "usable past." This goal is important not merely on the symbolic level, but also because of the actual value of the substantive insights of past theorists. One finds in nascent or developed form contestations of male theory that later generations have been able to draw upon intellectually.

Finally, there is the attempt to develop new conceptions of the polity that make explicit, through the mapping of the full dimensions of female subordination, what would be required to incorporate women into the body politic on a basis of real moral equality. For some feminist theorists, these conceptions involve the reworking of distinctions within a traditional framework on the assumption that existing theory, when purified of its gender biases, can be adopted by women. For others, the problem is not merely that the application of the theories has been contingently sexist, but that the very way of looking at the world is necessarily corrupted by the exclusion of women's experiences and concerns. Thus, the innovation—coming originally from radical feminism and later being adopted more broadly—of reconceptualizing the polity as a patriarchy, a politico-economic system of male hierarchy and female subordination has to occur so that the political is extended to include the personal and so that the dynamics of gender relations (heterosexual intercourse, marriage, pornography, rape) emerge as political practices in need of theorization. Within this framework, the sexism of traditional male political thinkers can no longer be seen as merely contingent—embarrassing but conceptually insignificant prejudices to be quickly passed over while the rest of the theory remains intact—but as the organic ideational outcome of a structure founded on female subordination, which thus affects the character of the theories.

Can these feminist strategies for rethinking Western political philosophy be emulated by those of us who seek to theorize race and relations between the First World and Third World? I believe they can and that the differences between the subjects on some points should actually make the task of rethinking easier. The origins of patriarchy remain a subject of bitter dispute, but even if it is not traceable to the origin of the species, as radical feminists claim, it is obviously far older than white racial domination and arguably more foundationally embedded in human interrelations. Thus, in some respects at least, racism has been less taken for granted than sexism and so requires less work to be made conceptually visible. Moreover, the long struggle against racism and European domination has been documented amply, so a reconceptualization of orthodox political philosophy that takes this history into account is the task to be addressed.

As far as reexamination of the canon is concerned, there already exists a body of literature that constructs genealogies of racism[7] and analyzes the racist views of various famous philosophers, though it does not approach in volume and depth the body of feminist revisionism. Such research needs to be expanded. On the empirical level, what is needed is an equivalent to what was done for women many years ago—the putting together of an anthology collecting Western philosophers' statements on race and the non-European world.[8] On the theoretical level, what is required is a framework for situating such views and for showing that—at least in the modern period—they are not incidental, but rather are linked to a crystallizing sociopolitical system.

With respect to locating oppositional texts as both symbol and resource, theorists of race have the tremendous advantage of being able to draw on a long history of resistance movements and of work based on those movements: Native American resistance; the abolitionist and antisegregationist movements; slave narratives; nationalist and anticolonial struggles in Latin America, Asia, Africa, Australasia; and already articulated ideologies such as Pan-Africanism and *indigenismo*. When they map the political, Western political philosophers do not usually consider these writings, but this neglect is arguably because of the mapmakers' deficiencies rather than the writers'.

Finally, perhaps the most interesting point of differentiation is that those critical race theorists who seek a global reconceptualization of the polity that would correspond to the feminists' *patriarchy* already have a concept at hand, *white supremacy*. In order to name the system of male domination, feminist theorists who sought reconceptualization had to redefine an old term that once had quite a different meaning. But white supremacy, the domination of whites over nonwhites, was originally proclaimed quite openly and under that very name. In a sense, then, the initial work has already been done for those who find this approach useful. When the perspective shifts, however, the system will be negatively rather than positively valorized, the survival of white supremacy beyond its officially proclaimed demise will have to be demonstrated, and the mechanisms by which it sustains and reproduces itself will have to be mapped.

I suggest, then, that one possible strategy for developing critical race theory within political philosophy will be to self-consciously theorize a *racial polity*—in this case, a *white supremacist polity*—and to rethink the political around the axis of race.

Why are these questions of reconceptualization important for political philosophy? After all, in the orthodox Anglo-American analytic framework, political philosophy is usually represented as properly concerned only with normative claims rather than the factual claims of political science. But in the classical Western tradition, political philosophy has always sought to explain as well as to prescribe. Thus, Jean Hampton, invoking this tradition, rejects an exclusivist focus on normative questions and argues that political philosophy also seeks to "understand at the deepest level the foundations of states"—how political societies arise and how people in these societies are bound together. Matters of fact do legitimately enter the ambit of political philosophy, though usually at a higher level of abstraction than in political science. One needs, in Hampton's words, to go beyond mere "surface description" to excavate the sociopolitical "deep structures" that generate "not only forms of interaction that make certain kinds of [resource] distributions inevitable but also moral theories that justify those distributions" (*Political Philosophy*, xiii–xv).

And these factual questions (low-level empirical assertions or, more usually, abstract theoretical claims) will also almost always play some role in the normative disputes. Only rarely is there a factual consensus among political philosophers about the social picture, with the debate being purely about rival sets of values. Typically, there will be disagreement about what the facts are. And once there is any kind of radical normative challenge to mainstream political thought—as there is, famously, with Marxist and feminist theory— the clash of political philosophies usually reveals itself in the systematic *con-*

testation of the ostensibly neutral, "apolitical" empirical and theoretical assumptions that have hitherto framed and underwritten the debate. Different political philosophies will have different stories about the past and present of the polity, its origins and its workings, and these divergences will have implications for its moral assessment also.

Consider, for example, the minimal statement that "women are oppressed," which Alison Jaggar takes to be the common premise defining all feminisms, no matter what their other theoretical differences *(Feminist Politics and Human Nature)*. The claim is descriptive as well as normative. It makes a moral and political judgment about the situation of women predicated on an alternative to conservative accounts that would represent women's position as the result, say, of free and informed choice, innate cognitive deficiency, or natural sex roles. Different feminisms offer different accounts of the origins of this oppression; see class or gender or both in tandem as foundational; have rival perspectives on domestic labor, heterosexuality, rape, the market, the state, or male political theory. But in all cases, the findings of social theory and different views on those findings are indeed relevant to the normative enterprise. In the words of Jane Mansbridge and Susan Moller Okin, "Feminist theory . . . has one overarching goal—to understand, explain and challenge [men's systematic domination of women]" ("Feminism," 269). For feminist political philosophy, as noted, one theoretical key to conceptualizing this domination and developing this normative challenge is provided by the idea of patriarchy.

Diana Coole suggests, "It is the concept of patriarchy which marks the most distinctive and innovative contribution by feminism to political thought. . . . By using patriarchy as a descriptive term, all the interlocking structures which had been previously identified as constituents of sexual domination could be integrated" *(Women in Political Theory: From Ancient Misogyny to Contemporary Feminism*, 259). By bringing the household and all that comes with it—the family, sexual relations, the division of reproductive labor—into the realm of the political, feminists not only radically transform our mapping of that realm, but also give us an external metatheoretical vantage point from which to understand the previous (male) mapping. The sexism of the tradition is seen to be not at all contingent, but structurally related to the unnamed system of patriarchy that the tradition—whatever else it is doing at the moment—generally serves to rationalize, because male freedom and equality in the public sphere are overtly or tacitly predicated on female servitude and inequality in the private sphere. This "functionalist attitude" toward women pervades the assumptions of political theory (Susan Moller Okin, *Women in Western Political Thought*, 10). In this deep and interesting sense the theorizing is "male":"maleness" is a location in a system of power that generates a certain corresponding outlook, rather than just a characteristic set of chromosomes.

The point is, then, that a political philosophy necessarily involves factual (descriptive and theoretical) assumptions as well as normative claims about the polity, and if the former are not explicitly stated and highlighted as integral to the political philosophy, it is often simply because they are part of a conservative, background "common sense" that its proponents take for granted.

The Blackwell editors' inclusion of entries on economics, history, law, political science, and sociology in their philosophy collection shows that they recognize this descriptive dimension of their subject. But as one would expect, these entries are no more neutral and politically disengaged than the listing of major ideologies. The economics and history of imperialism, colonialism, slavery—the law, politics, and sociology of imperial rule, white settler states, Jim Crow, apartheid, racial polities—make no appearance in the collection, either. The "whiteness" of the text—of this vision of what political philosophy is and is not—inheres not in the "biological" whiteness of (the vast majority of) the authors, but in the political whiteness and Eurocentrism of the *outlook*, one that takes for granted the truth of a certain account of world history and the centrality and representativeness of the European experience to that history. The pattern of exclusion is thereby complete, the theoretical circle closed. Given such a framework, it is hardly surprising that issues of race and Western domination are mentioned in neither the political philosophy nor the special subjects sections and that a political reference work produced in the last decade of the twentieth century can make next to no reference to the political issues that have for several hundred years engaged the majority of the planet's population.

Determining the cartography of the political is therefore itself a political act, insofar as it demarcates what is judged political, worthy of theoretical attention, central, interesting, and perhaps subject to a transformational human causality from what is dismissed as apolitical, residual, marginal, uninteresting, naturally ordained. *What* one views the polity as, *how* one sees it working, *which* of its features one takes to be most crucial, *why* one includes certain phenomena and excludes others are all organically related to one's orthodox or radical conceptualization. Correspondingly, reconceptualizing the polity can be a radical, even revolutionary undertaking because it names differently; it identifies different ontologies and alternative categorizations; it brings to light connections unknown or ignored; it offers different spatial and temporal maps; it privileges a subordinated set of experiences; it raises different questions; it points factual and evaluational inquiry in different directions. From the perspective of race, one can then see the events of the past few hundred years as bringing into existence a polity of a kind not described by Plato or Aristotle, Hobbes or Rousseau, Locke or Marx, Rawls or Nozick. It is thus unsurprising that the political philosophies of these writers, at least in their unmodified form, are of limited use in theorizing this "other" polity. The name of this polity is *white supremacy*, a political structure both global and national.

Race as a Global System and Modern Western Political Philosophy

Let us begin, appropriately, at the global level. Far from being new, the idea of race as a global system can be found practically at the inception of the oppositional black tradition. The pioneering Pan-Africanist Martin Delany complained in the mid-nineteenth century that though "there are two colored persons for each White man in the world . . . the White race dominates the colored" (quoted in Immanuel Geiss, *The Pan-African Movement: A History of Pan-African in America, Europe, and Africa*, 164). Half a century later, W. E. B. Du Bois's appeal "To the Nations of the World" at the Pan-African Conference in 1900 described the global problem of "the color line, the question as to how far differences of race . . . are going to be made, hereafter, the basis of denying to over half the world the right of sharing to their utmost ability the opportunities and privileges of modern civilisation" ("To the Nations of the World," in David Levering Lewis, ed., *W. E. B. Du Bois: A Reader*, 639). In our time, Frantz Fanon observed that "it is evident that what parcels out the world is to begin with the fact of belonging to or not belonging to a given race" (*The Wretched of the Earth*, 40).

Radical black and colonial intellectuals have always seen race in international terms as a set of relations to be understood not merely locally—in the particular setting of the Caribbean or the United States or Africa—but as the global outcome of a historic process of European imperialism, settlement, and colonialism. Whereas the white left has tended to treat race as an epiphenomenon of class domination, one finds in the work of black Marxists such as C. L. R. James a repudiation of both class-reductionistic Marxism and foundationalist racial essentialism: "The race question is subsidiary to the class question in politics, and to think of imperialism in terms of race is disastrous. But to neglect the racial factor as merely incidental [is] an error only less grave than to make it fundamental" (*The Black Jacobins: Toussaint L'Ouverture and the San Domingo Revolution*, 283). I take this statement as an assertion that race is both real and nonfoundational—that it is, in the contemporary vocabulary, "constructed" and that this construction, resulting as it does from European imperialism, is global.

Thus, Gary Okihiro talks about the emergence of "transnational identities of white and nonwhite" linked to "a global racial formation that complemented and buttressed the economic and political world-system," thereby "transcend[ing] national boundaries" (*Margins and Mainstreams: Asians in American History and Culture*, 129–33). Similarly, Paul Gilroy argues for the notion of a "black Atlantic," an "intercultural and transnational formation" that reflects the reality that Pan-Africanism and Black Power signified resistance to "a hemispheric order of racial domination" (*The Black Atlantic: Modernity and Double Consciousness*, ix, 17, 27). There is no world government as such, so one cannot speak of a global polity in that formal sense, but there is a set of *transnational* relations of domination that transcend the First World nation-state and for which race is the bearer. These relations are not merely internal—between colonizers and aborigines, slavemasters and slaves—but global, between one continent and the others, between European civilization and non-European barbarism, so one *can* speak of a "virtual" planetary polity. From the modern period onward, with the simultaneous domestic emergence of liberalism and the external expansion of Europe, pronouncements on race and the non-European world thus became theoretically significant because they had to be seen in the context of this crystallizing racial world system. Transactions of an economic, cultural, moral, and even metaphysical kind linked the European and non-European and contributed to making them both what they are.

Economically, wealth is extracted through the seizure of bullion and the expropriation of land by means of slavery and colonial labor. "[W]hiteness is ownership of the earth," comments Du Bois acerbically ("The Souls of White Folk," *Du Bois: A Reader*, 454). As Eric Williams argued half a century ago in his work on capitalism and slavery, and as numerous Third World and some renegade First World scholars have argued since, the profits from conquest, the slave trade, and colonial exploitation were to a greater or lesser extent crucial in enabling the European takeoff now misleadingly known as "the European miracle." [9] In Jim Blaut's words, the rise of Europe has been represented as resulting "essentially, from historical forces generated within Europe itself" (*Colonizer's Model of the World: Geographical Diffusionism and Eurocentric History*, 59). Correspondingly, cultural myths of origin have represented Europe as self-sufficient, autochthonous, with the contribution of Afro-Asia written out of the history books. "There never was a civilized nation of any other complexion than white," boasts Hume. [10] Ancient Greece becomes a self-contained fountainhead of wisdom, removed from its actual origins and influences, and its Enlightened heirs go out into the world as historied and cultured Europeans encountering peoples without history and culture. [11] Progress, liberalism, and Enlightenment for those peoples on the home continent morally rest on color-coded principles that turn out to be somewhat less applicable to those peoples from other continents. "The slave-trade and slavery were the economic basis of the French Revolution," points out James (*Black Jacobins*, 47). Finally, the planet as a whole is tectonically divided by a racial metaphysic that partitions persons from subpersons, linked by a reciprocating ontological engine. "[T]here was virtual unanimity that subject races should be ruled, that they *are* subject races. . . . [This assumption was] buttressed by a cultural discourse relegating and confining the non-European to a secondary racial, cultural, ontological status. Yet this secondariness is, paradoxically, essential to the primariness of the European," observes Edward Said (*Culture and Imperialism*, 53–59). Thus, white Lockean, Kantian, Millian persons who own themselves and their efficient nature-appropriating labor—who are rational noumenal other-respecting beings, individuals whose freedoms must be guaranteed by the modernist liberal state—emerge not merely in contrast to but to a certain extent on the backs of nonwhite subpersons thousands of miles away, whose self-ownership is qualified and whose labor is inefficient, whose phenomenal traits limit their rationality and consequent moral autonomy, and for whom, accordingly, slavery and despotic colonial rule are appropriate. As Paul Gilroy concludes, conquest, colonialism, and African slavery must then be seen not as the "special property" of nonwhites, but rather as *"internal"* to the West, integral to European modernity, "part of the ethical and intellectual heritage of the West as a whole" (Black Atlantic, 49, 9 [emphasis in original], 7). In certain respects, the real political system is global.

As with gender, then, this reconceptualization of race provides a framework for illuminating and explaining the silences, evasions, misrepresentations, and double standards of (most of) the important figures of modern Western political theory. These phenomena can appropriately be seen not as marginal deviations uninteresting to a later and (supposedly) more sophisticated audience but as part of the general project of justifying the global white racial polity and the exploitation of the rest of the planet for the benefit of Europeans at home and abroad. Locating First World thought within the context of the consolidation and reproduction of this system then puts us in the metatheoretical position of being able to track how the dominant theories, central concepts, and crucial moves of Western political philosophy are in general shaped by (and shape) the overall European project. Essentially, a racialization is manifest both in the explicit derogation of nonwhites and in the appearance of a dichotomous logic that restricts the principles of liberalism to domestic European space or to its implantation as civilized outposts in non-European space.

Consider social contract theory, classically seen (Hobbes aside) as the main vehicle by which European liberalism challenged absolutism. Contractarianism grounds the polity on the consent of free and equal human beings. The basic apparatus is simple: a presociopolitical condition (the "state of nature"); abstract "men" residing in this condition; a normative background of natural law; a voluntary decision to bring into existence society and the state; the institution of the constitutionalist sovereign and the corollary creation of *political* "men." The writings of the four most important contract theorists—Hobbes, Locke, Rousseau, and Kant—cover the period usually judged to be the golden age of contract theory, 1650–1800 (*Leviathan* [1651] to *The Metaphysics of Morals* [1797]). But this century and a half of the emergence of Western liberalism—from the seventeenth-century English "Glorious Revolution" to the eighteenth-century U.S. and French revolutions—coincides with the period of modern (rather than feudal Spanish and Portuguese) European expansionism. So even though the men who make the social contract are equal (bourgeois) persons rather than members of ascriptive feudal estates, they cannot be raceless; *they are, in effect, white men.*[12] "Wildness" and "savagery" are innate and necessary for non-Europeans, but external and contingent for Europeans (if they ever were in that state in the first place).

The racialization of the contractarian apparatus thus manifests itself in the following assumptions: a presociopolitical state of nature that is real and permanent for nonwhites but either hypothetical or just temporary (and in any case long past and not usually that bad) for whites; "men" who are by no means abstract, but coextensive with "white men" as against "savages"; a normative moral background that only whites are fully capable of recognizing; a decision to bring the polis into existence that whites are the only ones qualified (strong version) or at least the ones best qualified (weaker version) to make; and the institution of a governmental and legal system that either is necessarily white because white men are the only ones who can be political men (strong version) or is at least the superior system that others need to emulate (weaker version). Because the realm of the political is reserved for those who are capable of leaving the state of nature to create political/civil society, nonwhites who are savages (as in the white settler state) are then permanently nonpolitical ("wild," even if superficially tamed and civilized). If they are to enter the polity, they can do so only through the intervention of the political beings, the whites, who then have the responsibility of speaking for them and of ruling over them via the white sovereign. As James Tully summarizes this process:

> In the stages view of human history, all cultures and peoples are mapped hierarchically in accordance with their location on a historical process of progressive development. European constitutional nation states, with their distinctive institutions and cultures of manners and civility, are at the highest and most developed or improved stage. . . . [T]he modern constitution and its associated concepts are defined in contrast to what Michel-Rolph Trouillot calls "the savage slot," which is filled by the non-European "other" who is defined as lower in development and earlier in time: in a state of nature, primitive, rude, savage, traditional or underdeveloped, depending on the theorist. . . . The founding of a modern European constitution and the existence of modern European political institutions are used to define sovereignty and so to dispossess the Aboriginal nations of their equal status. . . . The legitimacy of European settlement and dispossession was assured. (*Strange Multiplicity: Constitutionalism in an Age of Diversity*, 64–65, 78–79)

Contract theory seemed to have expired by the end of the eighteenth century, partly in response to utilitarian and historicist critiques. But as with assumptions about gender, the broader framework of metatheoretical political assumptions about race is independent of any particular contractarian or anticontractarian commitment. Hume, the proto-utilitarian and critic of the contract endorses polygenesis and judges "negroes and in general all other species of men" to be "naturally inferior to the whites" (quoted in Immanuel Chukwudi Eze, ed., *Race and the Enlightenment: A Reader*, 33). John Stuart Mill, spokesman for individualism and the need for personal autonomy, excludes "barbarians" from the scope of his famous antipaternalist "harm principle" and recommends "despotism" for them (*On Liberty; with the Subjection of Women; and Chapters on Socialism*, 13–14). The most famous historical philosopher of the nineteenth century, Hegel, denies that sub-Saharan Africa has any history and suggests that blacks were actually morally improved through the experience of slavery (*The Philosophy of History*, introduction).

So although there are some laudable exceptions, the overall record of the philosophical tradition as a whole is one of complicity with the establishment of the global racial system. To make a point that should be obvious, but is often unappreciated: opposition to the ill treatment of indigenes is not the same thing as opposition to European expansionism itself. One can sincerely condemn cruelty to people viewed as less than equal, but nevertheless continue to think of them as less than equal. Insofar as European racial superiority is taken for granted by Western theorists—insofar as the colonization, expropriation, and settlement of the world are seen as legitimate—these theorists are apologists for the establishment of global white supremacy, however they may differ on the particular forms it should take and on how humanely nonwhites should be treated. To the extent that their political philosophies—and the adaptation of these philosophies to the exigencies of the states created by European expansionism—take nonwhite inferiority as natural and nonpolitical or as political and justifiable, they are broadly committed to the creation and perpetuation of the racial polity, a polity that generally subordinates nonwhites to the interests of whites.

The United States as a Racial Polity

Let us turn now from the informal global racial polity to a formal local one, the United States. One might expect that in a nation founded as a "white man's country," where white domination has been ramified in the legal system and in the moral and sociopolitical universe, race would be dealt with systematically and given the centrality it deserves. But these expectations would, at least until recently, have been disappointed. The best-known treatment—by an establishment scholar—of white supremacy under that explicit name is by a historian, George Fredrickson and, though very valuable, is an empirical rather than a theoretical work (*White Supremacy: A Comparative Study in American and South African History*). In mainstream theory, the term *white supremacy* does not appear, except perhaps in reference to the distant past. One has to turn to maverick writings by marginal black and minority thinkers or a few leftist white scholars to get a theorization of

the architecture of white domination. Globally, a pattern of neglect and evasion in sociopolitical theory in the United States has afflicted even the more
empirically oriented disciplines of sociology and political science.

In sociology, whether in the influential 1920s Chicago school of Robert
Park or in the postwar "melting pot" model discussed by Nathan Glazer and
Daniel Moynihan, the tendency has been optimistically assimilationist.[13]
Often, race has been blurred into ethnicity, with the qualitative distinctions between the nineteenth-century immigration and integration of (white)
European-Americans and the exclusionary subordination of (red/black/
brown/yellow) non-European Americans being ignored or played down.
Racism has been conceptualized as individual prejudice, a hangover from
premodern ("caste") assumptions; attributed to ignorance, lack of education, or a certain ("authoritarian") personality type; and expected to disappear with modernization. It has not been seen, as it should be, as the ideological correlate of a fundamental organizing principle of the *modern*
Euro-implanted social order. Correspondingly, the analysis of racism as a
whole is usually confined to the level of attitudes and ideas. Summing up this
literature, David Wellman concludes, "with few exceptions, social scientists
studying racism as prejudice do not consider racial division as a form of
stratification built into the structure of [American] society. In this view the
roots of racial division are not located in the structure of the division of labor or in the organization of political power. . . . The primacy of race as an
aspect of social structure in America is not recognized" (*Portraits of White
Racism*, 39). White Marxists, who would ideologically be more sympathetic
to structural analyses, have generally reduced race to class; black scholars
who favored such accounts—for example, Du Bois *(Black Reconstruction
in America 1860–1880)* or St. Clair Drake and Horace Cayton *(Black Metropolis: A Study of Negro Life in a Northern City)* were marginalized.

In political science, there has been a similar and indeed not theoretically
unrelated pattern. As two black political scientists, Michael Dawson and
Ernest Wilson commented some years ago, "while the place of race in the
practice of American politics is, arguably, quite central . . . the place of race
in the *study* of American politics is surprisingly peripheral" ("Paradigms and
Paradoxes: Political Science and African-American Politics," 189, emphasis
in original). Rogers Smith argues that the explanation for this silence is that
from the time of Alexis de Tocqueville, analysts of the U.S. social order have
been most struck by the absence in the New World of the ascriptive hierarchies of the Old World ("Beyond Tocqueville, Myrdal, and Hartz: The
Multiple Traditions in America"). Operating with the transplanted categories of European sociopolitical theory, which counterpose liberal egalitarianism to feudal status, these commentators have seen the United States as a
paradigmatic incarnation of the democratic dream of freedom and equality.
Themselves white, inhabiting a white discursive universe, they have characteristically treated the massive exclusions of race—Native American expro-

priation, African slavery, Mexican annexation, anti-Chinese discrimination, post-World War I non-"Nordic" immigration restrictions, World War II Japanese internment, general nonwhite subordination—as marginal, minor inconsistencies in a tradition somehow essentially still inclusive and colorblind.

Hence, a long series of distinguished writers (Alexis de Tocqueville, Gunnar Myrdal, Louis Hartz) has presented a "whiggish narrative" in which the (supposed) "anomalies" of systemic, juridically backed, and morally and theoretically rationalized discrimination would eventually disappear as part of the teleological working out of the universalist promise of the founding documents. "For over 80% of U.S. history, its laws declared most of the world's population to be ineligible for full American citizenship solely because of their race, original nationality, or gender," Smith notes. Yet mainstream "anomaly" theorists see no need to explain "why the exclusionary policies that have prevailed during most of U.S. history should be identified as 'exceptions' (however 'huge') to its ideals" and not as rival norms ("Beyond Tocqueville," 549, 557).

It should be unsurprising, then, that if such cognitive myopia has been possible even in practitioners of what are supposed to be empirical disciplines, their noses pressed to the world's facticity, the room for evasion has been even greater in philosophy, traditionally regarded as inhabiting the realm of the nonempirical, the abstract, and the otherworldly. In neither of the two important U.S. political philosophical works that originally staked out the spectrum of respectable political debate—John Rawls's *A Theory of Justice* (1971) and Robert Nozick's *Anarchy, State, and Utopia* (1974)—do U.S. slavery and U.S. white supremacy and what is correspondingly necessary to correct for their legacy figure in more than a marginal way. Rawls's decision to locate himself on the terrain of "ideal theory" generates a hypothetical contractarianism in which the implications of the racial exclusions of the original U.S. "contract" are not confronted, and Nozick's idealized Lockeanism ignores (except in an endnote) the real-life history of illicit aboriginal expropriation and property in stolen African persons (*Anarchy*, chap. 7, n. 2). Nor has this evasion of race changed dramatically in the intervening years. Race is abstracted even more thoroughly out of the philosophical models of the polity than out of their political science counterparts, reproducing the silences and lacunae of European theory.

Bringing race into U.S. political philosophy, then—or, more accurately, recognizing the ways in which the typical conceptualizations of white U.S. political philosophy *already* embed and encode race in a particular evasive way and so need to be rethought—would mean beginning from a different, more realistic starting point. The notion of a New World "fragment" of an idealized European nation-state[14] would be, if not displaced altogether, at least contextualized in the global and local relations of racial power typically minimized in mainstream political conception. It would mean drawing on recent (and older) revisionist work in history, political science, sociology, legal theory, and cultural studies that recognize how the invention of the white race, starting from the invasion of America, created a "Herrenvolk democracy" (Pierre van den Berghe, *Race and Racism*, 18), a white republic in which whites are the ruling race (James Oakes, *The Ruling Race: A History of American Slaveholders*). The wages of whiteness motivate the color-based division of the polity into two nations so that in the moral sphere of right and wrong, whiteness itself is property to be duly protected by the racial state[15] in this racialized universe of white *Recht*. Above all, it would mean rejecting orthodox frameworks and explicitly trying to work out the internal logic of a racial polity. Here is where political philosophy plays its distinctive explanatory role, abstracting away from the surface contingencies of party politics and parliamentary dispute (the terrain of political science) in order to articulate concepts that elucidate Hampton's "deep structures," the underlying struts and girders that make the polity what it is.

Both mainstream/liberal and oppositional/Marxist political theory have been conceptually inadequate in the theorization of race and racism. For orthodox liberalism, as I have briefly sketched, the United States is basically an egalitarian liberal democracy (though with a few admitted flaws), and racism is "prejudice" scheduled to disappear with enlightenment. For orthodox Marxism, the United States is basically a class society; race is unreal and ideal, attributable to the instrumentalist manipulations of the bourgeoisie to divide the innocent workers, and is thus scheduled to disappear with class struggle. In both cases, therefore, race is essentially external and ideational, a matter of attitudes and prejudicial misconceptions—having no essential link with the construction of the self, civic identity, significant sociopolitical actors, systemic structural privilege and subordination, racial economic exploitation, or state protection. In neither theory is there an adequate conceptual recognition of the significance of race as sociopolitical group identity.

In the alternative view on race (sometimes characterized as the "symbiosis" view), which is long established in the black radical political tradition, the orthodox liberal picture of deviations, aberrations, and anomalies is upended.[16] The nation's founding is placed in the demystified context of the European invasion and the conquest of America, in the course of which the earlier religious/medieval categorization of the enemy ("heathens") is gradually secularized into race (Francis Jennings, *The Invasion of America: Indians, Colonialism, and the Cant of Conquest*). In effect, the subtext already present in the work of classic contractarians is elevated by the Founders into the text so that a distinction is made between political white men and apolitical nonwhite savages. George Fredrickson emphasizes that "liberal conceptions of polity and citizenship were originally based on the tacit assumption that 'the people' being provided with 'equal rights' were citizens of a culturally and racially homogeneous national community. . . . In the minds of most white Americans of the pre-Civil War era an invisible color qualification appeared between 'all' and 'men' in the [Declaration] (*Black Liberation: A Comparative History of Black Ideologies in the United States and South Africa*, 15)." The contract is thus a racial one, a contract between civilized whites, producing a white republic from which the "merciless Indian Savages" of the Declaration and the 60-percent-person black slaves of the Constitution are legitimately excluded. As Richard Delgado points out, critical race theory begins with the simple but politically revolutionary insight "that racism is normal, not aberrant, in American society" (*Critical Race Theory: The Cutting Edge*, xiv).

Race thus emerges as *central* to the polity of the United States. Instead of counterposing an abstract liberalism to a deviant racism, we should conceptualize them as interpenetrating and transforming each other, generating a racial liberalism. The result is a universe of white right, white *Recht*, a white moral and legal equality reciprocally linked to a nonwhite inequality. At the heart of the system from its inception, this relationship between persons and racial subpersons has produced the "Herrenvolk democracy" in which whites are the ruling race. Thus, as Herbert Blumer argues, racism should be understood not as "a set of feelings" but as "a sense of group position" in which the dominant race is convinced of its superiority, sees the subordinate race as "intrinsically different and alien," has proprietary feelings about its "privilege and advantage," and fears encroachment on these prerogatives ("Race Prejudice as a Sense of Group Position," 3–4). Race and white supremacy are therefore seen primarily as a system of advantage and disadvantage, but only secondarily as a set of ideas and values. The individualist ontology is displaced or at least supplemented by a social ontology in which races are significant sociopolitical actors. The ontology here is not "deep" in the traditional metaphysical sense of being necessary and transhistorical. It is a created, contingent ontology—the "white race" is *invented* (Theodore W. Allen, *The Invention of the White Race, vol. 1, Racial Oppression and Social Control*)—and in another, parallel universe, it might not have existed at all. But it *is* deep in the sense that it shapes one's being, one's cognition, one's experience in the world: it generates a *racial* self. Biologically fictitious, race becomes socially real so that people are "made" and make themselves black and white, learn to see themselves as black and white, are treated as black and white, and are motivated by considerations arising out of these two group identities (Ian F. Haney López, "The Social Construction of Race," 191–203). Perceived "racial" group interests (not self-interest)—"racial" interests—become the prime determinants of sociopolitical attitudes and behavior.[17]

Race, then, becomes the most important thing about the citizens of such a polity, for it is because of race that one does or does not count as a full person—as someone entitled to settle, to expropriate, to be free, or as someone destined to be removed, to be expropriated, to be enslaved. As white, one is a citizen; as nonwhite, one is an anticitizen. The two are interdefined. "Whites exist as a category of people subject to a double negative: they are those who are not non-White," summarizes Ian Haney López ("White by Law," 547). And because race is intersubjectively constructed, so that its boundaries are more volatile than those of class or gender, battles will be fought over race and how people should be officially raced (Haney López, *White by Law: The Legal Construction of Race*). Whites whose family trees have unacknowledged roots will be terrified of losing their civic whiteness; borderline European immigrants such as the Irish will fight to have themselves categorized as white; some blacks favored by the genetic lottery will seek to pass temporarily or permanently into the white citizenry.[18] The content and boundaries of whiteness will be shifting, politicized, the subject of negotiation and conflict, fought out in everyday cultural practices and given official canonization in national narratives (histories, novels, movies) of racial superiority, exclusion, and purity.[19] Moreover, the racing of humanness implies that these political struggles will have an ontological dimension not present in European mappings—a politics of personhood. Invisible humans unrecognized in the racial polity, blacks will also be engaged in a metaphysical contestation with whites whose own personhood is predicated *on* nonwhite, particularly black, subpersonhood so that the seemingly simple declaration on a civil rights protester's placard that "I AM A MAN" is itself a threat to the ground rules of the racial order.[20]

But the bottom line, the ultimate payoff from structuring the polity around a racial axis, is what Du Bois once called "the wages of whiteness." Particularly in the United States—usually viewed as a Lockean polity, a polity of proprietors—whiteness is *property*, differential entitlement, as Derrick Bell, Cheryl Harris, George Lipsitz, and others have pointed out.[21] The racial polity is by definition exploitative. Whiteness is not merely full personhood, first-class citizenship, ownership of the aesthetically normative body, membership in the recognized culture; it is also material benefit, entitlement to differential moral and legal and social treatment, and differential rational expectations of economic success. For a Herrenvolk Lockeanism, whites' full self-ownership translates not merely into proprietorship of their own bodies and labor but also into a share in the benefits resulting from the *qualified* self-ownership of the nonwhite population. The racial contract between whites is in effect an agreement to divide among themselves (as common white property) the proceeds of nonwhite subordination.

Thus, the society is characterized by an ongoing "exploitation," whose conceptualization needs no controversial Marxist notions of surplus value because such exploitation should be considered wrong by quite conventional (nonracial) liberal bourgeois standards. From slavery, federal land grants, and the homesteading of the West, through differential access to education, job opportunities, white markets, union membership, equal wages, and equal chances of promotion, chances to ghettoization, restrictive covenants, redlining, white flight, and differential allocation of resources to schools and neighborhoods, whites have historically been materially advantaged over nonwhites, particularly blacks.[22] In their examination of the huge discrepancy between black and white wealth, Melvin Oliver and Thomas Shapiro point out, "Practically, every circumstance of bias and discrimination against blacks has produced a circumstance and opportunity of positive gain for whites" (*Black Wealth/White Wealth: A New Perspective on Racial Inequality*, 51). Or in the vivid phrase of Henry Louis Taylor Jr., "the black job ceiling has been the floor of white opportunity" ("The Hidden Face of Racism," 397). The failure to see white supremacy as a politico-economic system has blocked apprehension of this global picture. Liberals and Marxists, imprisoned in their individualist and class categories, are in general unwilling to focus on how the white population as a whole has benefited (though unequally) from nonwhite subordination.[23]

Moreover, even when the overtly discriminatory patterns of the past have disappeared, the legacy of these practices continues so that the system is reproduced even with no racist intent. If employment and housing discrimination were to end tomorrow, for example, the fate of blacks in the United States would still be negatively affected for decades to come by the simple fact that they were, through discriminatory federal housing policy from the 1930s onward, "locked out of the greatest mass-based opportunity for wealth accumulation in American history"—the chance to buy their own home (Oliver and Shapiro, *Black Wealth*, 18). As a result, the wealth of the median black household is less than one-tenth the wealth of the median white household, so that Oliver and Shapiro can speak of a "sedimentation" of racial inequality, a structural perpetuation of group disadvantage.

Insofar as whites go along with a racially structured system that privileges them, they can be said to be complicit with it, giving a racialized tacit consent to the racial polity and indeed usually actively supporting it by their choices, by their resistance to change. Nor has the state been a detached bystander to this process. Whether through its original contribution to "making race" in the first place, its acceptance of the imposition of post-Reconstruction segregation, or its current failure to take the necessary measures to correct fully for the institutionalized discrimination of the past, the liberal-democratic *Rechtsstaat* of an ideal Lockean or Kantian liberalism, acting to protect the property and rights of its abstract citizens, functions here as the racial state, acting to protect differential white entitlement.[24]

Thus, a hundred years after the *Plessy v. Ferguson* decision was rendered, cities in the United States are more segregated now than they were then. One in three young black men is in prison, on parole, or on probation; "underclass" problems are seen as intractable; biologically determinist theories of race are making a comeback; and a white backlash is virtually ubiquitous. Racial polarization of attitudes is as bad as it has been for decades; race has emerged as "a single profound line of cleavage" in U.S. society, creating "divisions more notable than any other in American life," by reference to which "differences by class or gender or religion or any other social characteristic are diminutive by comparison. (Donald Kinder and Lynn Sanders, *Divided by Color: Racial Politics and Democratic Ideals*, 34, 252, 287).[25] Liberal and Marxist prognoses on the disappearance of race have been spectacularly disconfirmed, but within white political philosophy, the adequacy of the basic global political categories has still not been questioned.

Amnesiac about the history and significance of European imperialism and colonialism in shaping the modern world, disadvantaged by a conceptual apparatus inherited from officially "raceless" European theory, and blinded by its aprioristic commitment to seeing the United States as simply a flawed liberal democracy, white political philosophy has generally been hampered in its theorizations of the system, global and local. Racial exclusion, its long history ignored, has been accommodated by the categories of deviation and anomaly instead of being seen, as it should be, as *normative*, central to the system, and traceable to the European expansionist project. Although the fact, if not the complete extent of racism in the history of the West is now grudgingly admitted, the theoretical realization of its full significance is blocked by the categories of orthodox conceptual frameworks. A start toward the necessary reconceptualization of political philosophy, a start toward bringing race into the world of mainstream theory and toward bringing mainstream theory, accordingly, into the real raced world, will be the act of naming: the formal recognition of white supremacy—the racial polity—as a political system in itself.

2 *Fanon, Philosophy, and Racism*

LEWIS R. GORDON

> Only for the white is the Other perceived on the level of the body image, absolutely as the not-self—that is, the unidentifiable, the unassimilable. For the black, as we have shown, historical and economic realities come into the picture.
>
> —Frantz Fanon, *Peau noire, masques blancs*

> At times, this Manichaeism goes to its logical conclusion and dehumanizes the colonized, or, to speak plainly, it turns them into animals. In fact, the terms the settler uses when he mentions the colonized are zoological terms.
>
> —Frantz Fanon, *Les damnés de la terre*

> They issue orders without providing information.
>
> —Toni Morrison, *The Bluest Eye*

> "Ordered you?" he said. "He *ordered* you. Dammit, white folk are always giving orders, it's a habit with them. Why didn't you make an excuse? . . . My God, boy! You're black and living in the South—did you forget how to lie? . . . Why, the dumbest black bastard in the cotton patch knows that the only way to please a white man is to tell him a lie! What kind of education are you getting around here?"
>
> —Ralph Ellison, *Invisible Man*

The objective of this volume is to theorize the intersection of philosophy and racism. Such a task calls for a marked break from past misconceptions of the nature of philosophy and the nature of race and racism. Philosophy, it is often believed, is not of the world, whereas problems of race and racism are firmly rooted in the most tenuous of worlds, the social world.

What could possibly be philosophical about problems of race and racism?

To that query, philosophers in the field of critical race theory can respond: What isn't racist about philosophy?

Or perhaps worse, given racism's well-rooted place in the modern and contemporary worlds, how can we be certain that racism doesn't ultimately render much of modern and contemporary philosophy serious to the foolish and irrelevant to the wise? [1]

I find myself in an awkward position when I raise these questions. After all, I am a philosopher. I am also a critical race and liberation theorist. I consequently face the risk of a performative contradiction if I take too skeptical a stand. Yet, as a philosopher committed to a conception of philosophy that is ultimately a form of radical critique, I need consider these questions with all the gravity they occasion. How are theorists such as I—black and philosophical in theoretical orientation—situated by such questions?

In a session of a course I taught on Africana existentialism, I recall discussing passages on blacks from the work of G. W. F. Hegel and Friedrich Nietzsche. Not a pretty affair. Consider the following passages from Hegel's *Philosophy of History*:

> The peculiarly African character is difficult to comprehend, for the very reason that in reference to it, we must quite give up the principle which naturally accompanies all *our* ideas—the category of Universality. In Negro life the characteristic point is the fact that consciousness has not yet attained to the realization of any substantial objective existence—as, for example, God, or Law—in which the interest of man's volition is involved and in which he realizes his own being. . . . The Negro, as already observed, exhibits the natural man in his completely wild and untamed state. We must lay aside all thought of reverence and morality—all that we call feeling—if we would rightly comprehend him; there is nothing harmonious with humanity to be found in this type of character. (93)
>
> But from the fact that [among Negroes] man is regarded as the Highest, it follows that he has no respect for himself; for only with the consciousness of a Higher Being does he reach a point of view which inspires him with real reverence. For if arbitrary choice is the absolute, the only substantial objectivity that is realized, the mind cannot in such be conscious of any Universality. The Negroes indulge, therefore, that perfect *contempt* for humanity, which in its bearing on Justice and Morality is the fundamental characteristic of the race. (95)

From these considerations in the text's introduction, Hegel concludes:

> At this point we leave Africa, not to mention it again. For it is no historical part of the World; it has no movement or development to exhibit. Historical movement in it—that is in its northern part—belong to the Asiatic or European World. Carthage displayed there an important transitory phase of civilization; but, as a Phoenician colony, it belongs to Asia. Egypt will be considered in reference to the passage of the human mind from its Eastern to its Western phase, but it does not belong to the African Spirit. What we properly under-

stand by Africa, is the Unhistorical, Undeveloped Spirit, still involved in the conditions of mere nature, and which had to be presented here only as on the threshold of the World's History. (99)

Hegel has ironically done us a great service. He has clarified some themes of racist theory by embodying those themes so well in his thought. One of those themes is rooted in the relationship of History to universality. History, with a capital H, is universal and marches a course toward absolute self-realization. White people are universal, it is said, and black people are not. A people's greater universality or their greater particularity is contingent upon their closeness to whiteness in the former and their distance from blackness in the latter. "Colored" people of the Asiatic varieties have periodic appearances on the Historical stage, having at times stood below universality, but not to the point of being without relevance to the charted course of universality. Beyond universality and particularity, however, are the nonhuman zones of, at most, human similitude. In those zones, there is no History. In classical Aristotelian logic, the syllogistic divide between universality and particularity is as follows:

(a) Universal Affirmative   (b) Universal Negative
   (All Xs are Ys)   (No Xs are Ys)
(c) Particular Affirmative   (d) Particular Negative
   (Some Xs are Y)   (Some Xs are not Ys)

The logic is familiar. A particular negative *(d)* is the contradiction of a universal affirmative *(a)* To refute the statement that "All Xs are Ys," one need only show that at least one X is not a Y. And for the universal negative claim *(b)* that "No Xs are Ys," one need only show a particular affirmative *(c)*, that at least one X is a Y. Universal affirmatives and universal negatives are each other's contraries, and the particulars relate to their correlated universals as subalterns. Thus, the particular of *(a)* is *(c)*, and the particular of *(b)* is *(d)*. Note also that if the universal categories, the contraries, are both false, it doesn't follow that the particulars are false. Some trees are not green is true in a world in which it is false to claim that all trees are green and that no trees are green.

If, for Hegel, History is a universal affirmative embodiment of world spirit (which is Western European), his judgment on Asiatic civilization becomes one of a universal to its subaltern. His claim is, however, stronger than a regional or cultural claim, which is why he made sure to distinguish the cultural genesis of the northern regions of Africa. He is, in fact, talking about blacks, and Africa south of the Sahara is being considered a nadir zone because of its concentration of blacks. Europe or the Occident is here read, then, as white, with its "other" being the Orient and its neither-other-nor-self zone being "below," "southward," "dark," and eventually "black." The black is left to stand as either Europe's contradiction or its contrary. A problem with central and southern Africa's being Europe's contradiction is that they would stand as only an instance of world spirit that is not European. Hegel's claim, however, is that the truth of world spirit can only be embodied in the European, so the (black) African contradiction must be false. If there is not at least one case of a black embodiment of universality, then in Hegel's system, the (black) African stands also as Europe's contrary. The divide between the worlds is therefore not one of Being and less-Being, but instead one of Being and *no-Being*. Its divide is absolute. It is a divide between Being and Nothingness.

Because Eurocentric History (here capitalized to signify its centrism) supposedly emerges on the level of the universal, blackness or *the Black* (*le Noir*), as Frantz Fanon would say, is locked in a pit of *ahistoricity*. One would think that being ahistorical would mean that blacks could claim at least another form of universality, a universality not conditioned by the relativism of historicism; however, as we shall see, when it comes to racism, it is the nature of the beast to be not only perverse and cruel, but also ironic. The black's ahistoricity is ironically conditioned by History. Thus, even Hegel's declaration of there being no History in "black Africa" (an ascription with a drama of its own) was, unbeknown to many black Africans, one of their historical moments.[2] Because Hegel's "no History there" was, as we have seen, an antithetical *Keindasein* (no being there), it facilitated a consciousness of black Africa as a humanless place, a place without God, and hence, a place below and without humanity. On that basis, all the rest—namely, the stereotypes about blacks—was granted.

Nietzsche, thick browed and thick mustached and utterly in love with the notion of aristocratic values, provides a conclusion to the dialectic. Why should whites condescend to engagement with blacks in a struggle for recognition? Would not a collision of claims to universality with one's potential equals make more sense, as in the case of, say, whites of lower social and class status? For Nietzsche, blacks are, in the final analysis, irrelevant.[3]

Here we have two Manichaean points of relevance and irrelevance that place blacks in a peculiar relation to philosophy. Named after the Persian Mani, "the Apostle of God," Manichaeism is the doctrine that espouses a world of "objective," material good and evil.[4] In a Manichaean world, there are physically evil objects, physically evil "things." From such a perspective, there are also people who are materially good and others who are materially evil—not because of their actions and deeds but because of *who or what they are*. Existential philosophers refer to this attitude as the spirit of seriousness. It is the value system in which values are regarded as material conditions of the world . In such a world, notions of physical purity are paramount and must be maintained at all costs. Thus, bringing blacks "in" is like miscegenation in that it subverts philosophical purity and relevance, whereas keeping blacks "out" maintains those dimensions of philosophy.

Here, there is a rigid ontological divide between being and nonbeing, and in the manifestation of both in the evaluation of reason, nonreason, and un-reason. Fanon puts this attitude another way: when blacks walk in the door, Reason walks out.

If our project is the exploration of philosophy and critical race theory as compatible projects, the obvious concern that emerges is the classical theo-retical problem of defining our terms. Much of what can be done hinges upon what we mean by *philosophy* and by *critical race theory*. Although philosophy and critical race theory have been developed by many theo-rists—from the European "giants" and the classic Africana liberation theo-rists Wilhelm Amo, David Walker, Maria Stewart, Martin Delany, Edward Blyden, Alexander Crummell, and Anna Julia Cooper of the eighteenth and nineteenth centuries, to such twentieth-century luminaries as W. E. B. Du Bois, Alain Locke, Léopold Senghor, Amilcar Cabral, C. L. R. James, and Sylvia Wynter—the rest of my discussion focuses on the exploration of this question of reason and unreason as it manifests itself in a particular dimen-sion of the work of perhaps the twentieth-century's greatest critical race and liberation theorist: Frantz Fanon.

Fanon was an explosion in the philosophical study of race and racism. His thoughts and deeds manifested a full-scale war against the forces of oppres-sion. We can summarize his position on racism by his deceptively simple for-mulation of racism as fundamentally misanthropic. He writes in *Peau noire, masques blancs*:

> All forms of exploitation resemble each other. They all seek their necessity in some decree of a Biblical order. All forms of exploitation are identical because they are all applied against the same "object": man. When one tries to examine the structure of this or that form of exploitation on an abstract level, one masks the major problem, the fundamental problem, which is to restore man to his proper place. (71)[5]

We see from this passage that Fanon's normative position is a form of exis-tential humanism. His call for the "restoration" of humanity makes his ex-istential humanism a form of *revolutionary* existential humanism. Restora-tion is here full of irony, for Fanon would have nothing to do with what humanity may have been, but with what humanity ought to be and possibly could become. It is a restoration of what has never been. It is to struggle to-ward a new kind of future. For him, the Rousseauian remark of a humanity in chains is a lived reality, and the demand for a freedom achieved by greater *humanization* is a lived obligation of every human individual.[6]

Fanon was born on the island of Martinique in 1925, the same year in which, farther north, Malcolm Little—who was to become El-Haji Malik El-Shabazz, better known as Malcolm X—was born. Like Malcolm X, Fanon was a restless spirit. Like Malcolm, his struggle with himself and with others against the dehumanization of his fellow human being took him across three continents, into the hearts of many devotees, and against the grain of many enemies. Both were actively engaged in liberation struggles. Both focused much of their energy on Arabic culture—Islam in Malcolm's case, the Algerian struggle in Fanon's. Unlike Malcolm, however, Fanon was not assassinated, although many attempts were made, and the circumstances of his death suggest pernicious forces at work. He died in Bethesda, Maryland, from leukemia-related pneumonia, which he contracted when CIA agents held him for questioning for ten days without treatment. Fanon had an interesting life that has been embellished in several biographical texts, including a recent film by Isaac Julien.[7] Because my concern is with his contribution to the philosophical study of race, racism, and colonialism, I will not say more about his biography here.

To illustrate Fanon's significance to the philosophical study of race and racism, consider what the "discourse" on colonial and racial oppression was before he came on the scene. That situation was much like a Trinidadian story of an Anglican clergyman inspecting an Anglican school for boys. Entering the school's corridors, he encountered a little boy who regarded himself as minding his own business. The clergyman decided to seek some fruits of the queen's labors. "Young man," he asked the little boy, "could you tell me who knocked down the walls of Jericho?"

Our young man thought for a moment and gave what he considered an appropriate response to authority. "Not me."

The clergyman became outraged. "Who is your teacher?" he demanded.

"Mr. Smith, sir."

He dragged the boy to Mr. Smith's room, burst in, and asked, "Are you Mr. Smith?"

"I am, sir."

"Well, Mr. Smith, I just asked this boy who knocked down the walls of Jericho, and do you know what he told me?"

Mr. Smith became perplexed. He looked at the boy and then at the clergyman. "No, sir. What did he tell you?"

"He told me he didn't do it."

Mr. Smith got up slowly. He took off his glasses and looked at the boy and then at the clergyman. "I've known this boy throughout the time he has attended this school, sir. He is a boy of good parentage. If he says he didn't knock down the wall, then he didn't do it."

The clergyman then dragged the boy, followed by Mr. Smith, to the headmaster (principal) and complained, "I asked this boy who knocked down the walls of Jericho, and he told me he didn't do it. Then I asked his teacher, and you know what he told me? He said the boy didn't do it!"

The headmaster, dark-skinned and proud, a stern and fair fellow, stood up. His eyes met the eyes of the frightened little boy and then the concerned teacher's. "Father," he declared, "Mr. Smith has worked here for more than

ten years. I've known him for a longer time than that. He is a man of great
integrity. If he has vouched for the boy, I see no reason not to stand by him."

The clergyman then decided to appeal to "higher authorities." After a
few heated moments on the telephone, he got the office of the minister of
education.

"Hello. I am at the Anglican school. I've asked repeatedly, but nobody
here can tell me who knocked down the walls of Jericho."

"Just one moment," answered the minister of education. "I'll put you on
to Buildings and Water Works. . . ."

Philosophical encounters with racism have for some time now functioned
like an Anglican minister in a colonial school. Its modern epistemological dimensions have been such that its messengers have tended to ask questions
without an appreciation for context, and the questioned are often those who
feel as though they are perpetually on trial. By the time Fanon came along,
there was a shift in inquiry. We see this shift when he writes, "From all sides
tens and hundreds of pages assail me and impose themselves on me. Still, a
single line would be enough. Supply a single answer and the black problem
will lose its seriousness. What do human beings want? What do blacks
want?" (*Peau noire*, 5–6). This passage reveals a provocative challenge to
the intersection of philosophy and racism, for in raising the question of desire—of a point of view of those who raise the question—Fanon also raises
the matter of black subjectivity. But black subjectivity is an ironic proposal,
for there is, after all, a structural humanity that challenges the formation of
what blacks want. The structural humanity is that universal spoken of earlier—the universal that lays claim not only to what human beings really
want, but also to what counts as really human.

"What do blacks want?"

A black philosopher taps away at the keyboard while a white plumber
is busy in the bathroom working on the toilet in the philosopher's drab
old apartment. (Strange class dynamics here, given U.S. folklore on race
and class that demand a reversal of roles.) The plumber decides to pass time
with some small talk. He notices a pile of papers on the floor by the philosopher's computer and asks him what he is working on. The philosopher,
regarding himself as organically rooted with working-class sensibilities,
tells him that it is a book on antiblack racism. After exchanging a few words,
the plumber's face tightens as he lets out, with an irritated huff: "What do
blacks *want?*"

Does he *really* want to know? Listen to Jean-Paul Sartre: "When you removed the gag that was keeping these black mouths shut, what were you
hoping for? That they would sing you praises? Did you think that when they
raised themselves up again, you would read adoration in the eyes of these
that our fathers had forced to bend down to the very ground?" ("Black Orpheus," 291).[8] Indeed, what do black people want?

Fanon asked the question, but in his typical penchant for irony, he ultimately put the question on its head; in Fanon, whose colonized person recognizes the need for "replacement," for the last's becoming the first, there is ultimately no point pursuing *that* issue of desire because the question itself is rhetorical and therefore requires the revolutionary recognition and response: "Not what you, whoever you are on top, the first, are willing to give up."

We are now experiencing a period of heightened attention on Fanon's work. The standard description of this development is that it is a "resurgence" in Fanon studies. In my research on Fanon scholarship, however, I've noticed a steady stream of articles and books since the early 1960s. The list of articles and substantial sections of monographs and anthologies in political theory and Africana studies has also made a sizable bibliography of secondary material.[9]

The secondary literature reveals that Fanon studies have undergone five stages of development. The first stage—occasioned by such strange bedfellows as Albert Camus, Jean-Paul Sartre, Simone de Beauvoir, Huey Newton, Hannah Arendt, and Jack Woddis—was primarily reactionary: both Fanon and his thought were either monsters or saviors.[10] Inaugurated by Renate Zahar's *Kolonialismus und Entfremdung: Zur politischen Theorie Frantz Fanons*, published in Frankfurt am Main in 1969, the second stage focuses on Fanon's significance for political theory. That stage was in full bloom by the mid-1970s, with excellent work by such theorists as C. L. R. James, Pietro Clemente, Ato Sekyi-Otu, and Emmanuel Hansen, and it has remained influential to the present.[11] The third stage—set in motion by David Caute, Peter Geismar, and Irene Gendzier—is Fanon as good biography. His life as a revolutionary who conversed with the foremost African, French, Cuban, and African American intellectuals of his day provides much informative and "sexy" material for anyone interested in twentieth-century intellectual and political history. In addition, he was an attractive, irascible, complex, courageous personality, the stuff that makes great biography. The fourth stage has accompanied the emergence of postcolonial studies in the *academy*. Although dominated by the work of people such as Edward Said, Neal Lazarus, Benita Parry, Homi Bhabha, and Abdhul JanMohamed, the most influential metatheoretical text on this period is an essay by Henry Louis Gates Jr. entitled "Critical Fanonism." This stage is marked by the peculiar absence of monographical studies on Fanon and, among some of its adherents, a peculiar absence of memory and at times clear hostility to the historical-racial reality signified by Fanon and his politics—in other words, by his *blackness* and his revolutionary commitments. In this stage, Fanon as text emerges in the midst of a derision, except for in the work of Said, Parry, JanMohamed, and Lazarus, which are perhaps the most in line with much of Fanon's thought regarding liberation theory and praxis.

The more unfortunate side of this turn is perhaps best illustrated by an account I received of a three-day workshop on Fanon conducted at the Uni-

versity of Chicago by Homi Bhabha and his adherents. The presenters were
East Indian, Middle Eastern, and white. The audience consisted of college
instructors, many of whom were black. Bhabha opened his talk with a quip
that he was known for being abstruse, so he wouldn't disappoint his audience by being otherwise. When he was asked by a member of the audience
to relate Fanon's relevance to the experience of blacks in the United States,
his response was that it wasn't his area of interest. That East Indians, Middle
Easterners, and whites were on the panel wasn't the problem. The outrage
was the absence of the black dynamic, whether in representation or thought.

Many black philosophers, sociologists, and literary theorists who do
work on Fanon in the United States would have perhaps told Bhabha, as I
know I would have, that what they have to say on identity issues, which are
Bhabha's "interest," may be highly relevant. I suspect, however, that the exclusion of blacks may have been connected to the current climate of treating
black participation as intrusion. Blacks might make the identity waters
murky with talk of racism and struggles for liberation. Or, what has become
a popular refrain, discussions of racism must learn to go beyond the black-
white dynamic. We also find that when many writers who dominate the
postcolonial stage of Fanon studies raise issues of liberation and blackness,
they often raise them *against* Fanon and other black liberation theorists by
reconstructing them as essentially misogynous and homophobic.[12]

It is an irony of postcolonial studies that perhaps no group is more alienated from its developments than black people—the very people from whose
history, experiences, and bodies a thinker like Fanon emerged.

Then there is the current stage. This stage, which also had its roots in the
mid-1980s, consists of engagements with Fanon's ideas in a multitude of
fields. The first major work of this period is Hussein Abdilahi Bulhan's
Frantz Fanon and the Psychology of Oppression (1985). Bulhan not only
discusses Fanon's life and work, but also pursues their implications for
the problem of developing a social psychology of liberation. Adele Jinadu's
Fanon: In Search of the African Revolution (1986) and Tsenay Serequeberhan's *The Hermeneutics of African Philosophy* (1994) are also worth mentioning in this regard, for they explore the relevance of Fanon's *ideas* for the
project of an African revolution. In the 1995–97 period, however, there was
an explosion of work. My book, *Fanon and the Crisis of European Man*, appeared in the fall of 1995 and in a way signaled the beginning of a new
stream of literature. T. Denean Sharpley-Whiting, Renée T. White, and I
have edited *Fanon: A Critical Reader* (1996), a work that presents the first
collective philosophical effort in Fanon studies from a variety of disciplinary
perspectives (philosophy, literature, and the social sciences). This anthology
was followed by Alan Read's *The Fact of Blackness* (1996), a volume that
focuses on cultural studies and film representations of Fanon; Ato Sekyi-
Otu's beautifully written *Fanon's Dialectic of Experience* (1996); T. Denean
Sharpley-Whiting's critical engagement, *Fanon and Feminisms* (1997); Syl-

via Wynter's discussions of Fanon's sociogenic turn and its relevance in the struggle to forge new conceptions of life; and Paget Henry's stream of important articles on the relevance of Fanon's thought for the development of Afro-Caribbean philosophy.[13] And then there are the many texts to come, including Nigel Gibson's *Rethinking Fanon* and *Beyond Manichaeanism*. Again, the primary feature of this period is that it engages with Fanon's ideas rather than comments on Fanon himself.[14] It focuses on the usefulness of Fanon's ideas.[15]

Now, the reader may wonder why a short statement on the literature of Fanon studies precedes my discussion of Fanon's contribution to the study of philosophy and racism. It is because in these stages we can observe the routes usually taken by any thought-provoking theory and consequently by critical race theory. Critical race theory first responded to reactionary views of its *critical* positioning of race matters. It then undertook overtly political explorations of race—explorations usually rooted in sociology and public policy—and then shifted to biographical or "experiential" accounts of race and racism. From there, it turned to metatheoretical questions of the Kantian form: How might a critical theory of race and racism be possible? Immanuel Kant, we may recall, changed the course of Western philosophy by raising the question of how synthetic knowledge without prior experience is possible. Similarly, critical race theory began to focus its critique on its own metatheoretical assumptions. We can consider this dimension to be the positive outcome of the turn to postcolonial theory. And finally, there is the point of simply doing theoretical work, where a response to the previous question is performative, where its assessments are left to emerge from its practice . In Fanon's biography and thought, we find a portrait of the study of philosophy and racism in all of its dimensions. Moreover, in Fanon, at least for our topic, we have the dramatic edge of his being not only a psychiatrist and revolutionary, but also a social theorist and philosopher.[16] He embodies the tension between the universal and the particular in a profound way. Consider the following disjunction of the question regarding philosophy and racism: Fanon *or* Kant, Hegel, Marx, Nietzsche, Heidegger, Dewey, Wittgenstein, Sartre, Foucault, Derrida? Except for Marx and Sartre, explorations on philosophy and racism lead to Fanon through a classic disjunctive syllogism.[17] Many thinkers have explored racism, and many thinkers have explored philosophy, but the treatment of philosophy *and* racism as a conjunctive analysis calls for Fanon as it does for no other.[18]

What do we find in Fanon's work?

In Fanon we find an arsenal of criticisms of three fundamental assumptions of Western philosophical attitudes toward the study of racism: (1) that racism is irrational, (2) that modern Western human sciences can present a rigorous portrait of racism, and (3) that racism is a conflict between the self and the other. These assumptions explode from three of Fanon's theoretical advances: the sociogenic dimension of racism (and of all forms of oppression that appeal to a conception of human nature), the existential reality of oppression, and the phobogenic dimension of antiblack racism. These theoretical advances emerge through a phenomenological consideration that governs antiblack reality: the *epidermal schema*. On the epidermal schema, Fanon writes:

> An unusual clumsiness came upon me. The real world contested my place. In the white world the man of color encounters difficulties in the assimilation of his bodily schema. Consciousness of the body is a uniquely negating activity. It is a third-person consciousness. . . . Then the bodily schema, attacked from several points, collapses and gives way to a racial epidermal schema. In the train, it is no longer a matter of knowledge of my body in the third person, but in a triple person. In the train, instead of one, I am left with two, three places. (*Peau noire*, 89–90)

Fanon here describes what can be called, in phenomenological language, a form of perverted anonymity. To be anonymous means literally to be nameless. Namelessness is a commonplace feature of the way in which we each move through the social world. Our fellow human beings—as Alfred Schutz, Merleau-Ponty, and Maurice Natanson have observed—pass by us, and at times they say hello to us as nameless types, people of definite description with an inner life-world of mystery: the cashier handing us our change, the student hurrying to class, the unfortunate stranger whose hat was blown off on a cold, windy day, the attractive man or woman who gave us a smile. Our ancestors and our descendants, whom Schutz called our predecessors and successors, are part of this anonymity. Think of the joy of finding dusty letters in the attic, messages that give us a glimpse beyond the named Namelessness of old black-and-white pictures, or of the archaeologist's shock in finding ancient graffiti and pornographic sculptures and paintings in ancient temples. And our successors? Well, in them we find a profound level of anonymity—neither named nor understood beyond the fact that they will or, in more skeptical times, may one day exist.

Fanon is not, however, concerned primarily with these forms of anonymity. He is concerned with forms of anonymity that constitute forms of closure in which the epidermal schema plays an ironic game of cat and mouse. These are *perverse* forms of anonymity. In such cases, social relations are saturated with bad faith; they manifest an opposing rationality. Things become what they are based on what they are not, and they become what they are not based on what they are. The black is invisible because of how the black is "seen." The black is not heard because of how the black is "heard." The black is not felt because of how the black "feels." For the black, there is the perversity of "seen invisibility," a form of "absent presence." How is this possible?

I have argued elsewhere that seen invisibility or absent presence is possible through a form of believing what one does not wholly believe. This phenomenon is bad faith, which manifests itself in convincing ourselves of the nonhumanity of others and of ourselves. In ordinary anonymity, the human being is a form of presented invisibility. Part of what it means to be human is to be beyond, though not without—one's "outside." It is, as Merleau-Ponty has observed, to have an "other side" of one's body *(The Visible and the Invisible: Followed by Working Notes)*. Thus, typical human encounters always involve a presumption of transphenomenal experience: there is always more about the human other that each of us could learn. With antiblack encounters, however, the mystery or riddle of blackness is a function of its supposed worthlessness. Hegel's rejection of black Africa could, after all, be translated as "Es gibt kein Geist dort" (There is no Spirit there). Fanon summarizes the matter this way: "For Hegel there is reciprocity; here [with the enslavement of black Africans] the master mocks the consciousness of the slave. He doesn't want recognition from the slave but work" *(Peau noire*, 179, note 9). The correlate is what the farmer wants from the ox. Frederick Douglass clearly articulated this form of consciousness when he wrote:

> In a very short time after I went to live in Baltimore, my old master's youngest son Richard died; and in about three years and six months after his death, my old master, Captain Anthony, died, leaving only his son, Andrew, and daughter, Lucretia, to share his estate. . . . Cut off unexpectedly, he left no will as to the disposal of his property. It was therefore necessary to have a valuation of the property, that it might be equally divided between Mrs. Lucretia and Master Andrew. I was immediately sent for, to be valued with the other property. . . . We were all ranked together at the valuation. Men and women, old and young, married and single, were ranked with horses, sheep, and swine. There were horses and men, cattle and women, pigs and children, all holding the same rank in the scale of being, and were all subjected to the same narrow examination. Silvery-headed age and sprightly youth, maids and matrons, had to undergo the same indelicate inspection. At this moment, I saw more clearly than ever the brutalizing effects of slavery upon both slave and slaveholder. *(Narrative of the Life of Frederick Douglass, an American Slave*, 59–60)[19]

The epidermal schema represents a perverse reality of a denied "inside" to the life of the black. The antiblack racist regards the black world as a world of "surfaces." Listen to Fanon:

> I am overdetermined from outside. I am not the slave of the "idea" that others have of me but of my appearance. I move slowly through the world, accustomed to aspiring no longer to appear. I proceed by crawling. Already the white looks, the only true looks, are dissecting me. I am *fixed*. Having prepared their microtome, they slice away objectively pieces of my reality. I am disclosed. I feel, I see

in those white looks that it is not a new man who enters, but a new type of man, a new genus. Why, a Negro! (*Peau noire*, 93)

The black, Fanon observes, is locked in a world governed by a natural attitude of surfaces. The black is an epistemologico-ontological ideal. One can study the black, it seems, as one studies the surfaces of "things." This attitude governs the framework of normality in such a world; it infects and perverts what constitutes the "normal." On this basis, Fanon declares that a "normal" black child growing up with "normal" black parents in an antiblack world will still be an "abnormal" human being (*Peau noire*, 117). How could such a circumstance emerge? What can be done toward its *lysis* or elimination?

The first task is to recognize what Fanon calls the "sociogenic" dimension of the situation. In one sense, *sociogenesis* refers to the human contribution to human institutions. On another level, it refers to the role of human institutions in the constitution of phenomena that human beings have come to regard as "natural" in the physicalist sense of depending on physical nature. Sociogenic dimensions are meaning-constituting features of social life. To understand antiblack racism in this regard, we need to go through a thought exercise on the creation of the "object" of antiblack racism: the black.

In the history of racist literature, there is the structural posing of a rather odd question: How and when did black people come into being? (Note here the normative presumption of white people's having always existed.) Now, although the history of this question is also a portrait of pathology—where the decoded originating query regarding the black is, "Where did humanity go wrong?"—a legitimate variation of the question can be found in the lives and history of black people. If we shift from perverse anonymous behavior to the phenomenological sociological technique of imaginative deployments of anonymity, where we imagine what a typical human being would do in a typical instance of the social situation in question, we find an unusual tale. Nonperverted or ordinary anonymity calls for us to imagine being in the place of another. Among ancient and even medieval people of the continent that we now call Africa, there may have been multitudes of ethnic groups but no reason to see a continental racial identity of any sort. If we were to employ this interpretive phenomenological technique radically, it may be the case that we cannot even imagine what those people ultimately saw in terms of color.[20] For, locked in the epidermal schema, *our* imagination of "seeing," "smelling," and "feeling" heads straight to the skin—at least where Africans and their descendants are concerned. But the exercise is instructive because it behooves us to raise the question of what social forces were set in motion to articulate an identity that blocks our perception so severely. According to the sociogenic approach, a transformation of social reality itself has taken place, a transformation on both the ontogenic (individual) level and the phylogenic (group, species) level. It is a convergence of individual involvement in social processes and the imposition of social processes on individualization. It is, in other words, an existential sociodiagnostic.

Having stated the sociogenic dimension of antiblack racism, the other considerations of such racism and their significance become evident through a summary of Fanon's argument in his first major work, *Peau noire, masques blancs*. The work itself has received much attention in the past ten years, but unfortunately for many of the wrong reasons. Commentaries range from discussions of Fanon's supposed Lacanianism to analyses of his Hegelianism and Sartreanism. Such elements are there, true, but I suspect that the power of the book goes beyond these features. Its power, ultimately, is that it is a beautifully and provocatively written *theoretical* statement on the human condition in the face of unyielding obstacles. One is not used to seeing theory written this way—save, perhaps, in some of Du Bois's classic engagements—*The Souls of Black Folk* in particular. *Peau noire* is a bold text, with irony, pathos, fear, trembling, and hope, even though they are framed in an unabashed pessimism toward any response short of revolutionary struggle against what Fanon regards as the murdering of humanity. In that regard, one cannot help but agree with Derrick Bell, who observes: "Fanon's book was enormously pessimistic in a *victory* sense. He did not believe that modern structures, deeply poisoned with racism, could be overthrown. Yet he urged resistance. He wrote a book—perhaps to remind himself that material or cultural fate is only part of the story" (*Faces at the Bottom of the Well: The Permanence of Racism*, x).

Fanon's project in *Peau noire* is to read how occidental thought has read the lives of black and other colonized folk. His reading of reading is a theoretical move in which the metatheoretical question of theoretical legitimacy emerges. How does the introduction of the black or the colored affect the ways in which we read and write our conceptions of the human being?

Here is Fanon's argument: Blacks have attempted to escape the historic reality of blackness through language, which offers semiotic resources for self-deluding performances of emancipation. If blacks can speak the European language well enough and even use it against the European with the ferocity of Shakespeare's Caliban, perhaps they will "become" European and consequently "become" white. Value-neutral semiotic resources do not exist, however, in an antiblack world. Signifiers that overtly deny color are governed by a colonized life-world. On the level of class, for instance, a person who speaks the national language well is someone who "speaks like a book" from the proletariat's perspective. Racial impositions lead to a different formulation: from the perspective of many blacks, a black who speaks the national language well is someone who "speaks like a white person." Think of the discussion over Bryant Gumble's supposed "whiteness." Should a professional journalist speak otherwise? What should Gumble speak otherwise?

Yet the discussion on Gumble emerges from the identity formation he is claimed to have transcended. It is because Bryant Gumble *is* black that his failure to speak "black speech" becomes pronounced.

Fanon provides many examples of the black's effort to escape the reputation of the black's relation to language. From the antiblack racist's perspective, the black is an "eater of language." The effort to escape blackness through mastery of the national language leads to a comic tragedy of escapism, for the more the black has mastered the colonizing language, the more obscene he or she becomes. The language games that emerge are too serious to be ordinary manifestations of the language. In other words, the semiotic turn only leads to phony whiteness and pitiful blackness. In post-structural parlance, the black chases the signifer in the hope of becoming the signifier. The black discovers, however, that he or she is always already negatively signified by the system of signs that constitute antiblack racism.

The failure of such an avenue of escape in the public sphere leads to a retreat into the private sphere of love. Toni Morrison summarizes Fanon's position well in *The Bluest Eye* when she observes: "The best hiding place was love. Thus the conversion from pristine sadism to fabricated hatred, to fraudulent love. It was a small step to Shirley Temple. I learned much later to worship her, just as I learned to delight in cleanliness, knowing, even as I learned, that the change was adjustment without improvement" (22). Perhaps one can escape racial stratification in the eyes and bosom of a white lover and in the gift of acknowledgment they offer from a white world. Fanon's point is not that blacks should not be romantically involved with whites. He argues instead that the effort to escape blackness through such liaisons is a form of unhealthy behavior. The white lover's desire to serve as a transformation of blackness requires either (1) loving blackness or (2) hating blackness, but failing to see it in the beloved. The failure of the effort strikes both possibilities. The lover's loving blackness would devalue the lover's affections in the pathological black's eyes, for the pathological black's efforts were aimed at rejecting blackness in the first place. In the second instance, a white lover who hates blacks while denying the blackness of a black lover is lost in a game of self-deception. What is lost in both instances are what Willy Apollon has described in Lacanian psychoanalysis as "a certain quality of love—more precisely, words of love, certain words addressed to them as subject" ("Four Seasons in Femininity or *Four Men in a Woman's Life,*" 103). The antiblack context subordinates words of love into words of transformed, epidermal existence—words of assured whiteness:

> In fact you are like us—you are "us." Your thoughts are ours. You behave as we behave, as we would behave. You think of yourself—others think of you— as a Negro? Utterly mistaken! You merely look like one. As for everything else, you think as a European. And so it is natural that you love as a European. Since European men love only European women, you can hardly marry anyone but a

woman of the country where you have always lived, a woman of our good old France, your real and only country. (René Maran, *Un homme pareil aux autres*, 152–53)

In psychoanalysis, one must distinguish between what a woman wants and what a man wants, but the intersection with racism raises new forms of "unhealthy" behavior for women and men.[21] The effort to escape blackness through a lover's words of whiteness perverts love. The psychological resources needed to preserve the bad faith of such relationships require more than the private dimensions such relationships can sustain. Fanon provides examples of the pathological black's eventual efforts to seek *public* approval of the relationships—a black woman who insists on going to an elite ball with her white lover, a black man who seeks approbation through his lover's brother—which returns the black to the forces of institutional imposition. The desire marks the internal limitations of the relationships. They are not relationships premised on love.

The black may then try to evade the *historical* dimension of antiblack racism by appealing to constitutional theories of oppression, such as Dominique O. Mannoni's. The argument is that blacks are oppressed because of the type of people they *are*. Here, we are reminded of W. E. B. Du Bois's observation in *The Souls of Black Folk*: antiblack racists treat black people as problems instead of recognizing the problems faced by black people. That ideological rationalization recurs in many forms. The vogue of the culture-of-poverty argument is one instance, and writers such as Dinesh D'Souza attempt to defend racism in the United States by rendering black people producers of pathological culture. Fanon's response to this claim is that *historical* forces come into play, without which the *racist* dimension of the situation cannot be articulated. His example of Malagasy children's dreams is a telling case. Without the imposition of social-political racial realities, their dream contents appear to be symbols of phallic and paternal orders. Fanon points out, however, that the images of blacks wielding guns in those children's dreams are not symbolic but "real": the French used Senegalese soldiers to do their dirty work. A collapse of symbolic resources into material realities emerged. The "black" dimensions are claustrophobic.

By the time we arrive at the fifth chapter of *Peau noire*, "The Lived-Experience of the Black," we find that semiotic, erotic-narcissistic, and constitutional resources are ultimately irrelevant to the matter.[22] The black lives on a collision course with Western rationality. To avoid the collision, the black retreats from Western rationality *as* rationality, which leads to a glorified blackness *(négritude)* that inevitably realizes its self-deception: it is an essentialized blackness that intensifies white hegemony. The isolation of black specificity intensifies, and it is an isolation that continues to chase European Reason and eventually consciousness out the door. As Fanon observes in discussing Jewphobia and negrophobia, "The Negro is fixed at the genital [level]. . . . There are two domains: The [Jewish] intellectual and the [black] sexual [danger]. Think of Rodin's *The Thinker* with an erection; there's a shocking image! One cannot decently 'have a hard on' everywhere" (*Peau noire*, 134). The situation is moribund from the following *évidence*: "*Wherever he goes, the Negro remains a Negro*" (140, italics in original). In these times of metaphorical blackness, where even rich, conservative white men can be found complaining about being treated "like the blacks," Negroes signify a convergence of these metaphors to the point of stepping out of metaphors (so that they are no longer metaphors).[23] Negroes are, in other words, significations of the blackest blacks.

Fanon describes the isolated anonymity of this schema: "I feel in myself a soul as immense as the world, truly a soul as deep as the deepest rivers, my chest has the power to expand without limit. I am a master and I am advised to adopt the humility of a cripple. Yesterday, awakening to the world, I saw the sky turn upon itself utterly and wholly. I wanted to rise, but the disemboweled silence fell back upon me, its wings paralyzed. Without responsibility, straddling Nothingness and Infinity, I began to weep" (*Peau noire*, 114).

Fanon's conclusion leads to a profound critique of the use of the symbolic in the analysis of antiblack racism, for the black lives not as a symbolic reality but as what Fanon calls a "phobogenic" reality. What this means is that the black stimulates anxiety. In his play, *The Respectful Prostitute*, Sartre uses the character Fred as a spokesman for what we may call the antiblack phobogenic consciousness. Declares Fred, "A nigger has always done something." Fanon could add the black's perspective to the play: "A feeling of inferiority? No, a feeling of nonexistence. Sin is Negro as virtue is white. All those whites in a group, guns in their hands, cannot be wrong. I am guilty. I do not know of what, but I sense that I am no good" (*Peau noire*, 112).

The police officer follows the black because the black has crossed his path. The white woman fears rape because the black is close enough to touch her. The black is unqualified because a white wanted that job. The black is unintelligent because, as Kant once observed, he or she *is* black and, therefore, anything coming forth from such a mouth must be utterly stupid. "Research" emerges that explores black propensities for violence, laziness, idiocy, and pathological sex—lots of pathological sex. The black thus becomes the material manifestation of pathology, and mythopoetical "facts" of blackness emerge that run counter to the lived reality, the lived experience of the black. What phobogenesis allows is the breakdown of theory into a perverse play of terminology . Phobogenesis refers to the Manichaeism, the spirit of seriousness, we discussed earlier; it locks the black outside symbolic reality and ensnares the black into materially constituted realms of evil. The black *is* rape, nymphomania, crime, stupidity, moral weakness, and sin.

Where does all this lead?

Perhaps Fanon's most enduring contribution to philosophical considerations of race has been his sociogenic critique of traditional ontology and his critique of European Reason. On that matter, Fanon admonishes us against the use of traditional ontological claims: "There is, in the *Weltanschauung* of a colonized people, an impurity, a defect that forbids any ontological explanation. Perhaps it will be objected that it is so with every individual, but that is to mask a fundamental problem. Ontology, when it is admitted once and for all that it leaves existence by the wayside, does not permit us to understand the being of the black" (*Peau noire*, 88).

The reader will note Fanon's proviso, "when it is admitted once and for all that it leaves existence by the wayside." Here, we find the classic critique of system-centric ontology. Ontology is the philosophical study of being or, as W. V. O. Quine puts it, what there is.[24] In opposition, there is existential ontology, which recognizes the being-there of the human being as a question to the questioner. This form of ontology takes seriously the meaning of what there is and what there is not.[25] In Hegel's world, where we began our discussion, there was no-one-there when it came to the question of the black. There was no other. Antiblack racism, then, becomes unintelligible without the reality of this denial. Hegel saw no other and therefore saw no reason for a dialectic of recognition with the black. The antiblack epidermal schema, properly understood, takes the form of such a denial. Recall Hegel's encouragement to "leave Africa, for there is no History there." Fanon's reply? "Let us decide not to imitate Europe but combine our muscles and our brains in a new direction. Let us try to create the whole human being, whom Europe has been incapable of bringing to triumphant birth" (*Les Damnés de la terre*, 373).

Fanon's response, through black existence, requires an ontology of admission (critical good faith), context (situation), and social existence (sociogenesis of lived experiences). Philosophy that fails to account for existence is, therefore, trapped in a bad faith claim to universality. In Fanon's critique, then, there is a perspective beyond particularity and universality, a perspective that sees multiple worlds.

These philosophical sketches of racism in a neocolonial world return to Fanon here and there. For now, I close with his two famous encomia that are important for understanding philosophy as both a love and a struggle for wisdom and therefore as a radical practice that must be lived. At the end of *Peau noire, masques blancs*, he asks, "Was my freedom not given to me then in order to build [to edify, to inspire] the world of the *You*?" (emphasis original). And in that regard, he prayed: "O, my body, make of me always a man who *questions*" (emphasis original).

Like Fanon, philosophy must decenter itself in the hope of radical theory and become in its embodiment a critically self-questioning practice.

3   On Race and Philosophy

LUCIUS T. OUTLAW JR.

Concerns regarding raciality (various characteristics in diverse combinations, which, taken together, are thought to determine the features of a particular race) and ethnicity (characteristics that collectively are thought to distinguish an ethnie as a subgroup of one or more races) are among the most pervasive and challenging aspects of contemporary life. The ideas that there are different races and ethnic groups (or *ethnies*, as I will refer to them) and that each person is a member of one or more races and ethnies are taken for granted by most people. Difficulties of various kinds involving considerations of raciality and ethnicity are abundant. Yet, what characteristics determine a race or an ethnie and whether or not it is ever appropriate to take raciality or ethnicity into account when making moral judgments about persons are hardly settled matters, nor is the question of whether it is even correct to say that races even exist.[1]

These unsettled matters are an important aspect of prevailing difficulties. Raciality, especially, continues to be the focus of intense social and political struggle, and thus is presently a topic of equally intense and wide-ranging discussion. I wish to contribute to the discussion by showing why I find it important to consider raciality and ethnicity as real, constitutive aspects of determinate populations of human beings: that is, as aspects of the meaningful, valued composition of persons—of their "being" and "doings"—that "preserve, confirm, and augment collective identities and the natural order" for members of racial and ethnic groups (Joshua Fishman, "Ethnicity as Being, Doing, and Knowing," 65).

As a philosopher, I came at this discussion by way of my participation in certain professionalized practices and tradition mediations of philosophizing that over the centuries have been affected by racial and ethnic concerns in important ways and have made pernicious contributions, not always acknowledged, to invidious racializations (that is, practices of formulating and imposing identifying characterizations of a group of people as a distinct race in order to facilitate their subordination). This aspect of the history of philosophizing—in the West in general, in the United States in particular—must be considered before any leading role can be assigned to philosophers in addressing the serious and challenging problems confronting this nation and others that stem from valorizations of raciality and ethnicity.

In this essay I set out a consideration of raciality and ethnicity as being the results of ongoing projects that are definitive of human sociality and that must be recognized as such. Let me make clear at the start, however, that it is my very firm belief that we must continue to identify and to condemn all actions, beliefs, attitudes, and evaluations involving invidious considerations of raciality and ethnicity. But I also believe that it is very important that we continue to make use of the concepts *race* and *ethnie* (or *ethnic groups*) and of their derivatives *raciality* and *ethnicity* as important resources for continuing efforts to understand, critically (re-)construct, and maintain social realities. For in complex societies in which raciality and ethnicity continue to be factors at the heart of social conflict, it is as urgent as ever that we engage in such projects with careful mindfulness of complicated biologically and culturally constituted self-reproducing social groupings of persons identified (however, not always consistently) as races and ethnies, although sometimes it will also be important to have little or no regard for a person's or people's raciality and/or ethnicity. The delicate, complicated, but crucial task is to fashion ways to have appropriate regard for raciality and ethnicity while being guided by norms that we hope—and that our best judgments lead us to believe—will help us to achieve stable, well-ordered, and just societies, norms bolstered by the combined best understandings available in all fields of knowledge that have to do with human beings and secured by democratically achieved consensus.

It is a formidable task, indeed, especially given centuries of invidious, brutal, even genocidal histories of commitments and practices predicated on racial concerns. Perhaps a brief review of decisive ways in which notions of race were involved in these histories would be helpful.[2]

Of central importance to such a review is Arthur Lovejoy's *The Great Chain of Being*. As Lovejoy shows rather convincingly, throughout Western intellectual and social histories a crucial "unit-idea" in systems of knowledge of the natural world and of humans was that of a "Chain" or "Scale of Being." The idea originates with Plato (in the *Timaeus*), whom Lovejoy also regards as having contributed two closely related conceptions to the general stock of Western philosophical ideas in response to two questions—conceptions that were to play a decisive role in the development and history of the idea of a "Scale of Being." In response to the question "*Why* is there any World of Becoming, in addition to the eternal World of Ideas, or, indeed, to the one supreme Idea?" Plato reasoned that "a timeless and incorporeal One became the logical ground as well as the dynamic source of the existence of a temporal and material and extremely multiple and variegated universe." The One was a "Self-Transcending Fecundity." And to the question "What principle determines the number of kinds of being that make up the sensible and temporal world?" the response was that it was the principle of *plenitude*: for Plato, with respect to living things or animals, there must *necessarily* be "complete translation of all the ideal possibilities into actuality." Thus, from the One come Many: "the universe is a *plenum formarum* in which the range of conceivable diversity of *kinds* of living things is exhaustively exemplified. . . . [N]o genuine potentiality of being can remain unfulfilled. . . . [T]he extent and abundance of the creation must be as great as the possibility of existence and commensurate with the productive capacity of a 'perfect' and inexhaustible Source, and . . . the world is the better, the more it contains" (*Great Chain of Being*, 46–50, 52).

To this unit-idea, according to Lovejoy, Aristotle added the conception of *continuity* as a principle operative in natural history and suggested the idea of arranging animals in a single, graded natural scale according to their degree of "perfection" since any division of creatures with reference to some one determinate attribute manifestly would give rise to *a* linear series of classes (though, Lovejoy notes, Aristotle did *not* hold that all organisms could be so arranged and made no attempt to frame a single and exclusive scheme of classification) (*Great Chain of Being*, 56). Plotinus contributed to this developing notion of a "scale" by adding further support to the belief that difference in kind is necessarily "equivalent to difference of excellence, to diversity of rank in a hierarchy" (64). This Neoplatonism prepared the way for medieval thinkers, Augustine and Aquinas in particular, to add "the thesis of the inherent and supreme value of variety and existence as such" in service to agendas formed in the context of the theology and cosmology of medieval Christendom (67, 76).

But out of this mixture of conceptions, a major conflict of opposing motives emerged that would command the attention and energies of thinkers throughout the Middle Ages: accounting for goodness and evil while remaining consistent with a conception of God, the principle of plenitude (of Many from the One), and the Principle of Sufficient Reason (the *necessity* that there be both One and Many). If the Many come from the One necessarily, and the One is good and thus cannot be the source of evil, must not the Many be of equal value? Or, at the very least, how could any of God's creations *be* by necessity yet not be good in their own right? Further, what did the Principle of Sufficient Reason demand in fulfillment of the Principle of Plenitude? An infinite number of beings with no "gaps" in the chain of being? How to reconcile the necessity that there be an infinite number of beings in a finite, temporal world with the equally important necessity that there be both One and Many?

By the eighteenth century, two conflicting positions were taken on these questions. For some, notions of plenitude, continuity, and sufficient reason led to arguments against equalitarian movements: variety by means of in-equality was evidence of Infinite Wisdom. The social microcosm should thus reflect in its organization the principles ordering the macrocosm. Demands for social equality were, then, "contrary to nature" For others, the whole of creation was thought to be perfect and therefore good: "The limitations of each species of creature, which define its place in the scale, are indispensable to that infinite differentiation of things in which the 'fullness' of the universe consists, and are therefore necessary to the realization of the greatest of goods" (*Great Chain of Being*, 216). But in the latter, more optimistic view there was a paradox: *"the desirability of a thing's existence bears no relation to its excellence"* (222; emphasis in original).

This conflict was played out between the Enlightenment and Romanti-cism, between universalism and diversitarianism. For Lovejoy, the dominant tendency of the Enlightenment was devotion to the simplification and stan-dardization of life and thought by way of the confirmation of a principle be-lieved to be universal, immutable, uncomplicated, and uniform for every ra-tional being. From the 1500s to the 1700s, efforts were made to correct and improve beliefs, institutions, and art—guided by the assumption that in every phase of activity man should conform to such a standard as nearly as possible. "Nature" was most often the conceptual vehicle carrying the con-notation of universality and uniformity of content and was drawn out and expressed in ethical applications such as the "law of nature" invoked in moral and political philosophy (*Great Chain of Being*, 292, 289).

Romanticism reversed the values of the Enlightenment by substituting "diversitarianism for uniformatarianism as the ruling preconception in most of the normative provinces of thought." Working against the prevailing ideas of the Enlightenment and drawing out implications of the principle of plen-itude, Romanticism was characterized by the belief that not only are there diverse excellences in all areas of life, but that diversity itself is of the essence of excellence. One consequence of this posture was "the cultivation of indi-vidual, national, and racial peculiarities." This development, in turn, led to a revision of the notion of universality: from "uniform" to "expansive" uni-versality (*Great Chain of Being*, 297, 293, 306).

However, a latent danger in Romanticism emerged: a revolt against uni-versal standardization of life became a revolt against the whole conception of standards. Consequently, Romanticism . . .

lent itself all too easily to the service of man's egoism, and especially—in the po-litical and social sphere—of the kind of collective vanity which is nationalism or racialism. The belief in the sanctity of one's idiosyncrasy—especially if it be a group idiosyncrasy, and therefore sustained and intensified by mutual flat-tery—is rapidly converted into a belief in its superiority. . . . A type of national culture valued at first because it was one's own, and because the conservation of differentness was recognized as a good for humanity as a whole, came in time

> to be conceived of as a thing which one had a mission to impose upon others, or to diffuse over as large a part of the surface of the planet as possible. (*Great Chain of Being*, 312–13)

This was the context in which the notion of *race* was taken up by natural philosophers and other *philosophes* in the modern period. How—or why—it was that the word and concept of "race" came to be used to classify human groups is not entirely clear (see Michael Banton and Jonathan Harwood, *The Race Concept*, 13), but a number of contributing factors do stand out.

First, tensions within Europe arose from encounters among groups of peoples who differed culturally or, more narrowly, religiously. Second, a more basic impetus, intensified by these tensions, came from the need to account for human origins in general and for human diversity in particular. Natural philosophy gave way to the development of various modern natural and social sciences, including anthropology, as endeavors to meet this need. Third, there were the quite decisive European voyages to what would come to be called the Americas, the East, and Africa, and the concomitant developments of capitalism and the slave trade (Banton and Harwood, *Race Concept*, 14). These developments, combined with the rise of European nation-states and attendant nationalisms, particularly where the states were involved in efforts to fashion empires through colonialism, "gave powerful impetus to the natural tendency of nationalism to become chauvinism. And chauvinism, perverting to its uses the new sciences, could become and, where conditions were propitious, did become racism. The interaction between colonialism and this nationalism provided the necessary *milieu* for the emergence and development of racism" (Dave A. Puzzo, "Racism and the Western Tradition," 583).

The authority of *race* as an organizing, classificatory concept within the scheme of a Chain of Being was strengthened during the unfolding of the project of Western Modernity, in the eighteenth century in particular, when "evidence from geology, zoology, anatomy and other fields of scientific enquiry was assembled to support a claim that racial classification would help explain many human differences" (Banton and Harwood, *Race Concept*, 13). Use of conceptions of raciality contributed to "typological" thinking, which regarded individuals as instances of defining *types*, a mode of conceptualization at the center of the agenda of natural philosophy and which thus facilitated the classification of human groups.

Two significant achievements resulted from these efforts. First, drawing on the rising authority of the increasing explanatory and predictive success of the natural sciences as the realization and guardian of systematic, certain knowledge, there was the legitimation of *race* as a gathering concept for morphological features thought to distinguish natural varieties of *Homo sapiens*, who were supposedly related to one another through the logic of an equally natural hierarchy of groups ranked in terms of their capacity for and their development and display of species-determining factors (i.e., language, religion, art, and thought of certain kinds that exemplify "civilization"). Thanks to the preparatory efforts of some proponents of the idea of a Chain of Being, "fact and value became combined in the concept of race" (Jeanne Hersch, "The Concept of Race," 116). Second, there was the legitimation of the view that the behavior of a group and its members was determined by their place in this hierarchy.[3]

Thus, notions of raciality were authorized and legitimized by natural philosophers and scientists, and when combined with social projects that distinguished and ultimately controlled "racially" different persons and groups—as in the case of the enslavement of Africans—they took root and grew to become part of modern common sense, particularly as racial apartheid was institutionalized in Great Britain, the Americas, and elsewhere. Such notions became part of virtually taken for granted understandings undergirding almost all forms of knowledge, especially those that dealt with "Man," as history unfolded into the contemporary period. *The* problem of life in modern North America was indeed the problem of the "color line," to paraphrase W. E. B. Du Bois, the problem of relations between darker and lighter races. To be a North American, to be in North America, meant that one had to learn to negotiate the social landscape guided by a compass whose ordered and ordering points were in significant part matters having to do with race. Philosophers were not immune to these influences or exempted from their requirements; nor, therefore, were the practices and traditions that were constitutive of the discipline.

In what follows, then, I offer my contribution to the work of fashioning enhanced and reasonable ways of understanding raciality and ethnicity, and of referring to social collectivities as races and ethnic groups: "enhanced" in that these understandings are intended to facilitate the identification and valorization of racial and ethnic groups but not to rank order them; and "reasonable" in that they will satisfy criteria for reasoning about means and ends intended to promote human well-being and social justice. Such understandings, I believe, will enhance social relations and praxes in the continuous struggle to achieve stable and just societies in which humans might flourish. I take it to be the case that at least some professional philosophers, myself included, along with thoughtful persons in other walks of life can contribute to the clarifying work of developing social and political philosophies and policies that might help us fashion communities in which racism and invidious ethnocentrism have been minimized and curtailed (I do not expect either problem ever to be eliminated completely and for good), even while races and ethnies are both conserved and nurtured, without chauvinism, to the enrichment of us all.

❦

First, two extended quotes here offer thoughts about human racial groupings. Each prompts provocative, highly charged questions that have to be addressed as we work our way through the problematic aspects of raciality and
ethnicity:

> Once a race has become established as the principal population of a region, it
> has a tendency to stay there and to resist the genetic influences swept in by later
> invasions. . . . When two races come into contact and mixture occurs, one race
> tends to dominate the other. The local advantage that the genetically superior
> group (superior for its time and place) possesses may be primarily cultural or
> primarily physiological, or a combination of both. . . . There is, however, a third
> kind of dominance, expressed by the resistance of a population to the intrusion
> of large numbers of outsiders into its social and genetic structures. Call it xeno-
> phobia, prejudice, or whatever, people do not ordinarily welcome masses of
> strangers in their midst, particularly if the strangers come with women and chil-
> dren and settle down to stay. Social mechanisms arise automatically to isolate
> the newcomers as much as possible and to keep them genetically separate. . . .
> [This] is the behavioral aspect of race relations. The genetic aspect operates in
> a comparable way. Genes that form part of a cell nucleus possess an internal
> equilibrium as a group, just as do the members of social institutions. Genes in
> a population are in equilibrium if the population is living a healthy life as a cor-
> porate entity. Racial intermixture can upset the genetic as well as the social
> equilibrium of a group, and so, newly introduced genes tend to disappear or be
> reduced to a minimum percentage unless they possess a selective advantage over
> their local counterparts. . . . [W]ere it not for [these] mechanisms. . . , men
> would be not black, white, yellow, or brown. We would all be light khaki, for
> there has been enough gene flow over the clinal regions of the world during the
> last half million years to have homogenized us all had that been the evolution-
> ary scheme of things, and had it not been advantageous to each of the geo-
> graphical races for it to retain, for the most part, the adaptive elements in its ge-
> netic *status quo*. (Carleton S. Coon, *The Origin of Races*, 660–62)

> The American Negro has always felt an intense personal interest in discussions
> as to the origins and destinies of races: primarily because back of most discus-
> sions of race with which he is familiar, have lurked certain assumptions as to
> his natural abilities, as to his political, intellectual and moral status, which he
> felt were wrong. He has, consequently, been led to deprecate and minimize race
> distinctions, to believe intensely that out of one blood God created all nations,
> and to speak of human brotherhood as though it were the possibility of an al-
> ready dawning to-morrow.
>
> Nevertheless, in our calmer moments we must acknowledge that human be-
> ings are divided into races; that in this country the two most extreme types of
> the world's races have met, and the resulting problem as to the future relations
> of these types is not only of intense and living interest to us, but forms an epoch
> in the history of mankind.

It is necessary, therefore, in planning our movements, in guiding our future development, that at times we rise above the pressing, but smaller questions of separate schools and cars, wage discrimination and lynch law, to survey the whole question of race in human philosophy and to lay, on a basis of broad knowledge and careful insight, those large lines of policy and higher ideals which may form our guiding lines and boundaries in the practical difficulties of every day. For it is certain that all human striving must recognize the hard limits of natural law, and that any striving, no matter how intense and earnest, which is against the constitution of the world, is vain. The question, then, which we must seriously consider is this: What is the real meaning of Race; what has, in the past, been the law of race development, and what lessons has the past history of race development to teach the rising Negro people? (W. E. B. Du Bois, "The Conservation of Races," 176)

For several hundred years now, in intellectual and social life, most instances of concern with *raciality* and racial groups, as well as with *ethnicity* and ethnies, have been dominated by two endeavors: (1) the identification and rank-ordering of populations of people for purposes of exploitation of and invidious discrimination against those said to be lower in rank by those who thought themselves members of a race and or ethnie of higher rank, and (2) the denunciations of and struggles against *racism* and invidious *ethnocentrism*, as we have come to designate such practices, and against rationalizations of both. Between these two types of endeavor a third is presently barely able to sustain itself free of suspicion or involuntary conscription by racists or the inappropriately ethnocentric as support for their invidious projects. This third endeavor is the studied consideration of the varieties of human collectivities referred to as *races* and *ethnies* with no concern for rank-ordering, exploitation, or invidious discrimination—a consideration that instead seeks to add to the storehouses of credible and morally appropriate knowledge of human beings as we have been and have come to be in all ways: physically, biologically, and culturally, visibly as well as beneath the outer configurations that first meet our culturally socialized senses.

It is an endeavor of this third kind that I undertake here, one that is not focused on either racism or antiracism. Rather, I want to inquire into how and why humans form themselves into bonding, self-reproducing, social collectivities distinguished by sets of biological and sociocultural characteristics that are shared, more or less, by the members of each collectivity. These groupings sometimes grow larger and then form into subgroupings that interact in ways by which they come to form a relatively distinct, self-reproducing breeding population that is constituted as such by shared sociocultural systems. As these populations and their subgroups survive and reproduce themselves, thereby persisting in and across times and spaces, they devote significant efforts to perpetuating their cultural meaning systems and institutionalized practices, in either preserved or altered forms. In and through these systems and practices, both cultural and physical characteristics become valorized elements of the social and personal identities definitive of group members. The conflicts involved in these efforts are increased when there is contact with persons from physiologically and culturally "different" populations.

The complicated processes (biological, sociocultural, historical) by which such populations and population subgroups are formed and maintained are what I refer to as *raciation* and *ethnicization*. I regard raciation and ethnicization as normal, social-natural aspects of human evolutionary histories: that is, they are important aspects of the *anthropologically necessary and contingent* ways in which we humans, as social animals, organize meaningfully, give order to, and thus define and construct the worlds in which we live, our *life-worlds* (necessary for meaningful existence and contingent in terms of how the meaningful ordering is effected)—and do so in the process of surviving while subject to the evolutionary forces of social and natural histories.

I assume that these social collectivities and the processes of their formation and maintenance are better known to evolutionary and social biologists, paleontologists, and physical and cultural anthropologists than they are to people in the humanities. Many contemporary philosophers, myself included, have been seriously miseducated when it comes to our knowledge of humans as beings of complexly interrelated socially conditioned, natural-biological, and sociocultural histories. In seeking to understand raciation and ethnicization—relations that involve racial populations and their ethnic subgroups—as well as to understand the variability and historicities of these populations and subgroups, I hope to partially but significantly re-educate myself as a philosopher.

Once again I take inspiration and guidance from W. E. B. Du Bois, who recounts in his third autobiography that he "conceived the idea of applying philosophy to an historical interpretation of race relations." However, Du Bois distinguished what he regarded as "the lovely but sterile land of philosophic speculation" from the objects (and objectives) of the fields of history and the newly developing social sciences that were constituted by the realities of social life. For him, historiography and empirical sociology would provide the means by which he would gather and interpret "that body of fact which would apply to my program for the Negro." And this gathering and interpreting would be philosophy in the form of what he termed the "keen analysis" of his Harvard philosophy teachers William James, Josiah Royce, and George Santayana. In his study of race relations, Du Bois would especially continue to develop and apply James's pragmatism, combined with the historically informed empirical research methods that he learned from Harvard historian and teacher Albert Bushnell Hart, among others (including professors and other thinkers he encountered during his studies in Germany) (*The Autobiography of W. E. B. Du Bois: A Soliloquy on Viewing My Life from the Last Decade of Its First Century*, 148).

After having completed his graduate studies at Harvard and in Berlin, Du Bois put his plan to work in "The Conservation of the Races" as he posed and set out to answer the questions that he thought must be seriously considered: "What is the real meaning of Race; what has, in the past, been the law of race development, and what lessons has the past history of race development to teach the rising Negro people?" For Du Bois, in order to achieve a proper understanding of raciality one must "survey the whole question of race in human philosophy" to be able to form the guiding higher ideals and policies for dealing with "the practical difficulties of every day " (Du Bois, "The Conservation of Races," 176–77).

It is this Du Boisian approach to race and raciality that I wish to take up and to extend to the consideration of ethnicity and ethnies. In the process I hope to persuade others, especially professional philosophers, who are concerned with racial and ethnic matters in their philosophizing to give Du Bois's work the kind of careful consideration that is cultivated in attending to the works of canonical figures in academic philosophy. For I remain convinced that Du Bois's approach is especially promising for working out conceptions of raciality and ethnicity that could help articulate a political philosophy appropriate to a modern, liberal democratic society in which diversities of philosophical doctrines as well as of valued social collectivities, including races and ethnies, are normal and important features.[4]

For example, it crucial to note that in his effort to characterize a race, Du Bois took particular care to observe that although physical differences "play a great part" in distinguishing each race, "no mere physical distinctions would really define or explain the deeper differences—the cohesiveness and continuity of these groups. The deeper differences are spiritual, psychical, differences—undoubtedly based on the physical, but infinitely transcending them" ("The Conservation of Races," 179). Du Bois thought there were "forces" that "bind together" members of a race, and he took these to be: first, a racial identity and "common blood" (by which Du Bois means, as I read him, biological descent from common ancestor[s]); "secondly, *and more important,* a common history, common laws and religion, similar habits of thought and a conscious striving together for certain ideals of life" (179, emphasis added). A race, then, for Du Bois, is a collection of persons of common biological descent who are "bound together" by the meaning systems and agendas constitutive of shared cultural life-worlds. Understood thus, the development of different races he saw as processes of "growth" characterized by "the differentiation of spiritual and mental differences," even as processes resulting in "the integration of physical differences" (i.e., cross-racial breeding) were also having their effect (180).

Du Bois has frequently been misunderstood as a typical late nineteenth-century thinker who regarded raciality as being determined by a fixed set of heritable biological characteristics. However, he was hardly a "typical" thinker, either for the late nineteenth or the early to mid-twentieth centuries.

What remains instructive for me is the nuanced way in which he struggled to conceptualize sociocultural groups called *races* or *nations*. Though in general these groups tend to be distinct from one another in terms of physical features shared by their members, they cannot be distinguished precisely by such features, for there are significant variations in the distribution of the characteristics thought to be definitive of a race among persons identifying themselves as being in the same racial group. In addition, Du Bois noted that the physical characteristics that are thought to distinguish a particular race are "most exasperatingly intermingled" among those of other races ("The Conservation of Races," 178). For Du Bois, no definitive set of heritable physical characteristics suffices to characterize a race. This reality defeats the classificatory efforts typical of natural philosophers concerned with identifying the invariant, determining, essential natures of natural kinds—races included.

Du Bois decidedly cut against the grain of prevailing natural philosophy as he contributed to the development of modern social sciences. Mindful of the work of Charles Darwin, he understood the variability of heritable traits. He understood, as well, the permeability of the social and political boundaries established to mark and maintain racial groups, for he repeatedly drew from his own family history to note how frequently these boundaries were transgressed: he counted among his ancestors persons both white ("of Dutch descent") and Negro (Africans "descended from Tom, who was born in West Africa") with the result that Du Bois himself was often described as a "mulatto." Such transgressions resulted in the intermingling of physical characteristics and thus wide variations in the phenotypes of members of a given race (*The Autobiography of W. E. B. Du Bois*, 62). This, in significant part, is why Du Bois turned to the realms of history and sociology to identify the characteristics shared by members of a culturally—as well as sexually—constituted self-reproducing group that, when given significance by members of the group, act as "forces" to bind them together *as a group* and become part of the members' personal and social identities.

Understanding such groups requires a philosophical anthropology and social ontology that include an understanding and appreciation of senses of *belonging* and of a shared *destiny* by which individuals are intimately connected to other individuals in ways that make for the constitution of particular kinds of social collectivities, what I term *social-natural kinds*. Races and ethnies are such "kinds" of collectivities: raciation and ethnicization the processes by which they are formed and maintained; raciality and ethnicity the interrelated sets of historically contingent and conditioned, socially defined, always varying and contestable physical and sociocultural features relatively definitive of a race or ethnie.

I want to think seriously about the natural history—the evolution— of social-natural kinds: that is to say, the ways in which the natural and social evolutionary processes through which humans form and maintain biocultural social groupings intersect and the consequences of those intersections. In addition, I wish to argue against those who regard raciality and eth-nicity (and gender) as nothing more than arbitrary, fluid, socially conte-stable, fictive, imagined, or ideological social constructions that are not even *real*, even though real enough in their social or "material" effects. Such ap-proaches to the "socially constructed" involve conceptions of the *real* that are much too simple in that they generally regard only material kinds as real while allowing that the fictive or imagined can and does have real effects when played out through social practices. Approaches of this sort fail to ap-preciate fully the varieties of kinds of the *real* and the full range of social re-alities. As a result, they help to impoverish social ontologies and thereby to impair the development of a social and political philosophy appropriate to an ethnically, racially, and culturally diverse society. As I have noted already, a major concern for me is the articulation of just such a philosophy sup-ported by a combined social ontology and philosophical anthropology dif-ferent in important ways from those that have been at the heart of modern liberal individualism: that is, a social and political philosophy that has seri-ous, noninvidious regard for racial and ethnic groups that can be a resource for praxes that might help us realize social peace and harmony with justice.

To these ends, my concern, as was Du Bois's, is to work out an under-standing of raciality, ethnicity, and the processes of their formation and maintenance that is focused on the world-making of evolving humans. For, I think, it is in and through this world-making, driven by the will to survive and the competition for resources, that raciation and ethnicization develop: they are responses to the need for a life-sustaining and meaningfully accep-table *order* of various kinds (conceptual, social, political). Understanding these aspects of our species-being (to reinvoke a central notion from the early Karl Marx) will enable us, I think, to understand better how racial and ethnic groups come to be and how they go about defining and identifying themselves. With this understanding it will be possible to better appreciate some of what has gone on and what goes on in the past and present when racial and ethnic groups meet under various conditions and why these par-ticular forms of intergroup relations sometimes come to have such impor-tance that they lead to bloodshed.

The processes of establishing order in world-making certainly provide the context within which we can properly understand what are termed *racialism* and *ethnocentrism*: the belief that races and ethnies, particularly one's own, are both real and valued. But I am convinced that his belief is not necessar-ily and certainly not always practically pernicious and to be opposed auto-matically. Racialism neither is nor need become racism; nor must ethnocen-trism become invidious. In neither case should the one be conflated with the other: that is, racialism with racism, ethnocentrism with invidious ethno-centrism. Racism and invidious ethnocentrism are best understood as sets of beliefs, imaginations, and practices that are "imbued with negative valua-tion" and employed as modes of exclusion, inferiorization, subordination, and exploitation in order to deny targeted racial or ethnic groups full participation in the social, political, economic, and cultural life of a political community (Floyd Anthias and Niva Yuval-Davis, "The Concept of 'Race' and the Racialization of Social Division," 2, 15). Such beliefs and practices are contingent, never necessary, no matter how frequent.

Among engaged contemporary thinkers who have turned their attention to racial and ethnic matters are those who argue in favor of discarding the very term *race* because, they reason, it is now loaded with centuries of pernicious valorizations accumulated from dehumanizing mobilizations of sentiments and practices ranging from the merely impolite to the genocidal. Further, the term has no "scientific" validity, some claim (frequently without giving any account of what they mean by either *science* or *scientific*). Moreover, in racially and ethnically complex nations-states such as the United States of America there are no "pure" races, if there ever were any, nor any persons who do not have genes from one or more of the old, now increasingly intermixed racial groups. Consequently, they claim, identifying persons and groups as races cannot be accomplished with precision and is at best arbitrary, and doing so often results in more harm than good. Like some "social constructionists," some persons who appeal to the authority of undifferentiated "science" even go so far as to claim that there is no such thing as a race. However, in continuing to side with W. E. B. Du Bois's position in 1897, I share his concern for the "conservation" of races (and, I would add, of ethnic groups). Thus, I think it important that serious philosophical attention be devoted to an appreciative but critical rethinking of ethnicity and raciality.

But why legitimize, even if not "properly" justified, such a dangerous and seemingly discredited notion as *race* in philosophy in support of a possibly misguided quest to "conserve" racial and ethnic groups? For should not philosophizing, as has been claimed for centuries, be devoted to setting out principles and norms of reason which will guide human beings in fashioning forms of living through which they can become fully, flourishingly *human*? Various philosophers have long argued that if such principles and norms— of truthfulness and justice, for example—are to be binding on all, they must not rest on the valorization and privileging of the norms and life-agendas of any particular groups, races, or ethnies. Principles and norms for ordering social and individual life that grow out of and are dedicated to serving the life-interests of a particular people are always conditioned by and relative to those interests. The abundant evidence of anthropological diversity makes clear that human groups do not, simply by virtue of being human, share the same interests and agendas except in the most general of terms (as, for example, "to live and live well," "to see offspring live and prosper," "to not be treated unfairly by others"). Conflict emerges when, in contexts of intergroup life (and even within groups), different meanings and weights are given by members of different groups to those things about which they care and compete, and for which they are sometimes prepared to die. It seems,

then, that the only way to avoid having such conflicts become socially destructive is to have principles to guide practices and efforts to resolve disputes—principles that owe their source and validity, their truthfulness and
reasonableness, to the life-worlds and life-agendas of no particular people,
perhaps, but which can be binding on *all* persons and peoples by being
grounded on, say, the principles and normativity provided by reason alone.
For only then can the norms and principles ensure mutual well-being in a
shared world.

Why not, then, join the quest for such norms and principles and work
with others to help stave off what many regard as the resurgence of destructive racialism and ethnocentrism—or "tribalism"—around the world? Why
seem to provide honorific philosophical justification to balkanizing dehumanization by valorizing talk of "race" and "ethnicity" and thus contribute
to the dangerous politics of identity and difference-recognition?[5] Why not
work to save the political and economic revolutions of liberal democracy
and free-market capitalism by redeeming the modern Enlightenments' expectation that the resources of critical reason embodied in and exercised by
the mature, autonomous individual are our best and last hope for realizing
the good life of peace with justice for all?

These are indeed serious questions, as problems having to do with raciality and ethnicity continue to plague social and political life throughout the
world. Why, then, endow raciality and ethnicity with highly honorific philosophical significance? The answer, simply put: *because we must.* The increasing frequency of conflicts tied to valorizations of differences among
peoples that we characterize as "races" and/or "ethnic groups" ought to be
sobering, for contemporary philosophers especially. For many of us have
shared the expectations that the kinds of features that divide one group from
another would inevitably lose their weight and sharpness in modern and
modernizing societies, that there would be increasing emphasis on achievement rather than ascription, that common systems of education and communication would level differences, that nationally uniform economic and
political systems would have the same effect, and so on. The "liberal expectancy" flows into the "radical expectancy"—that class circumstances
would become the main line of division between people, erasing the earlier
lines of tribe, language, religion, national origin, and that thereafter these
class divisions would themselves, after revolution, disappear (Nathan Glazer
and Daniel Patrick Moynihan, *Ethnicity: Theory and Experience*, 7).

These expectations were born in the philosophical anthropologies and
political philosophies of modern European and U.S. Enlightenments and
were nurtured in the centuries-old liberal-democratic, capitalist, and even
socialist-communist revolutionary experiments with forming decidedly
modern societies and nation-states. These legacies continue to serve as reservoirs of hope for many who would complete the realization of the promises
of modernity.

But it has not come to pass that the physical and cultural differences by which peoples continue to be identified and to identify themselves as races and ethnies have either ceased to exist or ceased to be taken as highly important in the organization of society, especially in situations where there is competition for resources thought vital to lives organized, to significant extents, through racial and/or ethnic identities. Of course, there are those who protest that such identities are inappropriate, in part because the notions of the racial or ethnic group involved in them lack science-certified empirical confirmation or philosophically certified logical precision. However, it strikes me that these protesters, although well intended, are nonetheless misguided, for they have forgotten a very important injunction from Aristotle that for any given science or systematic attempt to achieve certified knowledge one should seek no more precision than the subject matter allows. Because races and ethnies are *populations* identified as such on the basis of the degree to which persons share *more or less* particular sets of varied and varying physical and cultural characteristics, care must be taken to specify what empirical criteria would be appropriate for determining when references to any particular race or ethnie are valid. These criteria will be those by which statistical frequencies are conventionally set as definitive for some population range. A combined social ontology and philosophical anthropology informed by the best empirical and interpretive work of this kind (provided by physical, cultural, and paleoanthropologists; evolutionary biologists and geneticists; and others), as well as by attention to everyday social life, will no longer support expectations that racial and ethnic differences and concerns will disappear—or justify efforts to ensure that they do disappear—as societies modernize.

On the basis of a revised philosophical anthropology that draws on an enhanced social ontology mindful of social collectivities, perhaps those who philosophize might not mislead themselves in thinking that the elimination of antagonisms tied to invidious valorizations of raciality and ethnicity can be facilitated by "lexical surgery" that removes the term *race* from usage and replaces it with references to, say, "communities of meaning," as offered by Kwame Anthony Appiah,[6] or to "ethnic identities," as he has proposed more recently, because, he claims, there is no such thing as a race (*In My Father's House: Africa in the Philosophy of Culture*, 45). It is as though "something awkward or troublesome can be got rid of by the mere process of calling it by another name" (K. L. Little, qtd. in Pat Shipman, *The Evolution of Racism: Human Differences and the Use and Abuse of Science*, 166).[7] I worry that efforts of this kind may well come to have unintended effects that are too much of a kind with projects of racial and ethnic cleansing in terms of their impacts on raciality and ethnicity as important means through which we construct and validate ourselves; that is, such efforts might contribute to the dehumanizing delegitimation of sociocultural groups constituted, in significant part, by valuations of relations of descent.

Of course, centuries of wrongdoing as a function of racism and invidious ethnocentrism have cost the lives of millions of people as well as the unjust curtailment of their lives and possible futures of millions more. And the wrongdoing continues, assisted now by wider distribution of ever more efficient weapons of human destruction and the less ostensive but still very potent new strategies, practices, and means—including coded talk—of mobilizing persons of various racial and ethnic groups into projects of defensive and offensive racism and invidious ethnocentrism. It is, indeed, the very reality of injustices and atrocities motivated by racial and ethnic concerns that highlights for me the need for venturing into these difficult waters. Appeals to "reason" have not been either an effective vaccine against the ravaging viruses of racism and invidious ethnocentrism or an antidote to the social ills they produce. In fact, both racism and invidious ethnocentrism are generally highly rationalized ventures. As was noted long before now, reason can be a whore who sleeps with anyone: that is, the capacity for reasoning is not governed by inherent norms of humane propriety that come into effect whenever it is exercised; rather, reasoning can be bent to any task, no matter how horrific.

I remain convinced that what success can be achieved in reducing racism and invidious ethnocentrism and their effects will not come as a result of declarations of the "illusory," "superstitious," or "misguided" nature of talk of race (or ethnicity). This position assumes that the terms have no proven or possible *real* referents, or that the living referents are actually constituted such that the demarcations intended by the term *race* are at best arbitrary social conventions which inscribe physical characteristics with meanings that cannot be anchored in any abiding biological or anthropological fashion. I agree: there are no "pure" races; nor are there several unique characteristics—physical and cultural—that could be included in any definition of a particular group as a race or ethnie and that can override the statistical frequencies of the appearance of various combinations of biological and visible physical and cultural characteristics of socially defined raciality; nor is raciality the function of an invariant, transhistorical, transgeographical, biological essence that makes races natural, unchanging kinds. Again, human populations and their subgroupings are better understood as *social-natural kinds*: that is, groupings of humans formed and named under contingent sociohistorical, cultural conditions, according to social conventions (often under conditions of conflict in which there are disparities of power possessed by those naming and named), groupings of biologically and socially evolving living beings who are also part of socially conditioned natural histories. For important reasons, we should understand races and ethnies as *natural*: that is, as particular types of biosocial collectivities that develop and evolve, like all things in the natural world, but in ways that are characteristically human.

Humans are biological beings, however we make sense of our biological aspects: that is to say, our biological makeup, in providing species-specific biological boundary conditions, is foundational to our very being even though this makeup does not determine how we are to give meaning to its various aspects. Certainly, in thinking of a population of individuals as a distinct race we can be freed of the mistaken notions that race-defining biological characteristics are shared equally by all members of a population; that the characteristics are unique to and thereby definitive of the race; and that biological characteristics completely determine the cultural productions, individual capacities and achievements, and moral significance of any group of people. However, it does not follow from this that we are required to give up all use of *race* as a group-identifying or group-characterizing term. We need only remember that it is not biology, certainly not in the *last* instance, that determines the cultural productivity characteristic of any group or that determines the moral significance of racial groups: that is to say, determines the regard we should have for racial and ethnic groups and their members, in themselves and in relation to one another.

Humans are also social animals: that is, we require associations of various kinds, associations secured by affections, loyalties, and attachments that are contingent and variable yet, on the whole, necessary for any person to become fully human. I am especially interested in exploring conceptions of raciality and ethnicity which include appropriate considerations of shared, heritable biological characteristics and shared sociocultural elements. Together these are important constitutive aspects of the meaningful orderings of a life-world, the base of which is a determinate social collectivity. Still, it must be remembered that the boundaries of all such collectivities, except for those that are completely isolated from other, different groups, shade off into those of other collectivities with which there have been contacts and exchanges (including exchanges of genes). As has been noted, races, as large populations of persons identified by the statistical frequencies with which certain characteristics are shared, "are always fuzzy around the margins" (Pat Shipman, "Facing Racial Differences—Together," B1–3).

I propose, then, an inquiry into raciality and ethnicity via a treacherous "third path" between racism and invidious ethnocentrism, on the one side, and antiracism, antiinvidious ethnocentrism, on the other. What I propose can help us recognize and nurture races and ethnies as we reconsider raciation and ethnicization as processes by which we humans produce and reproduce ourselves as crucial aspects of our social construction of realities (see Peter L. Berger and Thomas Luckmann, *The Social Construction of Reality*). In pursuing this path, I wish to think carefully about Carleton Coon's question (knowing that for some anthropologists and others Coon was a racist whose work was thus suspect): Why is it, after thousands of years, that human beings are not all "light khaki" instead of exhibiting the variety of skin tones (and other features) more or less characteristic of various populations called races? Is this the result of boundary-setting projects motivated by racism and invidious ethnocentrism? Might these populations be the result of biocultural group attachments and practices that are conducive to human survival and well-being, and hence that must be understood, appreciated, and provided for in the principles and practices of, say, a liberal, democratic society? If biodiversity is thought good for other species and for the global ecosystem, why not for the human species and its biocultural ecosystems? Might we find in Du Bois, then, a possible model of how we might work at understanding raciality and ethnicity, and at developing an appropriate philosophy by which, in his words, "to lay, on a basis of broad knowledge and careful insight, those large lines of policy and higher ideals which may form our guiding lines and boundaries in [meeting] the practical difficulties of every day"? ("The Conservation of Races," 176).

Facing up to these questions in pursuit of an understanding of raciality and ethnicity, in the light of past and present histories, is treacherous, indeed. But face them we must if we would not have these matters so dominate our personal and shared lives in their pernicious forms that they become the fires that consume us all. We are compelled, then, to philosophize: to pursue understandings to guide our praxis of daily life. We must also develop, as well, an understanding of the collections of practices, discourses, traditions, organizations, and media which constitute philosophizing—an understanding that is appropriate to the task of coping with problems involving raciality and ethnicity if the resources of the enterprise of philosophy are to be of assistance. For social and political philosophies suitable for and contributing to the realization of a stable, well-ordered, and just multiracial, multiethnic society must provide appropriate accounts of and appreciative provisions for the racialities and ethnicities of the members of such a society, but they must do so without either endorsing or degenerating into chauvinism.

Philosophizing—a term for various ways of thinking and discoursing about various things and matters—is a decidedly varied venture engaged in by various persons variously situated and is thus inherently contingent and conditioned socially and historically, thereby epistemologically and normatively. Consequently, any tradition or genre of philosophizing is characterized by diversity. And there are many such traditions. As A. J. Mandt has noted, contemporary professionalized, academic philosophy in the United States, for example, is a structured "web" of communities of discourse, "partly overlapping and partly discontinuous with one another":

> The totality forms a "great community" that is highly organized even though its constituent parts are largely autonomous. The great community has norms that define its limits, but these norms are equivocal and conventional. They are interpreted differently in various sub-communities. . . . Although in each locality norms operate productively as conventions that shape philosophical activity, their extension to the larger community makes them the basis for *merely* conventional justifications. (Mandt, "The Inevitability of Pluralism: Philosophical Practice and Philosophical Excellence," 91)

But in addressing matters of raciality and ethnicity, I think it important to shift from a consideration of philosophizing as manifested in various prevailing forms, agendas, and reconstructed histories to a consideration of phi-losophizing generally—that is, the intellectual activities engaged in by some individuals in virtually all human societies that are devoted to "figuring out" the means and rules for surviving, stabilizing living, and perpetuating the bi-ological and cultural reproduction of the society through successive genera-tions in certain spaces (both natural and built) in and through time. Such ac-tivities are to be found wherever and whenever self-reproducing groups of human beings worry about such matters. It is in considering the processes by which associated humans construct meaningfully ordered life-worlds that we find the appropriate context for understanding raciation and ethniciza-tion. And it is also here that we find the context for understanding the col-lection of practices and discourses that constitute philosophizing, or what I term the authoritative "figuring out" of the various means by which life-worlds are to be ordered and maintained. What follows is my own brief sketch of an account of the hows and whys of life-world ordering in and through which raciation, ethnicization, and philosophizing take place.[8]

Projects of "figuring out" that have come to be called *philosophizing* (other kinds include the various human, natural, and social sciences; arts, religions and theologies; mythical systems; etc.) will *always* be found among the ac-tivities of human populations and their subgroups that survive across time. For in surviving, humans are always faced with and must resolve the prob-lem of the *recurrent need for order* in and through which they *secure* living and living well in the face of and of constant change, especially in the form of entropy. Simply put: meaningfully ordered shared life is essential for hu-man survival and well-being.

With challenges to ordered life come experiences of anxiety, particularly when the challenges are such as to raise concerns regarding the survival of the social unit or of key aspects of a group's "way of life"—for example, the practices and legitimations ordering relationships through which biological reproduction is achieved and by which a population and its subgroups re-plenish themselves with new members, thus continuing their history into the future, or the preservation of meaning-endowed naturally and socially constituted environs thought vital to social (and individual) well-being. Challenges of these kinds, in their various manifestations, can be especially threatening because humans are not "hardwired" with the necessary re-sources for meeting all challenges successfully: that is, such resources are not part of our gene-based neurophysiological makeup. Rather, it is *only* out of the trial and error of living and learning that successful, life-ordering, and stabilizing strategies become knowledge-certified by some among those who survive the trials and are able to determine the whys and hows of failure and success. Under certain conditions, the results of these efforts get organized into order-producing and order-maintaining strategies and forms of explicit knowledge, which are further institutionalized as economies of stockpiles of knowledge and practices further associated with typified social roles. Together these provide the means, utterly necessary, for humans to control expectations and behavior in a social collectivity. Through the socialization of members into the collectivity, and the socialization of nonmembers, as well, about the collectivity, expectations and behavior are channeled into predefined patterns of rule-structured ordering that secure the social group against the threats and vagaries of entropy and the unfamiliar.

Culture is the term we speakers of English use to refer to the totality of these meaning-endowed and meaning-endowing, socially and personally identity-forming and socializing, socially binding, historicizing, time-and-space configuring, order-forming and order-maintaining and order-reproducing belief systems, practices, institutions, and structures that provide the historically contingent and dependent beings that we with the means of constructing necessarily meaningfully ordered life-worlds, especially important because as individuals we are thoroughly inept at birth and unable, for more than a decade, to provide for our own survival and well-being. This constructing work is accomplished within the boundary conditions of our evolving species- and subspecies-specific biological and anthropological compositions, which are in continuous interactions with socially conditioned natural and built environments and sociocultural worlds constructed in part by predecessors. These worlds must be maintained and even refined by persons in the present and in the future if life is to continue in the same condition as before or better—that is, with increased chances of survival and without at least some members of the collectivity having to start over from scratch, if they survive at all.

Group life, social life in general, and thereby individual lives depend on sociocultural repertoires as accumulations of tried and proven knowledges and practices and as a context for innovation. These repertoires are not just means for securing food, clothing, and shelter, but are the totality of (cultural) resources that provide the defining practices and fabrics of meanings which are vital for the formation and maintenance of anthropologically crucial personal and social identities and histories (i.e., biographies and traditions) that make individuals into viable, socialized persons and tie them together in the making and remaking of social wholes. And when we inquire into the social-natural histories of humans, we find that the subgroup or the population, not the individual, is the unit of survival and the bearer of group-defining cultural and physical traits.

Utterly decisive in this regard are the normed ways, first, in which a self-reproducing collectivity (and its subgroups, if any) has developed in its environments over time; and, second, in which the members of the natal collectivity and subgroups identify themselves, physically and culturally (physically through their culture[s]), and order life within their social spaces, especially if the collectivity or any of its subgroups live in proximity with "foreigners" who are decidedly "different" in ways that are important to how native individual and social life is ordered. Obvious examples include differences in terms of norms for dress, language, and other cultural practices. But of particular importance are norms of somatic aesthetics that help to regulate the preferences and practices by which partners are chosen for the intimacies that frequently (must) result in the birth of new members and by which the offspring are bonded with, nurtured, and socialized into the collectivity. In this area, especially to those who have the responsibilities of ensuring the collectivity's persistence across time, significantly different and objectionable strangers are likely to be seen as serious challenges to the preservation of the home group's embodied identity and thus to the collectivity's biocultural future as would be realized through its descendants.

Such challenges are hardly trivial. Embodied identities are vital aspects of "the order of things" in terms of which a biosocial collectivity's life-world is defined. So, too, are norms that define and regulate the relationships that determine descent because the socioculturally conditioned choosing of partners for the biological production of descendants is, to paraphrase Aristotle, the principal means by which many of us satisfy our desire to achieve relative immortality by leaving others behind after our death who look and carry on somewhat like ourselves. Thus self-reproducing populations share distinguishing physical and cultural features that set the demographic boundaries of a life-world, features which become part of the reservoir of normed resources drawn from in the construction and maintenance of personal and social identities. Thus also our identities become more or less tightly woven to our bodies and secured with webs of legitimations drawn from these cultural reservoirs and their sacred canopies of rationalizing, justifying "explanations." Consequently, neither the reservoirs nor the legitimations nor the identities can be trifled with if an established form of meaningful ordering is to be preserved in and across social times and spaces.

This historically contingent, yet anthropologically necessary, sociocultural matrix which must be appreciated in endeavoring to understand how physical and cultural factors are taken up and given social meanings so as to become mutually reinforcing in the processes through which social collectivities are "constructed"— that is, the processes in and through which geographically determinant populations and subgroups of sexually reproducing individuals become adaptively differentiated biologically and culturally. We have come to call such groupings *races* and *ethnies* (though there have been other designations for such groupings, in various languages, throughout human history). Such groupings are both social and natural (*social-natural kinds*). That is, humans are part of the natural world and subject to its laws as well as to species-specific limits and possibilities as set by evolving, culturally influenced biological and anthropological boundary conditions. Sociality—organized associations among humans—is a crucial aspect of these natural conditions of human existence: they are necessary for survival. Still, humans are without a fixed, preestablished "nature" that determines the historical particularities of existence and telos. Within the boundary conditions there is an enormous (though not infinite) range of plasticity that must—and can only—be developed and nurtured under social and cultural conditions guided by agendas whose particular goals and objectives cannot transcend but are not preset in their particularity by these same boundary conditions.

As with other species of living organisms, so too with humans in the long run: those populations or their subgroups that survive across generations and in various environments are the ones who are successful in building up, storing, and refining the life-sustaining, order-producing collections of knowledges and practices of particular kinds groupings groupings and in mediating them to contemporaries and successors. These collections must be distributed to and placed under the guardianship of particular persons who have the responsibilities of storing, refining, and mediating these knowledges while protecting them from loss or corruption. Among these resources are conceptions of the collectivity devised to define the members in ways that bind them together so that, through sanctioned cooperation, chances for survival are increased. Thus, the valorizing of descent associations with members of the natal subgroup and its extended population, of the defining ways of life of members as well as of the ways of life of others "significantly" different by descent, hence, in particular circumstances, by physical appearance and/or by culture. This is the basis of the normativity of social life that we call *ethnocentrism*. Extended to an entire (geographic) racial population, we might call it *racialism*. However, this is the same matrix from which are produced, under the pressures of challenges and competitions threatening "the order of things," those defensive mobilizations that take the form of invidious ethnocentrism and racism.

Now, as situations of living change, so must the knowledges undergirding social life be revised; otherwise, they become inadequate to meet new challenges. Still, as knowledges are "software"—that is, not part of our biological makeup or "hardwire"—they are especially vulnerable to corruption, entropy, or to becoming inadequate to changing circumstances, which is why knowledges must be protected and maintained, if not revised. So, too, must "the order of things" be protected. Hence, the necessary creation of a canopy (often sacred) of cognitive and normative interpretations that rationalize and justify—that is to say, "legitimate"—the knowledges that determine the constructed "order(ing) of things," including the determination of such crucial matters as what is spoken of as the *real* and the *right*, the *true* and the *good*, and each of their opposites.

The production of protective, legitimating canopies requires particular folks, of course—namely, those who "figure out" such matters. But their functions are socially vital, which is why their positions and roles must be valorized in ways to give them "authority" and, thereby, power: the power to *define the real, the true, and the good*, including the characterizing and identifying definitions of members of the group and of "others," as well as of the overall "order of things." Such persons direct the institutionalization of legitimated and thereby valorized knowledges and provide for their transmission by developing, over time and varying according to sociocultural groupings, various "conceptual machineries"—systems of myths, theologies, cosmologies, philosophies, sciences, therapies, and so on—through which to rationalize and justify "the order of things."

This, in general, is what I take to be the social location of those who have come to be called *philosophers*. Their self-assigned responsibilities have been to identify, codify, and stand guard over the rules for producing and certifying the knowledges needed to produce order and to sustain life against changes and variations thought to be inimical to "the order of things." Hence the fetishization by philosophers of various (but by no means all) traditions of univocal, universal, change-impervious Truth and Goodness, Right or Justice, and of the tools (e.g., systematized and formalized logic) and strategies (e.g., certain forms of "justification") by which these ideals are supposedly acquired. Here, too, is the source of the efforts to achieve legitimization (as in Plato's Myth of Metals) that would give to philosophizing in certain forms and practiced by certain certified persons its authority and honorific status. In contemporary, decidedly "modern" and complex societies, however, philosophers are generally all but ignored outside of classrooms and gatherings mostly of other philosophers and interested persons except in certain academic (and a few other) institutions when, on occasion, they lecture to crowds of varying sizes more or less respectfully anxious to hear the curious, perhaps interesting, and only very rarely the famous, speaker. The likes of Cornel West—a philosopher become public intellectual and international celebrity—are rare, indeed.

The legitimation of "the order of things" is crucial, especially for members of succeeding generations who, not having been present at the purported "beginning," are unusually naive and skeptical with regard to various aspects of "the order of things." This legitimation will be especially important if present orderings and productive arrangements (economic and political, for example) have, over time, made life less challenging and anxiety-producing: in part by securing what is necessary for survival, by routinely providing, in relative abundance, both the needed and the desired; in part by the society having become more complex, porous, and accommodating of the once "strange," thereby freeing up energies from defensive mobilizations and productive labor that can then be redeployed in various forms of learning-recreation, sometimes in avid pursuit of pleasures found in partaking of the "exotic" and "strange" or the just plain "new" and "different" (such as watching television programs from various countries and/or with characters played by persons of various races or ethnies, or just hanging out at the mall with the multi-culti posse). Under such conditions it is more difficult to convince the young (or the mature and "liberated" cosmopolites) that the "old" ordering of things should remain more or less "the same." All the more pressing, then, the need for convincing legitimations of "the order of things" to keep enough members of the group "at home" to ensure the viability and reproduction of the life-world and its members. In such circumstances and on behalf of those groupings, certain members may fashion and deploy various concrete and rationalizing practices by which to colonize for their exploitation larger and extended spaces and peoples in pursuit of their ordered lives. They may justify doing so by claims regarding the superiority of the race and its ethnies. In such instances, racialism or ethnocentrism, in the words of Anthony Appiah, has "gone imperial."

Unless legitimated order replaces anxiety with calm and comfort, if threats to order are not met and neutralized, anxiety can and will become terror as the loss of familiar and comforting practices that bring ordering proceeds to such an extent that it threatens the configuration and stability of the life-world as a whole. By endangering the life-world's key structures and processes, these threats, whether real or imagined and responded to as though real, arouse the prospect of serious decline, chaos, or complete loss of the order that gives meaning to unifying personal and social identities. For without such identities, persons come to feel that there is no meaningful present explained, justified, and made endurable by biographies, histories, and traditions that situate the present in connection to reconstructed pasts and hoped-for futures. And without connections of this kind there is but personal and social chaos leading to more and more desperate reactions to remove the threat and to restore order before the onset of psychic and physical death, which arrives slowly over periods of decline (best visible in retrospect, though this view is unavailable to the dead), quickly over relatively short periods, or abruptly.

Whether disorder and decline lead to death is a complex matter involving the anticipation and apprehension of the threat(s), of what is (or is thought to be) threatened, of the nature of the threat(s), and how they are responded to: in what ways, by whom, when, and for how long. Among the means used, regardless of the nature of the threat, must be forms of social organization and conceptual machineries that are devised to define while they order the known and the real. If the unfamiliar, the strange, and the undesirable cannot be accommodated into prevailing universes of meaning on acceptable terms, they will have to be placed in restricted zones—whether conceptual, physical, or social—and kept there in quarantine, or eliminated entirely (as in genocidal projects of racial or ethnic "cleansing") to prevent the biological and social influences that might presage undesirable and threatening changes to "our" traditions and "way of life." The keepers of the social orderings and conceptual machineries for maintaining "the order of things"—machineries appropriate, that is, to the threat and area threatened—must mobilize arsenals of weapons from knowledge stockpiles with which to meet and resolve the challenges to order, and they must do so by defining policies to direct actions and behaviors that neutralize the threats and maintain or restore order.[9]

Raciality and ethnicity, then, are indeed "social constructions." But we humans *must* construct ourselves. In doing so, we form social collectivities requisite to which personal and social identities are also formed. Along with other aspects of life-world cultural repertoires, these identities include valorizations of our bodies (of the shared features that distinguish members of the natal group and the collectivity). These identities are set in various ways, and they work—and are worked on—dialectically in the ongoing processes of regulating the reproduction and maintenance of shared, biocultural life. In their particular configurations and valorizations, such social and personal identities are not biologically determined; hence they are not, in this sense, necessary, but they are historically and socially contingent in their configurations and valorizations. Part of the regulatory work such identities perform is played out in mate selections leading to the birth of offspring. Depending on the "program" directing the processes of socialization of offspring and social life generally, these identities contribute, more or less, to the reproduction of the biocultural collectivity, that is, of the race or ethnie.

So it is that we are not all khaki, as Carleton Coon observed (though, again, there are times when, for quite good and important reasons, we should and do act as though we are), and why, generally (hardly universally), so much resistance exists to our *becoming* all khaki. Should this resistance be facilitated? Or, to put this important question differently: How might we work to conserve "colored" populations and subgroupings (and white is a color, as well), races and ethnies, without making it easier for racialism and ethnocentrism to "go imperial"?

I have sketched a case in terms of which such groupings can be seen as social-natural kinds whose valorizing legitimations are initially internal to the groupings. Though this internalization makes these legitimations and valorizings historically and socially relative and, because humanly based, certainly contingent, in multiracial and multiethnic societies we can still orient ourselves to live in important ways beyond the various socially constructed borders that give order and definition to our respective race and/or ethnie-based life-worlds. In this way, we can share a larger, more encompassing life-world, perhaps by agreeing to public political principles that have sufficient overlap with the various life-world orienting doctrines to which we may be committed. Such principles will provide a basis for a shared life, one that leaves each race and ethnie almost—though not quite—as they were and wish to be. (This is, of course, the old but recurrent problem of trying to achieve unity while preserving diversity, and a particularly vexing problem for liberal democracies.) [10]

Is the realization of such a shared life a practical possibility? Yes. Is doing so possible practically, all things considered? A definitive answer to this question cannot come from philosophizing alone, only from pursuing it, in practice, in everyday life.

II RACISM: PARADIGMS AND PERSPECTIVES

4   *Moral Asymmetries in Racism*

LAWRENCE BLUM

In debates about racism within the United States, some take the position that black people cannot be racist and that only white people can be racist. Others hold a very different view. They say that racism is not confined to one group, that members of any ethnic or racial group can be racist against members of any other group, and that racism on the part of blacks (or Asians or Asian Americans, and so on) is no better or worse than racism on the part of whites. All racism is equal, according to this second view.

These two views are sometimes thought to correlate with particular members of racial groups. So, it is said, blacks tend to hold the view that only whites can be racist, whereas whites hold the view that all racism is equal. This claim about the view of blacks and whites may be true as a broad statistical generalization, but it has many exceptions, and I would caution against the racializing of philosophical viewpoints. Many blacks hold the view that all racism is equal, and many whites believe that blacks (and possibly members of other nonwhite racial groups) cannot be racist.

At the same time, the widespread popularity of these two polarized and extreme views—the "only whites can be racist" view and the "all racism is equal" view—has stood in the way of communication across racial lines concerning matters of race and racism. I believe that these views are incorrect. I argue that blacks can be racist and that no ethnic or racial group is immune from racism. At the same time, I do not agree that all racism is equal. I argue for a "moral asymmetry" in manifestations of racism. Some instances of racism are worse than others, and the moral asymmetry sometimes has to do with whether the perpetrator or the victim of racism is white or black. More generally, I argue that in some respects white racism *is* worse than black racism, but in other respects it is not. In this sense, I am arguing for a view that lies somewhere between the "only whites can be racist" view and the "all racism is equal" view. I am hopeful that this proposal, in addition to providing a more adequate conception of the moral wrong of racism, will provide a framework better suited than either of its two competitors for facilitating cross-racial dialogue and understanding that acknowledges the differing historical and social experiences of different racial and ethnic groups.[1]

Racism

What is the "racism" about which the aforementioned views disagree? Unfortunately, I am unable to come up with a general definition that satisfies me, but I will point to some specific forms of racism that can serve to ground the discussion.

First, we must make the familiar distinction between *institutional* and *individual* racism. *Institutional racism* refers to specific institutions or pervasive social forms that embody racism or racial injustice—such as word-of-mouth recruiting at a mostly white company, which leaves potential racial minority applicants at a disadvantage; or educational institutions failing to provide an atmosphere and services sensitive to the experiential and cultural differences of racial minority students, thus failing to provide equal educational opportunity for those students.[2] By *individual racism*, I mean any racism on the part of individuals, which can include actions, beliefs, attitudes, even feelings. The most common forms of individual attitudinal racism are bigotry, prejudice, and a belief in one's racial superiority, and these attitudes prompt many forms of racist behavior. However, individual racist acts can be unintentionally racist, particularly in institutionally racist contexts, where an individual is simply doing her job or conforming with "standard practice" so that her actions have racially discriminatory effect, but not the motivation.[3]

In this essay, I am concerned with *individual* racism, not *institutional* racism per se (although I recognize that some individual racism occurs as part of institutional racism), but not because I think individual racism is *more important* than institutional racism. I do not really think it is meaningful to compare these two modes of racism in terms of importance, partly because they are so intertwined with one another. While the institutional mode is deserving of philosophical attention, my concerns are primarily with individual actions, attitudes, and beliefs.

The terms *racism* and *racist* are distinctly moral or morally charged. In speaking of a "racist remark", a "racist stereotype", or a "racist policy", we condemn in strong terms the object in question. In the dominant culture in the United States., to accuse someone of a racist action or a racist sentiment or belief is to charge him with a serious moral failure, and most people wish very much to avoid being thought to be or being called, "racist."

There is a difference, of course, between saying that Jo's *action* is racist and saying that *she herself* is racist. If Jo has committed a racist act, as bad as that is, it does not go as far as saying that she herself is "a racist." To say that a *person* is "a racist" is to say that she has deeply ingrained attitudes and beliefs that are racist, and that this racism pervades her attitudes and actions (though perhaps in subtle ways) toward the groups against whom she is racist. It is quite important not to assume that a person who commits one racist act is thereby "a racist." (We contribute to blurring this distinction when we say that "Jo is racist in doing X," as this expression simultaneously refers to a specific action, yet also seems to implicate the person's entire character.)

In this essay, then, I am *assuming* that to be racist is a moral fault, but at the same time I am also supporting that assumption to some extent by spelling out aspects of the moral wrong of individual racism. One implication of the assumption that racism is a serious moral fault is a suggestion that we refrain from attaching the term *racism* to every manifestation of racial discomfort or insensitivity. Thus, a white or Asian student who displays ignorance about black culture and thereby makes what seem to black students insulting or offensive remarks is, in the framework of this suggestion, not necessarily engaging in a racist act. Although the ignorance and insensitivity deserve criticism—and although they may in some sense reflect racist institutions—it is not helpful to refer to them with the heavily loaded term *racism*. (If the ignorance and insensitivity were deliberate and willful—for instance, if the white or Asian student were presented with ready opportunities to learn about black culture, but deliberately chooses not to avail herself of these opportunities—the act would come closer to being straightforwardly "racist.") It cheapens and degrades the seriousness of racism itself if every racial mishap and misunderstanding gets labeled with the term *racism*.[4]

Well, what then *is* racism? As I mentioned, I do not want to give a general definition but to indicate two distinct forms that individual racism takes, which most everyone will agree are examples of racism, even if they disagree about other cases.[5] The first is *racial hatred, animosity, or bigotry*—hating blacks or Jews, Croats or Hutus because they *are* blacks, Jews, Croats, and Hutus.

The second form of individual racism involves seeing another group as *humanly inferior* in some significant way. The paradigm case here is the way Westerners have seen blacks, especially since the advent of slavery—namely, as inferior in intellectual capacity and in certain moral qualities taken as essential to civilized life, such as self-control, moderation of passion, and the like. Other cases, however, are Japanese attitudes toward Koreans, even today, and "caste" attitudes, such as in India and to some extent in Japan toward what are taken to be "lower orders" of persons. White American attitudes toward Latinos and Native Americans have also involved this form of racism.

Hatred-based racism and superiority-based racism often go together. Nevertheless, they do not have to and do not always do so. Often, groups who are seen as humanly deficient are not so much hated as patronized, scorned, and pitied, but sometimes groups that are hated—such as Jews and Japanese Americans have been in the United States—are seen as "superiors" in some fundamental respects: they are "taking over," they work too hard, they have superior intelligence, and the like.

I suggest that both hatred (or animosity) toward another racial or ethnic group and belief in the inferiority of another group are standardly taken to be instances of racism. Whether or not a common denominator can be found for these two forms, or whether both can be seen as unified in terms of some larger framework, I leave aside here and proceed with the two forms as the paradigms of what I mean by *racism*.[6]

"Only Whites Can Be Racist"

First, let us examine the view that blacks cannot be racist, that only whites can be racist. This view is articulated by Joe Feagin and Hernan Vera in their book *White Racism*.

> From the perspective we take in this book, 'black racism' does not exist. We conceptualize racism in structural and institutional as well as individual terms. Racism is more than a matter of individual prejudice and scattered episodes of discrimination. There is no black racism because there is no centuries-old system of racial subordination and discrimination designed by African Americans to exclude white Americans from full participation in the rights, privileges, and benefits of this society. Black (or other minority) racism would require not only a widely accepted racist ideology directed at whites, but also the power to systematically exclude whites from opportunities and rewards in major economic, cultural, and political institutions. While there are black Americans with antiwhite prejudices, and there are instances of blacks discriminating against whites, these examples are not central to the core operations of U.S. society and are not part of an entrenched structure of institutionalized racism that can be found in every nook and cranny of this country. (ix–x)[7]

Feagin and Vera's view is quite at odds with our normal use of the moral vocabulary of racism. When Colin Ferguson, a black American from Jamaica, murdered several people on the LIRR in 1994 and left evidence that he hated whites and Asians, many people regarded his actions as racist in their motivations. Ferguson's actions were evil not only because they involved killing but also because we think they were based on his hatred of whites and Asians, which is something that we normally think of as racism, even though Ferguson was black. Similarly, Leonard Jeffries's views, as reported in several publications, that white people are inferior to blacks in human warmth and concern because they lack melanin in their skin, or Elijah

Muhammad's views, as reported in James Baldwin's *The Fire Next Time*, that whites are evil and devils, are rightly thought of as (superiority-based) racist views, even though they are held by blacks; just as R. Herrnstein and C. Murray's claims about the inherent and genetic inferiority of blacks in *The Bell Curve* are rightly thought of as racist views.[8]

Racism and Institutional Power

Let us now look at the rationale Feagin, Vera, and other authors present in favor of their view. They claim that only groups that have systematic power over another group can be racist against members of the latter group. However, this line of argument would seem to imply that in societies in which people of color hold power, members of the dominant group can actually be racist against other groups that they take to be of a different race. So in that society nonwhite people *can* be racist. For example, as mentioned above, ethnic Koreans in Japan have suffered from prejudice and discrimination at the hands of Japanese. Although ethnic prejudice cannot be fully identified with racial prejudice, in this context the commonalties are more relevant than the differences. That is, even though Westerners may see Japanese and Koreans as part of the same "race," within Japan discrimination against Koreans is bound up with the view that Koreans are a fundamentally different kind of—an inferior kind of—human being than Japanese.[9] This Japanese view of Koreans (not to say that it is shared by all or even most Japanese), like the Serbian view of Bosnians that has evolved virulently in the 1990s, involves a "racialized" form of ethnicity—which, in contrast to a purely cultural conception of ethnicity, sees (perhaps not entirely coherently) ethnic differences as heritable.[10]

To summarize, if systematic power to oppress on the basis of race (or something like race) is the central feature of racism, then racism cannot be confined to whites.

Suppose the view that only whites can be racist is understood to be confined to the West (as I suspect Feagin and Vera mean it to be), where whites are the dominant power group. Would Feagin and Vera's view be plausible then? I think not. Consider a largely black school and a class within it that has only one white student. Several black students exclude the white student from socializing with them by calling him a "honky" and derisively referring to him as "white bread." Let us assume that these students are genuinely bigoted against whites; they dislike them simply because they are white.[11]

Here, the black students have power over the white one, a power that stems from a majority-minority dynamic and that is very much part of how the black students' racist and exclusionary remarks serve to hurt the white student. This example therefore draws on the insight that the harm of racism is bound up with the power relations between the parties involved, but at the same time it throws into question the view that (in the United States) only whites can be racist. Although the example involves power, it does not involve an institutionalized structure of domination in the larger sense invoked by Feagin and Vera; in the wider society, whites are still the dominant group.

Even if whites are the dominant group in society as a whole, they are not the dominant group in every institution or context. Even if power were the sole arbiter of when racism can occur (a view that I reject), Feagin and Vera would have to allow that when blacks hold power, then they are capable of being racist. Also, restricting the consideration of power *solely* to the basic structure or institutions of society seems arbitrary. In the example just mentioned, the power of the black students' racial exclusionary remarks to hurt the white child does seem bound up with the power that blacks have over whites in that particular venue. In cities, for example, where blacks hold political power, they are capable of using that power to harm whites, and if they do so on the basis of race, it seems partially in accord with Feagin and Vera's own emphasis on power to see their actions as racist.[12]

Perhaps we should take Feagin and Vera's view to be that the forms of racial injustice endemic to the dominant institutions of society are of *greater concern* than individual racism. Even if this claim were true, it seems a different claim than that only whites or only those in power can be racist. In condemning individual racism, we do not ordinarily think that the grounds of condemnation lie *solely* in the contribution that these actions, attitudes, and the like make to structures of racial oppression and injustice. We also regard these actions, attitudes, and the like as morally repellent in their own right, and the ordinary use of the terms *racism* or *racist* carry this moral opprobrium.[13]

Racism and Ideology

The idea that only white people can be racist may also stem from the fact that the philosophy of racism as an explicit ideology justifying colonial expansion, slavery, segregation, exclusion and domination has been much more fully developed in the West than anywhere else. (Indeed, the term *racism* was formerly used primarily to refer to such a system of belief.) According to this view, in other contexts in which a dominant group has the power to oppress a subordinate group conceived of as in some sense a different people or group, this ideology may be similar to racism, but yet not racism—for example, the Hutu-led government of Rwanda persecuting and murdering Tutsis (and moderate Hutus, though this point is peripheral to the matter at hand); or Bosnian Serbs engaging in "ethnic cleansing" of Bosnian Muslims.

If these other instances of domination, not backed by fully developed racial ideologies are taken to be as morally objectionable as racism and for similar reasons, then it might not matter very much, at least from a *moral* point of view, whether we call them *racism* or not (though there might be some intellectual or analytical reason for confining the term *racism* to these Western systems of domination). Does the alleged involvement of an explicit ideology in the term *racism* generate a further moral evil beyond the mere fact of a form of domination based on some (perceived, lineage-based) non-ideologized difference from the dominating group? This matter raises complex questions I cannot pursue further here, except to note that confining *racism* to systems supported by fully developed racist ideologies would exclude many forms of racial hatred and animosity, even of whites toward blacks and Latinos—forms that lack ideological underpinnings, but that contemporary parlance unquestionably regards as *racist*.[14]

Racism and Prejudice

A third argument suggested by Feagin and Vera is that what I am calling racism is just prejudice, whereas the term *racism* should be confined to its institutional forms. (See Spike Lee's view in note 7.) Unless this argument is to be a merely semantic, it must be allied with the view that prejudice is something *much* less serious, much less a matter of moral concern, than racism. Such a view could be supported by several claims about the nature of prejudice. (1) Everyone is prejudiced in some way, so no one is in a position to criticize its manifestations in others. (2) Prejudice is part of human nature and thus ineradicable. (3) Prejudice just means prejudging, which may in some form be essential as a cognitive matter, and even when objectionable, it is not seriously so. (4) Prejudice is just another way of talking about a preference for "one's own kind"; it is generally innocuous, and even when it is not, nothing much can be done about it.

Some of these views are not consistent with each other, and some may be versions of others. However none is satisfactory. First, in its primary meaning in ordinary English parlance, prejudice in the sense of "racial prejudice" is *not*, the same as simply prejudging someone; nor is it simply a preference for one's own kind. Rather, it carries a connotation of animosity or some other strongly negative attitude toward or assessment of the group against whom the person is prejudiced. So, we distinguish between wanting to be with people like oneself (which in itself may be limiting in some ways) and actual *prejudicial attitudes* toward members of out-groups. Particular prejudices are not more ineradicable than is racism, even if the goal of a totally prejudice-free social order may be a pipe dream. Nor is everyone prejudiced to anything like the same extent.[15] Racial prejudice, then, *is* a morally serious matter, and its moral distance from what I am calling individual racism is much smaller than Feagin and Vera's (and Spike Lee's) remarks imply.

Though the terms *(racial) prejudice* and *racism* do contain some area of overlap, some elements of what I am calling individual racism go beyond what even an accurate understanding of racial prejudice betokens. To say that someone who *hates* blacks, Asians, or whites, or who declares blacks to be inferior based on race, is "prejudice(d)" is greatly understated, if not exactly false. Racism involves either bigotry or seeing others as in some fundamental way less human or less worthy, whereas prejudice may signify merely some negative attitude toward or negative belief about the other group. Although the arguments here understate the seriousness of prejudice itself, racist bigotry and attitudes of superiority are more morally vile than the term *prejudice* normally conveys.

It misleads, then, to say that people of color can be prejudiced but not racist. It is true that the notion of prejudice fails to capture what we mean by racism—not, however, because it fails to involve power, but because it refers or can refer to psychic attitudes that are weaker than the racial hatred, bigotry, contempt, and degradation involved in racism. To encourage the idea that people of color cannot be racist ˙s to discourage their realization that if they do come to hold some power, ⸌hey have as much potentiality to abuse that power by persecuting other groups as does any historical power-holding group.

Reactive Racism

A fourth reason sometimes offered for confining *racism* to whites is that when blacks manifest racial animosity and hatred, it is generally either *reactive to* or *compensatory for* white racism toward them. Let me comment only briefly on this complex matter. First, one would want to distinguish between being racist and being to blame for one's racism. A person whose racist attitudes have developed as a result of being the victim of racism may well be less blameworthy for her racism than someone whose racism has other sources. Nevertheless, this explanation does not mean that she is *not* racist, nor does it mean that she should not be held responsible to some degree for her current racist attitudes and, even more, for her actions. Also, we must distinguish between the reactive racist reacting to her own racist victimization or of persons close to her and the reactive racist reacting to the victimization of other unknown members of her group. The first seems a much more strongly mitigating circumstance—in regard to accounting blame for racism—than does the latter. We seem to make moral allowance for feelings of anger, hate, and vengeance arising from harms and injustices that touch the agent more personally.

Second, however, there is a large difference between hating someone who has himself victimized you, and hating others who belong to the same racial group as your victimizer, but who otherwise have no connection whatsoever to that victimizer. It is the targeting of a group and of persons merely for being members of it—rather than the targeting of someone directly involved in racist victimization against oneself—that is racist. I once saw a documentary in which a white man had been beaten and robbed in his house by two black men. He said that he now hated all blacks and appeared to regard this as an entirely reasonable reaction to his victimization. The idea that "reactive" racism is not really racism may be used to support this sort of bigoted attitude in whites, in addition to the sorts of cases those who want to absolve blacks of racism have in mind.

Furthermore, even if the genesis of an individual's racial hatred *does* in fact (though irrationally) lie in having once been a victim of racism, there nevertheless comes a point at which that individual fully "owns" that racist attitude and must be held responsible for it. Here, we must keep in mind the distinction made earlier between three things: (1) committing a racist act, (2) having a racist attitude, and (3) being a racist or a racist person. An individual who is victimized by members of group X may lash out at *other* members of group X by uttering racist phrases and epithets in self-defense, but without truly holding the racist attitudes of hatred or superiority that these phrases generally express. This defensive racist action does not necessarily betoken the more morally serious attitude of racial hatred or animosity, much less that the individual is actually a racist.

Still, no matter what its genesis, a person is to be held responsible for her racist actions, and once she comes to hold racist attitudes, then the fact that without her previous victimization by racism she would not have held these attitudes becomes irrelevant to whether she must take responsibility for them *as* racist attitudes. After all, many white people come to hold racist attitudes in a "derivative" manner, reacting to personal and social frustrations by scapegoating a group culturally available for that role. These white people do not simply generate racism out of malice; without their personal frustrations, they may have never come to hold racist attitudes.

In addition, not all racism on the part of victims of racism *can* be attributed solely to a reaction to that victimization. Many victims of racism at the hands of group X just happen themselves to have racist attitudes toward group Y, whether Y is a group that persecuted them or not. Moreover, elaborated racist philosophies(such as those of Elijah Muhammad, described eloquently by James Baldwin in *The Fire Next Time* (90–93) or the calculated anti-Jewish and antiwhite racist (not to mention sexist, homophobic, and anti-Catholic) remarks of a former lieutenant of the Nation of Islam, Khalid Muhammad—cannot be regarded as simply reactions to white racism against blacks. Such a degree of committed and elaborated racist ideology and cultural stereotyping involves a "proactive" and not merely reactive moral agency.

In summary, then, adequate arguments have not been provided to lead us to jettison the commonsense view that racial hatred and any belief in racial superiority are racist no matter which racial group manifests them. Members of all groups are capable of the racial hatred, animosity, or belief in superiority that constitute individual racism.

"All Racism Is Equal"

But some who agree with the view that racism respects no racial or ethnic boundaries go a step further and hold that all manifestations of racism are equivalent in their moral significance—that it is as weighty a moral offense for a black person to manifest racism toward a Korean or white person as it is for a white to do so toward a black or Korean. This is the second position from which I want to distinguish my own. Against the view that, with regard to the race of the perpetrator and victim, all racism is morally symmetrical, I want to defend a claim of "moral asymmetry" with regard to race. Although I have never seen the "all racism is equal" view explicitly articulated or defended—in contrast with the "blacks can't be racist" view—it seems to me to inform a good deal of popular debate concerning racism, on college campuses and elsewhere. Frequently in the course of a dispute concerning racism, people cite incidents of what they regard as racism on the part of persons of color. The thrust of such interventions often appears to go beyond making the more limited point that, indeed, racism is confined to no ethnic or racial group, to imply the stronger claim that all manifestations of racism are of equal moral weight and concern.

The claim worth examining here cannot be that, taking its full moral character into account, every individual instance of racism is of equal moral concern. Obviously, a racially motivated violent physical attack is morally worse than the use of a racist stereotype in a joke.[16] Without any attempt at comprehensiveness here, it may be worth mentioning a few dimensions on which we commonly make distinctions regarding the moral seriousness of manifestations of racism. One is the degree of actual or anticipatable harm caused by the act of racism in question. A second is how intentionally racist the act is; ceteris paribus, intentional racism is more morally problematic than unintentional. A third concerns the type or degree of the racist attitude in question; ceteris paribus, mild racial dislike is less morally bad than racial hatred. A fourth concerns whether a threat of violence is implied in the action or whether any *actual* physical harm is caused. A fifth is how mild or vicious a racial slur or stereotype is; stereotyping blacks as basketball players may have an element of racism in it (though not necessarily), but to do so is not as bad as stereotyping blacks as mentally weak. Calling Latinos "taco-eaters" is not as bad (again, everything else being equal) as calling them "greasers."

Thus, I will not treat the "all racism is equal" view to be the claim that every single manifestation of individual racism is morally equivalent to every other, but rather that the moral seriousness of a racist act is not affected by the racial identity of the parties to it. That is, racist acts of the same type and morally equivalent in all other respects are also morally equivalent independent of the racial identity of their target[17] and perpetrator. It is this view against which I argue that the racial identity of the target and the perpetrator generally is material to our moral assessment of the act.

In particular, I argue for the core truth regarding the "only whites can be racist" view—namely, that there is a general moral asymmetry between racism on the part of whites toward blacks and on the part of blacks toward whites. More generally, racism against vulnerable groups (and their members) is more morally serious than racism against dominant groups (and their members). This view can be established only by pointing to the disvalues instantiated by racist actions. As suggested earlier, proponents of a power/subordination-based conception of racism have generally failed to provide such an account, in part because they have suppressed, while also presupposing, the moral dimension of their view.

Three factors are, on the one hand, generally empirically linked with racial differences between target and perpetrator and, on the other hand, also affect the moral significance of an individual act of racism.[18] These three factors affect the nature or intensity of the moral offense involved in the racist act. They are the following: (1) historical legacy, (2) current relations of institutional advantage and disadvantage, and (3) patterns of racist act and attitude.

Historical Legacy of Racism

The first factor is the *historical legacy of racism*. An act of racism against a member of a group that has suffered a strong historical legacy of racist discrimination and oppression generally evokes in members of the target group a sense, implicit or explicit, of that historical legacy. It brings some of the weight of that history down against that group by directly invoking the memory of the opprobrium connected with that history or by carrying an evaluative and emotional valence that partakes of that history (whether directly reminding the target of that historical opprobrium and oppression or not). Either way, the damaging force of the particular act stems, in part, from partaking of that history. In either case the act involves a greater offense against respect for the dignity of others (the members of the target group) than does a racist act that carries no historical legacy effect.

Two examples of this effect. In 1990, after a young black man was killed in the Bensonhurst section of New York City, demonstrations were held to assert the right of blacks to travel anywhere they wanted in that city. The mostly black demonstrators were met by a large group of whites, some of whom waved watermelons in a contemptuous gesture of hatred toward the blacks. Here, the force of these residents' racist actions was intensified by their use of this historical symbol of slavery, a symbol generally understood to invoke an image of the supposedly happy, slow-witted, agreeable slave eating watermelons. In making use of this image those who wielded the watermelons evoked, and no doubt many of them intended to evoke in the black demonstrators, the fear, sense of oppression, and terror of slavery.

A second example is the impact of the swastika symbol on Jews. To most Jews, the swastika evokes Nazism and the Holocaust, a historical memory of terror and genocide. The psychic pain caused by the use of a swastika as a racist symbol is, to some degree, independent of whether the target actually believes that its particular display in the moment presages an attempt or desire to reinstitute some form of organized persecution of Jews, just as the psychic pain of racist symbols and words evoking slavery, Jim Crow, and other systems of racial oppression is partly independent of whether the target in a particular racist incident believes that the perpetrator's actions are a prelude or bear some causal link to a return to a similar form of historical oppression. The historical legacy effect operates by way of the target group members' group identity; the moral offense is against the group insofar as that identity is bound up with having suffered a particular history of oppression or discrimination.

By contrast, a racist action against a member of a group that has not inherited a substantial and live history of racial oppression, such as whites as a racial group in the United States, cannot carry this particular psychic effect. There is no weight of history to bring down against that group. This moral asymmetry tends to correlate with that between dominant and vulnerable groups—and, in any case, yields an asymmetry between whites and blacks or Christians and Jews within the United States.

My claim then is that the historical legacy effect contributes to the psychic pain and damage wrought by acts of racism, involves a more intense insult and attack on the dignity of the vulnerable group, and thus differentiates between otherwise comparable racist acts.[19]

The historical legacy argument may draw a response something like this: "Why go on about slavery, the Holocaust, the internment camps (for Japanese Americans), and the like? That happened a long time ago; living in the past is just wallowing in historical victimhood. It isn't constructive." Such an argument is often, though not always, advanced by persons who are members of groups without comparable histories of oppression or terror; nevertheless, it is not without merit. There can be too much involvement in the legacy of historical oppression of one's group, just as there can be a misassessment of the direct causal impact of that legacy on the current condition of one's group or a misassessment of one's own individual lot in life. However, the historical legacy argument is not undermined by the abuses to which it may be subject.[20] We must guard against these abuses, but at the same time recognize that the identity of some groups is, for stretches of historical time, partially constituted by the historical memory of legacies of oppression. This is just part of the larger truth that who people are is in part what the histories of their "people" are.[21]

Current Relations between Racial Groups

The second factor making for moral asymmetries between racial groups— in particular, between whites and blacks in the United States—concerns current relations between the groups in regard to societal advantage and disadvantage, and their power to shame members of the disadvantaged group. All racism that takes the form of declaring or implying that the victim is of an inferior race or is inferior because of her race is objectionable by its very form. It violates the demand to treat and regard human beings as equals, independent of race. Thus, Leonard Jeffries' statement that whites are inferior to blacks because of the lesser degree of melanin in their skin is racist and repulsive. However, beyond the fact that the message is racist in its own right, when that racist message is directed toward a group or member that occupies a disadvantaged or subordinate position in the society, then it acquires a further power to shame its target. It is thus a greater violation of the norm of respecting others as equals. It involves a more intense shaming by pointedly reminding the victim that the inferiority declared in the racist action is reflected in the social distribution of advantage and disadvantage. Such forms of racism are attacks on the self-worth of their targets and have a tendency (not always effective) to harm the targets' ability to see themselves as moral equals in society.[22]

By contrast, racism toward a member of a dominant group does not have this kind of shaming power. No actual social inferiority corresponds to the inferiority or devaluing declared by the racist remark. Although objectionable and hurtful, the racist epithets "white scum," "honkie," and "white bread"[23] are generally not reinforced by the larger social structure surrounding the perpetrator and victim of the remarks (but they can be by the more immediate social context; cf. The school incident discussed earlier). In fact the contemptuous put-down contained in the epithets are belied by the structure, which places whites as the dominant group, and thus provides a built-in psychic counterweight to the insult contained in the racial slur. In some contexts, the power relations between the different groups make it virtually impossible for a member of the subordinate group to actually succeed in scorning or insulting a member of the dominant group, even if she utilizes the linguistic forms of insult and scorn.

Hence, everything else being equal, racism against members of currently disadvantaged groups involves a stronger offense against treating people as equals than does racism against members of dominant groups. This point, in particular, applies to whites and blacks. In this respect, dominant-to-vulnerable racism is worse than vulnerable-to-dominant racism.

Patterns and Prevalence of Racist Acts

A third asymmetry of psychic harm concerns patterns and prevalence of racist actions, attitudes, and beliefs in the society. When an individual is the target of racism in a context in which she knows that she or people in her group are and will continue to be victims of similar incidents, the larger presence of these racist patterns is invoked in the particular incident at hand. The pervasive character of incidents of racism make fear, self-doubt, and concern about acceptance and equal treatment the more likely results of each individual instance of racism so that the individual instance thus constitutes a greater moral offense against a norm of respect than a comparable act in the absence of such a pattern. The patterns and the prevalence of the attitudes expressed in them contribute to a diminishing of a targeted person's ability to resist society's racist beliefs and stereotypes and to slough off the individual racist insult.

The point here is analogous to but independent of historical legacy in that it is at least theoretically possible that a group with a strong legacy of discrimination will not experience patterns of racist treatment in the present. Conversely, a group that is a contemporary target of racism may not have had a strong historical legacy of such treatment. In the latter case, current racist incidents will carry no historical legacy effect—anti-Arab racism during the Gulf War, for example—but the effect of the pervasiveness of prejudice will be implicated in each individual racist incident. In any case, the historical legacy effect and the pervasiveness effect are distinct; frequently, both are present in that many historically oppressed groups are also prime targets of current widespread patterns of racist action and beliefs.

The point here is not simply the obvious one that an individual or group is caused more harm (everything else being equal) by a greater rather than a lesser number of incidents of racism directed against her/them. It is that an *individual* incident is a greater moral offense and also derives a greater power to harm from its embeddedness in a pattern of incidents, or pervasive racist beliefs. If one is a target of an anomalous racist incident—a type of insult that does not normally happen to members of one's group and that is not an example of socially pervasive prejudices against one's group—it is much easier to psychically ignore the individual incident. Suppose, for example, that a Norwegian American is the target of a racist incident on the part of a Swedish American. Such an incident may be painful in its own right or at least unpleasant, but it is not likely to evoke the sense of fear, shame, or general concern about one's social acceptance or respect that would be evoked by a similar incident directed against blacks, Jews, Arabs, or Asians (Asian Americans). An individual incident can much less readily be psychically dismissed by a member of a vulnerable group.[24]

The intensified moral offense being described here is distinct from, though in some ways analogous to, the way individual incidents shame by invoking the relations of social dominance in one's society. In that case, the shaming is brought about by invoking the target's inferior status in the society and the way the culture at large takes that status to reflect the inherent inferiority declared in the racist action. In the pattern effect, however, the attack on dignity is produced by patterns of incidents or patterns of belief that the victim of racism has reason to regard as widely shared.

The point about patterns casts a wider net than the one about social advantage and does so in two senses. First, it encompasses a larger set of groups as targets—not only those groups that are subordinate, such as blacks, Latinos, Native Americans, but other vulnerable yet non-subordinate groups, such as Arab Americans, Japanese Americans, and Jews. Racism against the latter groups does not characteristically take the form of declaring them to be inferior in order to account for and justify subordinate positions in society. Rather, nonsubordinate, vulnerable groups are the target of racism in the form of race- or ethnicity-based hatred, resentments, or horribly offensive stereotyping. Vulnerable, nonsubordinate groups remain susceptible to the pattern effect because racist attitudes against them are widespread in the United States and not infrequently break out into discriminatory and harmful actions—painting of swastikas on synagogues, routing Arab Americans from their homes,[25] attacking Asian Americans and resenting their successes. The flip side of this situation is that the social disadvantage effect does *not* apply to these groups, which are not socially disadvantaged by standard measures of economic and educational standing. (To be more precise: the effect does not apply to some Asian American groups, but does to others—for example, Southeast Asian immigrant groups). Thus, the second sense in which the pattern effect casts a wider net than the social disadvantage effect is that the forms of racism yielding the former effect are broader than those yielding the latter.

I have mentioned three factors—the historical legacy, the social disadvantage, and the pattern effects—that constitute asymmetries in the moral significance of racism with regard to different groups and that also tend to correlate to whether the victims of racism are dominant or vulnerable in racial status. Such factors provide grounds for saying that incidents of racism involving them are morally worse, at least in some significant respects, than those that do not. Thus, this correlation underpins a general—everything else being equal—moral asymmetry between racism against vulnerable racial groups and racism against dominant ones, a moral asymmetry that cannot be summarized in a single, all-things-considered moral judgment.

What I have not yet mentioned, however, are effects of individual racism on the general structures and patterns of racism. In the case of social subordination, each individual incident not only offends by invoking the subordination, but also strengthens the subordination itself. Similarly, with regard to the pattern effect, each incident not only invokes the pattern, but lends it support as well. Anti-Semitism in general is strengthened each time an anti-Semitic remark remains unchallenged. Racism against dominant groups does not strengthen pervasive racism against such groups because such racism does not exist. (However, it can be argued that any incident of racism, no matter against whom it is directed, strengthens *racism in general*, even if the effect is not as direct as the way in which incidents of racism against group X strengthen racism against group X.)

Subordinate-to-Subordinate Racism

The key identity-related factor in the dimensions of moral asymmetry discussed here is the racial identity of the *target* of the racist action. I have argued that, everything else being equal, it is racism against blacks or subordinate groups more generally that is worse than racism against whites. What are the implications of the argument for the racial identity of the *perpetrator*? Do the asymmetries apply to them as well?

I do not think a general answer can be given to this question. When members of subordinate or otherwise vulnerable groups commit racist acts against members of other such groups, the three effects discussed above generally apply to nearly as great a degree as they do when the perpetrator of the act is a member of a dominant group. However, in many cases, they do not.

Consider, for example, a Korean American's racist act against an African American in which she says or somehow conveys the view that the African American is dirty and stupid. It seems to me that such an act would still to some degree instantiate the historical legacy, social disadvantage, and patterns of racism effects. Even though the Korean American is not white and may herself be the target of racism from whites, nevertheless her antiblack racism partakes of the force of dominant group (white) racism. If she uses historically (in the U.S. context) infused racial epithets and reminds the target of the inferior social position of his group, then the moral offense of treating him as an inferior will be similar to the offense rendered by a white person making the same remarks. If the target (or his group) is a target of patterns of racism, the pattern effect would apply as well. The perpetrator, implicitly if not explicitly, aligns herself with the dominant group's racism against the target group. In fact, subordinate group racism is often a product of a desire, conscious or not, to align oneself with the dominant group, precisely by distinguishing oneself from another vulnerable group. Immigrant groups—from the "white" southern European groups of the late nineteenth and early twentieth century to the people of color arriving since racial restrictions were struck down in 1965—have often been given the message that their status could be enhanced by distancing and strongly differentiating themselves from African Americans.

Still, the racial identity of the perpetrator *may* make a difference. Insofar as one of the harms of a racist act is the message that the members of a target group are not accepted as equals by the mainstream culture of the society, that message may well be less forcefully conveyed by members of other subordinate or vulnerable groups than by members of dominant groups. The

Korean American's racism may seem less hurtful to the extent that the African Americans who are its targets do not perceive her as having sufficient power to represent that mainstream culture. The case of antiblack racism on the part of Jews is a more complicated case because Jews, even though themselves a vulnerable group (to anti-Semitism, a form of racism in the terms of this essay), are generally seen by blacks as "white," hence as aligned with the dominant culture, so the three effects will in general be as strong if the perpetrator is Jewish as if she is white but not Jewish.

Both the historical legacy effect and the social disadvantage effect might well be somewhat different than the usual cases of dominant-group racism if the perpetrator is a member of a vulnerable group and the *content* of the racist message is less reminiscent of dominant group racism—perhaps drawing on a racist content more specific to the ethnic culture of the vulnerable-group perpetrator than to U.S. culture. The content might then be less evocative of the particular tradition of historical oppression and of the particular racist ideology and imagery that are reflective and justificatory of current relations of advantage and disadvantage. If so, the historical legacy effect and the social disadvantage effect would likely be less powerful. Still, simply by being the target of racism at all, the member of the vulnerable group would tend to suffer some of the three effects.[26]

Remember that I am not discussing whether vulnerable-to-vulnerable racism constitutes a moral wrong. All racism offends against norms of respect, shared humanity, and equality, no matter who the perpetrator. The point at issue is whether the offense is in some significant respects less serious if the perpetrator is from another vulnerable group than if she is a member of a dominant group.

Thus, it is difficult to generalize about the greater or lesser moral evil of racism with respect to the racial identity of the *perpetrator*. But it is not necessary to do so. We must simply be alerted to the fact that the racial or ethnic identity of the perpetrator is a possibly relevant factor in particular cases, even though there is not as clear a moral asymmetry as in the case of the target of racism.

Still, the moral asymmetries attaching to racism's target do have some implications of their own for the moral agent or potential perpetrator in relation to racism. If certain kinds of moral offense characteristically involved in racism against vulnerable groups are absent in racism against dominant groups, then it is incumbent upon moral agents to be aware of these harms. We cannot confine ourselves to the evils of racism that are *independent* of the vulnerability status of targets of racism, though these evils—prejudice, hatred, violence, social division—are more than significant enough. Moral agents must also recognize the *intensification* of these evils or the *further* moral evils involved in the historical legacy, current social disadvantage, and pattern effects. Moral agents must be held accountable for these moral wrongs as well.

Conclusion

Part of my concern in arguing for these moral asymmetries is to contribute to the effort begun by a number of African American philosophers to establish that racial identity is a morally significant form of identity, one that raises a host of philosophically important issues. Although literary criticism, sociology, anthropology, and history have focused closely on race and racial identity, philosophy is a field that has insufficiently risen to the challenge of trying to shed light on what Du Bois rightly predicted would be a central problem of the twentieth century.

Yet I am also concerned that establishing the moral and philosophical relevance of racial identity not contribute to a reification and essentializing of that identity. In addition to the frequently made point that race is a scientifically invalid concept, and in light of the consequently historically contingent character of racial identity, I want to emphasize that racial identity underpins the moral asymmetry thesis as a locus of various distinct and historically contingent factors, not as a sui generis form of identity. The historical legacy effect, for example, is not a timeless and unchanging feature of racial identity. For one thing, it is localized to a particular country or tradition rather than applying to *every* member of the "racial" group. Blacks in Africa have a different historical legacy than Caribbean blacks. Historical legacy is not "built into" racial identity per se, though it may arguably be built into the claiming and consigning of a racial identity in a particular time and place (as David Roediger in *The Wages of Whiteness: Race and the Making of the American Working Class* and Ruth Frankenberg in *White Women, Race Matters: The Social Construction of Whiteness* have argued).

Similarly, the pattern effect is a very historically contingent and changing one. The treatment of different racial/ethnic groups has undergone great change, often for the better, though sometimes for the worse; so the ethical significance of the pattern effect at any given time and with regard to any particular group is thus quite variable. When prejudice and discrimination toward a particular group have weakened, the pattern effect regarding any given racist incident is thereby weakened. The treatment of Chinese Americans in the United States is just one example of this variability. There have been periods of more and less intense patterns of anti-Chinese racism, though the pattern effect with regard to Chinese Americans has also been affected by general trends of anti-Asian and to some extent anti-immigrant sentiment.

The current social disadvantage effect is also clearly subject to similar contingencies as the degrees of and relations between the advantages and disadvantages of different groups change. The point I want to emphasize here, then, is that in trying to establish racial identity as a morally significant identity, I have given an argument that applies in principle to other kinds of group identities and at the same time eschews the treatment of racial identity as a timeless and reified construct. In both senses, *race* is not a unique or sui generis concept.

Beyond my philosophical concern, the moral asymmetry thesis is meant to negotiate a territory of great controversy in the racial politics of our day. Recognizing moral asymmetry is a way of avoiding the popularly held yet untenable views that only whites can be racist and that the racial identity of parties to racism is irrelevant to racism's moral standing (or "all racism is equal"), yet it is also a way of preserving a core of truth in each of these positions and thus of accounting for the popular appeal in both.

Yet I still fear some implications of the *political* position in which these intellectual concerns have left me. As a political stance, the view that "racism against blacks is worse than racism against whites" can be taken in quite regressive directions. Someone might treat it as implying that racism against whites is not of much concern or that we should be more tolerant of the racism of people of color. Nothing in my argument implies either of these positions. First of all, although the argument has set up a comparison between these two types of racism (to oversimplify a bit for the moment), in the world of moral choice we are not normally faced with having to jettison a concern with one for a concern with the other. I have not attempted to establish this point in my essay, but I believe that we need to be more concerned than we are now *both* with racism against whites *and* with racism against blacks or any other groups. I do not think that there is a fixed and constant quantity of moral concern for racism so that apportioning it to one class of victims necessarily denies it to some other. Concern for racism is not a zero-sum game. The point is to remind us of moral wrongs involved in cases of dominant-to-vulnerable racism that would be masked if one's paradigm of racism is vulnerable-to-dominant racism—implied, whether acknowledged or not, in the "all racism is equal view."

Moreover, it must be kept in mind that the target-based racial asymmetries I have discussed here constitute only one part of the sources of moral concern regarding racist actions and beliefs. I have mentioned some other dimensions—the degree of physical harm or threat of physical harm, the intentionality of the act, the content of the racist message. Moreover, race remains only one of many sources of the power and subordination relationships that have framed the variables with which I have been concerned. An individual subordinated by race may be powerful in political, occupational, or educational position, or by class or gender, or by citizenship or immigration status, and the totality of asymmetries might ultimately go the other way in his case. The ceteris paribus character of my claim of moral asymmetry must be kept in mind here. The racial asymmetries are only one set of factors affecting the moral seriousness of racist actions. They are powerful ones, to be sure, in general if not in every particular case, but they far from exhaust the field of such asymmetries.[27]

5 Racism: Paradigms and Moral Appraisal (A Response to Blum)

MARILYN FRIEDMAN

Is racial identity ever salient to the moral appraisal of racist acts? More specifically, are the racial identities of the agents or targets of acts of racism ever relevant to the moral appraisal of those acts?

Lawrence Blum is one philosopher who thinks that they are so, and his defense is worth considering.[1] In Blum's view, the racial identity of the target and the perpetrator of racism are factors that can either mitigate or aggravate the degree of wrongness of a racist act. Blum rejects the view that "all racism is equal" ("Moral Asymmetries in Racism," chap. 4 in this volume). He writes: "racism against blacks or subordinate groups more generally . . . is worse than racism against whites." This asymmetry is true of both forms of racism that he identifies: first, *racial hatred*—that is, hatred directed toward someone because of her race—and second, a regard for someone as being lesser or inferior in some important human dimension because of her race, an attitude that I call *racial scorn*.

Blum does not believe that only whites can be racist or that racism by blacks is impossible. In his view, blacks *can* be racist; furthermore, such racism would be morally wrong. He believes that "All racism offends against norms of respect, shared humanity, and equality, no matter who the perpetrator." Nevertheless, some racist acts are worse than others on grounds that have to do with the racial identities of those involved and the sociohistorical backgrounds of their racial identities.

Blum lists three factors that intensify the wrong of racism when the target is a member of a socially vulnerable or subordinate group: (1) a historical legacy of racism that has been directed against her racial group, (2) current patterns of relative societal and institutional disadvantage experienced by her racial group, and (3) prevalent patterns of racism being directed against her racial group.

Blum presents a compelling case in support of the conclusion that acts of

98

racism are not equally wrong and that the degree of wrongness depends partly on the identity of the target of the racist act. I part company, however, with one presupposition that appears to underlie his account of how to appraise acts of racism. Blum's account appears to presuppose the wrong conceptual paradigm of a racist act.[2] In the first part of my discussion, I propose an alternative paradigm of racism that I believe to be more plausible than the one Blum invokes, but that sustains the same conclusions Blum defends about the relative moral wrongness of different racist acts. In the second part, I consider whether "reactive" racism—that is, racist acts committed in reaction to racism and by those who have been its victims—ever has positive moral worth.

Paradigms of Racism

Is the wrongness of an act of racism intensified when it is directed against a type of person commonly targeted for racism? An affirmative answer such as Blum's seems to decompose the possible wrongs of racist acts into two parts. First, there is the core moral wrong of racial hatred or scorn that is conceptually *isolated* from any socially prevalent pattern of racism. Second, there is an intensification of that core moral wrong in virtue of the social prevalence of such acts. For Blum, three factors in particular epitomize such prevalence: historical legacy, societal disadvantage, and prevalent racist patterns.

In this sort of approach, isolated incidents of racism become the basic standard for determining what is wrong with racist acts as such and in general. This moral wrongness is intensified when the person targeted for racism is indeed the member of a racism-targeted group, but that group-based racism is not part of the core moral wrong of racism properly so-called. We could say that for Blum, racism against whites is already very bad, and racism against blacks is even worse.

This approach to the moral appraisal of racism has certain drawbacks. To see why, let us consider what an incident of racism might be like when isolated conceptually from a social pattern of racism. In such a case, a perpetrator would express or enact hatred or scorn toward a targeted person in virtue of her race, but there would be no history or prevalent pattern of racism that pertained to the target person's racial identity. There would be no commonly known stereotypes of members of the target's racial group. There would be no commonly known slang words available for insulting such persons. In addition, if the targeted person were not relatively socially disadvantaged, it would be difficult to shame her on economic grounds, let alone associate that shame with her racial group. There would simply be no race-based context of hatred or scorn for making sense of such an act.

A conceptually isolated act of racism becomes little more than an act of mere hatred or scorn that happens to be prompted by the race of the target person quite independently of the culture in which it occurs or the history of that culture. Such acts are not logically impossible, nor are they empirically nonexistent, especially if we broaden the concept to include all group-based identities. I would venture to bet that just about every important group-based human identity has been the basis for hatred or scorn by someone, somewhere, at some time.

I can still recall a certain classmate of mine in elementary school in the Uptown district of Chicago. Let us call him Richard Hoffmann. Richard *hated and scorned everyone*, not merely those of us who made easy targets because we could be called "kikes" or "dagos," two of Richard's favorite taunts, but also our Scandinavian American classmates, who really challenged Richard's invective imagination. The strongest insult he could manage in those cases was "dumb Swede."

Anti-Scandinavian insults in the United States, for the past half century at least, have invoked no significant (recent) history or prevalent patterns of racism.[3] For that reason, such acts do not seem to exhibit the central moral wrongness of racism. When hatred and scorn are based on group identities not commonly the target for racism, it is unclear how this basis can make any difference to the moral wrongness of the act. If the target of racism has experienced no significant pattern of racism, then her racial identity seems incidental to the core moral wrong involved. Her racial identity would not have for her the vulnerability that it has for someone whose racial identity is frequently targeted for hostility. If isolated incidents of racism form the defining standard of what is wrong with racism in general, then Blum's analysis of the core moral wrong of racism reduces to the view that racism in general is wrong merely because it expresses or enacts hatred or scorn. Hatred and scorn by themselves become the primary offenses against the moral requirements to respect other persons and to treat them as moral equals.

Formulated in this way, Blum's view has two dissatisfying features. First, his general standard of racism, the notion of an isolated incident of hatred or scorn that happens incidentally to be based on race, does not seem bad enough to ground an analysis of what is wrong with racism in general as the evil that we ordinarily understand it to be. Second, this approach seems to marginalize the very forms of racism that are most troubling, forms such as antiblack racism that do evoke a serious, preexisting pattern of racism.

First, the question of hatred and scorn in themselves. Now, I hate hatred and scorn scornfulness as much as the next person. I am not certain, however, that hatred or scorn in and of themselves seriously violate our obligations to respect the dignity of others and to regard them as moral equals to ourselves. Such strong emotional attitudes as hatred or scorn are usually linked in some way with the experiences and/or psychologies of those who harbor these attitudes. In some circumstances, they might be justified or at least understandable and pardonable attitudes. It does not seem wrong to hate those who behave in vicious ways—who, for example, oppress, abuse, or exploit others. It does not seem wrong to scorn what is truly humanly inferior, such as deeply corrupt moral character. For practical reasons, hatred and scorn might not be the best attitudes to express in such cases, but they do not unequivocally violate the dignity or moral equality of their targets, mainly because they appear morally *justified* in those cases.

Blum could respond to this point by observing that hatred or scorn based simply on someone's race identity is surely unjustified. No racial identity, in and of itself, is hateful or scornworthy. Although certainly correct, this modification would still be insufficient to save what I have taken to be Blum's paradigm of the core moral wrong of racism. If I hate someone merely because she is of race R, but race R has never been the target of significant racism, then once again the racial basis of my unjustified hatred seems on the face of it inconsequential to the moral evaluation of my act.[4] My act would be wrong simply as an act of unjustified hatred.

The core moral wrong of racism, according to my suggested clarification of Blum's view, is mere unjustified hatred or scorn—hatred or scorn based on features about the target that simply do not warrant hatred or scorn. This failing is no different from the wrong of hating someone because of, say, her height or her pronunciation. Although such an act of groundless hatred or scorn can certainly amount to a moral infraction, it does not by itself constitute the major offense against the target's dignity or moral equality, of which I assume most of us, along with Blum, believe to lie at the heart of racism.

The second problem with analyzing the wrongness of racism in terms of unjustified hatred or scorn is that it moves the most common and most troubling cases of racism to the periphery of the analysis. In Blum's view, a context of racism makes the wrongness of racial hatred or scorn worse than it would otherwise be, but the context is not what constitutes the moral center or defining feature of racism. What a black person commonly experiences throughout her life in the United States ceases to be a *standard case* of racism. The specific meaning of racism seems to be decentered by this analysis.

When racism is a serious practical problem, it is so usually precisely because it is widespread and not confined to one or a few isolated incidents or to the behavior of an isolated perpetrator. Isolated incidents and isolated perpetrators, provided that they do not cause or threaten physical harm, can often be laughed off. Like my former classmate, Richard Hoffmann, trying to insult Scandinavian Americans in late 1950s Chicago, isolated perpetrators of unfamiliar racism are even a bit ridiculous. For serious cases of racism, however, it does not seem possible to disentangle a moral wrong that is independent of a prevalent *pattern* of racism.

The racist acts in the real world that should occupy our attention are those in which the target of the act is a member of a racial group commonly targeted for racism. Such acts do more than merely evoke a racist pattern; they also instantiate it. Instantiating a pattern of racism seems to be a definitive feature of racism in the paradigm cases that trouble us in everyday life. It makes sense for moral analysis of what is wrong with racism to take those pattern-instantiating cases as the standard for determining what is wrong with racism in general. In the alternative approach I am recommending, the wrongness of a racist act depends *centrally* on the pattern of racism that it instantiates.

When there is no prevalent pattern of racism, instead of the standard case of racism as suggested by Blum's analysis, we have a palefaced version of racism properly so-called, a version from which something important is lacking. Like Blum, we could still consider such incomplete forms of racism to be less morally wrong by comparison to our standard, or paradigm, case. The difference, however, is that where Blum takes palefaced, isolated-incident racism as his standard case and argues that racism against, say, blacks is *more* wrong, we would now regard racism against blacks as a standard case and consider the palefaced version to be *less* wrong. It is less wrong because it lacks a central feature of the standard case—namely, a racist context.

My formulation and the one suggested by Blum's analysis imply the same comparative conclusions about particular cases. Both approaches entail, as Blum asserts, that "racism against blacks or subordinate groups more generally . . . is worse than racism against whites." [5] However, my alternative formulation, which treats antiblack racism as a standard for determining what is wrong with racism in general, has the advantage of seeming to resolve the two problems that I noted earlier. First, our analysis would now focus on an undoubted evil—namely, racist acts that instantiate patterns of racism. Second, instead of being marginalized by the analysis, those most damaging sorts of racist acts would now become the moral center of the analysis. In my approach, the less serious, palefaced, isolated-incident types of racism, such as racism against a white person in the United States, would be moved to the periphery of the analysis.

Metaethically speaking, this issue is about *paradigms* and the ways in which they illuminate and guide moral thinking. Among those acts that do instantiate a racist pattern, racism is less wrong the less severe that pattern. If the racist act were a human novelty, instantiating or evoking no pattern whatsoever, its wrongness *as a case of racism* would diminish down to the vanishing point. It might still be wrong as an act of unjustified hatred or scorn, but not as an act of racism properly so-called.

The Moral Appraisal of Reactive Racism

If we agree that the wrongness of racism is a matter of degree depending on the circumstances and targets of its occurrence, we might go on to wonder whether the wrongness of a racist act, whatever the degree, is a prima facie wrong that can be balanced against other possibly worthwhile considerations. This thought prompts a question related to Blum's project, but which he himself does not raise. Are acts of racism ever, in any respects, morally positive? Is rightness, virtue, or value ever promoted or realized by racism?

In my estimation, what I regard as paradigmatic cases of racism, such as antiblack racism, are so bad that it is difficult to imagine their badness ever being overridden by positive considerations, and it is thus almost inconceivable that they might ever be justified on balance. But what about nonparadigmatic cases of racism—cases that, by my definition, lack a significant racist context and that are therefore less wrong than the standard cases? What about, say, racism against whites in the United States? The wrongness of these nonparadigmatic cases might be so minimal that any positive moral worth they had might be enough to make such behavior, all things considered, morally permissible.

Let us focus specifically on reactive racism as an example of racism that seems to fall outside the paradigm I have defended.[6] *Reactive racism* is a reaction against what I call *primary racism*. Primary racism is the *initiation* of race-based hatred or scorn toward members of a group that has not previously exhibited racism toward one's own group. Reactive racism, by contrast, is a reaction to primary racism inflicted on one's own group and is directed against those whose racial group has widely perpetrated that primary racism.[7] In our society, racism by a black against a white would be a paradigm case of reactive racism. Racism by a black against a Latina or a Navajo in general would not.[8] My question is whether there is ever any positive moral value or rightness in reactive racism.

First, a crucial caveat that I cannot overemphasize: my discussion aims as far as possible conceptually to extricate the wrong of racism as such from other moral wrongs that might be involved in its occurrence. Granted, this endeavor may prove to be difficult, if not altogether in vain. Nevertheless, one proviso is crucial. My focus is only on acts of racial hatred or scorn, such as verbal insults or social exclusion, that involve neither physical violence nor the violation of any legal rights. I am especially not asking whether there is moral worth in (reactively) racist acts of physical violence.[9] I do not rule out the excusability of violent or illegal acts of reactive racism—particularly as a reaction to severe primary racist violence. I am not considering that possibility here, however.

So, are (nonviolently) reactive racist acts ever, in any respects, morally worthwhile? One possible value provided by acts of reactive racism is the psychological satisfaction of the perpetrator. Remember that the perpetrator of reactive racism is someone who has been vulnerable to primary racism for a long time. A lifetime of being targeted for primary race-based hatred and scorn and of experiencing the social disadvantages that usually come with them must surely generate powerful attitudes such as resentment, frustration, and anger. To express such powerful attitudes, especially to someone who is a member of the group that systematically perpetrates the primary racism, is likely to be at least a relief and probably a gratifying indulgence.

How many of us are immune to the seductive allure of getting even with someone who has treated us unfairly or caused us much pain?[10]

Second, apart from the psychological satisfaction they would feel, the targets of primary racism might also feel empowered by acting in a reactively racist manner, an empowerment that is likely to bolster their self-respect. Someone who has been sorely victimized by racism in the public worlds of government, education, employment, and mass media—who has felt that she was unable to control the racial hatred or scorn directed against her—has likely suffered diminished self-respect as a result. Blum's argument supports this point: racist acts in the context of familiar cultural patterns of racism are wrong precisely because the targeted people are disrespected as human beings and treated as moral inferiors. It is not easy to maintain one's own self-respect in the face of frequent disrespect by others, especially if one has experienced this disrespect all of one's life.

For the target of pervasive racism to salvage self-respect in the face of frequent and *deep* disrespect by many others is a challenge indeed. One way in which she might be able to restore her self-respect is to act against those who oppress her. She can certainly regain a sense of her own effectiveness as an agent if she does not suffer passively the indignities inflicted on her.

There are, of course, a variety of ways to assert oneself against the primary racism that one might experience, many of which responses are not at all racist in turn. One can, for instance, challenge the derogatory stereotypes of one's group and debate the morality of racism itself. This rather defensive response to indignity, however, might not fully repair the damaged self-respect of a victim. For full self-respect to be restored, there is nothing like taking the offensive and directly attacking one's oppressors. (Remember that I am not referring to physical attacks.) One way to attack oppressors nonphysically is to express hatred or scorn for their group identities. This sort of response would indeed constitute reactive racism. Thus, a possible second moral value of reactive racism is that it might restore self-respect to victims of primary racism.[11]

Third, reactive racism might have educational value for the *perpetrators* of primary racism. It might awaken those primary perpetrators to a consciousness of what it is like to be victimized by racism. This raised consciousness might, in turn, promote remorse in them for inflicting such treatment on others. The remorse might then lead them to diminish the racism that they continue to inflict on others. In that case, reactive racism would have helped to reduce the total amount of racism in the world in the long run. (I do not deny that this suggestion is exceedingly optimistic.)

Fourth, reactive racism could constitute a kind of punishment or retributive justice for primary racism. Of course, the paradigm institutions for exacting retributive justice in our public culture are the judicial and penal systems. These institutions, however, are notoriously limited in their reach. At best, their scope extends only to acts either formally criminalized or actionable in civil court. Despite our much vaunted history of civil rights legislation, a great deal of primary racism is not criminalized (e.g., social exclusion) and would not be recognized as the basis for a civil suit unless the target could prove that she had been harmed in some measurable way. Even then, it would often be the harm and not the racism as such that would be the basis for a civil action. You cannot sue someone merely (!) for disrespecting you as a person or for treating you as a moral inferior. Certainly, the *verbal* expression of race-based hatred and scorn is not illegal and indeed in the United States has received substantial First Amendment protection,— as we continue to see in case after case in which the U.S. judiciary invalidates hate speech codes.[12]

Despite decades of struggle by legions of people in our society against race-based hatred and scorn, primary racism continues to flourish. Given the limited reach of legal retribution, it seems morally reasonable to think that private individuals are entitled to undertake their own retributive justice— provided that they think carefully about what they are doing and to whom. Reactive racism directed toward primary racists could well serve as one kind of retributive punishment. (Recall once more that I am not defending violent reactive acts.) Call this *vigilante retributivism*, if you will. In a world of imperfect moral rectification for wrongs done, to say the least, the idea of reactive racism as vigilante retributivism has a distinct appeal.

I have found four reasons in favor of thinking that reactive racism has positive moral worth: first, the satisfaction of the perpetrator, who is by definition someone long vulnerable to primary racism; second, the perpetrator's restored self-respect; third, the educational value for the target of the reactive racism, who is by definition a member of a group that has perpetrated primary racism; and fourth, vigilante retributive justice. I do not claim that this list is complete.

To balance the discussion, we should ask whether there are any reasons for thinking that reactive racism as such is morally wrong. Other than being wrong as a type of racism in general, is there something distinctively wrong with reactive racism, something that prevents the positive moral values I just listed from overriding even the diminished wrongness that such acts have as acts of racism per se?

First, reactive racism could fail to have an educational effect on the perpetrators of primary racism and, instead, provoke only a hostile reaction. Many white men are in open rebellion today against the cultural messages that hold white people responsible for historic and still prevalent white-against-black racism and that hold men responsible for historic and still prevalent male-against-female domination. Some perpetrators of primary racism will not "get it" no matter how often they are subjected to reactive racism. They will respond instead by fomenting a backlash that might seriously hurt the cause of fighting primary racism. Consider, for example, the current assault on affirmative action programs.

Rather than pondering whether or not they are guilty of primary antiblack racism, many white men today simply protest that they have become the new beleaguered minority.[13] Any acts of genuinely reactive racism against white people—that is, acts of hatred or scorn directed at white people simply because they are white—would appear to them to confirm their fears. If reactive racism bolsters primary racism by provoking a primary racist backlash then reactive racism is in that regard a moral problem.

Second, particular acts of reactive racism might be unjust as acts of retribution because they punish the wrong targets. They might reach only white people who are genuinely antiracist. I have witnessed a few incidents in which black individuals expressed racial scorn against whites whom I knew to have been long time, dedicated civil rights activists. Or, if you doubt the sincerity of white civil rights activists, consider instead that reactive racist acts might well reach only the minor and more vulnerable primary racist offenders, leaving the most powerful Kluxers and white supremacists quite unscathed.

Third, the character of reactive racists themselves might deteriorate if they pursue their reactive racism through the obsessive cultivation of such damaging attitudes as resentment and hatred. Reactive racism might too easily sink to the level of a Nietzschean "slave morality," the outlook of an oppressed person who can do no better than merely to *imagine* herself the moral superior of her oppressors and to *pretend* that their powers are moral shortcomings. It is certainly true that primary racists are morally corrupt *in respect of perpetrating the wrongs of (primary) racism*. It does not follow, however, that those primary racists are morally worse in all respects than those they oppress. It is a mistake, in general, to romanticize the condition of the oppressed. After all, if oppression made us better people, then why would it constitute a moral outrage? We should all get in line.

The concern I am raising is of a virtue-theoretic sort. It involves asking what costs for the oppressed themselves lie hidden in their own reactive racism against those who dominate them. Even if the *targets* of primary racism really are better people than primary *racists*, it does not seem that those targets do themselves a favor by obsessing about this moral ranking. As tempting as it often is to demonize people who treat us badly, we must also beware of the possible corruption of our own characters that comes from fixating on the wicked ways of others.

Granted, it is often difficult to resist the allure of thinking ill of people who do us wrong. It is not always easy to control our reactions to being oppressed. Daily survival in such cases calls for a clear grasp of the limits of human goodness and the distinct possibility of human brutality. We each need a robust awareness of the moral failings of others sufficient for our own self-protection as we move through the world. If I were frequently the target of racism, I would do well to distrust anyone or any group who is likely to threaten me. The problem is to maintain this self-protective state of alert without letting it swamp my emotional and behavioral repertoire. Otherwise, reactive racism might become an obsession that does little to stop primary racists, but instead devours me, the one who harbors it.

Fourth, the form of argument that seeks to excuse or justify reactive racism is a dangerous line of thinking that can easily be abused. Anyone who thinks she has ever experienced a race-based grievance or a group-based grievance of any sort, however isolated, could use this form of reasoning to try to legitimate revenge against whomever she thought had done her wrong. Primary racists have already availed themselves of this form of thought. Nazi philosophy, for example, construes itself as a kind of reactive racism. Nazis regard Jews as filthy, selfish, cunning thieves who have plundered Aryan culture, robbing it of its proper strength and greatness. Understood this way, the "Final Solution" was merely reactive racism on a grand scale. Justifying racism of any sort, reactive or not, is thus a perilous enterprise that we should undertake with the greatest caution.

I have found four reasons against reactive racism: first, it might provoke a primary racist backlash; second, it might take the wrong targets; third, it might contaminate the character of anyone who harbors reactively racist attitudes; and fourth, it provides a model of justification that can be dangerously abused.

What is the verdict about reactive racism, all things considered? My own tentative and wishy-washy conclusion is this: reactive racism might *sometimes* be morally permissible—provided it is done under the right conditions, confined within the right limits, and directed only against the right people. Aristotle meets multiculturalism.[14]

6 Contempt and Ordinary Inequality

David Haekwon Kim

> Ever since the birth of our nation, white America has had a schizophrenic per-
> sonality on the question of race. She has been torn between selves—a self in
> which she proudly professed the great principles of democracy and a self in
> which she sadly practiced the antithesis of democracy. This tragic duality has
> produced a strange indecisiveness and ambivalence toward the Negro.
> —Martin Luther King Jr., *Where Do We Go from Here?*

Many whites in the United States deplore the "tragic duality" of
the past that Martin Luther King Jr. describes in the epigraph, and they deplore the hate organizations that are the apparent vestiges of this past. They
optimistically believe that the democratic self of the United States is now as-
cendant and that its supremacist self is becoming obsolete. If we staunchly
oppose bigots, hate crimes, hate speech, and the like, the United States will
finally be its one true self. Anticipating such a response, King continued, "it
is necessary to refute the idea that the dominant ideology in our country even
today is freedom and equality while racism is just an occasional departure
from the norm on the part of a few bigoted extremists" (*Where Do We Go
from Here?* 68).

If we wish to understand the persistence and sheer ordinariness of racism
in the United States, we must supplant the hate or animosity paradigm, for
racism involves a psychology broader, more nuanced, and in certain respects
deeper than this naïve paradigm suggests. In addition, racism has a structural dimension in which institutions and fields of interaction maintain
racial hierarchy. In this essay, I attempt to provide an account of one of the
deep agent structures that undergird today's informal segregation. I argue
that a *contempt matrix* lies at the heart of many forms of personal racism.
Variations in this structure—different racist alloys—are explained (1) by its
absorption of other emotions, such as hate, sympathy, or resentment, and,
in some cases, (2) by the incorporation of a powerful drive to avoid guilt or
shame. Although many factors contribute to the schizophrenic system of

racial distance, the historical legacy of racial contempt is among the most potent.

My essay has two parts. I first characterize the structure of contempt and introduce the concept of a contempt matrix. I then use the notion of a contempt matrix to highlight unity among and differences between the psychic alloys of white supremacists, ordinary visceral racists, and paternalistic racists. I attempt neither to cover all forms of personal racism, nor all forms of the three types that I do discuss. In my final remarks, I discuss the question of whether, in the present situation, nonwhites can be racist against whites and argue that they cannot.

The Matrix of Contempt

For an understanding of emotion, I turn to Aristotle:

> The emotions are all those feelings that so change men as to affect their judgments, and that are also attended by pain or pleasure. . . . We must arrange what we have to say about each of them under three heads. Take, for instance, the emotion of anger: here we must discover what the state of mind of angry people is, who the people are with whom they usually get angry, and on what grounds they get angry with them. It is not enough to know one or even two of these points. . . . Anger may be defined as a desire accompanied by pain, for a conspicuous revenge for a conspicuous slight at the hands of men who have no call to slight oneself or one's friends. (*Rhetoric* 2.1.1378a, 21–28)

In my analysis of contempt, I accept and adapt the following features of Aristotle's account. Emotions are states of persons that involve feeling, evaluative content, and desire. An analysis of a particular emotion should include an account of (1) the psychological state characteristic of the emotion, including its telos or desire, (2) the typical targets of the emotion, and (3) the grounds or normative structure of the emotion. Moreover, I take the emotions to be socially constructed in the sense implicit in Aristotle's description of anger: the characteristic ways in which people respond emotionally involve evaluative perspectives that reflect social norms. Emotions such as contempt, however, also structure identities and social relations in ways that lead me beyond an Aristotelian analysis to the identification of a contempt matrix that is both individual and social.

The Nature of Contempt

Let me begin my characterization of contempt with two quite ordinary examples:

(A) Janice and Courtney are assigned as each other's chemistry partner. Unfortunately for Janice, who works hard and is on the verge of getting an A, Courtney is a D student, sloppy, and a procrastinator. Janice knows this. When she is partnered with Courtney, Janice feels not just fear of losing her chance for an A, but also an acute sense of Courtney's inferiority—more specifically, an inferiority that is in obnoxiously close proximity. Janice finds herself edging away from Courtney, moving an extra few feet as they discuss the project.

(B) Albert meets his fiancee's parents for the first time when they dine together at one of the finest restaurants in the city. As they eat hors d'oeuvres, Albert's future father-in-law cringes at the sight of Albert using the wrong fork without the slightest embarrassment. With diffuse agitation, he also notes that Albert's enunciation lacks crispness and that his countenance fails to communicate a certain manly ease and intelligence. Albert's prospective father-in-law muses, "Ill-breeding. We'll have to work on that." As they part, he offers Albert a solid hand squeeze with two staccato shakes.

These scenarios clearly illustrate some common features of contempt. First and obviously, contempt involves negative judgmental regard, but so do mere dislike and antipathy. Perhaps the phenomenological character of contempt differentiates it from dislike and antipathy. Albert's prospective father-in-law and Janice act as if they are repulsed by an offensive odor. They psychically and even physically distance themselves from the object of their contempt. I would argue that contempt involves a feeling of offense, whereas mere dislike and antipathy need only involve a sense of something being disagreeable or negative. The presence of offense in antipathy would suggest a contemptuous antipathy toward or a loathing of the other. I take contempt, in its clearest forms, to be marked by a sense of offense toward somebody in virtue of some negative feature he or she possesses.

Resentment, too, however, carries a sense of offense due to some negative feature of the object. Insult, especially without good reason, evokes resentment. The resentful agent feels offended by the undeserved harm (Jeffrie Murphy, "Forgiveness and Resentment"). Further, that agent is likely to distance himself psychologically and physically from the perpetrator of the insult. How, then, does contempt differ from resentment?

The second distinctive feature of a clear case of contempt is the emotion's vertically or hierarchically organized phenomenology of the emotion. Resentment obviously involves a sense of offense, though more like irritation and anger than revulsion. But one typically does not feel superior in resenting an other. Indeed, proper resentment seems to involve an insistence on equality, reciprocity, and fair treatment. In contempt, one does take oneself to be superior to an other, sometimes feeling filled, empowered, or buoyed. One might say of the contemptible, "That's beneath me," or with powerful irony, "He is beneath contempt." The sense of offense that constitutes contempt is the sense of being agitated or repulsed by some inferior, low, or degraded feature felt to be beneath one's self or one's dignity. Insofar as a particular case of resentment has a haughty character, it is a contemptuous resentment. The hierarchical phenomenology is contributed by the attendant contempt, and not by the resentment proper. Note also that even the strongest form of antipathy—that is, hatred—need not proceed downward, for one may hate precisely because of an appreciation of a superior feature of the hated. I conclude that contempt is a sense of offense toward an other due to the perceived inferiority of the object or target.

It is illuminating to consider the extensive vocabulary we can use to express contempt. I have isolated just seven roughly independent, sometimes overlapping, lines of evaluation that reflect the affective hierarchy of contempt:

1. *Pathetic, Feeble*: gross incompetence or inferior passivity
2. *Perverse, Degenerate*: violation of a deep natural or natural-normative order
3. *Cheap, Lousy*: greatly lacking in value or cost
4. *Coarse, Uncivilized*: lacking in sophistication or depth
5. *Ugly, Grotesque*: opposite of beauty
6. *Rotten, Spoiled*: dangerously impure or polluted
7. *Disgraceful, Ignominious*: opposite of honorable or noble

To attribute any of these qualities is to regard the target, in whole or in part, as base, low, inferior. If the formal object of contempt is the contemptible, this extensive array of attributions marks out a variegated set of proper objects. Because *baseness* is sufficiently broad to cover these lines of evaluation and a thicker term than *inferior*, I shall describe contempt's robust hierarchical outlook in terms of *base* and *debasing* qualities. Contempt involves a sense of offense due to the perceived baseness of its object or target.

One other sentiment to which contempt has been closely linked is disgust. Psychologist Paul Rozin has argued that disgust is constituted by an intrusion and contamination sensitivity ("Disgust, Contagion, and Preadaptation"). The evolutionary basis for this affective structure is the survival conductivity of heightened concern for the integrity or purity of one's bodily boundaries, so basic visceral disgust is localized to one's various bodily orifices, particularly the mouth. The intrusion of spoiled food in one's mouth or stomach triggers oral expulsive musculation, nausea, and a vomiting reflex. Moreover, as anyone who has had food poisoning can testify, one's body revolts against similar types of food long after the initial encounter, even when one knows that the later servings of the food are safe. The phenomenology of disgust has moral analogues. One example is provided by Rozin: few people with any sense of moral integrity would feel comfortable touching, let alone wearing, one of Hitler's sweaters, even though he died some time ago and even if it has been laundered several times. One's moral sensibilities revolt against it as if it carried some kind of moral contagion. The only thing that might vaccinate it, as it were, is if Mother Theresa were to sanctify it or wear it for some time. For some, even the Mother Theresa treatment may fail to eliminate the sweater's moral pollution ("Disgust"; see also Paul Rozin, Jonathan Haidt, and Clark McCauley, "Disgust"). All this suggests that disgust is a defense against contamination. Disgust involves a harsh, often nauseous, sense of offense at the intrusion or proximity of a physically or psychologically deleterious contagion and impels the agent to expel the contaminant, a characteristic effect of which is a spewing facial expression.

Contempt resembles disgust in its visceral phenomenology and its sensitivity to contamination. Janice seems repulsed by Courtney as if by a bad taste, and Albert's prospective father-in-law can muster only a classic interview shake, which suggests that, to an extent, contempt shares an underlying structure with disgust. But contempt also involves a sense of hierarchy that is not felt when the target is merely perceived to be spoiled or potentially sullying. In contempt, the target is not simply distasteful or defiled; it is felt to be beneath one's self and, sometimes, to have the potential to lower one's self. Although Janice may not exactly be disgusted by Courtney, she feels Courtney's inferiority or baseness to be encroaching or potentially debasing, especially if their connection is more intimate or prolonged. Hence, naturally, the goal-directed character of Janice's contempt is detachment or recoil from the debasing contagion. Status preservation may take a number of forms:

1. simple avoidance of the contemptible
2. fending off the contemptible in a scornful or hostile manner
3. fending off the contemptible without overt hostility: snubbing or being snooty
4. marking a distance or boundary from the contemptible—e.g., cold handshakes, minimal or unreciprocated affection, only the most formal expressions of goodwill
5. impaling: holding the contemptible up before one's sarcastic amusement or sadistic delight, tormenting the contemptible
6. extinguishing: hatefully exiling, incapacitating, or killing the contemptible
7. circumscribing: embracing or drawing inward a deftly contained contemptible other

Thus far, all my examples have supposed that the agent and target can be located on a shared axis of evaluation. They have all been examples of *comparative contempt*, widely discussed in the literature, but not fully adequate to an analysis of racism. When a black person under Jim Crow violated one of the implicit rules of race relations, that individual may have elicited not just resentment but also contempt on the part of whites. That black individual would have been seen as not knowing his or her place in the world. This instance is not an example of comparative contempt, however, because whites were not under Jim Crow; there was no shared standard of evaluation. Here the contempt is felt because the black person has demeaned himself by violating a role unique to blacks. Similarly, when men contemptuously criticize women for being unmotherly, there is no implication that the men too must adhere to standards of femininity. Clearly, the contempt is elicited because they perceive such women to have debased themselves by violating the gender order. What I shall now call *order contempt* is felt upon perceiving an other to have violated some norm, standard, or role that, along with other such valuational structures, constitute the contemptuous agent's normative world or order without being symmetrically imposed on the agent.

To summarize, in its clearest forms, contempt is a defense *against* debasement in virtue of being a defense *of* an elevated status, which is why its telos is vertical differentiation or detachment from the inferior, low, or mean. It functions this way in the psychic economy. In reference to Aristotle's "what, with whom, and on what grounds," I have maintained that *contempt is a sense of offense toward an object or target in virtue of perceived base and infectiously debasing qualities of that target, accompanied by a drive to effect an elevated distance.* The target of contempt is an individual who is positioned below the contemptuous agent due to features of the target that register on the low end of some scale valued by the agent. Alternatively, the target of contempt can be an individual who has violated some norm or role that is important to the contemptuous agent's normative order but to which the agent is not necessarily symmetrically bound. Having thus characterized contempt, we can see that it is a finely blended compound of disgust and pride. Although contempt involves a concern with contagion, it parts company with disgust by configuring that threat perspective with the moral and interpersonal complexity of status maintenance.[1]

The Contempt Matrix

Emotions presuppose interests or needs. Emotions, therefore, involve susceptibilities. One feels anger often because some goal has been frustrated, or one feels fear because one must respond to the possibility of bodily damage. A being who has no goals or who is invulnerable to harm would not become angry or frightened. Moreover, emotions involve points of view or schemata that convey the agent's interests or needs and are projected upon situations that may affect these interests or needs. Schemata are important because they constitute the representational contents of emotions and are involved in the activation of emotion dispositions. Fear involves a danger schema. When an object is considered to fall under the danger schema, fear may be produced. Once generated, the affect embodies the schema so that the agent's emotion is fear *of* the dangerous entity.[2]

It is important to note that schema projection is not sufficient to produce emotion.[3] One may be severely depressed or physically exhausted to a point where a joke is judged to be funny but does not elicit amusement. Moreover, the schema applied may underdetermine which emotion is generated. Although a joke may fall under the humor schema, one may find the joke offensive rather than amusing. One's companion, in virtue of having a different personality, may find it hilarious. Similarly, a roller coaster may be regarded as dangerous and therefore exciting and fun. For another person, that danger may generate terror. The backdrop in which a schema is embedded mediates the production of emotion. I call the schema together with its backdrop an *emotion matrix*. *Point of view*

Due to its stability and binding organizational properties, the contempt matrix is far more interesting than episodes of the emotion proper, for sometimes an emotion will be unconscious. Sometimes, it will be fused with another emotion, the result of which may be an ambivalent overall affect at the level of consciousness. On other occasions, it may not be precisely conscious or unconscious, but have a ghostly background presence like the subdued sense of bodily posture when we read or drive. In yet other cases, the occasion for the activation of the emotion is lost due to conditions such as depression. What remains constant throughout these vicissitudes, however, is the matrix of the emotion.

In addition, focus on the matrix is important because it gives us a framework for understanding the common phenomenon of blended or mixed emotions. Here are four examples: (1) sympathy and contempt may produce pity; (2) hatred and contempt may produce loathing; (3) terror and contempt/disgust may produce horror; and (4) resentment and contempt may produce scorn of impudence. We might say—perhaps artificially—that sympathy, hatred, fear, and resentment have been absorbed by a contempt matrix, for in each case the presence of contemptuous regard robustly influences the phenomenology. The individuals who are hated, resented, feared, or sympathized with are represented, to a variable extent, as base or inferior. This contemptuous presentation of the target is then delivered to the other emotions.

Now clearly, not all contempt matrices are alike. One crucial dimension along which contempt matrices differ is the degree of invulnerability to the psychological ingress or proximity of the apparently base object to one's self, for threat of debasement is centrally a function of degree of ingress. The distinction between a contempt matrix and episodes of contempt is important because an agent may regard an other as being distasteful or defiled without actually feeling contempt. The absence of palpable contempt would not then indicate the absence of debasing regard. The other who is regarded as inferior may not be a sufficient threat to the agent's purity or elevated status. Agents in positions of power often have the psychic, social, and material resources to obviate the threat of debasement by either psychologically distancing the other or by introducing positive paternalistic feelings toward the other, which has the effect of not precisely distancing but of carefully circumscribing the other once that other is drawn inward to an extent. Circumscription may be a vitally important skill when there is reason for guilt or shame in derogating a certain class of others. Later in this essay, I highlight the importance of these ingress-control maneuvers for racial regard.

Personal Racism as Constituted by a Contempt Matrix

Many people take personal racism to involve prejudice in the form of racialized trait ascriptions. Such ascriptions are troubling because they are typically demeaning and, hence, in themselves morally unjustified. In addition, they reflect and help to sustain a system of derogating racial meanings in a culture. Further, they help to generate, in an entrenched and ramified manner, a host of negative social conditions. In a powerful theory of racism, Adrian Piper has characterized personal racism as a defective theory of personhood sustained by a need to maintain the self's conceptually unified integrity ("Xenophobia and Kantian Rationalism," 209–14).[4] Anthony Appiah has explained personal racism as an ideological schema of trait attributions motivated by the need to rationalize and preserve unearned privilege (*In My Father's House: Africa in the Philosophy of Culture*, 13–15). Many would concur with elements of both characterizations.

I maintain, however, that, from the Klansman to the ordinary racist who loathes the Klan, a range of personal racisms is constituted by a racially configured contempt matrix. Now, it is true that racism does involve a theory of sorts of what a person is and how nonwhites fail to be full-fledged persons. Certainly, even if evidence of some kind can be marshaled in favor of this quasi-theory, it is, *as a theory*, false and unjustified and perhaps incoherent. But can we seriously suppose that the core of racism is cognitive deficiency brought on by deep-seated interests? Persons who fit this characterization would be deeply psychologically warped, for there would be persistent judgments of inferiority and baseness without corresponding emotion. In the same way, someone who never felt fear when deeming something dangerous would be at best an odd person. In fact, one is hardpressed to see how such racists could have cognition-warping interests without any attached emotional meaning. As noted earlier, emotions bridge interests to salient elements of a situation. Nor is it straightforward how such persons could judge racial others to be base or sullied because these concepts require an appreciation of affective meaning, the special charged sense in which something inferior is not simply inferior, but *base* or something defective *sullied*. Clearly, then, racist regard is a kind of emotional regard, and the complex cluster of cognitions, warped as it surely is, comprises an important part of the emotional matrix. Although many discussions of prejudice allude to contempt, I contend that contempt is central to some of the dominant forms of personal racism and, moreover, that many racist trait ascriptions are best understood in terms of contemptuous regard.

The vast majority of us would hold that racism is concerned with far more than just theory; it is a fundamentally emotional phenomenon. Person schemata or trait ascriptions are only a part of the picture. Many individuals have claimed that racism is hatred of racial others, but there are too many counterexamples to this claim. There are too many people who certainly regard racial others negatively, but never with anything like the commitment and depth of involvement entailed by hatred. Others, seeking to capture as many cases as possible, contend that racism is at heart a deep fear of racial others. This contention, too, fails as it can be too strong for some cases. The benevolent or paternalistic racist likes and wishes to befriend racial others, not to fight or take flight from them. In other cases, a fear analysis is too weak (neo-Nazis hate racial others), and in most cases, it is too ambiguous or coarse-grained, for two reasons. First, the fear schema differs from the threat feature of the contempt/disgust schema. Whereas fear is centrally about the possibility of harm to one's body or one's goals, contempt is about the perception of baseness. Although the threat element of contempt overlaps with fear, it has a very specific phenomenology calibrated to the baseness schema: a threat of debasement. Second, what is assumed to be pure fear is often fear tinged with contempt/disgust. Often, homophobes are taken to have fear of gay men or lesbians, as the very title *homophobe* suggests. This is too coarse an account. I don't think I need to argue that, typically, homophobes experience deep revulsion toward homosexuals. The physical and psychological intimacy between homosexuals is perceived to be deeply unnatural or perverse and, thereby, contemptible or disgusting. Although a male homophobe may fearfully entertain the fantasy of being raped by a gang of gay men, it is typically a fear laced with disgust. With regard to the notion of blended emotions and the contempt matrix, the emotion felt by the homophobe is likely to be horror rather than terror. Similarly, many racist white women are disposed to view black men, especially when they are alone with them, as potential rapists. Is the fear of rape by black men the same as the fear of rape by white men? Perhaps in some cases. But it also seems that many racist white women will perceive black men differently than they perceive white men, their feeling may be more like fear blended with contempt/disgust—horror.[5]

Let me be clear about what drives my conception of personal racism. *From the view of moral agency and accountability, racism is centrally about individuals who see difference and inferiority in racial others.* Given this conception, what emotion could better capture the import and complexity of many of the forms of racist outlook than the interpersonal, order-affirming, and hierarchical emotion of contempt? The racist, even the ordinary garden variety, will often experience offense at the detestable character of the racial other or of some racialized aspect of the other. And again, it is an offense constituted by the threat of being lowered or contaminated by the other's baseness. This threat will generate a response in which the racial other is literally, symbolically, or imaginarily put in her place. If the contempt is sufficiently strong, the racial other will be harshly and maybe enjoyably subdued. The racist will stand unsullied, retaining and maybe slightly gaining some purity and respectability. This description may be exaggerated. It is clear, though, that a haughty negation of the racial other is often experienced by those who express racial contempt.

Racial contempt may be instigated by the demeaning regard of slanted eyes, dark skin, a "broken" accent, the inability to exude American cool, and other deviations from white normalcy. Often, contempt or even disgust is felt by ordinary racists toward miscegenation, even though he or she may get along fine with, say, black colleagues. The contempt or disgust in such individuals reveals their degrading perspective. In this vein, Adrian Piper contemplates a "litmus test" for racism: staring intently at someone's face, point out and compliment "black" facial features and ask if he or she has any blacks in her bloodline ("Passing for White, Passing for Black," 19–20). The elicitation of deep disgust or contempt upon being forced suddenly to identify with black bodies would be profoundly revelatory of the person's racism.

Sometimes, racist contempt is directed at generalized racial others and can coexist with purported race neutrality. An ordinary racist may identify strongly with the neighborhood community where he has lived for some years, feeling solidarity or camaraderie with his white neighbors. He may regard as debasing the increasing number of black or Latino homeowners in the same neighborhood. If there is an accompanying sense of offense and fear of contamination, then the neighborly individual is in the grips of racist contempt, even if he attempts to produce apparently rational, race-neutral justifications for leaving the neighborhood. The same analysis can be applied to identification with one's country and the subsequent formation of contempt at the thought of mass immigration of Latinos and Asians and of the ensuing change in national demographics, a change understood not solely in terms of, say, economic complexities, but also in terms of the degradation or pollution of the country. Monolingualism, the pressure to purify English usage, and the preservation of the Western canon can, in some cases, offer further examples.[6]

Sometimes racist contempt is prefaced by racial praise. Consider Jean-Paul Sartre's depiction of the anti-Semite: "But the way is open to me, mediocre to me, to understand what the most subtle, the most cultivated intelligence has been unable to grasp. Why? Because I possess Racine—Racine and my country and my soil. Perhaps the Jew speaks a purer French than I do, perhaps he knows syntax and grammar better, perhaps he is even a writer. No matter; he has spoken this language for only twenty years, and I for a thousand. The correctness of his style is abstract, acquired; my faults of French are in conformity with the genius of the language" (*Anti-Semite and Jew*, 24).[7] This fascinating passage suggests that one can concede inferiority only to insidiously reassert superiority. Yes, blacks are great athletes, better than whites, but can they excel at gentlemanly sports? The Asian grasp of math and science is legend, but a broad, humane, liberal wisdom it is not. Other examples can be easily multiplied.

Clearly, not all forms of personal racism are alike. There are marked differences between neo-Nazis and ordinary racists as I have characterized them. What accounts for these differences? I maintain that many of the differences should be understood in terms of different emotional alloys formed by the different emotions that are absorbed by the contempt matrix. Extremist racists, such as members of the Klan, have an alloy of contempt and hatred. More precisely, these types of racists have contemptuous hatred, a profound loathing, of racial others. Hate need not proceed downward, for it may be possessed because of an elevated regard for some feature of the hated. In the case of the white supremacist, however, the racist is affectively enflamed with a commitment to diminish the racial others in order to avoid what he or she perceives as a degrading contaminant.[8] Such an affective militancy is difficult to maintain and often needs a special social setting, such as a supremacist organization, to nourish the hate.

Most racists, however, are unexceptional. These average North American citizens are constantly brushing elbows with each other in the engagements of daily life, attending or delivering a biology lecture, participating in a PTA meeting, heatedly debating the merits of union membership over a lunch break, rooting for the home team at a peewee league game. Many—though not all—of these citizens may profess an authentic commitment to liberty and justice for all people in the United States. And some may even be at pains to show that they are entirely unblemished by racist attitudes and, perhaps, advert to the now proverbial "black friend." These ordinary racists find the cost of hate too much and find themselves disgusted by supremacist organizations. Their disgust is directed more at the violence and style of these organizations than at the contemptuous racial outlook of these organizations because their own contempt for racial others is less alloyed with hatred.

Contempt is a world-ordering emotion. It provides a vision of the normative structure of the world. The sharing of contempt is a powerful social exercise as it binds people together in political solidarity and provides a basis for self-esteem and belonging. The fellowship of racist contempt is no exception. Racist griping, joking, gossiping, and lay theorizing constitute a pastime in the United States that unites people in affirming ways. One can easily picture a groom-to-be shooting the breeze with his father-in-law about how Latinos have criminal tendencies and how sad he and his fiancée were to reject a wonderful house in an increasingly Latino neighborhood. Or one can think of a group of workers complaining about affirmative action and how they have to deal with "incompetent" black coworkers. The shared resentment of the white backlash movement is powerfully binding, but more so when it is mingled with contempt. There is some muffled sense in which nonwhites are not supposed to be the rivals of whites. Correlatively, such whites may even feel shame when they are surpassed by a black colleague, as blacks are not supposed to be that capable.[9] Or we can imagine two mothers sharing in the castigation of black women as so-called welfare queens. This communion of contempt is obviously racist, and it is exceedingly ordinary.

Even within the class of ordinary racists, however, important distinctions can be made. For example, there is a difference between the openly contemptuous, such as the individuals described in the previous paragraph, and the racist who has positive emotions toward some racial others. Though many ordinary racists are openly contemptuous, there is pressure to maintain decorum because they may feel devoted to equality and find that the epithet *racist* carries a nasty stigma. The racist alloy in such an individual is a contemptuous paternalism, a positive, caring, affiliating regard for racial others, where the care proceeds downward rather than horizontally as between equals. On their own behalf, they may cite the fact that they have good rapport with nonwhite coworkers and have nonwhite friends or have dated nonwhites. These "facts" are taken to have prima facie force for showing an absence of racism but there is no reason to think this unless one conceives of racism centrally as hatred or animosity. Care and debasing regard are compatible.

Care and contempt may coincide when, for example, care may be the more ostensible emotion, whereas contempt remains subconscious or takes up a diffuse, hardly noticed background presence. The occurrence of subconscious emotion is a normal phenomenon, especially when its explicit occurrence is forbidden. A persuasive argument for the general phenomenon of hidden emotions can be found in Helen Block Lewis's detailed work on suppressed shame, *Shame and Guilt in Neurosis* (see chap. 7). Many cases of contemptuous paternalism may fall under this type of phenomenon, but there may be still subtler cases of racism in which contempt is not experienced even subconsciously. These unusual cases, too, can be understood as contemptuous paternalism, however.

To see this, we need to return to the idea of a contempt matrix, setting aside particular episodes of contempt for just a moment. As noted earlier, a central concern of the contempt matrix is the degree to which the perceived base object may have psychological ingress. The greater the ingress, the greater the threat. Once a certain threshold is crossed, contempt is experienced. One exception to this description—there may be others—is when a good deal of ingress is allowed but the base object is deftly circumscribed so as not to be a real threat. Returning to an example at the start of the essay, we might suppose that Albert's prospective father-in-law relies on his class standing, charisma, and status as a potential in-law to ensure his own comfort around Albert. In fact, he may take Albert on as a project of sorts. Having noticed in pictures that Albert likes to wear a baseball cap backward, he may point out how the men across the street look undignified with their backward caps. They are making, he remarks, a crass attempt to experience again their youth long faded, but then hastens to add that Albert's full head of dark blonde hair gives him a certain force or presence. We might suppose further that Albert's prospective father-in-law begins to like Albert a great deal. He may think that, contrary to his initial impression, Albert is not like others of his social class. He needs only a little coaching in the right direction. With this turn of mind, Albert's father-in-law-to-be has not abandoned his class snobbery and contempt, for he still regards lower classes as base. He simply takes Albert to be an exception. Albert has been safely contained.[10]

I maintain that so long as care proceeds from an assumed position of superiority, the contempt matrix has not been abandoned. Rather, as just suggested, strategies of threat elimination are deployed. One obvious form of power is an agent's ability to have and express prejudice with impunity. A subtler kind of power can be found in an agent's ability *not* to feel prejudicial sentiments with any regularity or forcefulness. Such an agent will have the capacity to stave off the psychological encroachment of degrading racial others in virtue of having the means to avoid racially mixed neighborhoods, shop at mostly white stores and malls, interact mostly with racial others who are below him or her on the workplace ladder, and so on. More interestingly, many whites are in a position where racial others depend on them for job security and advancement, intellectual affirmation, mentoring, spiritual/moral counseling, essential cooperation in a group endeavor, and so on. This situation is awkward for racist whites. In light of the plasticity of the human mind and the peculiar pressures of such support-demanding but downwardly oriented relationships, we can expect, in most cases, sympathy and benevolence to issue from the racist white toward dependent racial others. But these sentiments will be structured by the contempt matrix, which will be made evident by when they occur and their representational content. So long as the racial other does not transgress acceptable bounds of containment, no contempt need occur because there is no offense or threat of a degrading contagion. Perhaps de Tocqueville had this idea in mind when he asserted:

> In the South, where slavery still exists, the Negroes are less carefully kept apart; they sometimes share the labors and recreations of the whites; the whites consent to intermix with them to a certain extent, and although legislation treats

them more harshly, the habits of the people are more tolerant and compassion-ate. In the South the master is not afraid to raise his slave to his own standing, because he knows that he can in a moment reduce him to the dust at pleasure. In the North the white no longer distinctly perceives the barrier that separates him from the degraded race, and he shuns the Negro with the more pertinacity since he fears lest they should some day be confounded together. (*Democracy in America*, 374)

In the present, so long as the newly appointed black professor conforms to the informal rules of her white department and does not have a racial chip on her shoulder, she is contained and is responded to with care and colle-giality. Once she starts doing things "her way" or demands "too much," she may become distasteful, a defiling element, and, hence, someone to be toler-ated, coped with, or socially subdued. Or perhaps her white colleagues are a little more flexible, for who wants diversity without genuine difference? They may not mind that she challenges the departmental status quo, under-mines the canon, or begins to surpass many of her colleagues by an objec-tive criterion (such as number of publications). As long as she is a force of one, she may yet be contained in their psyche in ways that are unthreaten-ing. Their new and uppity colleague may even add a certain spice to the de-partment or be someone they can talk about at conferences to show that theirs is a really liberal department. Moreover, given her objective progress, they may even view her with a pleasurable fascination, almost like a speci-men under a slide: she's black, female, and *very smart*. However, imagine if one or two more transgressive racial others join the department. That num-ber may engender a containment breach. The psychic resources for staving off the debasing element may be depleted, so offense and threat of defilement may ensue. Was there no contempt before? Perhaps not, perhaps not even subconsciously. However, given the structure and evolution of the relation-ship, it seems clear that a contempt matrix was in play the whole time, shap-ing the care and collegiality. Prior to uncontainability, the black colleague was the recipient of care and benevolent feelings under the description of *a "good black"* or *a "black that enhances the diversity and, hence, status of the department."* [11]

But imagine if the black professor conformed to the desires of her col-leagues. We can easily suppose that she would be embraced as an exception to the general rule; she's not like *them*. There is contempt here—contempt whose content is keyed to a group, namely blacks, rather than to this ex-ceptional and, for this reason, likable individual. Paternalistic racism typi-cally has this structure, but I think more is involved in such a situation. Even the "good black" may be an object of deeply suppressed contempt.

The above example displays the operation of a suppressed contempt ma-trix within the confines of departmental roles. There are, however, role-in-dependent ways of revealing the clandestine contempt that shapes overtly

positive feelings. We need cases in which a high degree of intrusion of baseness is forced upon the racist paternalist. Piper's litmus test has been offered
as one way of revealing contempt, and I offer a concrete example of its effectiveness. When I was a young child, I noticed that a baby girl had what I
thought were slanted eyes rather like Asian eyes, so I innocently asked her
mother, "Is your husband Oriental?" She was deeply perplexed and replied,
"No." I then said, "Oh, because the baby has Chinese eyes!" Her response
puzzled me. It was wholly nonverbal: a look of revulsion and dismay.

The significance of Piper's test and my story of Chinese eyes lies in the
sudden and complete neutralization of the distancing or circumscribing maneuvers that structure the racist's contempt matrix. Piper's litmus test drives
blackness into the very heart of the racist's self, forcing the racist to self-
identify directly with blackness. The case of Chinese Eyes is slightly different
in that it forces the racist to identify deeply with Asian-ness via her powerful parental identification with her child. The elicitation of revulsion conveys
dramatically that such individuals cannot bear to *be* black or Asian, no matter how well they get along with blacks or Asians. Their vision of the world
squarely places racial others within the contemptible. The upshot is that in
spite of amiable relations, there may yet be contemptuous regard. If, as Aristotle claimed, a true friend is another self, many well-meaning and caring
white racists are constitutionally incapable of authentic interracial friendship. Care is care only under a certain description: the racial other must fall
under the description of *a self like oneself*. Racist contempt militates against
the possibilty of this description. Perhaps the reason why so many whites
claim to regard their nonwhite friends as *individuals*, pure and simple, and
claim not to see their race is that these whites can regard the racial other as
a self like oneself only by raising both the self and the other to an ethereal
plane divested of the concrete features that would ultimately divide them.
Deracination, then, may be obscurantist, in many cases.

Conclusion

I have suggested that contemptuous regard is central to many forms of personal racism. Moreover, I have maintained that even so-called benevolent
racism may not lack contempt. Given that contempt is an order-imposing
emotion, the world of the racist is one in which racial others serve as reference points in a social schema for the distasteful or sometimes the degenerate
and sullied. If I am right, there is something problematic when whites accuse
nonwhites of antiwhite racism. It is often claimed that nonwhites cannot be
racist against whites because nonwhites lack power broadly understood.
From the standpoint of structural relations between whites and nonwhites,
this may well be the case, as they typically do not have the power to "back
up" their prejudice. But there is more. *From the standpoint of moral agency,*

nonwhites are rarely, if ever, racist against whites, for in what does the non-white's contempt of the white consist? Typically, when more than resentment is felt, it is a contempt for the white's racist thoughts, racist feelings, and racist actions and inactions. It is a *moral* contempt laced with resentment, as it is *localized* to the moral failings of certain whites. Of course, a nonwhite may contemptuously and culpably tag an innocent white as racist. The impropriety is in its application, its hitting the wrong target. White racist contempt, by contrast, is in its very constitution disturbing and immoral. Even when some nonmoral aspect of whiteness is seen to be distasteful, at no point is the contempt expressive of an antiwhite world. White racism regards nonwhiteness as intrinsically base. Nonwhite "racism" demands moral accountability for a world that debases.[12] Perhaps when "nigger," "gook," and "spic" sound as silly as "honky," "whitey," and "round eyes," we will have achieved a level of racial symmetry such that there could be reverse racism. Until then, ours is a racial regime. Insofar as I am right, the allegation of nonwhite racism involves a serious loss of contact with (racist) reality. If I am wrong, an account of reverse racism surely ought to make a mockery of the racism that continues to be inflicted upon nonwhites.[13]

7 Colonial Racism: Sweeping Out Africa with Mother Europe's Broom

Nkiru Nzegwu

My own feeling is that he used his mother's broom to sweep out his father's house.

—Pascal Kyoore

Late-twentieth-century British-Ghanaian philosopher Kwame Anthony Appiah begins the first chapter of *In My Father's House: Africa in the Philosophy of Culture*, a narrative of cultural politics, with the following:

> On 26 July 1860, Alexander Crummell, African-American by birth, Liberian by adoption, an Episcopalian priest with a University of Cambridge education, addressed the citizens of Maryland County, Cape Palmas. . . . [I]t is particularly striking that his title was "The English Language" and his theme that the Africans "exiled" in slavery to the New World had been given by divine providence "at least this one item of compensation, namely, the possession of the Anglo-Saxon tongue." Crummell, who is widely regarded as one of the fathers of African nationalism, had not the slightest doubt that English was a language superior to the "various tongues and dialects" of the indigenous African populations. (3)

With this opening gambit, Appiah quickly moves into a polarizing discussion on race and racism. He shows that the man who "initiated the nationalist discourse on Africa in Africa" (5) is an African American émigré in Liberia with pejorative views of Africa, its languages and traditions. Appiah uses critically selected passages from Crummell's speech to dwell on the latter's laudatory views about the Anglo-Saxon tongue, which he thinks is "su-

perior to the 'various tongues and dialects' of indigenous African populations; superior in its euphony, its conceptual resources, and its capacity to
express the 'supernal truths' of Christianity" (3). At the same time that Appiah represents Crummell's vision on language as prophetic, he neatly un-
dercuts the legitimacy of that vision by presenting it as tainted by racism. According to him, "At the core of Crummell's vision is a single guiding concept:
race" (5). Appiah argues that Crummell is both a racialist and a racist and
that Crummell and others like him "inherited a set of conceptual blinders
that made them unable to see virtue in Africa. . . . *[T]hey conceived of the
African in racial terms* . . . and they left *us*, through the linking of race and
Pan-Africanism, with a burdensome legacy" (5, my emphasis).

Many have rightly critiqued Appiah for his superficial understanding of
ideology of race relations in the United States.[1] Nevertheless, he is correct in
stating that "colonial Africans experienced European racism to radically different degrees in differing colonial conditions, and had correspondingly different degrees of preoccupation with the issue" (6). The problem in Appiah's
position is not just that he failed to give credit to African intellectuals such
as Kobina Sekyi, who (as Appiah's father, Joe, also knew) eschewed racial
categories, underscored the importance of culture,[2] and by 1925 had rejected the racial basis of Pan-Africanism.[3] In my view, the central problem is
that Appiah deploys the inclusive "us" to appeal to our (Africans') sense of
indignation at Crummell's prejudices, while he masks the depth of his own
implication in the structures of experience and racial ideology of his Anglo-
Saxon matriclan (7).

So what is the rationale for Appiah's appeal, even though his view on
Africa's material culture and life is fundamentally similar to Crummell's?
What is the motivation for his kinship identification with Africans? And why
is it necessary to explain Africa to the world by route of individuals whose
experiences were substantially formed in the New World? The objective of
these three questions is to raise and keep in sharp focus the link between
scholarly agenda and the declared ethnic, racial, and national identities of
the philosopher. This link is needed to understand the relevance to "us" Africans of Appiah's extended discussion on a biology-based, body-focused
conception of race and the relevance it has for "the possibilities and pitfalls
of an African identity in the late twentieth century" (x). Because Appiah
starts his book with issues of race, the questions we have to consider are:
Does *race* as it is theorized by "New World natives" (21, Crummell) and
other "natives" of the United States have the same resonance for "us" "Old
World natives" in Africa as it does for "them" in the New World? Were the
theorizations of these emigrés to the Old World from the New World (e.g.,
Crummell and Edward Wilmot Blyden[4]) ever affected by their experiences
in Africa, the changing historical conditions of the time, and their personal
growth? Moreover, what are the consequences for theoretical discourse if we
start any analysis of Africa with a New World conceptualization of race and

racism? If, as Appiah suggests, "our" experiences of European racism are radically different from the experiences of "New World natives," why would the New World variant of racism be a starting point of analysis and an urgent issue of concern for "us" Old World natives? And lastly, what exactly does the New World variant of racism and its recent preoccupation with mixed race identities and global interconnections have to say, for example, about African identity and women's concerns in this last decade of the twentieth century?

Contemporary discourses on race and racism in West Africa often fail to distinguish sufficiently between colonial racism in Africa and racism in the United States, where New World slavery defined the ontological and epistemological framework of racialization and infused meaningfulness to the concept. Lacking empirical and historical specificity as well as geographical accuracy, theoretical debates on race fail to provide a textured sociohistorical understanding of events in West Africa and to account for Africans' bewilderment over the venomous character of racism in the United States. When we treat the U.S. model of physiognomy-based racism as the exemplar for all possible kinds of racism, *race* becomes a catch-all, homogeneous category in which all forms of racism are restricted to or must approximate that variant. Not only is this theoretical move artificially restricting and colonizing, it is epistemologically flawed. It mistakes the character of a particular social phenomenon for the genus.

In not making this qualification, many contemporary discourses on racism fail because they cannot sufficiently account for other modes of racism, nor can they detect the ways in which these forms thrive in their own radically different terrain. Empirical evidence reveals that the language and culture of racism do not exist only in contexts where the racialized identity is constructed in negation and where blackness or a black body is a focus of stigma and devaluation. In the interracial contact between colonial West Africa and Europe, racism thrived even when African identity was not constructed in negation, when Africans in Africa were the normative order, had the power to wield "the Look," and were sources of meaning and value.[5] In this essay, therefore, I examine the philosophical dangers of exclusively conceptualizing racism through the prism of Africans in diaspora. Using Appiah's classic book, I explore the complicated manner in which colonial racism is inverted so that Africa's values, practices, beliefs, and responses are swept out of scholarly consideration with Europe's explanatory broom. I conduct my argument in seven broad moves. In the first move, I examine the nature and formal character of colonial racism, as well as its various sites of operation, and in the second move I establish the West African variant of racism. The third move deals with the invidious ways in which a set of assumptions about race initiates a search of explanatory narratives that obliterate the African conceptual scheme. In the fourth move, I consider a particular historical moment in Asante history to articulate an alternative conception of race that is nondiscriminatory. The fifth move focuses on how colonial racism is inverted so that one's own embodies a racist ideology, and in the sixth move, I examine the deployment of the sexist dimension of the racist ideology against African women. In my seventh and final move, I explore the results of this virulent strain of racial discrimination in the demonization of African women and in their subsequent elimination.

Colonial Racism

Racism in United States, as African American theorists have consistently and correctly argued, is a supremacist ideology of power that exploits visible physiognomical and phenotypic differences to promote a political relation of dominance. Racism in general is not merely about individuals' intrinsic and extrinsic prejudices and biases (Appiah, *In My Father's House*, 17–20), or about a temptation to be resisted (ibid., ix), as conservatives and some liberal individualistic ideologues contend.[6] Quite to the contrary, racism is about the sociopolitical institutionalization of racial prejudice and the implementation of social policies from that base. In establishing a relation of dominance and oppression, race becomes the central axis of social life, and racism derives its power from the valorization of a constructed physiognomical and phenotypic trait, such as whiteness.

A review of recent literature by black critical race theorists in the legal field demonstrates the palpable flaw of the position that equates racism with individuals' racial prejudice. In "The Race/Class Conundrum and the Pursuit of Individualism in the Making of Social Policy," Jennifer M. Russell methodically maps out the race-conscious character of individualism in the United States and establishes that in "valoriz[ing] the individual as the primary moral, political, and legal subject" (1361–62), "American individualism endowed the population with inalienable rights in a racially discriminatory manner that favored whites . . . over blacks" (1395). She reveals that the ensuing form of racism, based as it is on physiognomy, "contributed to a constitutionalization of the 'outsider' status of blacks that would prove resistant to future reformatory efforts" (1398). In "Whiteness as Property," Cheryl Harris approaches the issue from another angle and argues that the structural processes of color codification in U.S. social polity is such that political and juridical categories are indelibly racialized and are formally implicated in the racist agenda (1707, 1716). Unraveling the idea of racial characteristics as property, she exposes the hidden structure of U.S. racism and shows that the presumption of freedom is implicitly built into the white color of the skin, whereas the "presumption of slavery" and, by extension, the denial of entitlement are inherently built into the black color of the skin (1720). In the United States of America and Canada, body-based racism is socially expressed in negative stereotyping, invidious segregation, social disenfranchisement, political discrimination, white nepotism in employment, restriction of access to jobs, resources and entitlements for blacks, and covert and overt resistance to racial equality.

In the United States and Canada, where physiognomy is an important organizing principle of social classification, racism is an endemically entrenched process of oppression manifested in every aspect of life. Blacks and other racialized groups occupy a structurally inferior position to whites in income levels and wealth, physical well being, employment rates, and incarceration rates. The racial imperative of both the historical and the contemporary principle of classification in the United States is that, technically, whites have no nonwhite ancestry (the positive criterion of *absence*), whereas a person is black once a black ancestry can be traced (the negative criterion of *presence*). Regardless of its numerous disguises, permutations, and transformations, this obsession with white racial purity, or whiteness, is the pivot of morbidity on which U.S. and Canadian racism and race discourses revolve. Negrophobia (or U.S. whites' pathological fear of absorption by blacks) is theoretically elaborated and historically refined in the Aryan supremacist theories of Johann Blumenbach, Comte Joseph Arthur de Gobineau, Adolf Hitler, the Mississippi Black Codes, and Jim Crow laws.

Interesting as this concept of negrophobia and its social consequences may be, it is largely irrelevant to the lives of the Mande, Akan, Yoruba, and Ibibio, whose conception of self are defined on positive grounds and for whom colonial racism played itself out on other grounds. Equally, the same can be said for Nigerians and Ghanaians, for whom the racial concept of *blackness* (the negative criterion of presence) lacks intelligibility and for whom being black is not a badge of inferiority. The character of racism in the United States and the sorts of question it raises about racial identity may resonate in South Africa given the similarity of its apartheid structure to the U.S. policy of segregation. They do not, however, translate easily to other environments, particularly West Africa because the familiar U.S. and Canadian conception of the term *racism* as connoting the pathologization of the black body does not constitute the sole definition of the term. In its U.S. manifestation, John Pittman makes it clear that the race question for African Americans is tied up with issues of (body) identity as black people in United States. As he puts it, "*identity* [his emphasis] is not for us simply a philosophical problem about ontological sameness and individuation but a question of *our hard-fought collective relation to a social designation devised and enforced by a hostile culture*" ("Introduction," my emphasis). Indeed, the defining features of racism in the United States is the black body, people's experience of collective enslavement and its aftermath, and their "hard-fought collective relation" to "a hostile culture." Given this definitional emphasis, it needs to be underscored that this specific form of social and racial identification did not extend to regions of Africa, such as West Africa, that were environmentally hostile to the white man, hence did not support a white settler community as in East and southern Africa.

On the West Coast of Africa, which was also known as "the white man's grave," historical evidence shows that the occurrence of U.S.-type racism and its obsessive preoccupation with racial (body) identity were low on the priority scale. Russell's articulation of the "outsider status of the black body" within the U.S. experience and such racial imperatives as the positive criterion of absence do not exist in this region. For example, if Charles Mills's concept of "subperson'" is deployed in discussions in West Africa, especially in Nigeria, not only would whites be the racial other, they would also end up in the "subperson" category. In many areas of this region, whites, according to Mills's approach, are perceived as entities that "because of phenotype, seem human in some respects but not in others ("Non-Cartesian Sums: Philosophy and the African American Experience," 228). Incidentally, his statement that a human in the subperson category is "not fully a person [because his or her] moral status was tugged in different directions by the dehumanizing requirements of slavery on the one hand, and the (grudging and sporadic) white recognition of the objective properties blacks possessed on the other" (228) is interesting. With the substitution of greed and avarice for slavery, the first half of Mills's description captures West Africans' perception of the white man in many parts of West Africa.

Consider that for most of the nineteenth century, Obanta, the national deity of Ijebu-Yoruba, decreed that Europeans were evil. As a consequence, Ijebus saw white people as subpersons who lacked proper behavior and a cultured presence, and whose humanity was even in doubt. Ijebus then and many Nigerians today would agree that in regard to morality, the white man is indeed tugged in different directions by greed and avarice, on the one hand, and the objective property of his pallid white skin on the other.[7] Constantly looking the worse off for the hot humid weather, or routinely being laid low by malaria and dysentery, or facing defeat at the hands of Asante generals in the nineteenth century, or being held as captives in Kumasi in 1870s, or being by their minuscule presence constrained to a few places on the coast, Europeans (hence, European white skin, like that of the albino) were perceived as basically deficient. In the late nineteenth century, the setting of Appiah's first chapter, many West Africans viewed the white man as uncultured and his skin as an indication of aberration. Thus, in a context where Africans were demographically dominant and constituted the normative order, whiteness was not the definitional force. It was the "outsider's category," the quintessential color of marginality and social devaluation, and the marker of otherness, gullibility, duplicity, moral depravity, and cultural devaluation.[8]

This is not to say that racial conflicts were absent in West Africa in the late nineteenth and early twentieth centuries, but that they wore a different face. Philosophically, this difference calls into question the legitimacy of assuming that the U.S. conceptualization of race—its pathologization of the black body, and its pathological race relation—is the norm. In its ubiquity in this last quarter of the twentieth century, CNN may convey the impression to people in the United States that U.S. culture is everywhere, but certain U.S. cultural habits, institutional traits, and sociopolitical experiences do not easily cross international boundaries or retain their relevance outside the social space of the United States. It is important, therefore, to underscore that in a social order in which West Africans are the norm, black as a category of identification is unintelligible. No one is a black Mande or a black Fanti or a black Yoruba or a black Igbo. Even the idea of a black Nigerian or a black Sierra Leonean or a black Senegalese is ludicrous.[9] In a region in which Africans are numerically dominant and in which their history and culture have remained intact, the category of difference and differentiation is *white*: only the white man and the white woman are colored. The truth is that even when we acknowledge that the ideological concept of race and racism came with colonialism, physiognomy-based racism was never an organizing category of life, for instance, in imperial Asante from the eighteenth century to the late nineteenth century or of the Asante Confederacy under colonial rule in the first half of the twentieth century, as it was in the same historical period for blacks in the United States.

Racism thrived in other ways in British West Africa, ways in which bodies were seldom racialized. People were visually identified by culturalized means such as modes of dress, facial markings, names, and language; hence, colonial racism targeted culture. It is true that in pre-1880's Europe, racist narratives provided moral and political justification for intervention in African affairs, which eventually led to colonization. These narratives emerged in propaganda campaigns in European parliaments, literary and scholarly texts, pamphlets, newspapers and trade journals; they were stories of savagery, cannibalism, bestiality, and primitivity that were manufactured as justifications for colonization.[10] Such stories were targeted to the European audience and thus had no immediate impact on the majority of West Africans, who remained unaware of them and were dismissive of Europeans. On the Gold Coast, where some Fantis could read the European newspapers, the savagery stories received some approval because the target of demonization was their enemy, the Asante.[11] For literate Asantes in Cape Coast, however, such stories were treated with contempt, given the authors' clearly ignorant and self-serving objectives. As Agnes Akosua Aidoo, a Ghanaian historian, has argued, the British constructed demonic histories of Asante in which they represented themselves in the best possible light so as to mask their bankrupt trading practices and policies ("Political Crisis and Social Change in Asante Kingdom, 1867–1901," 170). Concurring, Ivor Wilks reiterates that British historians led by W. W. Claridge, constructed a "Whig interpretation" of Asante history to accord with the British political establishment's Whiggish preconceptions of the Asante as cruel, militaristic, and despotic (*One Nation, Many Histories: Ghana Past and Present*, 29–43). Indeed, such rhetoric functioned as a moral cover for imperial aggrandizement. It was especially prevalent just before the partition of Africa as agents of European trading establishments frantically sought to expand their firms' monopolies, and European military officers and spies tried to justify their adventurism.

Establishing the West African Variant

To grasp the character of racism in West Africa, it is important to understand the nature of African-European interaction during the colonial period. Equally, we must avoid the classic error of conflating British colonial racism in the region with body racism as articulated in the United States. Indeed, Saburi Biobaku's work on the Egbas and the British consuls, E. A. Ayandele's history of the Ijebus, and Omoniyi Adewoye's work on the litigious letter writers in the judicial system of southern Nigeria between 1854 and 1954 reveal the error in the conflation.[12] These studies show explicitly the extent to which the British were marginal in the lives of the people and the extraordinary reliance of the British on different African interest groups to further their cause. Owing to this dependence, it would have been politically short-sighted to target the body as the site of racism. Without a doubt, the U.S.-type racial ideology would have antagonized and alienated the entire populace and effectively undermined the administrative policy of divide and rule that depended on collaboration to pit one cultural, ethnic or interest group against another. Given the absence of a settler community, the beleaguered British could ill afford to pathologize the body; hence, they selected culture as the target of difference.

Colonial racism, then, is a historically specific form of cultural racism practiced against non-Europeans. It was operationalized in West Africa during European colonial rule and had the weight of governance behind it. The reason these and other subtler forms of racism seem to be nonracist is that they do not approximate the banality of the overly crude U.S. model. Thus, the term "colonial racism" is useful because it makes a sharp distinction between the body racist experiences of African Americans and the culture racist experiences of Africans. Also, it provides a way to open up discussion about other types of racist policies that derive from a pathological fear of racial pluralism and that are much more damaging to humanity. The racist politics of erasing Africa's conceptual schema and of discriminating against certain bodies, certain cultures, certain knowledges must be uprooted, but first of all we have to understand the different manifestations of racism, including those manifestations that exploit the illusion of modernity and progress in order to produce a mass of "apologetic imitations of the Englishman or the American" (Kobina Sekyi, cited in J. Ayodele Langley, introduction to *Ideologies of Liberation in Black Africa, 1856–1970*, 32).[13]

The glaring contrast between the sociocultural realities of the two geographical locations—Africa and the New World—raises two important questions. The first, what good reason can be adduced to justify the conflation of these two different social environments? And second, what would be the epistemological consequences of taking seriously the radical differences between the two locations? Although no plausible reason can justify the conflation—a completely misguided project—taking the radical differences seriously can lead to an elucidation of the nature and character of colonial racism.

Between 1890 and 1910, the overtly racist rhetoric that provided the cover for colonization went into abeyance as Europe smugly surveyed its colonial possessions. This lull allowed highly educated Saros in Sierra Leone, Fanti in then Gold Coast, and Yorubas in Nigeria—who saw themselves as the rightful political heirs to the colonial government—to move into the upper echelon of the civil service in British West Africa. After World War I, however, a policy reversal occurred following the intensification of colonized peoples' demands for self-determination. At this juncture, the colonial relationship of Britain and some of its colonies increasingly took on racist overtones that violated British moral principle and their postwar "Ideal of the Brotherhood of Man." At the formal structural level, Britain developed a two-tiered colonial system in which Canada, Australia, South Africa, and New Zealand were treated differently from colonies (India, Pakistan, Ghana, and Nigeria) in which the restive "natives" were a majority. The proof that colonialism is really about power and dominance and that it need not entail racism can be seen in the very different relationship Britain had with its predominantly white colonies Canada, Australia, and New Zealand, where the native population had been severely decimated. Invoking racial and cultural homogeneity, Britain protected these white colonies from the institutionally backed rights violations meted out to the non-European natives in the African and Asian colonies.

For the West African colonies especially, Britain deployed the negative conception of race that it had refined during the transatlantic slave trade era, and thus administratively discriminated against the indigenous majority in very subtle ways. The absence of a white settler community, as existed in India and southern Africa (thanks to malaria), and the high turnover of officials meant that Britain could not afford the cost of demonizing the black skin. It, however, problematized the people by representing their cultures as primitive and retrograde, which meant that the axis of British body-targeted racism was stretched across international space and hardly impacted on the lives of West Africans.[14] Unlike the situation in the New World, West Africans in their own cultural region and the British on their own cultural island did not share the same local and national space, and so were not in competition for national resources and entitlements. West Africans had to travel to the British metropole to actually experience racist conditions similar to those in the United States. Geographically insulated from the racism of the British public, this spatial buffer created a critical difference between racism in Britain or the United States and racism in West Africa. At home in their own nurturing cultural space and minimally affected by the easily befuddled colonial district officers, West Africans maintained a positive conception of themselves. They were not overly threatened by what they considered to be ludicrous comments of ignorant white administrators, whose stay in the region was usually temporary and whom they connived to get into trouble with the Colonial Office in London when they thought these officers had stepped out of line.

The epistemological consequences of this geographical feature have to be factored into theoretical analysis. In British West Africa, colonial racism was moderately experienced through administrative policies in which culture rather than the body was the site of racism: Lord Frederick Dealtry Lugard's racialized policy of indirect rule; the residential segregation of senior British colonial officials from the African population (white merchants lived with Africans); the establishment of a two-tiered civil service structure; the abolishment of meritocracy so that barely competent white men could be promoted; the portrayal of African culture as anachronistic; and the proscription of sexual contact between senior white colonial male officials and African women, on the one hand, and between African men and white colonial female officials, on the other.[15] Rationalizations for these "administrative" policies were advanced when subjected to interrogation by the West African press which gleefully created political storms out of the inequities. On such occasions, a discomfited Britain was forced to reconcile the poster image of herself as a civilized, law-abiding nation and her real image as an imperialist oppressor. Bearing in mind that there is a disjunction between colonialism and racism, and that not all colonial policies were racist, the ones that were racist were condoned just as long as they did not jeopardize imperial interests. Where conflicts arose, as in marriage and inheritance laws, compromises were made to avoid political unrest and economic destabilization.

Thus, it is a testimony to the minority status and vulnerability of Europeans in West Africa and an indication of the very different character of colonial racism that the primary audience for British racist stories and arrogance were the European populations in Europe, not the Africans for whom the Europeans were objects of eccentricities. Relatively speaking, then, colonial racism in British West Africa was institutionally practiced in a measured and calculated manner, unlike the body racism practiced during the post-Reconstruction period in the United States. The basic difference between West African and U.S. racism is that in the New World the emphasis has historically been on the negation of the black body and personhood. In pre-independence West Africa, by contrast, the emphasis has been on the negation of African culture and cultural dignity. This vital difference between body-targeted racism and culture-targeted racism explains the divergent views, responses and attitudes between West Africans and African Americans on matters of race and racism. Having been racialized for centuries on the basis of physiognomy, African Americans are thoroughly exasperated at what they perceive to be West Africans' apathy over the polarizing politics of color that characterizes life in the United States. Comfortable with who they are, West Africans are bemused at what they perceive to be African Americans' hypersensitivity on issues of "color and race," and their seeming inability to "get on" with life.

For us in West Africa, colonial racism has played itself out at the comprehensive, macrolevel terrain of culture, where invidious cuts and slights nebulously have taken place out of sight, often with the collaboration of well-known locals, whereas in the New World, body racism has systemically targeted the black body, problematizing and degrading it to create a traumatic inner crisis of individual identity. In West Africa, colonial racism attacks the dynamic elements of a culture, fossilizing and stultifying it to create a graduated collective crisis of identity. Whereas the black body has become the site of repulsion and negativity in the United States, African cultures have become the site of shame and aversion for many Africans, who now see their culture as primitive (which explains why some Africans can never understand why some African Americans are fascinated with customs and traditions they think are outdated). Culturally inferiorized many Africans are thrown into a quandary over the stasis and functional failure of their culture, wheras bodily inferiorized African Americans have been thrown into a quandary over the institutionalized questioning of their social relevance and existence. Though the two sites are radically different, the end products are the same—the destabilization of the psychic equanimity of peoples of African descent.

The philosophical import of these two manifestations of racism must be integrated into theoretical discourse and must guide our understanding of the specific experiences of life in West Africa. Contrary to the supposition made by race theorists in the United States, the body is not the sole and exclusive site of devaluation. Nebulous things such as cultural norms and patterns, socialized behavior, legal entitlements, and the environment may be attacked once the focus is shifted from skin pigmentation to the community and the society.[16] The epistemological implication is that negrophobia is not really the cause of racism, but its symptom. It is true that racism in general stems from racial prejudice, but its institutionalization stems from a deep-seated, pathological fear of relationally extending one's identity in a plural society. The visceral fear of absorption—which to the small individualistic mindset connotes annihilation and death—is indicative of a severely diminished vision of reality. This fear of relationality and extension bespeaks of an impoverished psyche unable to appreciate difference in other human beings.

Shifting the burden of racism to its rightful place, the psychic center of whiteness, means that the white skin cannot really be conceptualized as a signifier of superiority. Around the world, whiteness has actually been the prime racial signifier of difference. Precisely for this reason, superiority was never defined in West Africa by white bodies per se, but by the technological efficacy of the European culture at a given historical moment. Responding to this logic in the 1890s, Asantehene Agyeman Prempeh sought to technologically develop Asante economy without culturally transforming the society (Wilks, *One Nation, Many Histories*, 54–55).[17] However, once the British colonial administration realized that science and progress could mark racial superiority equally well, it effectively deployed the ideal of modernization in the colonizing game. Through the racist educational policy devised by Lugard, modernization and progress came to offer a pseudo-pathway to political representation and cultural equality.

Missionaries too played a vital role in this process of colonization. Haranguing country folks to convert from heathenism to Christianity, they widely disseminated the idea that native cultures were reprobate and evil. They insisted that conversion to Christianity and literacy would produce the requisite educated souls to uplift their kin and thus end up modernizing the societies. Paraphrasing K. A. Busia's penetrating analysis on this point, colonial racism was practiced through the idea that loyalty to the values, religion, and lifestyle of Europe signified modernization, whereas loyalty to values, religion, and lifestyle of Africa was misguided and heathenish ("The Political Heritage," 447–57, see especially 451).

Obliteration: Alienated Discourses on Africa

The epistemological consequences of taking seriously the radically different histories of Africa and the United States are having far-reaching effects. For one, the experiences of colonial racism and the politics of area studies in the United States are increasingly forcing African scholars to interrogate the motives of scholars who purport to be responsive to the best interests of Africa and Africans, yet who end up creating an alienated discourse *of* Africa rather than *about* Africa. This interrogation is primarily a response to the invidious de-Africanization that results from the works of both the old-time Africanists and the New Africanists, whose knowledge of Africa tends to be breathtakingly superficial.[18] The consensus of opinion is that this de-Africanization process is a colonial strategy that has effectively been used for decades to gain control of the production of knowledge about Africa. In de-Africanization, the conceptual categories of the different African nations are obscured, then the political, economic, social, and philosophical issues are conducted on the basis of Western categories and interests. If Africa were really placed at the center of such analyses, as it rightly should, it is debatable that old-time and new Africanists would begin with the currently used set of research issues and assumptions. In fact, it is very probable that Appiah would not have begun with the race issue and the historical moment that he did.

Discourses on colonial racism are conceptually skewed once scholars attempt to theorize West Africans' political reality through the experiences of émigré intellectuals from the New World. The calibrated frame of reference introduces a dichotomy between the so-called traditional African state and the modern period of state formation, and the resulting analyses are heavily colored by New World experiences of enslavement. The twin shortcomings of this intellectual orientation are that the ensuing analyses are really a dialogic response to certain European intellectuals and that such an orientation innocuously deflects attention from the normative moral, social, and political issues on the ground in West Africa. Although the theoretical disputes about African's humanity waged by Crummell and certain European intellectuals are certainly engaging and definitely a part of the intellectual history of West Africa, they nonetheless remain a miniscule part of a much larger history. What is exceptionally grievous in Appiah's deployment of Crummell's race-focused debates is not just that he obscures the substantive issues of concern to the normative African center, but that he conceals the racist European side of the dialogue, which created Crummell and provoked his response in the first place. The effect of the concealment is that the body-based racism Appiah identifies in the writings of Crummell and Edward Wilmot Blyden really has its roots in the racist claims and theories of European scholars, phrenologists, politicians, church leaders, and traders. Had the thoughts of these individuals been properly contextualized, it would have become clear that Appiah's critique is misplaced. His argument breaks down at precisely the point he presents Crummell as racist, effectively ignoring the political force of the racist arguments of John Locke, David Hume, George Berkeley, Immanuel Kant, G. W. F. Hegel, Blumenbach, Gobineau, and others. Shifting the blame to the African American Crummell places the victim on the same level as Locke the profiteer, who financially invested in slaving companies, and as Hume, who provided the theoretical justification for the debasement of Africans.

Interestingly, the assumptions underpinning Appiah's position cause him to ignore the relevance to his analysis of Edward Blyden's cultural nationalism, his advocacy of Krio as a national language, his support of African customs, and the other conceptual transformations that he and other émigrés experienced as they adapted to conditions in Africa.[19] No doubt, incorporating these materials would immediately have informed Appiah's twentieth-century readers of the racism of the European church establishment, the European Christian missionaries in Africa, and the European and U.S. politicians and adventurers. To provide a textured image of New World émigrés in Africa, it is important to convey to late twentieth-century readers the exact features of racism, colonialism, and Christianity in the late nineteenth century because knowledge of these features would enable us to appreciate the historical, institutional, and ideological issues faced by these émigré intellectuals and why they believed in the modernizing role of imperialism. We can then follow how they could argue for cultural modernization and the adoption of European languages even as they rejected the central premise of European racism, which is that African peoples were at the lowest rung of the human evolutionary chain, constituting a link between humans and apes. Despite their championship of cultural modernization, these nineteenth-century intellectuals attacked the conceptual flaws in European theorization of culture. It is definitely helpful to know that many years before Kobina Sekyi contended that "Africa was old when Europe was young: therefore reflection is Africa, whilst impulse is European" ("The Future of Subject Peoples," 251), the New World—born James Africanus Beale Horton had made a similar point.

While acknowledging the reactive posture of these New World émigrés, we need to note too that they failed to adequately connect with the indigenous cultures—hence, erasing them. We need to remember that Americo-Liberians and African Americans in the United States were Crummell's primary focus of interest. Influenced by their race experiences in the New World and seduced by the rhetoric of education, modernization and Christianity, some of these intellectuals failed to see that, as Sekyi puts it, "they cannot get thoroughly into the secret of success of applying [their science and learning] unless they acquire the vices of Europe and America" (ibid., 247). In Sekyi's view, these antisocial vices, rather than science and learning, would eventually undermine the integrity of Africa's social institutions and bring about the collective loss of people's humanity, mainly because of the debasement principle at the heart of European civilization. He contends that European civilization and its notion of modernization and wealth are predicated on the "exaltation of one nation and the debasement of all other nations" (ibid., 244).

Far more pressing from the point of view of this essay is the importance of centering Africans' reality and experience in historical and cultural analyses. Restoring indigenous perspectives and cultural histories shifts the axis of research to the sorts of studies undertaken by Fante intellectuals such as John Mensah Sarbah and Kobina Sekyi, or Yoruba scholars such as Bolaji Idowu and Olumide Lucas. The question we need to pose at this juncture is: What were the issues of concern to the Africans who constituted the normative political and social order in 1860, the major historical moment Appiah chose to open a discussion of the affairs of "his father's house"? What were the flaws in their theories of nation-state? Was body racism of vital concern to them? Focusing exclusively on the Asante, what conception of race, if any, underpinned the strategies of political figures such as Kwaku Dua I, Asantehemaa Afua Kobi, and Yaa Akyaa?

In a Different World

Historical evidence reveals that the political figures of imperial Asante and members of the Fanti Confederacy were respectively engaged in a conversation with each other about their respective nationalities, about what it means to be Asante or Fante, and about their conception of the larger world.

Conducted in the form of military and political maneuverings, these conversations provide a unique angle from which to view and understand the issue of race in an indigenous setting.

By 1859, forty years old and affluent, Afua Kobi came to the stool as the Asantehemaa (Queen Mother) after having survived the second major purge of Asantehene Kwaku Dua I. She replaced her mother as the Asantehemaa. Her mother, Afua Sapon, the Asantehemaa and sister of Kwaku Dua I, and her brother, Osei Kwadwo, had been charged with treasonable felony and had had to commit suicide. On ascending the stool, Asantehemaa Afua Kobi became the royal genealogist and a full member of the Asanteman Nhyiamu (National Assembly) and of the Asantehene's inner council. By virtue of the constitutional duties vested in her office, she had to be present for all important matters of state, especially when cases requiring Asante oaths were on the table for decision and action. One of her major responsibilities was to advise and guide the Asantehene, and she alone had the authority to criticize and rebuke him to his face and in public. Failure to perform this restraining duty effectively could have contributed to her destoolment (Aidoo, "Political Crisis," 191).[20]

In 1867, seven years after Crummell's speech at Cape Palmas, a far more momentous event occurred in Asante. Kwaku Dua I died. His carefully designed plans for succesion by his grandson (who was also his grandnephew) suffered a set back. Asantehemaa Afua Kobi exercised her constitutional prerogative and nominated her son, Kofi Kakari, to the Stool. The candidature was approved by the Kumasi chiefs and Amanhene (state chiefs, another cadre of Asante chiefs), and Kofi Kakari became the next Asantehene. According to Aidoo, "the joint rule of Afua Kobi and her son took place in the most critical of circumstances? ("Asante Queen Mothers in Government and Politics in the Nineteenth Century," 69). Kofi Kakari was reputed to be a profligate who lacked "noticeable administrative skills; [and] his government was controlled by his subordinates" (Aidoo, "Political Crisis," 286). That he ruled Asante as long as he did, seventeen years, was possible because of his mother's political astuteness, which kept him on the Stool (Aido, "Queen Mothers," 69). When Afua Kobi finally withdrew that support in 1874, after learning of Kakari's sacrilegious and unconstitutional rifling of the gold in the royal mausoleum, Asantehene Kofi Kakari was destooled. She conceded to the destoolment to preserve her dynasty, but quickly regrouped and placed her younger son, Mensu Bonsu, as Kakari's successor.

Eyewitness accounts of the period reveal that Asantehemaa Afua Kobi was "the most influential person at court," enjoying "unusual influence both with the king, her son, and with the people, and [was] a woman of great ability and shrewdness" (Aidoo, "Political Crisis," 194). British intelligence reports describe her as "a prudent though warlike woman" and "the only moderating influence on Asantehene Kakari" (Aidoo, "Political Crisis," 195).[21] From recorded speeches, Aidoo establishes that Asantehemaa Afua Kobi was critically aware of her place in history and possibly for this reason adopted a strong moral framework in monitoring and evaluating the actions of the government within the imperial borders and in their interracial relations with the Dutch and the British. This sense of moral responsibility is evident in her speech of November 20, 1873, in which she urged that the European prisoners of war (F. A. Ramseyer, J. Kuhne, and Marie Joseph Bonnat) should be released because all the stipulated conditions had been met.[22] Disagreeing with Dwabenhene Asafo Agyei, who suggested that the prisoners should be kept "for curiosity," she stated:

> I am old now; I lived before Kwaku Dua, and I have now placed my son on the Asantee throne. . . . I do not wish for our successors to say my son was the cause of the disturbance of the sixty *nkurow* [towns of the whole Asante]. From olden times it has been seen that God fights for Asantee if the war is a just one. This one is unjust. The Europeans begged for the imprisoned white men. They were told to wait until Ado Bofo (the general who captured them) returned. Adu Bofo came; then they [the military chiefs] said they wanted money. The money was offered, and even weighed. How then can this war be justified? . . . Taking all into consideration, I strongly advise that the white men should be sent back at once, and God can help us. (Ivor Wilks, *Asante in the Nineteenth Century*, 507)

Lest it be assumed that Asantehemaa Afua Kobi was a pacifist, the notes of the Dutch mulatto representative, Henry Plange, recalled the swift manner in which she decisively called him to order during his address to the Asanteman Nhyiamu of September 2, 1872. Unable to conceal his anti-Asante prejudices, Plange had spoken curtly to the Asantehene and his counselors, prompting Asantehemaa Kobi to spring to her feet to insult, not the messenger, but his European bosses (Aidoo, "Political Crisis," 1975). She threatened menacingly: "I am only a woman, but would fight the governor with my left hand" (220). Soon after this event, in which Afua Kobi weighed in on the side of war, a detachment of forty-eight thousand troops left Kumasi in December 9, 1872, to invade the South.

Afua Kobi was a skilled political strategist. The point of this historical narration is not to debate this point or to raise the issue of the gender status of the Asantehemaa in the Asanteman Nhyiamu. It is not the concern of this essay whether or not she represented women because that would be to raise an inappropriate issue. Nor is it of concern whether or not the anthropological writings of R. S. Rattray and Meyer Fortes placed undue emphasis on the notion of motherhood in describing the office of the Asantehemaa. It is interesting, though, that these anthropologists' adoption of the Anglo-Saxon gender framework was what really caused their conceptual devaluation of the Asantehemaa as it deprived her office of its full legal and political power.[23]

What is critical at this point is the full philosophical implications of the Asantehemaa's argument, particularly her employment of a moral argument to insist on the release of the prisoners. Its epistemological premises reveal that Afua Kobi recognized the Europeans as humans and as inhabiting the same ontological and moral universe as the Asante. This significance is conveyed by the statements, "This one [war] is unjust," and "The Europeans begged for the imprisoned white men." The entailment relation between the two statements shows that there was a clear recognition and acceptance that, though the prisoners were enemies, the same moral codes bound the word of the Asante to the white solicitors of the white captives who had begged for mercy as bound the white men's word and their God.

The legitimacy of this interpretation derives from a number of interconnected ideas. The first is that the basis on which Afua Kobi declared the war unjust was tied to the failure of the Asante to keep their word to the Europeans, who had begged for the prisoners. Consider, if the Gods could abandon the Asante because they failed to keep their word to the white man, then the white man had to exist within the same moral sphere as the Asante, regardless of his skin pigmentation. This sort of consideration was not given to animals, which were regarded to be outside the morality codes of humanity. Second, only those who were recognized as human beings could be said to beg. Third, the Asante could hear and make sense of the white men's entreaties only if the white men were human. Although the white prisoners were enemies, and Afua Kobi seemed to take their subject status for granted, she heard their entreaties and evaluated the justness of Asante action by it, which proved that she accepted their humanity and the implication that humanity had for political action. In her view, once certain demands had been met, no further ethical moves could justify failing to keep one's side of the bargain.

Regardless of the larger political issues at stake during this period, Afua Kobi's tactical speech can be said to embody a conception of race that was politically deployed in monitoring and evaluating the actions of Asante nation in the last quarter of the nineteenth century. There is no doubt that she saw the white men as both strangers and enemies. Yet, this powerful combination of events did not provide a negative basis for racialization that would justify debasing the European captives as subhuman in the way Africans were debased by Europeans. The reason for this treatment, one could argue, is that she knew the death of these men would be avenged in a way that would be disastrous for Asante nation and in a way that would not occur if the captives were Fante. The point here is that Europeans were by far the dominant military force in the region; hence, they had to be feared.

Unfortunately, historical evidence does not entirely support this analysis. First, although the tide was slowly turning against the Asante in the *Sagrenti* war of 1873, the Asante were still the dominant military power in the region; after all, in 1824 they had routed the British at the Battle of Asamakow, in which the British commander, Governor Sir Charles MacCarthy, was killed. In the Battles of Esikum and Bobikum in 1863, Asante General Owusu Koko had defeated all the allied forces supported by the British (Aidoo, "Political

Crisis," 168). Second, there was no reason to suppose that a military loss for the Asante in 1874 was not a temporary setback from which they could extricate themselves once they restored their balance with the Gods. Third, the Dutch at Elmina were Europeans, but they were vassals of imperial Asante. They regularly paid tribute to Kumasi even in the process of secretly negotiating the transfer of Elmina to the British. Fourth, the Asante treated the Fante much more harshly than they treated Europeans, not because the Fante were local people, but because of the depth of animosity and the long-standing hostility between the Asante and the Fante. Studies on the history of Asante imperialism, trade, and socioeconomic change show that numerous other local groups, such as the Dagomba, that did not resist or contest Asante power were treated very mildly. Thus, it has to be conceded that Asante treatment of non-Asante people (both local and white) was based on substantive principled grounds rather than on skin pigmentation.

This exceptionally evenhanded principle of the Asante imperial policy contrasts sharply with Britain's biases and racist relationship with some of its colonies. As discussed earlier, the British treated colonies of white settlers (Canada, Australia, and New Zealand) with dignity and with respect that they did not extend to colonies populated with indigenous peoples. This discrepancy stems from the fact that Britain pursued racist discrimination in its imperial policy, whereas the Asante did not. It was not even an issue for the Asante. What was most important to them were strategic matters of national interest and the role of others in advancing or constraining that interest. Situated as Asantehemaa Afua Kobi was within the Asante conceptual universe, she had no problems in recognizing the racial difference and enemy status of the white prisoners or in according them their humanity. Imperial Asante maintained relationships with different racial groups, and it is this more than anything else that shows it neither had nor employed a negative conception of race in its imperial relationship with others. Unfortunately, the same principled stance was not taken by the British. Commanders Garnet Wolseley and Francis Scott, Governor Richard Pine, and other agents acted in racist ways and smugly took their "integrity" and "civilized behavior" for granted while constructing false pictures of Asante as a barbaric, bloodthirsty despotic state. Their relentless representation of the "natives" as primitive and uneducated was a racializing strategy utilized to control the production of knowledge about Asante and to obscure those elements of a culture and a people that are of vital importance to scholarship and humanity.

If events in Africa had truly driven the orientation of Appiah's research, he would have undertaken a serious study of Asante and British imperialism, the relative merits of the structures of government, the implication of both for theory building, and the conditions under which citizenship was attained. Or he would have exposed both the error of associating political modernity with colonialism and the formation of the colonial state, as well as the mistake of treating the Asante political institutions as outdated and premodern. In using the U.S.-driven discourse on race to begin his study, Appiah lends weight to the idea that African-centered issues are of marginal importance. The lessons of history can be ignored only to our peril. In hitching his wagon on issues of body racism, Appiah ignores the denigrating racist objectives of the administrative policy of indirect rule. He misses the underlying racist intent in the creation of chiefs where there were none and with sole allegiance to their colonial creators. Appiah also fails to appreciate the need to explore the racist disruption of the sociopolitical order of indigenous West African states caused by the colonizers' removal of constitutional checks that had prevented the rise of autocratic traditional rulers. Like Appiah, many scholars and the Sandhurst-trained military officers of West African origin, still do not see the long-term racist effect of introducing into Africa the idea of a military as a standing army of occupation. Nor is it clear to many people how the absence of a progressive policy of education and the simultaneous colonial insistence on the importance of a unitary national government and active promotion of ethnicity are varieties of racism. Lastly, many people have ignored the exploitation of the illusion of modernity and progress to produce a mass of "apologetic imitations of the Englishman or the American" (Sekyi, "The Future of Subject Peoples," 443).

Inverse Racism in an African Philosophy of Culture

In studying the structural effects of colonial racism in West Africa in this last decade of the twentieth century, we need to simultaneously engage in a corollary study of the cumulative effects of the racist policies on Africans. Such a study would facilitate an understanding of how Africans are responding to the racializing forces of neocolonization and globalization. Over the course of sixty years, in which Britain ruled parts of West Africa, colonial racism facilitated the erosion of cultural memory as new cultural formations created a consciousness of subjugation. The term *colonial mentality* describes the psychological effects of colonization, identifying a debilitating complex of inferiority in which the colonized perceives the oppressor as a god. Education is one arena where the acquisition of this complex begins. Children are overwhelmed as materials underscore their cultural inferiority. In this section, I explore how colonial racism is inverted in post-independence Africa so that nationals are unable to see virtue in Africa. I use Appiah to elucidate how the transnational, transracial New Africanist identity embodies a racist ideology from which individuals become agents of neocolonialism.

Because colonial racism attacks cultures rather than bodies per se, its character continually changes with historical times. The neocolonial variant is an inversion of colonial racism because nationals rather than foreigners are the racists. It appears in its most quintessential form when the white colonizer is literally reproduced as one's relation. Inverse racism is not a biological process. It is fundamentally a sociological phenomenon with sociological causes, goals, and objectives. Neocolonial racism draws its strength from Western imperialism and the economic rewards offered to individuals by that structure of dominance. I have argued elsewhere that New Africanists aspire to make Africa intelligible to the West, but they do so by projecting their analyses on the basis of the latter's interpretive categories, and in the process they erase Africans' conception of world-being (Nkiru Nzegwu, "Questions of Identity and Inheritance: A Critical Review of Kwame Anthony Appiah's *In My Father's House*"). The intellectual politics of New Africanist scholars establishes a connection between colonial (culture) racism and neocolonial racism. Because colonial racism is culture racism, it deploys concepts and interpretive categories that erase Africa's conceptual scheme. Some Africans become agents once they align themselves with the racializing global structures of domination. Inverse racists have emerged from the deployment of racially hostile actions toward the cultures of Africa.

The sociological process by which racism is inversed and one becomes a racist toward one's own people is infinitely complicated. It incorporates a range of processes that includes self-interest, institutional rewards, education, facile cultural knowledge, cultural shame, close mothering bonds, separation from specific cultural experience, feelings of loyalty, family history, intellectual ideas, cultural values, and the cumulative impact of all of these on one's personality. In response to cultural devaluation and racialization, cultural shame provides the spark that activates restructuring. Feelings of shame and inadequacy cause racialized individuals to evince hostility toward their own culture. Through the complex process of introversion, they imagine themselves into identification with the supremacist culture. They construct a transcultural identity from a smorgasbord of Europology myths, colonial master narratives, and theories that push all other cultures to the margin.

Appiah's New Africanist identity stems from a set of factors. As a child of two cultures—imperial Britain and imperial Asante—Appiah, unlike most Africans, has had to deal with the violence of one arm of his ancestry (the British) on the other arm (Asante). In the course of coming to terms with this conflicted history of the British subjugation of the Asante and his hybrid identity, he is made aware of the ways in which his mother's Anglo-Saxon tribesmen marched into Asante under Francis Scott in 1895. After looting the royal treasury and rifling the gold in the royal mausoleum, they exiled the Asantehene, the Asantehemaa, and key Amanhene to the Seychelles Island in the Indian Ocean. As he confronts the disreputable actions of his maternal kinsmen, Appiah also learns that the organizing principle of his father's Asante culture required mothers to claim their children and to bestow on them their cultural identity. He learns of the ways in which his father's family "was and was not [his]" (*In My Father's House*, 183) and in what ways he has to separate from it. As he fully grasps the implication of this social principle, he knows that the only way he can really claim the matrilineal heritage of his father is to sweep out or supplant the social norms and structures of the Akan with his mother's Anglo-Saxon culture. Indeed, to effectively claim his father, according to the ideology of Victorian paterfamilias, he has to metaphorically reenact Scott's 1895 replacement of the Asante political order with British imperial rule.

Appiah is infinitely knowledgeable in the intellectual tradition of his matriclan and has immense affection for a culture that has given him so much: a first-rate education from its equally first-rate intellectual tradition and a global language that is "superior to the 'various tongues and dialects'" of the world. Because he was born in England and nurtured from his postelementary school days by the upper-class English culture of his Anglo-Saxon matriclan, the Europhonic side of his heritage overwhelms the Akanphonic side. When we dwell on these family issues, we appreciate the extraordinary weight of British intellectual and cultural legacy on Appiah, as well as the importance of the pedigree ancestry of his Anglo-Saxon mother. His father, Joe Appiah, was exceedingly proud of his marital coup and of his wife's privileged "blue blood": "She was the grandchild of Lord Parmoor on her father's side and the daughter of Sir Stafford Cripps, 'The Iron Chancellor' of Yeoman stock. Her father's mother was a Potter, a sister of the famous Beatrice Webb and descendant of great merchants who built up the cotton trade in Manchester and helped build the Canadian Pacific Railway. Her mother, Lady Cripps, G.B.E., holder of China's oldest and highest decoration—the Order of the Most Brilliant Star of China, First Class—was a Swithenbank and grand-daughter of the great chemist Eno, inventor of Eno's Fruit Salts, famous all around the world" (*Joe Appiah: The Autobiography of an African Patriot*, 193).

This "blue blood" ancestry provides Appiah with a venerable platform from which to take over his father's house. Appiah, however, goes to great lengths to conceal from his readers this impressive heritage as he writes in a culturally ungrounded way about Africa, thus alerting us to an unstated agenda. He has many reasons for taking over and restoring order to "his father's house," the first of which is his love for his father; the second is the disreputable condition of the house; and third is what he sees as the backward state of cultural traditions. In the shaping of his identity, Africa has never really offered him anything that it has not tried to take away. It gave him a father whose culture cast him to his mother; then it produced a corpus of narratives about British expeditions that represented his matriclan as duplicitous. And in this late quarter of the twentieth century, it has produced relatives who slaughter sheep to cast powerful spells against him (181). To be sure, the continent has become an embarrassing sore; its impoverished inhabitants are now scavenging food from most parts of the world including those countries where their kith and kin were enslaved. By contrast, the Anglo-Saxon culture of his matriclan continues to grow, confounding its former colonial subjects' prognosis of its impending demise.

Pascal Kyoore's pithy comment that Appiah used his "mother's broom to sweep out his father's house" is a perceptive identification both of the Anglo-Saxon core of Appiah's identity, which he passes off as African, and of the displacement of Africa with Anglo-Saxon categories. As Appiah awes his readers with the scope and brilliance of his knowledge of canonical texts and master narratives (read: European), people see a new enlightened African worthy of taking over and restoring order to the chaotic African "house." But as Kyoore's comment acutely reveals, unsavory consequences follow the simulation of an African identity to mask a europhonic identity. The "broom" to which Kyoore refers is not the biological aspect of Appiah's maternal ancestry but the powerful combination of conceptual, cultural, and global forces that comprise his matriclan, which Appiah unleashes to radically restructure the "father's house" along Anglo-Saxon lines. Kyoore's comment addresses not only the issue of identity misrepresentation at the heart of Appiah's project, but also speaks to the problem of representing Africa without understanding it. In exposing the dissimulation of reality that readers might ignore because their attention is on Appiah's name and physiognomy, Kyoore alerts us to the ongoing neocolonial racism evidenced in Appiah's cultural attacks.[24]

Conceptually Euro-nativist in his thinking, yet African by virtue of his biracial heritage, Appiah is the perfect foil for a neocolonial racist agenda. He holds proprietary claims to Africa that cannot easily be challenged, and he needs no official mandate from anyone to function as Africa's spokesperson. Whatever anyone may think, he is still Joe Appiah's son. But on what basis is he taking over "the father's house"? What sort of order is he going to restore? And to whom does he account?

We need to revisit the core of Appiah's identity to ascertain the extent to which his knowledge of Africa is culturally based. Appiah clearly requires an array of concepts, language skills, narratives, shared histories, feelings of loyalty, family bonding, pungent smells of place, memories, food flavors, sexual hunts and peccadilloes, and a corpus of infinitesimal minutiae to fill the gestalt of his Africaness—that is, to fully establish his credentials. The experiences from holiday visits to Ghana, in which he is driven around Accra and Kumasi with white friends in tow, are interesting, but they do not offer sufficient sociological details to fill a cultural gestalt.[25] Because he was socialized more in England than in Ghana and immersed more in the intellectual and cultural tradition of Europe than of the Akan, the African aspect of his social reality and identity is subordinate to and exists in an unequal relation with his developed, carefully nurtured Anglo-Saxon side. Because he was substantively socialized and educated in the intellectual norms of his matriclan, Appiah's body, memory, and conceptual scheme are refined surfaces on which Anglo-Saxon morality codes, norms, values, sentiments, and social laws are indelibly etched. In short, he supremely instantiates the attributes and qualities of the white racial other.

For the global audience culturally uninformed about Africa, the alienated identity is especially difficult to detect, especially given the general lack of knowledge about Africa. With Africa hardly present in people's consciousness, a racist system easily creates experts by lending the aura of an Ivy League institution to an anointed intellectual. Such institutional affiliation bestows profundity and expertise on the latter's ideas and encourages establishments such as the *Village Voice*, the *New York Times Book Review*, the *Washington Post Book World*, the *Weekly Mail* (South Africa) to do the same. Lacking an African reference frame necessary for substantive evaluation, critics confuse knowledge about Africa with institutional location, so they are dazzled by *In My Father's House*. To highlight the colonizing logic of the racist system, however, it is necessary to ask the following questions: How can reviewers who lack an understanding of Africa's cultural life, historical condition, and conceptual scheme legitimately have determined the "groundbreaking" and "ground-clearing" nature of Appiah's work? In what domain of scholarship are the opinions of the conceptually uninformed represented as informed? The answers to these questions lie in why Appiah's book has given reviewers a strong sense of comfort. Can it be that it speaks more about things they actually know and less about Africa? Or that the author's analyses confirms their assumptions about Africa?

Appiah's negative attitude toward Africa's material cultures overlaps with Crummell's inability "to see virtue in Africa" (*In My Father's House*, 5). Like the Cambridge-trained Crummell, the Cambridge-trained Appiah responds to global concerns and opinions about Africa in his attempt to make it intelligible to the world. The tacitly expressed modernizing influence he seeks is always from Europe to Africa. That this assumption is embedded in Appiah's framework of theorization is obvious from the unequal power relations he takes to hold between Africa and the West and between Akan culture and Anglo-Saxon culture. We can glean his assumption of the inherent inequality of Africa and Europe from his not too positive attitude toward "traditional African cultures," from his expectations as to how they should change, and from the way in which the suggested direction of change replicates the current global power relations between nations. As implied in Kyoore's comment, Appiah's "housecleaning" (restructuring) objectives do not allow for the fact that there is anything that Africa can offer the world or that Europe and the United States can learn from Africa. The trajectory of change implicit in chapter 6, "Old Gods, New Worlds," is wholly unidirectional and embodies stereotypical assumptions about Africa inherent in the Western intellectual structure of knowledge. This unidirectionality exposes a colonial vision that has already ruled on the inefficacy of "traditional African cultures" and the efficacy of modern Western culture.

Sexist Racism in the Philosophy of Culture

Numerous sociological studies establish that the Western intellectual structure of knowledge embodies a sexist ontology.[26] Subtly diffused through criteria, paradigms, and perspectives, this racist ontology is accepted as legitimate by both uncritical scholars and those who are invested in the survival
of that structure of knowledge. Unfortunately for inverse racists who affirm
the superiority of the European cultural scheme, a major defect of the intellectual structure exposed by feminist scholarship is its endemic sexism. Because my interest in Appiah's work derives primarily from my location as an
African and a woman, I have noticed the complex interplay of racism—particularly, the complicated structure of inverse racism—and sexism in his approach. I am especially concerned about his masculinist ethos and textual
enactment of male bonding, and the ways these features direct attention
away from female subjects, concerns, and interests. In pondering the reasons
for the near total erasure of African women in Appiah's book, I have to ask
the following questions: Why are African women absent in his father's
house? What does he understand to be the identity issues of concern to African women in this last quarter of the twentieth century? Surely what Ama
Ata Aidoo, Flora Nwapa, Mariama Bâ, and Bessie Head have to say on the
subject of identity are relevant to all Africans? So why are the voices of African females silenced in this house? What forces are militating against their
presence or forcing them into reticence?

With the inversion of colonial racism and the emergence of neocolonial racists, patriarchy defines the frame for relating with African women.
Through the patriarchal lens, women are inferiorized and presented as unworthy of public office and public attention, even though the women of the
Asante royal family, at least, were actively involved in political affairs of the
state. The sexist gaze of the neocolonial racist renders women invisible. This
absence of African women in Appiah's book is most troubling because of the
systematic and thoroughgoing way they are cut out. First, Appiah frequently
cites an all-male cast of scholars, producing a tightly regulated homosocial
environment that emphasizes male concerns, male voices, male thoughts,
and male theorists.[27] In this artfully constructed homosocial discourse, African women's concerns are elided, suggesting that they have nothing to
say and that the issues discussed by him must be important to them.[28] Second, Appiah cites only one book by an African woman in his bibliography,
though nothing in Ifi Amadiume's *Male Daughters, Female Husbands* was
referenced in the text, which calls to question the reason for its listing in the
bibliography. Third, in the few cases where Appiah mentions women in the
text, his manner of naming contrasts sharply with his formal presentation of
his male characters. His overly familiar treatment of the few women characters in the book, his failure to fill out their identity profiles robs them of any
dignity. For instance, in the preface, an "Auntie Jane" is mentioned and

identified as the stepgrandmother who baked bread for hundreds of people (*In My Father's House*, vii). This mode of description frames her identity as a person by the "domestic" nature of the task she performs, not by the commercial or business value of baking. Another senior family relative, a great-aunt remains nameless, although her husband is formally named. In a tone more patronizing than intimate, Appiah describes this great-aunt as the "first wife" of the Asante king, Prempeh II, suggesting that her marital relationship to the king is all that matters in framing her identity. What her name is and why she sometimes calls him "Akroma-Ampim" and sometimes "Yao Antony" are irrelevant within a sexist scheme that presents women in the subsidiary role of wife. What seems to matter to Appiah is that as the wife of the Asantehene Prempeh II, she lived "up the hill" (vii), a geographical location that signifies power, and that she is connected to an individual who embodies political power. In the epilogue, one encounters his Auntie Victoria, whom he represents as devious and wicked, whose full name we never learn, and who lacks an identity outside of the men in her life. She is constantly referenced either by her connection to the Asantehene or by her relationship to his father.

Appiah's disparaging description of the women "in the house" represents a carefully directed attack on the matrilineal principle of Asante, which he portrays as anachronistic. It constitutes a patrilinealization of Asante culture and the projection of the social, political, and philosophical ideologies of his European matriclan on it.[29] This demonization of his Aunt Victoria, Akua Afriyie, the *obaa opanin* (female head) of the Akroma Ampim *abusua* (matriclan) derives from her opposition to his Euromorphic housecleaning and from her embodiment of the matrikin principle that threatens his presence in his father's house. To the extent that Appiah champions the patrilineal principle of his Anglo-Saxon matriclan, he exposes himself as a colonizing agent.

Among the Asante, as among many other Akan societies, a person is an individual with relational links to the abusua or matrilineage. The abusua is a corporate collective to which members owe their identity and are loyal. Each part of the corporate collective works in a synergy for the advancement and benefit of their collective objectives and corporate identity. Because the Asante are matrilineal, the organizing family principle privileges the women of the lineage, first, by shifting the attention of male members from themselves and their conjugal unit to the offspring of the women in the family and to the wider abusua. Second, because the principle of consanguinity overrides conjugality, kins have more say in the family. Third, a man's identity is relationally defined by matrifocused kinship ties and his name and memory are relationally preserved by his sister's children, not by his own. A child inherits both from the mother and her brother, and the brother's child inherits from the mother and the maternal uncle. This nullification of the primogeniture rule of inheritance means that the father-child bond is de-emphasized. Because men's emotional investment in their ego and progeny are displaced, the social consciousness facilitates the production of male siblings and *opanin* (male head of lineage), who are custodians rather than quintessential patriarchs.[30]

This matrilineal consciousness underlies the funeral crisis discussed by Appiah in the epilogue. Like Akua Afriyie, Appiah's father, Joe, was a corporate member of the Akroma Ampim matrilineage: in fact, he was its opanin. Her mother and Joe Appiah's mother were from the Akroma Ampim *abusua*. After the death of her parents in her teenage years, Akua Afriyie—like Joe Appiah—was raised by Yao Antony, the opanin of the Akroma Ampim abusua and her maternal grand-uncle (Akua Afriyie, "The Personal Queen of Otumfuo Opkuware II," 33–42). Like Victoria, however, Joe owes his education, his wealth, and his strong career prospect to the lineage. Although Joe Appiah and Akua Afriyie stand in a similar relationship to Yao Antony, Joe Appiah's children are ineligible to inherit from the Akroma Ampim abusua. Only the children of the daughters have full rights of inheritance in an abusua. Thus, although Akua Afriyie was the wife of the Asantehene, Otumfuo Opoke Ware II, the fifteenth occupant of the Golden Stool of Asante, her children with the Asantehene are the direct descendants of the Akroma Ampim lineage and heirs to its fortune.

In matters of inheritance, Joe Appiah and his children stand in exactly a similar relationship to Yao Antony, the former head of the Akroma Ampim abusua. Though Joe Appiah became the male head of the matriclan and like Yao Antony succeeded to the corporate wealth of the lineage, his children, like Yao Antony's, cannot inherit from the Akroma Ampim estate. Notwithstanding the elaborate nature of his installation ceremony, Joe Appiah was appointed to administer the considerable fortune and assets of the estate, which included accounts in the bank, timber and gold-mining concessions, plantation farms, real estate and rental properties, and commercial businesses. According to Joe Appiah, during his management of the estate, Yao Antony had expanded the family's wealth into "a prosperous business with his headquarters in London and branches in New York, Zurich, Prague, Liberia, Ivory Coast and the Belgian Congo" and Ghana (*In My Father's House*, 104).

This clarification of the rules of inheritance is important because it puts in proper perspective the benefits that individuals derive from their abusua and explains their emotional investment in it. The clarification also underscores the obligations and responsibilities of the opanin to the younger members of the abusua. As the administrator of the matriclan's wealth, Joe Appiah was morally entrusted with the educational responsibility of nieces such as Nana Ama, in the same way that Yao Antony had overseen his own and Akua Afriyie's education. Thus, Appiah's representation of matters in the following passage is highly problematic: "My cousin Nana Ama, whom I had always thought of as good-natured and put-upon, revealed the depth of feeling in the *abusua* when she warned us coldly to consider the future welfare of our mother. 'Be careful,' she said to my sisters and I. 'You do not live here. We are here with your mother.' When my sisters challenged her . . . asked her if she remembered how my mother had watched over her education— she shouted defensively" (189). This construction of Appiah's mother as "watching over [Nana Ama's] education"—without acknowledging the latter's entitlement to the corporate wealth of the abusua or, in other words, making it seem as if Joe Appiah's responsibility to his niece is entirely charitable—automatically highlights the beneficent nature of his Anglo-Saxon mother. Yet, by virtue of her status as ward, Nana Ama is rightfully entitled to an education just as Joe Appiah and Akua Afriyie had been. It is most revealing that in building a villainous profile for the women of the matriclan, Appiah misrepresents the presence of Nana Ama in his parent's home. He portrays her as a poor relative who would not have been educated but for the magnanimity of his mother. Miffed by Nana Ama's loyalty to the abusua rather than to his mother, he sidesteps the more central issue of the ways Nana Ama has been made to serve Joe Appiah's family in order to receive her entitlement.

Appiah's neocolonial representation demonstrates poor knowledge of familial relations and obligations in a culture he claims as his own. Familiarity with the reciprocal ties of obligations of African family systems should have told him that the household comfort of Joe Appiah and his wife was secured by the services and ministrations of younger family dependents such as Nana Ama. Totally ignoring this principle of reciprocity, Appiah masks the obligatory duties of his father to dependent members of the abusua in order to get back at Nana Ama for placing loyalty to the abusua higher than loyalty to his Anglo-Saxon mother. In his neocolonial racist role, Appiah's ignorance of Akan culture shines through as he mystifies the culture in ways that enhance his transnational objectives.

Strategies of erasure are also enacted in Appiah's account of the strained relations between his father and his aunt. An examination of the funeral controversy exposes his muddled cultural knowledge, which lends weight to his sexist stance. In demonizing his aunt, Akua Afriyie, Appiah discloses very little about the inheritance dispute at the core of these strained relations. However, his cryptic summary that his father "had a dispute with my aunt over properties left to them and their sister Mabel in the will of my great-great-uncle, Yao Antony . . . [and] my aunt had refused to come and make peace with her brother even on his deathbed" (183), successfully shifts the blame to his aunt. So what exactly is the basis of the dispute that it should cause Akua Afriyie's to refuse to make peace with her brother even on his deathbed? What specifically did Joe Appiah do with the properties to elicit such an implacable response from his sister? What could have motivated Akua Afriyie to remain adamant in the face of her brother's failing health?

To obtain answers to these questions we need to revisit the inheritance principle of the matriclan as Joe Appiah himself presents it in his autobiography. He provides sufficient clues of the inheritance issue in his autobiography. Waxing eloquent about his fortunate position in the Akroma Ampim abusua he asserts that "as far as the family lineage is concerned, only the issue of my grannie mattered" (*Joe Appiah*, 104). As explained earlier, the children of Yao Antony—grannie's brother and then *opanin*—did not matter because they could not inherit from their father's abusua. Although Joe Appiah's account of events makes it seem as if the wealth is an outright inheritance, it is not. It is custodial. Given that Joe Appiah's quarrel with Akua Afriyie is related to properties and is strong enough to thwart reconciliation, it must have touched the core of the abusua. Akua Afriyie's implacable opposition to Joe Appiah tells a different story. At the very least, it tells us that there is a fundamental problem both with Appiah's and his father's representation of these family properties as if they are nonfiduciary assets.[31] Moreover, because the properties are really the corporate assets of the Akroma Ampim abusua and are fiduciary properties, they are not available for redistribution as if they were personal properties. Hence, Akua Afriyie's strong response could be a reaction to Joe Appiah's conversion of the abusua's property into a personal one.

In her role as the *obaa opanin* (female head of the abusua), it would be clear to her that this property appropriation is contrary to the matrilineal principle of the family. Her response is understandable because she has a personal stake in the matter. Only her children and Mabel's children (if she has any) are heirs to the abusua fortune, not Joe Appiah's.[32] Hence, if Joe Appiah were allowed to appropriate a considerable part of the estate for his conjugal family, not only would he substantially reduce the fortune of the Akroma Ampim abusua, but more importantly he would have divested her children of their inheritance and restructured the abusua along the lines of his wife's Anglo-Saxon culture. Thus, Afriyie's refusal to make peace comes from a need to secure the inheritance rights of her children, which they are in danger of losing should the cultural patrilinealization go unchallenged. It is therefore imperative to check her brother because as the wife of the Asantehene, she knows that her children cannot inherit from their father's abusua. Given that the Asantehene represents Asante traditional norms and therefore no "modernizing influences of patrilinealization" can alter the inheritance lines of the royal families, it is understandable that Afriyie would refuse to accede to her brother's attempt to extend the resources of the lineage to those excluded from it.

The accuracy of this interpretation is confirmed by the loaded graveside eulogy of the Ghanaian head of state, Ft. Lt. Jerry Rawlings. As reported by

Appiah, Rawlings admonishes the audience not to disturb the widow and the children over questions of property (192). What is important in this is not the executive rebuke, but Appiah's sexist utilization of it to undermine his aunt's integrity and to minimize the importance of women in the family.

Following the death of grannie, Akua Afriyie became the obaa opanin, as revealed by the prominent role she played at Joe Appiah's installation as the opanin. As we saw with the Asantehemaa, it is the obaa panin's duty to stop the opanin should he attempt to violate the cohesive force of the abusua. Afriyie is described as a woman of "strong personality and refreshing candour" (Afriyie, "Akua Afriyie"), and her dispute with her brother constitutes a rebuke that challenges his patriarchalization scheme. Her strong personality provides her with the courage to take on an equally feisty opponent. Chagrined at his aunt's audacity, Appiah initiates processes for her demonization. He aligns himself, his Anglo-Saxon mother, and the church on one side, and Akua Afriyie, Nana Ama, the abusua and the Asantehene on the opposing side. Insofar as the church and Christianity are aligned on their side, Appiah textually proclaims that Joe Appiah's family is on the side of God, goodness, and rightness. Because the logic of contrast arraigns the opposition on the side of demons, witches, darkness, and evil, Appiah textually pronounces as archaic and evil the central matrilineal organizing structure of Asante's social cohesiveness.

Switching Gender Norms and Codes

Within this complex interplay of racism and sexism and of colonialism and Christianity, the demonization of Akua Afriyie attains its fullest expression. Readings of colonial writings confirm the existence of sexism and the regulation of African women's bodies and their social space in diverse regions of Africa. Even after the demise of historical colonialism, conceptual colonization continued in the treatment meted out to them in academic circles, including in the writings of feminists. Aligning himself with this colonial racist tradition, Appiah unleashes his sexism. He uses his father's codicil to textually restrain his aunt and to justify her vilification.[33] What Appiah neglects to reveal is that it is irrelevant whether or not Joe Appiah and Akua Afriyie made their peace on Joe's deathbed. What is important is that Joe Appiah is an opanin of the abusua, and as Akua Afriyie appreciates, the burial of the dead is one of the prime duties of the lineage, with the living head supervising the funeral rites of its deceased. Knowing that it is not the place of a son alone to bury the father, yet spurred on by his objective to complete the patrilinealization of Asante, Joe Appiah wrote a codicil, secure in the knowledge that the Anglo-Saxon-derived laws of Ghana he invoked would prevail over the Akan-derived rights of the abusua.[34]

The endowment of Anglo-Saxon values and norms with supervenient force to override Akan family law constitutes an instance of the still unresolved aspects of colonialism. It is important to underscore this point in order to graphically highlight the complicity of locals in the colonial process and the invidious ways colonial racism continues in operation long after the end of historical period. Through the injection of conflicting foreign norms and values, social havoc has been created in most postindependent nations. This point cannot be overemphasized because it shows that Akua Afriyie is acting neither disruptively or extrajudicially in insisting on burying the deceased male head in accordance with the norms of the abusua of which she is the head.

Considered in this light, Joe Appiah's codicil is the hostile instrument for weakening the abusua. The metaphorical "broom from his mother's house" is utilized to sweep out and suppress the nonpatrilineal elements of the father's house and culture. It provides the basis for the son's textual lynching of the woman who stands as an obstacle to his father's appropriation of the abusua assets. For too long, African women have had to endure uncomplainingly the systematic erosion of their rights, resources, and power, by colonial administrations, egoistic male relatives, and husbands who, in the name of administering family properties, often convert such resources to their own personal use. Too often, such acts of well-educated men have reduced sisters, mothers, aunts, wives, and girlfriends to a pitiable state of penury and servitude.

Throughout the colonial period and even in these neocolonial days, the image of African women was and has been negatively represented. It is fashionable in these postmodern, postcolonial, psychosexual days to theorize on the body and vulva of the African woman. Where Alice Walker leads the way in collapsing the vagina with African female identity and in "discovering" the mutilated vaginas of African women, Appiah, the philosopher, understandably distances himself from women's sexuality and chooses the head, the seat of reason and rationality, as the site of his attack. Well-versed in the European intellectual tradition of his matriclan, he sets up a similar ideological framework for Africa in which "true" rationality is male and emotion is female and in which female rationality and power are deviant. On this recessed Europhilic framework, he irrationalizes his aunt's rationality and astuteness. Substantially drawing from his matrikin's intellectual heritage, he attempts to domesticate, contain, bind, and neutralize what he perceives as the "threatening," "unrestrained" female power of his aunt. Appiah's discourse on his aunt's activities is conducted in a manner that suppresses the Akan conception of women as full members of the abusua, and as independent, resourceful individuals who have sole ownership of the wealth they generate. Using the Anglo-Saxon model of women as subordinate and imageries of them as subject to the will of their master-husbands, he problematizes his aunt's business acumen and independency and constructs her as an overly ambitious woman. This illicit substitution of Anglo-Saxon gender codes for Akan gender codes enables him to portray his aunt as beyond restraint and outside the legitimate control of her husband.

Within the Anglo-Saxon boundaries of Appiah's intellectual and social life, the power of women is typically depicted as deriving from witchcraft. Men's exercise of power is proper and normal, but women's is deviant and abnormal. As a marker of the boundary of legitimate power, Appiah's construction of his aunt as a wicked witch also becomes a useful way to totally bind and dispossess her of that power. It is pertinent that in one of her constructed identities, the aunt emerges as an evil witch, sending out poisoned food and casting devilish spells on her poor innocent nephew and nieces. In a scene straight out of some fairytale that bespeaks an encounter between good and evil, Appiah becomes an Anglo patriarch, standing tall and strong in the midst of his constantly weeping and tearful sisters. In all this raucousness, the son protects the dignity and virtue of the beloved Anglo-Saxon mother from the "irrational," "unrestrained," threatening wrath of the "undomesticated" African woman. As he puts it, nothing is to be allowed "to disturb my mother upstairs" (188).

Appiah's choice of vocabulary, imageries, and language of discourse raises troubling questions about his conception and role of African women and his representation of them. In a seeming dislike for female industriousness and assertiveness, he portrays his aunt as a vainglorious, unbalanced woman who is more concerned about the negative publicity she will receive at her loss of face, than about the death of her brother. In a climactic portrayal, the height of his aunt's madness is made to appear when she is placed before us as unbalanced African woman sitting on the throne beside the "castrated" Asantehene. With elegant Oscar Wildean sarcasm, we are prodded to see in her a poor unworthy substitute of the colonizing Queen Victoria, whose name she "dishonorably" bears. In Appiah's reproving patriarchal eyes, this assertiveness is dangerous and polluting: "'That woman,' I said pointing at my aunt, 'and that man,' pointing now to her cohort Uncle George, 'are trying to use Nana [the Asantehene] to get their way; to force the Church to do what they want.' We were not going to be party to such an abuse of the stool; we were leaving. . . . I told him that I had indeed been brought up to respect the stool and its occupant; that I was still trying to do so, but that the stool was being 'spoiled' by my aunt; and that after what I had seen today, it was hard for me to hold Nana himself in respect" (186).

In constructing Akua Afriyie as a pollutant, Appiah conveys the depth of his anathema for African women. His barely concealed loathing emerges in the following description of her: "Auntie Vic made her weight felt around the town, driven around in one of her fleet of Mercedes-Benzes, cultivating a faintly plutocratic aura" (189). The language and subtext of his description is an exhortatory call to arms for his aunt to be restrained and bound by the gender codes of Anglo-Saxon matriclan. He astutely manipulates his readers into sharing his disgust at Akua Afriyie's "lack of gentility" and "proper behavior." He justifies his characterization of her as a witch by indicating that she unabashedly forces her will on others and sends out poisoned food to achieve her objective (189). Then in melodramatic rage, we are informed that she is a Jezebel dominating and ruthlessly manipulating her husband, the Asantehene. In this domineering role in which she "spoils" the Stool (186), Akua Afriyie is presented as a diabolical being. As if all this is not enough, her nephew indicts her for castrating her husband, the Asantehene, declaring: "she has influenced Nana [the Asantehene] to make bad decisions in chieftaincy disputes. . . . [H]is decisions could be bought by paying off his wife" (187).

It is not that Appiah cannot conceptualize love between an African couple, it is more that he has removed it from the sphere of African women, reserving it only for his father and his Anglo-Saxon mother, Peggy Cripps. In his conceptual scheme, Akua Afriyie's forty-eight years of marriage and devotion to her husband, the Asantehene, is not based on devotion and love, but on domination. However, Peggy's ironclad influence over Joe Appiah—an influence that caused him to formally break with his abusua after benefiting from it—is described in touching terms and presented as a perfect picture of spousal love and fidelity. Appiah gushes, "When [my father] entered into the house he was once more my mother's Joe, and our papa" (190). Caught in his picture-taking pose, Appiah misses the implication of the possessive pronoun he used to describe his parents' marital relationship. Insofar as the pronoun "my" in "my mother's Joe" establishes a possessive relationship and exposes the underlying power lines of the relationship, Appiah unwittingly reveals the dominant role of his mother in the union.

Thus, to assert that *In My Father's House* is the diversionary title of a diversionary tale is to acknowledge the sexist and inverse racist moves of Appiah's anti-African narrative. Demonizing matrilineality allows him to uphold the supremacy of Anglo-Saxon patriarchal values by presenting it as the best possible option. The carefully positioned objective of displacing Africa for Europe is supported by a stellar array of eulogists. Wole Soyinka, the Nigerian Nobel laureate in literature, describes it as "an exceptional work, whose contextual sweep and lucidity ushers in a new level of discourse on race and culture." The eminent white U.S. philosopher, Richard Rorty, who does not believe that African philosophy exists, lavishly praises the book for its range of reference and the vigor of its argumentation. In Rorty's Europhilic view, the book is an absorbing, path-breaking, and impressive work that rescues the philosophy of culture from Herder. Johannes Fabian, a major figure in anthropology, offers an enthusiastic endorsement that portrays Appiah as an intellectual leader in articulating the situation of African intellectuals. According to Fabian, nobody has defined the situation more sharply than Appiah, and nobody has built so many bridges to a discourse that is universally shared. Lastly, the African American sociologist Orlando Patterson asserts that it is "a major intellectual event in the discourse on race, identity, and culture," a "desperately needed antidote to the resurgent chauvinism that threatens the conditions of black peoples in Africa and the Americas." [35] In short, given the surreptitious nature of the author's anti-African agenda, *In My Father's House* is a brilliant postcolonial work that ushers in a new form of colonization and sexism. [36]

8 Reading the Colonizer's Mind: Lord Lugard and the Philosophical Foundations of British Colonialism

Olufemi Taiwo

There are two moments in the colonial whole: the colonized and the colonizer. Much attention has been directed at the situation of the colonized. Numerous studies have detailed the impact of colonialism on its victims, their mindscape, their landscape, and so on, but few attempts have been made to go behind the mind of the colonizer. Of course, I am aware of histories, biographies, and such like that do. However, concerning examinations of the ideas that inform the colonial practice whose impact on the colonized has been much studied, the pickings are very slim indeed.[1] It is time to take seriously the other moment of the colonial totality: the colonizer. After all, as both Frantz Fanon and Albert Memmi so eloquently tell us in their works (*The Wretched of the Earth* and *The Colonizer and the Colonized*, respectively), there would have been no colonized had there been no colonizer. This acclaimed symbiosis between the colonizer and the colonized underscores the need to unearth the motivations behind the colonizer's activity.

The colonizer moment of the colonial whole is itself a whole with several determinations. Albert Memmi identifies three such determinations: "a colonial, a colonizer and the colonialist" (*The Colonizer and the Colonized*, 10). Fanon, too, never failed to point out the many demographic and other groupings in the ranks of the colonizer. For the purposes of this essay, though, I would like to focus on other possible determinations of the colonizer whole. When we speak of the colonizer we may mean any of three membership categories: *missionaries*, *administrators*, and *traders*. The man whose views are analyzed in this essay belongs to the second category, administrators. The character of colonialism and its principal lineaments were fashioned by administrators, which is why it is important for us to make sense of their views and, where available, their justifications for them. Additionally, acquainting ourselves with those views might enable us to make better sense of the policy options discernible in the practice of colonialism. Thus, however odious the views held by the colonizers, however much they discomfit us, we ignore them only at our own peril insofar as they had consequences on colonial practice. It is an unargued assumption of this essay that those views had such consequences.

I interpret the colonial enterprise as it was established in Africa, to be an integral part of the outward march of *modernity* from Europe. One reason why commentators do not often make the connection between colonialism and modernity is that they pay too much attention to the self-serving rhetoric of the colonizer about bringing modernity to the colonized. It is easy to argue that the colonizer didn't do anything of the sort, but to so argue is to ignore the complexity of the colonial situation. Yes, one category sought to achieve this purpose: missionaries. But the fact that the traders and administrators were the real policymakers in the colonial enterprise confirms Hegel's linking of modernity and colonialism *(Philosophy of Right)*. Lip service would later be paid to the notion of bringing the fruits of civilization to the colonized. Ultimately, however, despite their rhetoric, all categories of colonizers agreed to exclude the natives from this new life. Based on this assumption, I suggest that one consideration, among others, that motivated various colonizers was the need to bring the fruits of civilization to the natives. Needless to say, different colonizer individuals and groups were not affected to the same extent by this consideration, and each expected different rewards and consequences. For example, *traders* were interested in expanding markets for their products and finding new places to invest for maximum profits, nor must one forget their need for raw materials for industries back home. *Administrators*, many of whom like Lord Lugard started out as adventurers and hired guns for the companies, were possessed of the love of country that, as I presently show, made them want to stake out new territories as a way of enhancing the conditions of their fellow citizens and thereby the national prestige of their countries. Again, we must not forget the lure of lucre and the seduction of fabulous wealth. *Missionaries* sallied forth guided by the injunction to spread the good news to all corners of the earth and become fishers of native souls in the name of God. A by-product of this goal was the dissemination of Christian civilization (which by then was indistinguishable from modernity) in native lands.

It is customary to talk loosely of the Westernization of various Africans and of the impact of Western values on native cultures. However, things are not always as they appear to be. The business of the transposition of modernity to native shores is not an exception. Contrary to the received wisdom that laments how Western values have corrupted and distorted native cultures—usually what is meant when the epithet *racism* is evoked—I propose that the relationship between indigenous cultures and colonialism was much more complex. Yes, distortion and corruption took place, but there was another dimension—electing to leave indigenous structures "untouched" or "undisturbed"—under which colonialism managed to damage indigenous cultures. That is, even in *not* doing something, colonialism had an impact. I am suggesting that in its most benign form, colonial racism either did not allow the normal course-of-progress extinction of moribund social forms or actively fostered their preservation even when it was or ought to have been obvious that they had become outmoded. By so doing, colonialism inaugurated what I call the ignoble science of *sociocryonics*, the frozen preservation of outmoded and moribund social forms. I describe the consequences of this science in a moment.

For now I would like to contend that colonialism, British colonialism, never meant to make Westernization or modernity or civilization an option for its colonized wards. This contention is borne out clearly by a consideration of the divergent aims of the three major categories of colonizers: missionaries, administrators, and traders. Of the three, missionaries were most desirous and, in some cases, the more aggressive pursuers of the dream of making *modern* men and women out of Christian converts and freed slaves. Because I have made the case more fully elsewhere,[3] I only summarize my central claims here. The missionaries were interested in two significant elements of social transformation. First, they were desirous of creating an African middle class as the primary agents of civilization. As J. F. Ade Ajayi puts it:

> The desire of mid-nineteenth century missionaries to create an African middle class must be emphasized. It was reinforced by the argument that for reasons of climate and of expense, a large part of the missionary staff had to be African. But the aim was often pursued deliberately and for its own sake. "In the history of man," said the American pioneer missionary, "there has been no civilization which has not been cemented and sustained in existence by a division of the people into higher, lower and middle classes. We may affirm, indeed, that this constant attendant upon human society—gradation of classes—is indispensable to civilization in any form, however low or high." It was to the lack of this gradation of classes that he traced African backwardness. (*Christian Missions in Nigeria 1841–1891: The Making of a New Elite*, 17)

Second, in furtherance of this first objective and others, especially that of introducing civilization to Africa, some of them—organized as the Society for the Extinction of the Slave Trade and for the Civilization of Africa—had a program whose contemporary relevance is striking. They sought, inter alia, to

- adopt effectual measures for reducing the principal languages of Western and Central Africa into writing;

- prevent or mitigate the prevalence of disease and suffering among the people of Africa;
- encourage practical science in all its various branches;
- investigate the system of drainage best calculated to succeed in a climate so humid and so hot;
- assist in promoting the formation of roads and canals, the manufacture of paper and the use of the printing press;
- afford essential assistance to the natives by furnishing them with useful information as to the best mode of cultivation, as to the productions which command a steady market and by introducing the most approved agricultural implements and seeds. The time may come when the knowledge of the mighty powers of steam might contribute rapidly to promote the improvement and prosperity of that country. (listed in Sir Thomas F. Buxton, *The African Slave Trade and Its Remedy*, 8–16; and quoted in Ajayi, *Christian Missions*, 16–17)

Although the missionaries (especially those who came at the commencement of the second wave of evangelization[4] that began in the aftermath of the abolition of the slave trade—did considerably well in the implementation of various items on the above program,[5] their administrator and trader successors never implemented it on any scale. One may cite the dynamics of the evangelizing missions themselves and their relative penuriousness for the absence of implementation on a grand scale, but one must consider the machinations of the other constituents of the colonizer moment of the colonial totality: the traders and the administrators. The traders wanted new markets and new sources for raw materials, and in their search for both they aided the missionaries for a time in the latter's quest for the souls of the natives. They let missionaries take rides on their ships, and from time to time they shared stations and victuals with itinerant preachers. But this class of colonizers is not the focus of my interest here, for the missionaries and the traders both ultimately yielded to the last arrivals to the colonies: the administrators. It was what this third category of colonizers did that was to define the principal character of colonialism in the British colonies. The rest of this essay is devoted to the examination of the philosophical assumptions that informed the practice of the administrators. Let me sum up the discussion so far.

Strange as it may seem, in Britain's African colonies, the missionaries were the progressives, and the administrators—soldiers, residents, hired guns— were the reactionaries. The missionaries were not only the ones who felt it their duty to bring the native to civilization, but also the ones who were willing to put in place some of the most important institutions for the filtration of modernity into the colonies. So it is easy to see why they were the ones who insisted that the Africans *must* abandon their old ways in their entirety and embrace the new ways: little wonder that the Christianity of this period did not countenance coexistence with old ways of doing things. Now, I should not be misunderstood. I have argued elsewhere that this approach was fraught with danger for the Africans' engagement with modernity.[6] Yet I also must insist that the revolutionary nature of the missionary enterprise stands out in sharp contrast to the reactionary, conservative nature of the administrators' enterprise. I can cite several indices. Christianity[7] recruited from the outcasts, the marginal elements; the administrators favored recruits were mostly of chief provenance. Christianity wanted to wipe the slate clean, to implant new forms of social living, new ways of being human, new ways of seeing the world and of naming it; administrators inaugurated sociocry-onics with its attendant consequence of preserving or shaping existing institutions, regardless of their state of health or relevance, to subserve their limited needs for low-cost empire building. Christianity had an expansive view of its mission—the implantation of civilization; administrators had a narrow view of their mission—do whatever would redound to the glory of the motherland and the profit margins of those who funded their activities. Most important of all, missionaries were willing to commit the resources required; administrators were content with doing the minimum.[8] If my thesis is plausible, then there is some warrant for investigating the enabling views of the latter category of colonizers, the administrators.

In the rest of this essay, I examine one such set of enabling views held by a man whose career as an imperialist and colonizer few could match: Frederick Dealtry Lugard, later Lord Lugard. He worked in India, East Africa, and later West Africa. It was in West Africa that he became the principal philosopher of Empire. His philosophy was distilled from his practical engagement with the exigencies of empire building first as a hired gun deployed by commercial interests to stymie the eastward advance of the French in West Africa at the end of the nineteenth century and later as the administrator who amalgmated the components of what is now Nigeria through his becoming a peer and elder statesman of the British Empire until his death in 1945. His service alone qualifies him for scholarly interest, but his attempt at providing some philosophical justification for colonization and his authorship of the theoretical guidebook for the practice of colonial administration are what qualify him for philosophical treatment.

I propose to analyze critically his two major theoretical works: *Political Memoranda*, which has been described in the following way by one of the principal administrators whose own practice was built on the book: "Granted the inherent difficulty in separating the influence of the model [of indirect rule] outside Nigeria from the book which embodied the whole system down to details of routing, the importance of *Political Memoranda* lies not in their use as a blueprint of British colonial policy but in a considerable measure as a highly rewarding illustration of Lugard's own perfectionist view of Nigerian administration in practice. To this extent alone, granted Lugard's respected place among the proconsuls of empire, *Political Memoranda* may be consulted as an index to colonial thinking" (A. H. M.

Kirk-Greene, "New Introduction," in Frederick D. Lugard, *Political Memoranda*, xx).

The second work is *The Dual Mandate in British Tropical Africa*, which was published in 1922. In it, Lugard describes his object thus:

> The object which I have had in view in setting down these notes on adminis-
> tration in British tropical Africa is twofold. In the first place, I have hoped to
> put before those who are interested in the development of that part of the Brit-
> ish Empire beyond the seas for which Great Britain is directly responsible, an
> outline of the system under which those responsibilities have originated and are
> being discharged, and some idea of the nature of the problems confronting the
> local administrator. In the second place, in discussing these problems I have
> ventured to make some few suggestions, as the result of experience, in the hope
> that they may be found worthy of consideration by the "men on the spot"—in
> so far as the varying circumstances of our Crown colonies and protectorates
> may render them in any degree applicable. (b)

It is easy to construe the first text solely as a handbook of administration, and it is often so construed. But interspersed with the book's plethora of administrative and policy guidelines are numerous and wide-ranging summations of principles behind and justifications for specific administrative choices and the reasons why alternative paths were shunned. It is possible to tease out of these reflections and guidelines some of the philosophical views that provided the background and justifications for colonial practice. In the case of the second text, the author set out to provide a philosophical justification for British colonialism. The title itself is a shorthand description of what he took to be the charge the British had in colonizing Africa. On the one hand, the "dual mandate" refers to the responsibility that it had pleased God and history to bequeathe to Great Britain, to make available to Europeans and the rest of humanity the riches and resources of Africa, which "lay wasted and ungarnered . . . because the natives did not know their use and value. Millions of tons of oil-nuts, for instance, grew wild without the labour of man, and lay rotting in the forests. Who can deny the right of the hungry people of Europe to utilise the wasted bounties of nature, or that the task of developing these resources was, as Mr. Chamberlain expressed it, a 'trust for civilisation' and for the benefit of mankind?" (Lugard, *The Dual Mandate*, 615). On the other hand, Great Britain must bring the light of civilization to the blighted heathenish peoples of the "Dark Continent." "As Roman impe-rialism laid the foundations of modern civilisation, and led the wild barbarians of these islands [Britain, that is] along the path of progress, so in Africa to-day we are repaying the debt, and bringing to the dark places of the earth, the abode of barbarism and cruelty, the torch of culture and progress, while ministering to the material needs of our own civilisation" (618). Apparently, this idea was not original. The epigraphs in the frontispiece of his book are:

"It will be the high task of all My governments to superintend and assist the development of these countries . . . for the benefit of the inhabitants and the general welfare of mankind" (HIS MAJESTY THE KING); "The wellbeing and development of peoples not yet able to stand by themselves, form a sacred Trust of Civilisation" (*Covenant of League*, Art. 22); "We develop new territory as Trustees for Civilisation, for the Commerce of the World" (JOSEPH CHAMBERLAIN). What Lugard did in the text was to present a case for these sentiments and to write a full-blown justification of colonialism as he worked from what seemed to be a ferment of opinion in the late nineteenth and early twentieth centuries.

My task in the current essay is to present in as coherent and integrated manner as I can the philosophy of colonialism that inheres in these texts, but before I do, it is important to lay out in some detail the circumstances of Lugard's departure for Africa, what sorts of views he had of Africans when he arrived, how those views were altered or reinforced by his experiences in Africa and of Africans. I consider these earlier views important because I argue that the policy options he adopted and the practice of colonialism he embraced were influenced by them, if not directly determined by them. That is, what administrative structures were deemed suitable for the natives in Africa, outside of the constraints of limited resources, and what types of institutional practices were considered appropriate to impose on the natives were profoundly affected by Lugard and his cohorts' ontological commitments and philosophical predilections. This is one situation where it truly can be said that ideas have consequences. In the conclusion of the essay, I submit that an exploration of the formative views of the colonizers is apt to shed some light on why some of the institutions that are the legacy of colonialism do not behave the way we expect them to based on our view of their originals.

Bound for Africa: Formative Views

Lugard's initial departure for Africa occurred in inauspicious circumstances. He had been extremely ill, so as he put it, "finding myself unfit to discharge purely routine duties satisfactorily, I applied to be placed on temporary half-pay, and this course was permitted to me on the recommendation of a medical board. The question then was, what should I do? What I felt I needed was active hard work—rather than rest—in order to recover from the strain" (*The Rise of Our East African Empire*, vol. 1, 2).[9] What hard work did he find? He went in search of adventure: "So with fifty sovereigns in my belt, and with practically no outfit at all except my favourite little .450 rifle,—which had done me service already in many countries, for some years,—I got on board the first passing ship, as a second-class passenger, and sailed I knew not whither" (*The Rise*, 2). Although it was true that he knew not whither he sailed, there was little doubt that he wanted to see action and, to this end, was on offer as a hired gun. The ship he boarded sailed for Naples, which suited him well. He had wanted to join the Italians for military service, but distrust would not let the Italians give him a commission. He had a fallback position: "My hope was, that I might embark in some useful undertaking in Africa, if possible in connection with the suppression of the slave trade" (11). So this hired gun was available for service to the Italians, who were engaged in an imperialist dance of death with Emperor Menelik of Ethiopia at about this time, which culminated in their defeat at Adowa in 1896. Failing that, he was available to anyone who would use his service to suppress the slave trade. This seeming ambivalence between wanting to push back the imperial frontiers, British or Italian, and at the same time feeling morally indignant at the traffic in human beings was to characterize Lugard's entire career in Africa. For this reason, it is important to not fall into the trap of dismissing him all too easily as an archimperialist scoundrel. I have no doubt that he meant his protestations of interest in and desire to rescue the African from the infamy of slavery, but this desire was based on an evolutionistic characterization of the African as belonging to the infancy of the human race. He brought this characterization with him to the continent, and it remained largely unchanged through his many tours of duty in Africa, with the only exception being his selection of the Fulani in northern Nigeria as, at least, belonging to the pubescence of the human race. What were the elements of this characterization of the African that provided him with an ontological template from which the architectonic of colonialism was constructed ?

Lugard can speak for himself, however. After his arrival on the East African coast in the first quarter of 1888, he sailed south to Zanzibar and later to Mozambique. He was on his way to the interior in the area of present day Malawi in order to cut at its root the Arab-run slave trade on the East African littoral. "On board the Dunkeld I met for the first time a South African 'gold prospector.' . . . He told me success in African travel depended entirely on prompt and resolute action. He begged me to remember his words—'On the first signs of insolence,' he said, 'or even of familiarity, kick them under the jaw (when sitting) or in the stomach. In worse cases shoot, and shoot straight, *at once*. Your life in Africa depends on such prompt measures!'" (*The Rise*, 20). Lugard did not need to be taught this lesson again, for, as I have suggested, his views about the relative ranks and merits of natives and of Europeans, especially of the British variety, were already well formed ever before he went to Africa. In the same book, with relish he retells the story of an earlier incident, the elements of which show that what the South African prospector told him could only have reinforced, not shaped, his own views:

Before leaving Mozambique an unfortunate incident occurred. An Indian Mohammedan trader had brought some goods on board for shipment. The officer of the vessel had been working for many hours in the heat transferring cargo, and had sat down for a few minutes to rest. The trader demanded in an insolent manner that he should immediately rise and attend to him. He declined and the native then made some gross remarks in Hindustani, which I understood, but the officer did not. Extremely indignant at such an affront, I asked him if he could tamely submit to be thus insulted by a native? He replied that if he resented it, he would be "run in" and would lose his ship; that the Portuguese authorities encouraged such action, and were absolutely sure to take the part of the native against an Englishman, and the British India Company would hear no excuses. I, however, had no ship to lose, and I cared not for the Portuguese authorities. I therefore told the Buniah, in Hindustani, that had he used one-half the insolence to me that I had heard him use towards the ship's officer, he would have had cause to regret it. Thereupon he included me. Not liking to strike a native with my fist, I gave him a heavy box on the ear. He seemed inclined to show fight, for he was a strong-built man, but received another similar cuff, which effectually silenced him, but unfortunately broke a bone in my hand, spraining also my thumb and wrist against his cast-iron head. (*The Rise*, 19–20)

Let us examine this passage for some of the pointers to Lugard's view of what natives are. First, what gave offence was that this native had been insolent to a white man. In the second place, when he, the native, had the good fortune of being shown the error of his ways by a more cultured European, he did not have the good sense to step back and apologize. Quite the contrary. Now, fortunately for this insolent native and for his education in civilization, he had present a good teacher and an adult who would not flinch from cracking the whip to teach him how to behave properly. But behaving "properly" was not a matter of not being rude to anybody or treating everyone with respect. Rather, it was a matter of knowing one's place and its duties. In this instance, it was out of place for a native to speak insolently to his superior, the white man. This idea that the peoples of the world were organized in a hierarchy, atop which sits the white man, is the lynchpin of the worldview with which Lugard arrived on native shores. The South African's admonition was a mere reminder, not a fresh disclosure, of how the African was to be viewed from the perspective of a nineteenth-century white man. For Lugard, as for his contemporaries, the African belonged, if at all, to the infancy of the human race. Worse still, he was a savage, an animal who was able to mimic humans. Throughout his career, Lugard never abandoned this view of the African.

He was unwavering in his detestation of the human slave traffic. Simultaneously, however, he cautioned against undue haste in emancipating African slaves because, according to him, it might do more harm than good. He excoriated his fellow Europeans for their hypocrisy at condemning the Arab slave trader when they themselves had engaged in similar activities for so long. He argued that they thus had "a duty of expiation to perform towards the African" (*The Rise*, 27). Yet this belief did not stop him from issuing the following caution:

> That in our efforts to perform this duty, we must recollect how the African has been wedded to slavery through centuries on centuries, so that it has become the product, as it were, of the blood-stained soil of the land. . . . The nature of the African, moreover, is not of that stamp which chafes at the yoke, like the nations of Teutonic blood. Let us accept all this, and clear the ground of all high-coloured nonsense—of "kingly hearts" beating in the bosoms of slaves, and so forth; and taking the African as he is—as centuries of wrongs have made him—apply ourselves to raise him to a higher level. (*The Rise*, 27–28)

The theme of the African's natural suitability for bondage, for being ruled, continued to dominate Lugard's thought right till the end of his life. Witness the following entry of September 10, 1888, in which Lugard quotes himself from his own diary:

> "These savages do not think or act as we do. They are, in truth, like 'dumb driven cattle.' With the slave caravan they suffer uncomplainingly starvation, the scourge, and all the painted horrors of so many writers. They meet a European *safari*, and they hide in the jungle and rejoin the Slavers. Like cattle, they will face any misery but dread the unknown. They are brought on by us—fed, clothed, and spoken kindly to; they bolt. Why? . . . I think, however, it is merely the dumb brute's instinct to wander which makes them go. The long, hot, dusty march, &c., is a bore. They wander off as cattle do, regardless of stall and food, of danger from lions, of danger of a cruel master, instead of a kind one. The very immediate present is the only thought, and sooner than march tomorrow to the unknown, they slip off to-day, and follow the caged bird's instinct, and, like it, they perish in their ill-advised liberty; but, who blames the foolish bird?" I have copied the passage *verbatim*, though it is somewhat lengthy, and perhaps those who read it will begin to understand that the African must be treated differently from the European with centuries of culture to his making, and that coercion is sometimes necessary for their own good. (*The Rise*, 309–10)

In addition to the repeated characterization of the African as a savage closer to the lower animals than to the higher races, he continually regarded and described Africans as belonging to the infancy of the human race. To Lugard, they exhibited a childlike nature characterized by innocence, a lack of appreciation of danger, a basic lack of understanding of and concern for the future, and a penchant for leading a carefree existence marked by sexual abandon and unbounded happiness:

> The happiness of these people is quite phenomenal. Nothing seems to distress them for long, and ties of love and affection sit lightly upon them. Their intel-

lects are not strong enough to enable them to suffer acutely from *anticipation* of evil, nor to *realise* danger till it is actually before them. Hence they live a careless, happy life, laughing incessantly all day, dancing all night; supremely happy, if meat is abundant; able to endure hunger like the beasts of the field, if food is not to be got; plucky, because believing themselves invulnerable by reason of their *dawa*; undisturbed by hopes and fears of a hereafter; rarely subject to those ills that flesh is heir to—headaches, toothaches, and their kindred woes—by reason of their strong animal physique. Such are the Manganja, and with some minor alterations in detail, such is the typical savage of Africa. (*The Rise*, 40)

Elsewhere, he states:

The African holds the position of a late-born child in the family of nations, and must as yet be schooled in the discipline of the nursery. He is neither the intelligent ideal crying out for instruction, and capable of appreciating the subtle beauties of Christian forbearance and self-sacrifice, which some well-meaning missionary literature would lead us to suppose; nor yet, on the other hand, is he universally a rampant cannibal, predestined by Providence to the yoke of the slave, and fitted for nothing better, as I have elsewhere seen him depicted. I hold rather with Longfellow's beautiful lines—

"In all ages
Every human heart is human;
That in even savage bosoms
There are longings, yearnings, strivings
For the good they comprehend not.
That the feeble hands and helpless,
Groping blindly in the darkness,
Touch God's right hand in that darkness."

That is to say, that there is in him, like the rest of us, both good and bad, and that the innate good is capable of being developed by culture. (*The Rise*, 75)

Once again, we confront the insistence that although the African may be way down on the human ladder, she is not completely off it. On the road to becoming more human, what she needs is guidance and tutelage by advanced humanity, with the British being the most advanced. Several implications can be drawn from this premise. In the first place, the metaphor of the child and the requirement of "the discipline of the nursery" were aptly chosen. In exactly the same way it would be irresponsible for parents to let their children grow anyway they wish, it would be irresponsible of civilized races not to take the African in tow and lead him carefully and firmly to civilization (through all the social equivalent stages of pubescence, adolescence, to adulthood). Additionally, the discipline of the nursery sometimes requires its enforcer to be rough with his ward. (I show later how this idea came to provide some philosophical justification for the infliction of punishments on Africans that civilized opinion in the nineteenth century considered to be opprobrious. At that point, I also draw the policy implications.) Third, we do not ordinarily put before children complex social rules or expect them in infancy to comprehend the principles that enable and justify those rules. We do not hold children responsible for many of their actions, and we therefore exclude them from much of responsibility discourse.

> For the rest, if we are in earnest in our efforts to benefit the slaves, we must be content to accept, as a part of the task, the natural apathy of the people, and their indifference to a yoke, which to us would be terribly galling. We must realise that the ties between husband and wife are often of the loosest kind; that a greater affection is said to exist between man and man than between the sexes (as is often seen among the lower animals); that mothers, and more especially fathers, do not feel so intense a love for their children as Europeans generally do, and hence ruthless separation from relatives or family, though it may involve some grief, cannot be said to be so terrible an ordeal as we should imagine by analogy with our own feelings; that when once these ties are ruptured, and the slave transported miles from his own home, he has no resource in himself, no object in the recovery of his freedom and thus his master's house is his sole refuge. His apathetic and submissive nature adapts itself to his surroundings, and he often ceases to desire to be free. (*The Rise*, 191)

If indeed Africans were the children of the human race, they could not be held accountable in the same way that adults are accountable, and it would be a mistake to try to put before them in their childhood the "subtle beauties of Christian forbearance and self-sacrifice." After all, in good Christian ethics, it is unbecoming to cast pearls before swine! This attitude, which cautioned against putting the pearls of civilization before the unschooled African swine, dictated Lugard's opposition to the activities of many Christian missionaries in the nineteenth century, activities that to him were instances of such inappropriate pearl casting. (I have more to say about this later.)

Lugard's complaints about the missionaries were not groundless. In the early to mid-nineteenth century, many missionaries not only thought that Africans were capable of doing exactly what Lugard held they could not do—that is, "appreciate the subtle beauties of Christian forbearance and self-sacrifice"—but also went ahead to create ministries with Africans playing principal roles. They held that if the progress of evangelization was to accelerate, Africans must be sought and trained to perform the task. Most controversially, perhaps, they held that Africans were ready for the fruits of modern civilization and its attendant opportunities.[10] Lugard would have none of it. He did share the missionaries' belief that the African was part of the human family, but he did not share their view that the African had marched in tandem with the rest of humanity and might therefore be in a position to appropriate quickly the fruits of civilization.

One word as regards missionaries themselves. The essential point in dealing with Africans is to establish a respect for the European. Upon this—the prestige of the white man—depends his influence, often his very existence, in Africa. . . . In my opinion—at any rate with reference to Africa—it is the greatest possible mistake to suppose that a European can acquire a greater influence by adopting the mode of life of the natives. In effect, it is to lower himself to their plane, instead of elevating them to his. The sacrifice involved is wholly unappreciated, and the motive would be held by the savage to be poverty and lack of social status in his own country. The whole influence of the European in Africa is gained by this assertion of a superiority which commands the respect and excites the emulation of the savage. To forego this vantage-ground is to lose influence for good. I may add, that the loss of prestige consequent on what I should term the humiliation of the European affects not merely the missionary himself, but is subversive of all efforts for secular administration, and may even invite insult, which may lead to disaster and bloodshed. (*The Rise*, 73–74)

What I have done in the preceding section is to present Lugard in his own words from the time of his first landing in Africa. His views did not change much, if at all, throughout his tenure in Africa till his death in 1945. When he arrived in Africa, he was the bearer of the following interrelated views. (1) The human race was organized into a hierarchy of races. Each race had its own genius and a nature appertaining to it. But these geniuses were not coordinate. On the contrary, the hierarchy of human groups mimicked an evolutionary ladder in which some races were at the top and others were at the bottom, with any number of others on the intervening rungs. Whatever Lugards' views about other races, one thing is clear from the passages previously cited: for him, the European was at the top of the hierarchy and the African was at the bottom. But because this is an evolutionary structure, the European exhibited what was best about what humanity could become and had become up till that time. Simultaneously, to the extent that the European represented the measure of the best possible, he was also a lawgiver to mankind beneath him. The more removed from the European and the more unlike him you were, the closer you were to animals, and the less human you were. But there was hope: you could become more like the European if you had the good fortune of being colonized or imperialized by him, and if you learned your lessons well on how to be human. If, on the other hand, you had the misfortune of being imperialized by a slightly less inferior race—for example, the Arab—the longer it would take you to cover that distance between your animal-like existence and the God-like existence of the European.

(2) The African world, as Lugard apprehended it, was not a human world. It was a world peopled by "primitive savages" who, though they had human hearts beating in them, would require wholesale makeovers before they could be seated as full members of the comity of humans. By the same token, the European, who found himself charged with the onerous but honorable responsibility of rescuing the African from the thrall of savagery, had to watch out for any signs in him or his cohort of slipping back into the infancy of the race, resist any atavistic tendencies, separate himself mentally and physically from the natives, and at the same time execute his responsibility. The African world had to be made livable for the European—humanized as it were—and those areas that were made livable had to have a *cordon sanitaire* erected around them to make sure that they were not infested, polluted, or otherwise muddied by the disease-carrying primitive savage. This idea of the animal and natural character of the African world would later have grievous but widespread implications for colonial policies concerning the spatial organization of the colonies and protectorates.

(3) As a result of the first and second views, the relation of the European and the African in the colonial world could not be *direct, immediate*; it was always *indirect, mediate*. For example, given the first view, the African first had to move away from the depredations of his animal nature before he could be suited to appreciate the "subtle beauties of Christian forbearance and self-sacrifice." As nonselves, Africans had to become selves before they could become Christians. As children, they had to grow and *mature* before they could be admitted as members of the adult community. Given the second view, it would be foolish to install the principles of liberty, egality, and fraternity in a world populated by savages. Thus, the only logical procedure was to hold off on the introduction of these principles until one was sure the savage was humanized and one could therefore make sense of them. This combination of philosophical anthropology and social ontology, I argue, had serious consequences on the evolution of colonial structures and ideologies.

In light of the preceding philosophical predilections, we should be less surprised that Lugard authored the kinds of policies that are to be found in the *Political Memoranda* or that he chose the options that he did in the African colonies where he worked. In the next section, I present and examine the policy options that Lugard chose and the types of administrative mechanisms that he deemed suitable for the Africans in his charge. Of course, I take care to show that, contrary to the apologias of his biographer, Margery Perham, or of Anthony Kirk-Greene, one of the men who operated the system that he set up and shared his mindset about the African, alternate paths in the colonies could have been chosen, but were not. What were the policy options that were chosen in the colony? It is time to introduce the *Political Memoranda*.

Racism as Administration: Political Memoranda

The subtitle of *Political Memoranda* is *Revision of Instructions to Political Officers on Subjects Chiefly Political & Administrative*. As a handbook, it has little interest for those of us who are not administrators, but because the instructions themselves come with explanations of and justifications for particular policy choices, as well as several observations and ruminations on the nature of the African native, indigenous institutions, and so on, we may use the book as Kirk-Greene has suggested—"an index to colonial thinking." There are thirteen memoranda in the book: "(1) Duties of Political Officers and Miscellaneous Subjects; (2) Books, Returns and Office Records; (3) Judicial and Legal; (4) Education; (5) Taxation; (6) Slavery—forced labour, etc.; (7) The use of Armed Force; (8) Native Courts; (9) Native Administration; (10) Lands; (11) Townships; (12) Goods and Vessels in Transit; (13) Forestry" (6). To consider each of these topics in their several subsections would be impractical, so instead I have chosen the ones that, in my estimation, illustrate the general frame in which colonial policies were formulated or reflect the combination of philosophical anthropology and social ontology I have identified as the template from which the architecture of the colony was constructed—in particular, memoranda 1, 3, 4, 8, and 9.

The first memorandum contains an early restatement of the aim of British colonialism as it pertained to the natives. According to Lugard, political officers—residents and district officers and their subordinates, administrative officers—were the executors of the aim and objectives of British colonialism, stated as follows: "3. The British role here is to bring to the country all the gains of civilisation by applied science (whether in the development of material resources, or the eradication of disease, &c.), *with as little interference as possible with Native customs and modes of thought*" (9, my emphasis). The underscored portion points up the ambivalence I already identified in Lugard's attitude to Africans. How, on one hand, was the country to get "all the gains of civilisation by applied science" and, on the other, escape with as little interference as possible in native customs and modes of thought? This recommendation is more curious still when it is recalled that Lugard regarded Africans and their native customs and modes of thought as being out of the loop of civilization; he called them savages. I submit that in light of the philosophical anthropology and social ontology that governed his views, one half of these twin objectives could not have been seriously meant. That is, the resolution of the apparent paradox was to ignore the injunction to bring all the gains of civilization to the natives and thus to leave them little improved. The justification for this choice is easy to find.

Recall that the colony was populated by primitive savages relative to the European superior. Among these savages, however, some had climbed higher than others on the evolutionary ladder. Hence, in the colony, Lugard identified "advanced tribes" and "backward tribes" (11–12). Advanced tribes were those that had hierarchies, atop which sat chiefs or similar functionaries. Backward tribes lacked this simple marker. "Applied science" was to be done in accordance with the relative standing of the tribes concerned in the hierarchy of races, a standing that was itself determined by how well or ill the social organization of the tribe mirrored the example of the advanced British. So those tribes that had chieftaincy systems were judged "advanced," and those that did not were judged "backward." Additionally, even among those adjudged "advanced," the closer their institutions and practices were to those of the British, the more approval Lugard extended to them—hence, his almost irrational preselection of the Fulani as the most gifted rulers among the tribes of Nigeria and consideration of the Yoruba as not as good. Given this schema it should not be surprising that Lugard worked hard to extend the administrative reach of native Fulani authorities to areas of Northern Nigeria that had successfully resisted the Fulani encroachment on their territories. Where there were no chiefs, the political officer was literally invited to invent them. "If there is no Chief who exercises authority beyond his own village, [the political officer] will encourage any village Chief of influence and character to control a group of villages, with a view to making him Chief of a district later if he shows ability for the charge" (11). But it was not only with reference to native administration where the preference for "as little interference as possible with Native Customs and modes of thought" trumped the requirement "to bring to the country all the gains of civilisation." I would like to suggest that this happened in all the areas of activity in the colony and protectorates of Nigeria.

For example, like memo 1, memo 9—"Native Administration"—was virtually a blueprint for restoring the Fulani aristocracy in Northern Nigeria after they had been militarily vanquished by the British. "1. The cardinal principle upon which the Administration of Northern Nigeria was based was what has been commonly called 'Indirect Rule,' viz., rule through the Native chiefs, who are regarded as an integral part of the machinery of Government, with well defined powers and functions recognised by Government and by law, and not dependent on the caprice of an Executive Officer" (296). The policy of indirect rule is usually celebrated as the evidence of Lugard's genius. For many, the preservation of indigenous modes of governance was symptomatic of Lugard's appreciation of native administrative and political development. For others, the savings to the British colonial treasury that accrued from not having to employ regular modern-trained civil servants meant that the colonial adventure could proceed on the cheap. I take a different view of the practice. Contrary to received wisdom, I argue that the reason that the option of using modern-trained civil servants was foreclosed was that the natives—savages that they were—were not deserving of such benefits of applied science and, in any case, were not ready for institutions of governance founded on the principles of accountability, meritocracy, and strict adherence to rules and procedures.[11] Lugard states the policy as follows:

> The *de facto* rulers who after the British conquest of Northern Nigerian had been reinstated or appointed to the various Emirates, and all other *de facto* Chiefs who had been recognised by Government, were to be supported in every way and their authority upheld. Already in Memo. 1 it had been laid down that it was the duty of a Resident to rule through the Chiefs, to endeavour to educate them in the duties of rulers, to seek their co-operation and to maintain their prestige.
>
> It was laid down, however, that no independent or revolted Pagan tribes were to be included in the jurisdiction of a Moslem ruler without the express sanction of the Governor.
>
> The Native Chiefs thus recognised were not to be regarded as independent rulers. They were the delegates of the Governor whose representative was the Resident. The Central Government reserved to itself the sole right to raise and control armed forces, to impose taxation of any kind, to make laws and to dispose of such lands as are, under Native law and custom, vested in the paramount power. These limitations were specifically set out in the letter of appointment under which each Chief of the higher grades held his office. (297)

It is only on a generous interpretation of the above directives that one can hold that Lugard was preserving native institutions. In the first place, it should be obvious that the rulers who were kept in place were not kept in place on terms that reflected their preeminence in the preconquest days. On the contrary, they had become "civil servants" of sorts, interposed between the British resident or political officer and the people over whom the latter ruled. That the native chiefs were not to be regarded as "independent rulers" and owed their appointment to the administrative fiat of the British governor or his representatives was made clear by the issuing of "letters of appointment" in which the terms of their appointment were stated. One may therefore conclude that instead of seizing the opportunity of the defeat of the erstwhile absolute, paramount rulers to put in place new forms of administration based on modern principles, as had happened in Europe, Lugard chose to revivify modes of governance that were well under way to withering. Moreover, to have sought a modern bureaucracy peopled with beneficiaries of meritocracy, of careers open to talent, would have violated one of the cardinal principles of Lugard's philosophy: the natives were not ready for the twentieth century, and a direct relationship with natives would mean extending to them the benefits and courtesies of *citizenship*. Hence, the philosophical anthropology that dominated his view of the natives precluded the option of bringing to them all the benefits of civilization. This conclusion is supported by the following prescription: "4. Subject to these limitations it was the declared policy of the Government to restore to the Chiefs the prestige and authority which they had lost by the British conquest, or forfeited by their own previous mal-administration. I was not myself very hopeful of far-reaching reform among the men who had for a lifetime been used to other methods, and who would necessarily chafe under the restraints imposed by British rule and the curtailment of their despotic power" (297). And it is not an accident that Lugard offers the following justifications for the policy: "5(c) [T]he obvious folly of attempting any drastic reform which would cause a dislocation of methods which, however faulty, have the sanction of traditional usage, and are acquiesced in by the people, until we had an increased knowledge both of Moslem methods of rule and of Native law and custom" (298). At every point at which the imperative of bringing all the gains of civilization to the natives dictated severe reorganization of native life and practices, the weight of Lugard's evolutionary thinking led him in the opposite direction of preserving institutions and practices were frankly moribund.

Even more noteworthy was the record of decisive movements in the area of law away from the substitution of new forms of social ordering and away from the implantation of new institutions and practices that would have ensured for the natives all the gains of civilization. Doubtless one of the most significant gains heralded by modernity was the triumph of the Rule of Law. Under it, formal equality before the law was guaranteed, even if only in theory, to different classes whose relative social power may have varied widely. By the same token, given that the law is supposed to be no respecter of persons, those who lay down the law were not exempt from the strictures of the laws that they made. Finally, it marked the triumph of process whereby rules and adherence to them were considered the ultimate hallmarks of a good municipal legal system. Ordinarily, one would have thought that the colonial authorities would make haste to induct the people into the system of law that is usually considered one of the jewels in the crown of modernity.

But what did Lugard do? There were two types of courts in the colony: British courts and native courts. In the British courts, the governing laws were "the Common Law, and the doctrines of Equity (administered concurrently), and the Statutes of general application, which were in force in England on January 1st, 1900. This is modified by the proviso that British Courts shall in Civil causes affecting Natives (and even non-Natives in their contractual relations with Natives) recognise Native Law and Custom when not repugnant to natural justice and humanity or incompatible with any Ordinance, especially in matters relating to marriage, land and inheritance" (memo 3.2, 83). On the face of it, British principles of justice provided the benchmark for the administration of the justice system in colonial Nigeria, and this benchmark at least in theory applied to the second category of courts: native courts. "3. The fundamental law in the Native Moslem Courts of Nigeria is the Maliki Code of Mohammedan Law, and in the Native Pagan Courts it is the local Native law and custom. Both are subject to the proviso that all judgments and sentences must not be repugnant to natural justice and humanity, or to any Ordinance of Nigeria. In Criminal Cases, however, the penalties awarded are not strictly limited by the Criminal Code" (84). The reader should note the exception inserted at the end of the passage just quoted because once again it illustrates the divergence that I have pointed out between the stated aim of bringing to the natives all the gains of civilization and the failure to put in place the types of institutional mechanisms that would enable the attainment of this aim. On the one hand, native law and custom would be recognized only as long as it did not conflict with the benchmark set by British notions of natural justice and humanity. On the other, the same principle was not to apply in criminal cases. Why this inconsistency? Again, the answer is to be found in the philosophical anthropology that supplied the background for Lugard's views. If Africans were closer to animals than they were to humans, they were sure to be impervious to the logic of arguments but amenable to the logic of the prod. In part II, section 23 of memo 3, Lugard wrote: "Under British rule the principle of reprisal and mutilation has of course been abolished, and imprisonment has become the commonest penalty. Flogging for theft and other offences for which it cannot be inflicted in a British Court is not, however, illegal in Native Court. It used to be common in Native Court returns to find that the sentence for theft (mutilation being illegal) was 'to return value of articles stolen.' Native judges should be told that this is an insufficient sentence and that a punishment should always be added to restitution" (93).

It is curious that flogging, dehumanizing enough to be restricted in British criminal cases, was not adjudged to breach the requirement of conformity to natural justice and humanity, but that levying accused persons the equivalent value in lieu of articles stolen, humane as it obviously is, was considered inadequate by Lugard. This exception in criminal cases is merely an instance of Lugard's general refusal to extend to the natives the benefits of civilization that he took to be one of the principal justifications of British colonialism in Nigeria. This particular refusal—that is, to implant new legal systems—is significant in other ways.

Few would deny that law in its dirigiste dimensions is a vital instrument for orienting people's behavior. And it is equally true that one of the most definitive achievements of modernity was the installation of the Rule of Law as the principal mode of rule in civilized societies. Even in the Britain of Lugard's time, the king had become a constitutional monarch, and British subjects did not take kindly to anyone trifling with their hard-won rights under the Rule of Law. This was why many of the remedies that Lugard wrote into his memoranda would have been considered ultra vires under a regime guided by the Rule of Law. Now, it was not that Lugard did not try to replicate some of the institutions that entitled Britain to regard herself as lawgiver to the rest of the world. There were so-called British courts, as already pointed out. In those courts, at the apex of which was the Supreme Court, formalities and procedures were standard; there was representation by counsel and the native elite were particularly enthusiastic about the opportunity to embarrass the colonial authorities using the instrumentality of law.[12] Although the operation of the British courts did not follow the standards set by their originals in Britain, they at least aspired to until Lugard set them back with so-called court reforms in 1914. Here, the native courts are most interesting because, as usual, they provide us with another example of the institutional face of what Lugard thought of the natives in his charge.

Native courts were set up for two reasons. First, the dearth of personnel trained in British law and practices made impossible the establishment of British courts for the entire territory. Second, making British law available to all people within the territory would have made it impossible for the colonial authorities to prevent the natives from raising uncomfortable questions about the legitimacy of British rule. To be sure, this was what happened with the native products of missionary-inspired "Western" education. In light of Lugard's evolutionist predilections, it should be obvious why, using the first reason as a shibboleth, he would settle on native courts that would be palpably inferior to the British courts and would be kept so. Let us bear in mind that the principles that made the Rule of Law such an enticing ideal include the following: equality of all before the law, those who make law are not above it, meticulous adherence to procedure and rule following, and so on. What was to be found in the native courts, though?

The jurisdiction of the native courts was restricted to natives, except in criminal cases and in those cases involving natives who were "not ordinarily subject to Native Courts": "The practice and procedure of Native Courts is in accordance with Native Law and Custom, and *no unnecessary formalities may be introduced.* . . . No legal practitioners may appear in a Native Court" (memo 15, 89, my emphasis). I have already mentioned that forms of punishment that would be unacceptable under British law were to be allowed under native law and custom. Lugard reinforces the injunction not to introduce unnecessary formalities in his description of how to keep native court clerks in check: "Members [of native courts] will be taught that the clerk's self-asserted knowledge of procedure and of English law is of no account in the eyes of Government, *which sets no value on forms and procedure,* which will be simplified as much as possible. It will be impressed upon them that *a knowledge of English law is valueless since the Court administers Native law only*" (memo 8.24, 275, my emphasis). One must resist the temptation to regard the underscored sentiments in the passages quoted as mere pragmatic cautions. In the general context of Lugard's thought regarding what was suitable for the Africans, given their retarded development, these sentiments meant that he held any attempt to introduce the intricacies of forms and procedure to a people who were not ready for them as a recipe for disaster for all concerned.[13] He not only restricted the jurisdiction of the

Supreme Court as part of his court reforms in 1914, but also eliminated representation by counsel—to prosecute or defend—from the provincial courts that he created. This was a significant step backward, especially in the western part of Nigeria, where the legal profession was growing.[14] Why discourage natives, especially those who had benefited from missionary education, from trying, if they saw any value in the new mode of life to which they had been introduced, to incorporate into the operation of the native courts any forms and procedure that they might have learned from English practices? The argument about means or costs is less persuasive given that Lugard himself states: "It has occurred to me that in many centres in the Southern Provinces, where there are mission schools, an intelligent youth of the local population who had learned to read and write would possibly be the best selection as Native Court clerk, and would be less likely to attempt to domineer over the Court. The Resident, Oyo, reports that the experiment has been a success" (275). If there were such nodes for possible transformation of social forms in the legal area, it was a disservice to discourage their development. In affirming that the natives were not ready for forms and procedure, in terms reminiscent of his earlier insistence that the Africans were incapable of comprehending the "subtle beauties of Christian forbearance and self-sacrifice," Lugard arrested the growth of African institutions in directions that might have made Africans beneficiaries of "all the gains of civilisation."

Even more curious, the native law and custom that the native courts were charged with enforcing was hardly recognizable to many people who were supposed to be bound by it. Indeed, for the most part, the native law was whatever the relevant chief said it was, if he was able to persuade the resident to take his word for it. And as we have seen, in areas without chiefs, the colonial authorities created them as "warrant chiefs." In other cases, many natives were bitten by the bug of modernity and fancied themselves worthy of British citizenship and so claimed it, but were forced to submit to the jurisdiction of native courts, which they considered *infra dignitatem*. In fact, Lugard fought a running battle with educated natives who thought that they were the advance brigade of the new civilization in their communities. Although he made use of them when it served his purposes—for appointments as court clerks, for example—he always saw them as bad parodies of Europeans who had become sundered from their moorings in native soils. He saw them as people who thought that they could run before they had learned to crawl.

In light of the foregoing, it is fair to conclude that the tension between the twin injunctions to bring to the natives "all the gains of civilisation" but to interfere with native customs and modes of thought as little as possible was resolved in favor of the latter. The problem, though, was that the latter option came too late for some parts of the country, specifically certain areas of southern Nigeria, where modernity under the tutelage of Christianity had already made serious inroads on both the landscape and the mindscape of the natives domiciled there.[15] In addition to Christianity, the principal medium through which this reordering of native life was effected was education, for it was a part of the educational agenda of the missionaries to create a native middle class equipped with the wherewithal to read, make, and buy the Bible and generally to afford the type and standard of life that would set them apart from the lower classes. By the time that Lugard was standardizing the administrative procedures represented in *Political Memoranda*, the area of Western Nigeria—especially Lagos, Abeokuta, and Ibadan—was home to a coterie of professionals in law, medicine, the building trades, the press, and education who fancied themselves as deserving of equal treatment with Europeans simply because they had proved their mettle as participants in the new dispensation. So how did education, given its importance just described, fare in *Political Memoranda*?

In memo 4, number 9, Lugard describes the principles of an educational policy thus:

> The primary function of education should in my judgment be to fit the ordinary individual to fill a useful part in his environment with happiness to himself, and to ensure that the exceptional individual shall use his abilities for the advancement of the community, and not to its detriment, or to the subversion of constituted authority. We are to-day beginning to realise our failure in this respect both in India and in West Africa. If the local Press may be taken as a criterion of the feelings of the educated communities in all the West African Colonies we must admit that education has not brought them happiness and contentment. It should be the ideal of a sound educational policy to exchange this hostility for an attitude of friendly co-operation, and to train a generation which shall be able to achieve ideals of its own without a slavish imitation of Europeans, and be proud of a nationality with its own definite sphere of public work and its own future. (130)

This passage encapsulates Lugard's attitude to the education of his native charges. No one can argue with the first part of his articulation of the principles of education that informed his policy. One can even go along with his insistence that education should suit its recipients to work for the advancement of their communities or that it should not be a training in subversion. Furthermore, one must not ignore the influence of the strictly hierarchical society from which Lugard came on his need to prevent subversion of constituted authority. But these cautions cannot explain his hostility to the educated African's insistence that he and his people deserved all the gains of civilization as well as a say in the constitution of the authority that bound them. What Lugard did not let out was the fact that the running battles he fought with the new educated elite in the southern parts of Nigeria turned on their justifiable horror at the extension to the south of the practice of indirect rule, which in reality was northern native administration system writ large. They also protested vigorously his court reforms of 1914, to which I

have already alluded, and their implications for the southern elites' understanding of what direction their progress should take. Against this background, Lugard's injunctions attain a more sinister coloration. Why de-
nounce Africans who saw value in the new ways of life as engaging in
"slavish imitation of Europeans"? If it was important to get the native elites
to substitute an attitude of friendly cooperation toward the colonial authorities, as was the case with the northern native authorities or with chiefs in
many areas of the South, why not address the grievances of the elites and,
given their predisposition to accept English ways of life, use them as the principal medium for the evolution of colonial rule? This was not what happened. On the contrary, Lugard presented policies that represented a clear
retrogression from the advances that had been made thanks to missionary
education. For instance, whereas the missionaries sought to transform local
languages to writing in order to facilitate literacy in the Bible among the natives, even though they continued to teach English to their native wards, Lugard took the opposite tack:

> In the South, and perhaps in some districts in the North, English must be the
> common language, and though, as Lord Kimberley said, instruction in English
> must, of necessity, at first be given through the medium of the vernacular, Gov-
> ernment encouragement should not be enlisted to stimulate or preserve the use
> of these Native tongues. The acquisition of sufficient knowledge of the vernac-
> ular to enable the British and Native Staff to teach English or Hausa presents
> difficulty, and is a cause of delay, but as their use will be confined to the simplest
> instruction given in the lowest classes, complete mastery of them will not be re-
> quired. Only one vernacular (other than Hausa) will be used in any school.
> (memo 4.4, 125)

It is strange that, on one hand, indirect rule was pledged to the preservation
of native modes of life and thought, but on the other, "Native tongues" were
slated to wither on the vine.

Stranger still was Lugard's failure to celebrate the unruliness of the beneficiaries of missionary education. If Lugard was right, they had become
exactly what the missionaries thought and desired that they would be: icon-
oclasts and rebels against the old ways of doing things. We must trace Lugard's hostility to his evolutionist orientation according to which the Africans were not yet ready for freedom or reason. Thus, he championed the
type of education driven by the nitty-gritty requirements of servicing the
colonial system, not the type that would open the minds of its recipients to
new ways of being human or make them question, with a view to improvement, immemorial customs. For example, he held that purely secular education was ill-suited to the level of development of Africans:

> The examples of India and China, as well as of Africa, appear to demonstrate
> that purely secular education, and even moral instruction divorced from reli-

gious sanction, among races who have not the atmosphere which centuries of Christian ethical standards have produced in Europe, infallibly produces a class of young men and women who lack reverence alike for their parents, their social superiors, their employers, or the Government. They lack self-restraint and control, and they lack the foundation on which the best work is based, whether of public usefulness or private effort. . . . It remains more than doubtful how far the African is capable of being restrained by moral precepts divorced from the incentive of religious sanctions, and I am impressed with the belief that the African boy requires every force which can be brought to bear if his natural proclivities are to be overcome, and he is to learn self-control and discipline. (memo 4.14, 135)

Hence, he supported religious instruction in schools. Here again, we confront another inconsistency. Earlier, we are told in *The Rise of Our East African Empire* that the African was not yet at the stage where he could appreciate the subtle beauties of Christian forbearance and self-sacrifice. So how come the same African could learn Christian morality? With this question, I conclude my discussion of the policy options articulated in *Political Memoranda* and the philosophical justification for them.

Conclusion: Ideas Have Consequences

I have argued throughout this essay that when Lugard arrived on the African continent, he came with preconceptions about the African—preconceptions that ruled his policy choices in his role as an influential administrator in Nigeria. As a result of the play of these views, the tension in his characterization of the dual mandate component regarding the duty owed to the African by the British was resolved in a specific way that shortchanged Africans. Recall his declaration that "The British role here is to bring to the country all the gains of civilisation by applied science (whether in the development of material resources, or the eradication of disease, &c.), with as little interference as possible with Native customs and modes of thought" (*Political Memoranda*, 9). I have suggested that it would have been impossible to bring to the country all the gains of civilization without simultaneously interfering heavily with native customs and modes of thought, more so if we consider how he was already convinced that the native customs and modes of thought barely rose above the level of the lower animals. It is right to conclude that even though the opportunity was available to effect a total transformation of native life using the template of modernity, à la Christian missionaries of the early nineteenth century, Lugard either held back or went in the opposite direction. Colonial racism explains this unfortunate choice. What is left for us to do is to explore, albeit briefly, the philosophical grounds Lugard gave for the choices he made in what is considered his theoretical magnum opus: *The Dual Mandate in British Tropical Africa*.

Throughout the entire period that he served as an administrator in Nigeria, Lugard fought a running battle with a certain category of natives: the Western-educated elite made up mostly of returning slaves and indigenous converts to Christianity. He made few policy choices that did not attract complaint, criticism, or condemnation from this group of natives. Incidentally, most of the members of this group were to be found in the southern parts of Nigeria. Lugard and his cohorts fully reciprocated their hostility. His reaction to them was in sharp contrast to his fawning disposition toward the Muslim rulers of the northern parts who had been militarily defeated by the British. Lugard's favoring of northern Muslim rulers over southern Christians was somewhat counterintuitive. One would have thought that Lugard would have felt a closer kinship with those who not only had accepted the new civilization, but had gone to great lengths to become good at it and to become proselytizers on behalf of the new mode of social living represented by Christianity and capitalism. One can make a strong case for affirming this close kinship between Lugard and the Christianized native elite. Those who have studied this group of natives in the period before the dominance of the administrator-colonizer have made clear that the educated elite shared many of the philosophical justifications of the missionizing and civilizing activities of the Europeans. This attitude was most pronounced among the returned slaves who, although condemning slavery, sought to explain their initial capture as evidence of the hand of providence that had chosen them to be recipients of the good news and the new civilization that they adjudged superior to that civilization from which they had been taken in captivity. As a result of their education in the ways of being human in the modern sense—which, as I have mentioned, was coterminous with being Christian—they fancied themselves as the inheritors of the new civilization. They thought that the basis of the legitimacy of both the missionizing activities of the evangelists and the imperializing activities of the administrators was to be found in their claim to being the purveyors and embodiments of a superior civilization. Having been baptized and having acquired the other trappings of the new way of life epitomized by Christianity and capitalism— education, lifestyle, family forms, the English language, and so on—they were persuaded that they deserved to enjoy the privileges and benefits appurtenant to these acquisitions. Hence, they demanded that they be treated as British *subjects*, as citizens of the British Empire were then called. That meant, as far as they were concerned, the creation in Nigeria of the appropriate equivalents of modern British institutions, and they were willing to put their money where their mouths were. As is documented by both Ade Ajayi *(Christian Missions in Nigeria)* and E. A. Ayandele *(The Missionary Impact on Modern Nigeria, 1842–1914)*, the late nineteenth and early twentieth centuries witnessed serious efforts by this new elite to recreate as best they could the institutional forms of social living that they felt were required by their new cultural acquisition. They created schools, set up hospitals, publishing houses, and presses, and built magnificent structures that have remained monuments to their assiduity in their embrace of this new way of being human.

In addition to Ajayi's and Ayandele's works, a significant source of information about this new elite and their achievements in one location—Lagos—is Michael J. C. Echeruo, *Victorian Lagos: Aspects of Nineteenth Century Lagos Life.* In this work, the author attempted to "reconstruct the patterns of life and thought in Lagos during the second half of the 19th century, as reflected in the Lagos Press of that period" (1). I present some evidence from this source because the picture the press presents to us might offer a plausible approximation to what life was like at that stage of Nigeria's history before Lugard wrote his works. According to Echeruo, this segment of the elite in western Nigeria was very small indeed, making up about "only a tenth of the entire population" (*Victorian Lagos*, 30). But it is not their number that makes them important to us; it is what they represented:

> These Lagosians were usually very conversant with events in Europe and America, especially with the progress and consequences of the American Civil War. They maintained close contact with friends and other descendants of rescued slaves on the West African Coast. They had high hopes for themselves and for the Africa they were going to help civilize. They felt deep obligations to the hinterland, and yet considered the civilizing influence of British power sufficiently beneficial to justify the gradual control which Britain was gaining over Yorubaland. They wanted good education for their children, and fought to have Government subsidy for schools; they wanted their children to be "refined," and so they frequently sent them to England. These children had to be in the smart circles of Lagos, so they went into the right professions—law, medicine and the Arts. Educated Lagosians wanted to associate themselves with the usual recreations of a sophisticated Europe, and so went to the Races, to Fancy Dress balls, to the Gymkhana games, and to cricket. In the evenings, they went for "brisk walks" or for "short rides." On such occasions, (as an advertisement reminded them), they called first on "their friend, the hairdresser. Everything will be done to your taste and profit and you will come again PRO BONO PUBLICO."
> (Echeruo, *Victorian Lagos*, 30)

It was not only in the area of everyday expressions that these new converts sought to display their new adherence. Of greater significance to our discussion is what Echeruo has identified as "the intellectual context" of Victorian Lagos. This community was riven with tension between its "instinctive and deep-felt attachment to Yorubaland and to Yoruba life" and the fact that most of its members "had grown up in foreign lands—in Sierra Leone, in Cuba or in Brazil." The latter fact, according to Echeruo, placed them "at some advantage over their own people because of the opportunity that expatriation and education had indirectly offered them to acquire some of the characteristics of European civilization" (*Victorian Lagos*, 35). As inheritors of such characteristics, "they became, as it were, brokers for the new civilization and the new culture; the propagators of a 'higher' morality, a new way of life and a novel affluence" (35). Fierce debates were waged within the community concerning what the possibilities were of the African adopting European ways of being human and the consequences thereto:

> It is not difficult to identify the source of this disorientation. The educated Lagosian of the century was a typical creature of the times. His philosophers were Spenser and Darwin; his idea of progress was inseparable from the Victorian idea of evolutionary development. Where Europe, especially Germany and England, troubled itself about the future of civilization and of the chosen races, Lagosians sought to fit their community into a system which Europe had set up for its own convenience. In this scheme, their society was primitive, undeveloped. Accordingly they continued to see themselves in a pattern of world history reconstructed from the Darwinian hypothesis. (Echeruo, *Victorian Lagos*, 50)

Echeruo then presents evidence from the editorials and debates in the Lagos press of the day of the widespread acceptance of the Darwinian hypothesis concerning the place of the African on the ladder of evolution. The debate then turned on what the African had to do to secure a place on the "Progress Express" then hurtling toward the twentieth century. He concludes: "the Lagosian of the period thus saw Africa as a continent yet to evolve into something. He saw the customs, morals and institutions of his people as desperately in need of improvement through the use of good (probably European) models. And no effort should be spared in his search for these models and in his application of the whole self to understanding them" (41).

This passage marks a convenient point at which to get back to Lugard. On what can be deemed one of the most important philosophical points of Lugard's scheme—the African's need of tutelage in the ways of the new civilization—there was a remarkable convergence between the educated elite in Lagos and Lugard. So why did Lugard not see these gentlemen as the main agents with or through whom to bring all the gains of civilization to the natives? However we look at it, using them made the most sense: they met the requirement of using native agents; they were schooled in the language and ways of the white man; even if they were not proficient yet, the fact that they already had the appropriate foundations in place meant that it would require just an intensification of the way of life they have come to know and to adore; finally, they already saw themselves as "brokers for the new civilization and the new culture." The failure of the European colonizers to entrust this task to them was inconsistent with the colonizers' declared aim. This refusal to recruit native talent, but instead to hire unqualified Europeans at higher cost, made the *Mirror* (March 17, 1888) "remark, quite bitterly that 'one of England's noble objects in acquiring possessions in Africa, is to train the natives for self-government. Yes! we are trained with a vengeance, and strained into poverty, to be left ruined at last . . . The Colony is overburdened with needless European officials, and it cannot further withstand the strain'" (Echeruo, *Victorian Lagos*, 29). Why did Lugard not see this kinship, and if he did, why did he not celebrate it and put the Western-educated local elite in charge of the administration of the colony? I can provide a very simple answer.

Although there was a convergence between Lugard's view and the local elite's there was also a crucial divergence between them: *each placed the African on a different rung of the ladder of evolution*. For Lugard, the African had barely, if at all, emerged from the ranks of the lower animals and was, at best, still in the infancy of the human race. For the repatriates, their lives represented proof of the educability of the African and of the fact that he was willing, able and ready to assume the task of joining the rest of humanity in the race to progress. One may not accuse them of self-deception on this issue. After all, the evangelization of the southern parts of Nigeria had been accomplished under the superintendence of one of them: Bishop Samuel Ajayi Crowther. Here, then, we find the most significant demonstration of the power of the philosophical anthropology and social ontology Lugard formulated before he went to Africa. Even though the reality in southern Nigeria was completely different from his perceptions, his pretensions to science failed the supreme test of any decent empirical science: the priority of facts over theory. That is why he would write *The Dual Mandate* without feeling any need to change any of the formulations he had as early as his first contact with Africa in the closing years of the nineteenth century. The hold of racism on Lugard's mind was so strong that whole passages of *The Rise* were worked into *The Dual Mandate* virtually unchanged. In some other respects, *The Dual Mandate* even amplified some of the themes he emphasized in earlier works. It also helped explain some policy choices he made and described in the *Political Memoranda*. For example, it turns out that his preference for the Fulani as rulers had nothing to do with their genius for administration. They were preselected because they were light-skinned.

But for the most part the progressive communities adopted and owed their advance to the adoption of, an alien monotheistic religion, which brought with it a written language and a foreign culture. It is to the creed of Islam that this political and social influence has in the past alone been due. *It has been the more potent as a creative and regenerating force, because it brought with it an admixture of Aryan or Hamitic blood, and the races which introduced it settled in the country and became identified with its inhabitants. They possessed greater powers of social organisation than the negro aborigines, and may therefore claim to be of a superior race-type.*

In West Africa the conquests of the Arabs and Berbers from the north-east introduced the creed of Islam in the belt bordering the southern edge of the Sahara early in the eighth century. The modern history of the advanced communities of Hausaland and Bornu in Nigeria "may be said to date from the period at which they accepted the Moslem religion, though the purer black races had established their domination over the inferior, and ruled by force of superior intelligence and cultivation long before that time." They founded kingdoms which, in the zenith of their prosperity, rivalled the civilisation of Europe of that day. Their descendants, the Fulani, still form the dominant caste, and rule the Moslem States of Nigeria. (*The Dual Mandate*, 76, footnotes omitted, my emphasis)

This backhanded compliment to the Fulani and Hausa rested on their (s)kinship to the Aryan or Hamitic stock. If they looked like Aryans as a result of the admixture of Aryan or Hamitic blood with their original types, they must automatically share the latter's genius for administration and conquest. Given Lugard's a priori designation of the "negro" stock as closer to the animals, the more "this stock" demonstrated their capacity for the assimilation of the new way of life presaged by Europeans, the more they appeared to be irredeemable pathologies. It turns out that the animus directed at the repatriates and other natives who enthusiastically embraced modern European civilization arose not from their inability to wear the garb of civilization well, but from an a priori assumption that modern natives were misbegotten. Here is how he described the "Europeanised African": "The Europeanised African differs not merely in mental outlook from the other groups, but also in physique. Doctors and dentists tell us that he has become less fertile, more susceptible to lung-trouble and to other diseases, and to defective dentition—disabilities which have probably arisen from in-breeding among a very limited class, and to the adoption of European dress, which writers in the native press say is enervating and inimical to the health of the African" (*The Dual Mandate*, 79–80).

For corroborating evidence, he looked to the United States, where there were more "Europeanised Africans" (*The Dual Mandate*, 8182). He acknowledged the progress that blacks had made in the United States, but he attributed it to their living in close proximity to and their tutelage under whites. Even then, he misconstrued W. E. B. Du Bois's contention that blacks in the United States should not desire to be other than themselves. As for the insistence of the Europeanized Africans that they were the natural brokers between their people and the new civilization, he argued that "however strong a sympathy we may feel for the aspirations of these African progressives, sane counsellors will advise them to recognise their present limitations" (*The Dual Mandate*, 85). It is remarkable that he wrote this passage at a time when the Pan-African movement was afoot and the National Congress of British West Africa was already agitating for the extension of the rights of citizenship to West Africans.

If as late as 1922 Lugard remained unyielding in his perception of the African as being mired still in the infancy of the human race and as yet having a long road to join the ranks of humanity, I think I am justified in my insistence on the centrality of this view in an explanation of his policy choices in the colony. In light of my argument that reason dictated that he should have made common cause with the repatriates, his failure to do so may then be regarded as evidence of how his racism trumped the declared aim of one-half of the dual mandate: moving the natives along the path to civilization or bringing all the gains of civilization to them. Finally, in preferring to preserve old institutions even when reason dictated the substitution of modern ones, Lugard substituted the ignoble science of sociocryonics, the frozen preservation of outmoded and moribund social forms, for the genuine science of social transformation that would have ushered in, with all their attendant strains and stresses, new ways of being human for those Africans who found value in them. By embracing sociocryonics, Lugard distorted the old institutions for his own ends or bastardized them beyond recognition. Simultaneously, he deprived Africans of the opportunity to engage critically with their own culture for the purposes of moving it along, expunging those elements that had outlived their usefulness, keeping in altered forms those that remained relevant, and generally borrowing from other cultures whenever they felt the need for new forms that their indigenous structures lacked. Such critical engagement would have been the ultimate demonstration of self-government and would at the same time have been closer to the normal evolution of all human societies when they are not forced artificially to maintain a world in certain cases well lost.[16]

III MORALITY, IDENTITIES, AND "RACE"

9 Split-Level Equality: Mixing Love and Equality

LAURENCE M. THOMAS

> In all things that are purely social we can be as separate as the fingers, yet one
> as the hand in all things essential to mutual progress.
> —Booker T. Washington, *Up from Slavery*

The continual existence of social inequality is something of a mystery because just about everyone says that she or he believes in equality. Of course, people mean different things by equality, so in this light perhaps inequality's continual existence is no mystery after all because no common convictions can be found. I am not persuaded, though.

People often mean different things by good music, for example; yet, the convergence across peoples regarding what is excellent music is considerable. This is true of not only classical music, but of many aspects of popular music as well. The music of Mozart and Beethoven presents no contest when it comes to general agreement, but music from Diana Ross and the Supremes and the early Aretha Franklin, say, have widespread appeal among people who otherwise listen to very different popular artists. There is no reason to think that people's thinking about equality is any more divergent than their thinking about music, so if we can get considerable convergence regarding music, significant differences in musical tastes notwithstanding, we should certainly be able to find considerable convergence with respect to what is meant by *equality*. My suspicion is that inequality's persistence is owing, at least in part, to another factor having nothing whatsoever to do with different views about equality. What I suspect is that many people across all ethnic groups do not believe in equality to quite the extent that they say they do. As we shall see, this conclusion becomes manifestly clear when we consider the view of a great many people concerning ties of romance and friendship.

Let me emphasize here that I am talking about ethnic rather than cultural groups, even though we often suppose that there is a correlation between an ethnic group and a culture. But consider that although Arabs constitute an ethnic group, there are Christian and Muslim Arabs and therefore two different cultures within the same ethnic group. Finally, I should say that although I regard the notion of *race* as intellectually bankrupt from the point of view of science, I mean to use the term *ethnic group* as it is used in common parlance; and I assume that even common parlance can be refined, as indicated by the observation I just made regarding Christian and Muslim Arabs. Before getting under way, I want to make a few remarks concerning equality itself.

The Naturalness of Equality

Jean-Jacques Rousseau thought equality to be natural. He expressed this idea with the provocative claim that man was born free, but is everywhere in chains. Rousseau's point is that the first human beings were not born in society and, moreover, that all were free to use their natural powers as the circumstances permitted it. For him, the chains were the restraints of an unjust society. There is another way in which we may think of equality as natural.

With regard to the flourishing of the human species, skin color is irrelevant. *Flourishing* here can be understood as producing healthy progeny that in turn produce healthy progeny and, in each case, as providing the progeny with the proper care.[1] Any two fertile human beings of a female-male pairing can produce progeny, and no male-female-pairing within an ethnic kind is, on that account alone, more favored to produce healthy progeny. What is more, no infant cares about the physical features of its parents, just so long as the parents love and care for it. In general, a happy infant will be responsive to the warmth of any adult. This is quite amazing when one considers the matter. The differences among human beings are extraordinary within any given so-called race, to say nothing of across races. Yet, regardless of the pigmentation of a person's skin or the texture of person's hair or the bone structure of that individual's face, any generally happy infant will be most responsive to the warm interactions of an adult. No infant knows that it is white or black or yellow. None knows that it is African or Chinese or Arabic. What is more, from the standpoint of receiving love and attention, these things are quite irrelevant to it. That is why people of one ethnic background can adopt children of a different ethnic background, and all the love and affection in the world can develop between them. It is society that endows the aforementioned differences with great significance.

From an evolutionary perspective, that things are this way is hardly surprising. From the standpoint of physical features, the most salient difference between an infant and an adult is not skin color or hair texture or whatever, but sheer size and the concomitant differential in strength and power. (Recall Sigmund Freud here.) What is more, with recessive genes and the combination of genes from the mother and the father, the last thing that nature guarantees is that an infant will have the physical features of its parents. As a basis for the parent-child relationship, it is clear that nature would not warrant an infant putting much weight upon resemblance even if the infant could attend to these matters—which it cannot. So from an evolutionary point of view skin color and ethnicity are entirely irrelevant, which gives us what we may call equality by natural default. For all the fighting and animosity between groups, a most sobering truth is that any adult person of any ethnic kind can adopt an infant of another ethnic kind, and if they show that infant love and affection and provide it with the proper care and attention, then that infant will be most responsive to them. Indeed, it will love them in return. If the child should grow to be unsure of itself, to question its affection for its adoptive parents, it will only be because society or the community in which the child finds herself or himself has revealed its uneasiness with that young person's familial situation.

I call this *equality by natural default* because nature has not provided any arguments against the irrelevancy of skin color or hair texture or ethnicity or whatever in the parent-child relationship. Rather, in this regard, natural selection has simply not taken them into account. This is an utterly profound truth, however obvious it may be. Needless to say, the claim here is not that equality is natural by default in all respects, for that is surely false. But the point unequivocally holds in the context of the concerns of this essay, to which I now return. From the point of view of nature, it would be stunning if skin color, hair texture, and so on were utterly irrelevant in the case of parental love, but of enormous relevance in matters of friendship and romance.

The Rhetoric of Equality: Saying and Meaning

As we all know, people do not always say just what they mean. In fact, it is quite possible to mean the exact opposite of what one has literally said. Famously, whether the adjective *bad* is a compliment or a criticism depends on the context in which it is used. When said in the right way and context, "That was one bad performance last night" is the ultimate compliment. In all likelihood, the musicians had better be a group playing jazz rather than a string quartet playing Bach.

When most people say they believe in equality, what they actually mean is that they believe in ethnic equality only in the public sphere: ethnic preferences are thought to be out of order only when it comes to institutions that operate in the public sphere, such as schools, businesses, neighborhood housing, and so on. Even those who believe in affirmative action hold that in the ideal world ethnic preferences would have no weight in the public sector. By contrast, many people who are adamant about equality in the public sector hold that individuals are perfectly within their rights in marrying someone of their own ethnic kind and so privilege ethnicity as a matter of principle in the private sector. The thought seems to be that when it comes to matters of the heart, a person's preferences properly have sway unless, perhaps, one is about to marry an egregiously immoral person. So if an individual would only want to have romantic ties with or to marry a Purple (some ethnic group), then this individual does no moral wrong in so behaving.

In fact, some who relentlessly insist upon equality in the public sphere hold not only that it is morally permissible for a person to marry an individual of the same ethnic group, but that it is morally obligatory, so a person actually does what is morally wrong in marrying someone of a different ethnic group. There are blacks and whites who advance this stronger thesis. Some Christian religious groups have done so as well. Although I do not want to examine any of these arguments, I should point out that, strictly speaking, neither Islam nor Judaism nor Christianity should be understood as advocating the stronger thesis. Anyone of any ethnic group can be born into or become a member of any of these religious traditions. People who have allowed their preference for a marital partner of the Islamic or Judaic tradition to masquerade as a preference for a certain ethnic group do the religious tradition in question a grave disservice. Ideally, wanting to marry a Jew or a Muslim is more like wanting to marry a Christian (which does not readily associate the person with an ethnic group). This religious preference should not imply an ethnic preference. It is true enough in North America that when a white Jew asserts, "I want my child to marry only a Jew," a double-barrel assertion is often heard, namely "I want my child to marry only a Jew" and "I want my child to marry a white." But this double meaning has to do with certain aspects of North American Jewry, a discussion of which would take us beyond the purview of this essay.

At any rate, what is of interest to me is the fact that whereas preferences for ethnicity that are expressed in the public sphere are subject to considerable moral condemnation, such preferences in the private sphere are generally regarded as beyond substantial moral criticism. In the public sphere, it is not morally permissible to say that because Y is a Blue rather than a Purple, X will not be hired even though X is more qualified. Yet the parallel line of thought in the private sphere is morally acceptable. A person who is a Purple may concur that the Blue, say Leslie, is more intelligent than the Purple, that the Blue has a better moral character and is far more attractive than the Purple, and so on, without supposing that consistency, common sense, or moral considerations make it incumbent upon her or him to marry the Blue rather than the Purple. Indeed, the person may concede that were it not for the fact that Leslie is a Blue, then she or he would marry Leslie. To be sure, for any two ethnic groups, Purples and Blues, a person could surely find in either group an individual of similar qualities, whatever dimensions of qualities might be invoked. It would be one thing if a person of Purple ethnicity were to say, "I will not marry unless I can marry a Purple who displays the same brilliant qualities of so-and-so, who is a Blue." But to hear people tell it, what seems to be the case is that ethnicity may properly carry far more weight than personal qualities—so much so that, according to them, it would be better for a person to marry an individual of the same ethnicity but with obviously inferior qualities of mind, character, and physique than to marry someone of a different ethnicity but with far superior qualities along these dimensions. So, on this view, it is not just that it is morally permissible to have a preference for one's own ethnic kind. Rather, it is morally permissible to privilege one's own ethnic group as a matter of principle.

The above remarks should not be confused with a very different kind of consideration—namely, that love can be oblivious to many traits of qualities of intellect and so on. That seems true enough. We certainly have the right to marry the less attractive, less intelligent, less well organized person, but that is usually because the person "moves" us in some way. Contrary to all expectations, the person makes us feel good! Accordingly, what we would most certainly not say is that we would rather marry someone else but for the fact that they have or lack such-and-such quality. Indeed, one of the striking things about love is that when it gets a hold of us, lots of considerations that many think should matter seem not to matter—except, surprisingly, ethnicity. And that is my point. We even speak differently regarding this exception. In one instance, we say, "Although Leslie is not such-and-such, it is obvious that you truly love Leslie." In the other, we say, "It is obvious that you love Leslie, but (gasp! gasp!) Leslie is white or black or Asian." And so on. In the former case, the love is invoked as an explanation for how it is that one got past the fact that Leslie does not have such-and-such feature(s). In the latter case, the implicit question is, "How could you have let yourself become in love with Leslie given that Leslie is not a member of your ethnic group?" The equally implicit implication is that although it is understandable that love can be oblivious to a myriad of flaws, it is incomprehensible that love should be oblivious to ethnicity. Privileging ethnicity as a matter of principle is paradoxical in the sense that the idea seems to be that if a person is not of one's ethnic kind, then it cannot be appropriate to marry that person, even if she or he is otherwise right for one. Thus, the interethnic case is quite different from the case where the person with whom someone falls in love does not seem to have the sorts of features (ethnicity aside) so often deemed admirable in a marriage partner. In this latter case, we stop the complaints with the observation that the couple is happy together. In the interethnic case, even if it most apparent that the parties are happy together, the question seems to be: How *could* they be happy together even if they are happy together?

The only context where something analogous seems to hold with as much rigidity is in matters of royalty. Thus, Prince Charles could not have married a commoner or a nonvirgin and hold on to his claim to the throne, even if she were right for him in every way. Surely, so the idea goes, there was somebody of pedigree with whom he could find at least enough happiness. Together, these considerations show that privileging ethnicity as a matter of principle is not subsumable under the idea that people have a right to marry whom ever they please, so long as it makes them happy.

Now, when it comes to friendships as such, there is often the tendency to say that open-minded people will have friends from a variety of ethnic groups. Still, even in this regard, there is the strong feeling that individuals are perfectly within their right *to want* to form ties of friendship with only those individuals of a like ethnic background. Hence, the real problem that people have with skinheads, for instance, is the ideology that they embrace and not the skin color of the people with whom they prefer to associate. Once more, it is common enough among black people, certainly among black college students, to insist that blacks should form ties of friendship only with one another and not with whites or Asians. So with friendships, too, we have the view that it is morally permissible to privilege one's own ethnic kind as a matter of principle.

Let me acknowledge straightaway that whites (allowing only for the sake of argument that all whites belong to one ethnic group) are generally more vulnerable to the charge of racism for insisting upon marrying (or forming ties of friendship with) only whites than are blacks, Asians, and so on for insisting upon marrying only their ethnic kind. With regard to the issue under discussion, however, I hold that either we have an utter impropriety across the board, or we do not have one at all. If it is wrong for one ethnic group to privilege their kind as a matter of principle, then it is wrong for any and all ethnic groups to do so. Besides, the fact of the matter is that most whites marry whites, and it is the rare minority person who would insist that a white-white marriage is open to moral criticism on that account alone, although the minority person may have little or no reason to believe that the white person would have married any other ethnic kind.

It might be intoned here that when it comes to romance and marriage, precisely what people should be allowed to do is privilege their own ethnic kind because society has no business legislating such personal matters. True enough. Society should not legislate such matters. However, something can be quite wrong and yet not be properly subject to social legislation. If a child should become a multimillionaire as an adult, surely he should offer some assistance to his ailing parents who had been so loving and caring while raising him, but this decision is clearly a personal matter. All the same, not aiding his parents constitutes an egregious moral failing on his part, even though we should hardly want society to legislate that well-off children should care for their parents.

I am not about to suggest that society should legislate matters of friendship and romance. Such laws would be utterly incompatible with the cherished ideal of freedom of association between consenting adults. But having said this, it should be noted parenthetically that it was only thirty years ago, in 1967, that the U. S. Supreme Court (*Loving v. Virginia*, 388 U.S. 1 [1967]) struck down the ban on interracial marriages in the State of Virginia and, consequently, any such ban in the United States, the State of Virginia being one of sixteen states in 1967 prohibiting interracial marriages. The truth of the matter is that states do in fact legislate matters of the heart, claiming an invested interest in the survival of the family, which is why lesbian and gay marriages have not been legalized and why states felt entitled to prohibit interracial marriages. Whether having an invested interest in the survival of the family could ever justify legislating matters of the heart is beyond the purview of this essay.

The issue before us is whether there is a tension between, on the one hand, the ideal of equality in the public sphere and, on the other, the conviction that no wrong is done in privileging, in principle, our ethnic type in ties of romance and friendship. I argue that there is.

The Social Grammar of Cupid's Arrow

It is generally held that ties of romance and friendship are the most important ties in a person's life. Aristotle, for instance, famously wrote some two thousand years ago that a person without friendship had an incomplete life though she should possess all other goods in the world. Pushed to its apparent logical limit, Aristotle's thesis seems to be that it is better to be poor and otherwise without, but have a deep friendship, than to have all the wealth in the world and yet be without friends. This thesis and its apparent implication continue to strike a very responsive chord in our lives. Without at all challenging Aristotle's claim, many would hold that romantic ties are at their best only when the two partners are friends.

So if ties of romance and friendship are of such enormous importance, and we do no wrong in privileging, as a matter of principle, our own ethnic type in forming such ties, but it is impermissible to do so in the public sphere, then do we not have tension? Rhetorically, one might ask: How seriously can we be about equality in the public sphere if we believe that it is morally permissible to privilege our own ethnicity as a matter of principle in the private sphere and therefore in forms of social interaction regarded to be far more important—namely, ties of romance and friendship? Indeed, if ethnicity is allowed to be so terribly relevant in the private sphere when, instead, quality of character should certainly be the most relevant, how serious can we be about equality in the public sphere?

If the private sphere (where Aristotelian friendships would be located) is the most important aspect of a person's life, considerably more important than the public sphere, then to hold that it is morally permissible to privilege our own ethnicity in principle in the private sphere but not in the public sphere is to hold the following:

(a) Between the private and public spheres, we do no moral wrong in privileging our own ethnicity, as a matter of principle, in the sphere of social interaction that is of the greatest importance to us—namely, the private sphere.

Or, to put the point a different way:

(b) Between the private and public spheres, it is morally wrong to privilege our own ethnic type, in principle, only in that sphere of social interaction that is of the least importance—namely the public sphere.

Thus, our commitment to ethnic equality proves to be somewhat disingenuous. We judge that a person does no wrong at all in not being concerned with ethnic equality in the most important area of her or his life because we hold that equality matters only in the public sphere, which is less dear to our hearts. Let me repeat here that the issue before us is not whether society should legislate matters of friendship and romance. Surely it should not. But as I have already noted, the thesis that society should not legislate an action is perfectly compatible with a person being open to staunch moral criticism for failing to perform that action.

If it is so morally important that ideally we not see—that is, not give any weight to—ethnicity in the public sphere, what changes in the private sphere warrant the privileging of ethnicity? If from the moral point of view we should consider in the public sphere only the quality of a person's character and mind, then what is it about the private sphere that makes a person's ethnicity such a relevant factor? If love transcends all boundaries, then why are we so very conscious of ethnicity in matters of friendship and especially romance? There are no good answers to these questions that do not bespeak unjustified biases. Therefore, we must ask: Just how important can equality in the public sphere be to us, given that we privilege ethnicity in the private sphere, though by all accounts there are no good or justified reasons for doing so? The importance that we attach to ethnicity in the private sphere calls to mind the nonexistent substance that was referred to as *phlogiston*. We act as if there were surely a reason why ethnicity matters in the private sphere, though close scrutiny reveals that there is none.

It is in this context that we should be mindful of the distinction (owed to internet technology) between the virtual values of our ideological rhetoric and the real values that we transmit to our children. Our children learn both to parrot our virtual values and to imitate our real ones in their lives. What is frightening about skinheads is that their lives more closely reflect the real values of North American societies when it comes to marital matters than one would suppose given the virtual values of our idealized rhetoric.

At this juncture, I invite the reader to recall the biblical passage that reads: "Therefore shall a man leave his father and his mother, and shall cleave unto his wife; and they shall be one flesh" (Genesis 2:24). Far from being a digression, this passage is directly relevant to the argument that I am making. This passage reminds us that marital ties are formed when two biologically unrelated (or genetically distant) people join their lives together. The best source of biologically unrelated people is the public sphere.

So if it is morally permissible as a romantically uninvolved individual to privilege, in principle, her own ethnic kind in the private sphere, then to some extent it should be morally permissible to privilege, in principle, her ethnic kind in the public sphere. More poignantly, it should be morally permissible that the individual's ethnic kind has relevance in the public sphere because her potential romantic partner is most likely to come from the public sphere. Furthermore, this privileging of one's ethnic kind in principle gets played out derivatively: although X is already romantically involved, there are X's children or siblings or cousins, and X may privilege ethnic identity on their account in considering encounters in the public sphere that might give rise to a romantic tie. Or there are X's friends, who are of X's ethnic kind and for whom possible romantic ties constitute a reason to privilege X's ethnic kind in the public realm. (Of course, ethnic homogeneity does not follow from the existence of family ties; however, I leave this consideration aside.)

Suppose, then, that the Purples are the ethnic majority in a society and that Blues are a small ethnic minority struggling to achieve equality in that society. If Purples are allowed to privilege Purples in the private sphere, is it reasonable to suppose that when it comes to institutions in the public sphere Purples will choose between Purples and Blues without any biases whatsoever in favor of Purples? I think not. Consider a silly example. If Mary thinks that curly-haired people are the most sexually attractive, she is not going to cease thinking that when hiring someone for a position, given the continually borne out assumption that we prefer to be around sexually attractive people than people who have little or no sexual appeal. She may hire the curly-haired one because she thought that the person was more attentive to what she said, although the absolute truth of the matter is that it is she who was more attentive to the features of that person (who could be female or male).

If we privilege ethnic identity as a matter of principle in matters of romance and friendship, will we not get results that are analogous to the supposedly silly curly-haired example? So, to continue the previous example in which Purples are an ethnic majority, when a Purple executive is considering two candidates, a Purple and a Blue, will it not often turn out that to the executive, the Purple candidate will seem to have that ineffable "something special" that the executive is looking for in a management person, which the Blue candidate lacks, although the truth of the matter is simply that the executive found the Purple more appealing just because the person is a Purple?

The Purple candidate could indeed have that something special, but the executive notices it only because the executive paid more attention to the Purple person in the first place.

My contribution to the literature on equality is not the obvious upshot of these imaginary examples because their point is familiar enough. Rather, it is the thesis that such outcomes are unavoidable in a society where people are allowed to privilege, as a matter of principle, their ethnic kind in matters of romance and friendship. What is more, if both minority Blues and majority Purples embrace the principle that it is quite morally permissible to privilege one's ethnic kind in matters of romance and friendship, then the Blues themselves are an impediment in their very own struggle for equality.

In effect, what I have argued is that if we allow our ethnic kind to be privileged in the private sphere because matters of the heart are of considerable importance, then we have allowed ethnicity to have such a dominance in our lives that it is unreasonable to suppose that the ideal of ethnic equality can be realized in the public sphere. Now, values and their hierarchy are transmitted to our children and by our children to their children. I suggest that it is no accident that most of us have formed romantic ties with and most of our children will form romantic ties with persons of the same ethnic kind, for we continue to hold as morally permissible the privileging our own ethnic kind as a matter of principle. Likewise, I suggest that it is for precisely this reason that equality in the public sphere has remained no more than an ideal to which we continue to pay lip service rather than an ever present reality.

A final consideration here. Although ties of friendship and romance may be matters of the private sphere, these ties can be and in fact are the object of considerable public approval and disapproval. There can be stares of incredulity from strangers at the interracial couple or warm smiles of approval at the wife and husband walking along and holding the hand of the child between them. We can smile adoringly at the little black infant girl and the little white infant boy playing together and yet bristle at a married, adult representation of them passing by. And one naturally wonders: How deep can the commitment of a society's members be to public equality when they publicly and routinely endorse the privileging of ethnicity in the private sphere and frown with contempt upon all else?

Gender and Ethnicity

I should like to consider two objections that might be thought to reduce my argument to an absurdity. The first objection would suppose it to follow from what I have said that, as a matter of principle, persons should form ties of romance and friendship with persons who are not of their ethnic kind. Not so. What follows, rather, is that no ethnic kind should be privileged as a matter of principle. Therefore, on my account, the Purple who as a matter of principle will have romantic relations only with a Blue, and the Purple who as a matter of principle will have romantic relations only with a Purple are both problematic cases, albeit for somewhat different reasons. Love is simply too amorphous and complex a phenomenon for it to travel entirely along ethnic lines.

A stronger version of this objection would be that persons should not have any preferences at all, but nothing I have said implies such a thing. Indeed, it would be foolish to suppose that ties of romance and friendship are without preferences. Still, few things are more amorphous and complex than ties of romance and friendship. If we formed such ties only with persons who fit our fantasy images, then few ties of friendship and especially romance would ever be formed. Though people generally have preferences for this or that set of physical features, they often form ties of romance or even friendship with a person who does not exactly meet their fantasized ideal. So although Mary may prefer tall persons, it was that short wobbly Leslie who swept Mary off her feet. In this case, Mary's preference for tall persons does not privilege tallness as a matter of principle.

The second objection attempts a reductio by pointing out that when extended to sexual preferences, my argument entails that the in principle privileging of sexual orientation of any kind in the private sphere is also objectionable. But we might ask whether the extension is appropriate in the first place. For instance, suppose someone takes it to follow from my argument that a principled privileging of decent moral character is out of order. Surely, this conclusion would be a mistake. I have not argued that it is morally impermissible to privilege anything as a matter of principle. It most certainly is not morally impermissible to privilege as a matter of principle either good character or religious commitment.

Besides, the claim that it is wrong to privilege ethnicity as a matter of principle is entirely applicable to lesbian and gay relationships, yet no lesbian or gay person would suppose it to follow by analogy from this claim that it is also wrong for persons to privilege lesbian or gay preferences as a matter of principle. The following discussion sheds some light on why this is so.

Consider two claims:

1. Naomi says to Susan, "John is everything I ever wanted in a man, but he is a Purple [some ethnic kind]," and
2. Naomi says to Susan, "Leslie is everything I ever wanted in a sexual partner, but Leslie's gender is such-and-such,"

where (2) is not owing to

3. Naomi says to Susan, "I thought I was really attracted to one kind of gender, but my experience with Leslie has shown me otherwise."

My argument can be extended to sexual preferences only if claims (1) and (2) are parallel, and surely they are not. The first claim means something like Naomi found John to have the qualities of character that she wanted to find in a man, but the man does not belong to her preferred ethnic group. But what exactly does the second claim mean? That Naomi's sexual encounter with Leslie was what she had dreamed of, longed for, but, alas, it turns out that Leslie is a woman? Or a man? This statement may not make any sense because it is not at all clear that we can even speak of sexual satisfaction with another person independently of whether that person is female or male. Although males and females can do similar things, there is considerable divergence. What we fantasize about touching and doing to the other and having the other touch and do to us is not independent of the body parts that the person in our fantasy has. Thus, if Naomi's sexual fantasies genuinely involve a male (female), then a female (male) encounter will not even begin to approach the emotional take of her fantasies, which is why it is difficult to make sense of (2). The issue here is not whether people can be mistaken about the character of their sexual orientation. Surely they can be. Nor is it whether people are more fluid in their sexual orientation than perhaps they would like to believe. Undoubtedly they are. Rather, the issue is whether our ethnic preferences and our sexual orientation are properly viewed as parallel to one another and therefore whether an argument that privileging one's own ethnicity as matter of principle is problematic from the moral point of view can be extended to privileging one's sexual orientation as a matter of principle. It would seem that the two are not parallel to one another; for (2) is not owing to (3).

What is more, it is a matter of historical record that privileging sexual orientation as a matter of principle in the private sphere does not play itself out in the same way that similarly privileging ethnic kind in the private sphere does. Privileging heterosexual orientation has hardly meant equality for women. Quite the contrary, it is utterly astonishing just how much effort heterosexual men have put into forming and maintaining institutions and associations that ensured only male-male interaction. By contrast, privileging ethnic kind as a matter or principle in the private sphere generally results in favoring that ethnic kind over other ethnic kinds in the public sphere. The considerations in this and the preceding two paragraphs suffice to show that although there are indeed apt parallels, the fact remains that sexual orientation and ethnic preferences are fundamentally different personal and social phenomena. Together, these considerations suggest that the second objection fails because it is inappropriate to extend the argument regarding ethnic preferences to preferences for sexual orientation.

Lest there be any misunderstanding, I am hardly intimating that there should not be equality in the public sphere with respect to sexual orientation. On the other hand, I am supposing that because sexual orientation is different in fundamental ways, not spelled out in this essay, from preferences for an ethnic kind, then a distinction between the private and the public in the area of sexual orientation is a tenable one. After all, the argument of this essay is not that this distinction itself is without merit on all accounts. Presumably, it is one thing for couples of whatever composition to hold hands in public, and quite another for them to copulate in public. The bifurcation is a problem in considerations of ethnicity if ethnic type is properly deemed irrelevant on all accounts, but it is not a problem in considerations of sexual orientation. I argued in the first section that from an evolutionary perspective, skin color is simply irrelevant to the flourishing of the species. Parts of that argument do not—indeed, they could not—show that sexual orientation is irrelevant to the flourishing of the species, as gay and lesbian couples do not reproduce. Yet, with other parts of that argument, being lesbian or gay is utterly irrelevant, for just as the child takes no interest in the skin color or hair texture of those who love it or whether the parents be biological or surrogate, she also takes no interest in the sexual orientation of those who love her, except insofar as society makes this a salient factor for her.

Conclusion: Means-Ends

Although I am not a Kantian in my general moral outlook, I do accept the view that if we truly will a certain end that is within our reach, then we will the means for achieving that end (provided that we are adequately informed concerning both ends and means). Thus, by drawing attention to our abiding conviction that it is morally permissible to privilege, as a matter of principle, our own ethnic kind in the private sphere, I have tried to show that we are not as committed to willing the end of public equality as we profess to be, and therein lies the reason why equality in the public sphere remains so elusive, notwithstanding all that lip service paid to it.[2]

IO "Race" and the Labor of Identity

The description of racial identity as a "social construction" typically is offered as a challenge to the view that race is a biological feature (or a set of such features) present in every human being at birth and in virtue of which groups of humans are distinguishable from one another. On the social constructionist view, racial identity is not something one has in virtue of possessing some distinct and demarcated biological trait, but something one possesses in virtue of being subject to a process of racialization, a branding—a "representational process whereby social significance is attached to certain biological (usually phenotypical) human features, on the basis of which those people possessing those characteristics are designated as a distinct collectivity" (Robert Miles, *Racism*, 71). The meaning of the various racial identities and the criteria for ascribing them to people are dictated not by what is discovered to be true about the constitution of human beings, but by the need or desire to sort humans for certain social and political ends, to make them markable for certain kinds of treatment and not others. Howard Winant has pointed to ways in which the social construction of racial categories is revealed in their being subject to "reconstitution" or to "constant rearticulation and reformulation . . . in respect to the changing historical contexts in which they are invoked" (*Racial Conditions: Politics, Theory, and Comparison*, 18, 115).

The term *social construction* suggests something that humans make and that by its very nature needs maintenance and repair—Winant's "re-constitution," "rearticulation," and "reformation" suggest—requires renovation, remodeling, refurbishing. (Toni Morrison recently has referred to the "struts and bolts" keeping up "The House that Race Built" ["Home," 11].) That such a construction is not literally a building, not something we can drive nails into or put on the market to sell, does not mean it is any less a product of human labor than they are, though our by now sometimes facile use of the notion of social construction tends to obscure that fact. In this brief essay, I explore some aspects of the labor it takes to construct and maintain racial identities as part of the social fabric of life in the United States (and elsewhere, too, but the focus here will be on the United State). As a partial but very provocative set of reflections on relations between whites and blacks suggests, a pernicious form of labor is exacted from blacks in order to keep that fabric from being rent. Although such work is also exacted from other nonwhite groups, in this brief space the task of exploring and exposing the nature of this work is better served by examining ways in which the demands for such labor have been made on one group in particular in a variety of contexts.

I

Historically, a not uncommon experience of blacks in the United States has been the demand that they acknowledge whiteness as being by its very nature superior to blackness. As writers such as James Baldwin and Judith Rollins remind us, this particular construction of the meaning of white and black racial identities remains alive and well into the latter part of the twentieth century. Both Baldwin and Rollins offer detailed descriptions of the labor it takes to keep this piece of the social fabric from falling into disrepair.

Drawing from both his sense of the history of race relations in the United States and the details of his own life, Baldwin suggests in *The Fire Next Time* that whatever changes in the meaning of whiteness there may have been historically, many whites have understood being white as not only distinct from but also superior to being black. Central to such whites' sense of themselves as white is the certainty that they "are in possession of some intrinsic value that black people need, or want" (127)—"intrinsic" in the sense that "God decreed it so" (40). But as Baldwin sees it, such certainty only thinly covers a kind of fear: for most whites in the United States, he claims, recognition of blacks as anything but inferior to whites is not possible on pain of "loss of their identity," an "upheaval in the universe" in which "heaven and earth are shaken to their foundations" (20). (Baldwin does not in any way suggest that this fear in whites depends on their socioeconomic status.) To try to ward off such an upheaval, whites build into the very meaning of whiteness—and thus also of blackness—what they fear may turn out to be false about whites and blacks. They make the matter of white superiority something about which no evidence can be probative either way. If whites are by their very nature superior, blacks by their very nature inferior ("God decreed it"), then these are not matters for proof or disproof. The white inability to recognize blacks as human beings (101) is something entirely different from an inability or failure to gather the appropriate evidence. Indeed, in warning non-Muslim blacks about the folly of becoming as committed to black superiority as whites are to white superiority, Baldwin comments on how this kind of belief functions: "I suddenly had a glimpse of what white people must go through at a dinner table when they are trying to prove that Negroes are not subhuman" (100). At the same time, he points out that even what appears to be the assertion of fundamental equality in fact "overwhelmingly corroborates the white man's sense of his own value" (127): "It is the Negro, of course, who is presumed to have become equal" (127).[1] What such an affirmation from whites means is, "You blacks are just as human as we are!"

Baldwin suggests that the idea that whites are by their very nature superior to blacks is not the result of deep metaphysical understanding of natural kinds or of careful attention to the empirical facts, but the product of anxiety and self-delusion.[2] It functions to provide immunity from the possible onslaught of argument and evidence. Baldwin counsels his nephew that what whites believe about blacks, "as well as what they do and cause you to endure, does not testify to your inferiority but to their inhumanity and fear" (19)—fear that without such a guarantee of superiority, they will lose their identity.

The claim to innate white superiority, then, according to Baldwin, fails to command the acknowledgment and respect of those it is meant to cow into submission. The effort to secure independently of argument and evidence precisely what is feared can be taken away by argument and evidence is all too transparent. Moreover, the idea that whites are innately superior to blacks is treated by blacks such as Baldwin not as evidence of white superiority, but on the contrary as an invitation to pity those who embrace it. White people lack self-understanding; they "have had to believe for many years, and for innumerable reasons, that black men are inferior to white men" (19–20). In presuming that they have by nature a value that they are in a position to withhold or to grant to blacks, whites are depending on a value that "can scarcely be corroborated in any other way; there is certainly little enough in the white man's public or private life that one should desire to imitate" (127–28). Indeed, according to Baldwin, blacks in general have tended "to dismiss white people as the slightly mad victims of their own brainwashing" (137). At the same time blacks are fully aware that they cannot render such a dismissal with impunity in their everyday interactions with whites.

On several occasions in The Fire Next Time, Baldwin underscores his feeling of pity for whites rather than hatred of them. Given blacks' knowledge of whites, which Baldwin likens to the knowledge parents have of children (136), blacks should love whites rather than despise them. Baldwin believes that "it demands great spiritual resilience not to hate the hater whose foot is on your neck, and an even greater miracle of perception and charity not to teach your child to hate" (134). But blacks should love rather than hate not only because hatred toward whites simply reiterates white failures of humanity ("Whoever debases others is debasing himself" [113]), but also because whites desperately need the kind of love that "takes off the masks that we fear we cannot live without and know we cannot live within" (128). And because blacks will continue to be endangered as long as whites must live by the delusion of their superiority, "we, with love, shall force our brothers to see themselves as they are, to cease fleeing from reality and begin to change it" (21). Only this kind of love from blacks can free whites from their destructive anxiety, and until whites are free in this way, blacks cannot be free either (Baldwin here of course is nicely inverting the common phrase from the sixties about how no one is free until everyone is free, which was widely taken to mean that whites can't really be free unless blacks are).

In providing such counsel and direction to other blacks, Baldwin drives a stake into the heart of the idea of innate white superiority even while noting the ways in which blacks are supposed to affirm it (e.g., by greeting proclamations of equality with pleasure and gratitude). It is a notion forged of a desperate attempt to secure conceptually what it lacks empirically; it invites, indeed demands, a response of pity rather than worship or envy or desire to "be equal" to such "superior" beings; and the only solution, or anyway the best solution, to the problem of whites thinking they are by nature superior to blacks is for them to become subject to the ministrations of blacks' love—a love that does not leave whites as they are, but leads them into self-understanding and freedom from fear. The idea of innate white superiority is clear evidence of a kind of madness that can best be cured by those "inferior" blacks who have borne the brunt of such madness.

As James Baldwin sees it, then, the idea of innate white superiority is in several senses quite a piece of work. When he suggests that it would take a labor of love on the part of blacks to begin to unravel this piece of the U.S. social fabric, he is in effect urging blacks to engage in a different kind of labor than that exacted from them for centuries to keep it from unraveling. The nature of the latter kind of labor is illuminated in Judith Rollins's *Between Women: Domestics and Their Employers.*

In the early 1980s, Rollins completed a close study of the kind of work expected of black female domestics by their white female employers. In many cases, the black employees do not just clean house; intricately tied to the more obvious tasks they perform are required patterns of behavior and modes of appearance geared to attesting to the inequality of employer and domestic. The inequality the white employers want confirmed is not simply the delimited relative power of employer over employee in an unregulated and unprotected part of the labor market. What is supposed to be affirmed is an innate inequality (198), a distinction between persons of superior and persons of inferior human worth (203), of which the work relation is only a reflection. Though this inequality allegedly exists independently of any actual work arrangements, employers go out of their way to ensure that everything in the relation between employer and employee is to announce and reinforce this distinction in human worth (157, 162, 173, 180, 193, 194, 203).

In particular, the employers implicitly demand behavior on the part of their employees that expresses the employees' beliefs in their own natural inferiority and in their employers' natural superiority. Such arrangements can of course be used to try to reflect and reinforce notions of superiority and inferiority based on something other than race, as Rollins acknowledges and as workers in the service industry continue to attest.[3] But Rollins found that many white employers preferred dark-skinned (in her sample, black) over white domestic workers precisely in order to punctuate visually the difference between employer and employee.[4]

Focusing more finely on the nature of the superiority supposedly inherent in whiteness, Rollins enables us to see why insistence on its confirmation is so bizarre. Strictly speaking, there is nothing self-contradictory about the notion of something with which one is born and yet of which one needs confirmation. For example, someone might be born with a congenital disease, but she may not automatically be aware of it and for a variety of reasons may want to know whether she has it; for example, the availability of certain kinds of insurance may turn on confirmation or disconfirmation of such a condition. Similarly, we might wonder whether a property is inherent in something and come to confirm that it is—for example, the insolubility of copper.

Rollins clarifies how the superiority said to inhere in whiteness is not anything like a discovery after the fact. When Rollins refers to the apparently never satisfied need of the white employer to confirm the relative positions of white employer and black employee, she is alerting us to the fact that if there is anything to be empirically confirmed rather than simply agreed to on demand, it is not the existence of innate differences between white and black, but the power of the employer to arrange relations between them in such a way as to preclude the very possibility of empirical disconfirmation. Everything in the behavior or attire demanded of the employee as a condition of continued employment is geared to underscore the alleged inequality of white and black. The kind of confirmation referred to in the examples in the preceding paragraph (finding out whether one has a congenital condition or whether copper is insoluble) is one in which it is an open question whether someone or something has a particular property. The kind of confirmation Rollins is talking about (here echoing Baldwin) is one about which there cannot possibly be such a question. It precludes confirmation in the empirical sense and demands confirmation in the sense of affirmation, agreement, or at the very least no obvious disagreement. What is demanded is not empirical proof that whites are superior specimens of humanity, but proof that black domestics believe this about whites.

Rollins helps us, then, to unravel several bizarre aspects to the notion of innate white superiority: (1) The kind of confirmation of white superiority exacted from black employees in social interactions with their white employers attests to the employers' unwillingness to countenance confirmation or disconfirmation of a more empirical nature. Indeed, the conditions of employment are geared to preclude the possibility of disconfirmation: "The domestic's 'place' is below her employer in every way (except, of course, in her capacity for prolonged physical labor). Any hint of competition with the employer must be avoided by the domestic's being clearly non-threatening in all ways, including her physical attractiveness" (201). Not only must there be no competition, no hint of the employee having capacities or relationships that suggest something other than her innate inferiority to her white employer, but there must also be no sign that she disagrees with the employer's assessment of their relative worth as human beings. The employees Rollins interviewed had no doubt about the importance of their appearing to share the employers' beliefs about white superiority and black inferiority (164), but equally no doubt that such beliefs were false. Their apparent acquiescence is the price they must pay to get and keep their jobs (189–90). (As Ellis Cose recently highlighted in *The Race of a Privileged Class*, black lawyers, journalists, and other professionals are also expected to keep the warp and woof of white superiority from being damaged. Such expectation, of course, does not show up as part of their job description, but as an implicit condition of employment.[5])

(2) Because the kind of confirmation in question depends on what the black employees say and how they act, the white superiority being confirmed depends upon what is believed about whites by the very people those whites deem to be their inferiors. (3) Although the ability to exact such confirmation from blacks attests to the power of whites, its exercise reveals the very vulnerability it pretends not to have: it is power to get people to agree with you not because they believe what you say, but because it is too costly for them to disagree openly. (In this connection, no wonder Baldwin speaks about self-delusion: I know I have to make you agree, but I also take this agreement as a genuine expression of your belief.) (4) The nature of the confirmation of whites' belief in superiority suggests how ungrounded the belief is: it isn't really confirmation, but simply acclamation on demand.

II

Judith Rollins's analysis, like James Baldwin's, invites us to think seriously about the maintenance of the idea of white superiority and black inferiority as a kind of labor. The deference required of the black employees is not simply a condition of their employment as house cleaners. It is part of the larger sustained effort it takes to keep afloat the notions of innate white superiority and black inferiority—joint notions that have long been a piece of the social fabric of U.S. society. Because of that fabric, the whites Baldwin describes fear the overturning or the rending asunder of the world as they know it at the suggestion that whiteness does not carry with it any innate superiority to blackness. Not all parts of the social fabric are fabrications in the pejorative sense of being lying contrivances, but the notion of the innate superiority of whites and the innate inferiority of blacks surely is. Baldwin, no less than Rollins, reminds us of the labor of lies it takes to maintain this notion, and he insists that it would take the labor of love to undo it.

The words *work* and *labor* should not be understood as only metaphors here, though some common metaphors help us to understand the nature of this work. Think for example of the metaphor deployed in the idea—and a very common idea it is—of "the social fabric." The social fabric of our lives is not something that exists "in nature," independently of human beliefs, attitudes, behavior, language, gesture, and the many institutions that frame human interactions and survive the birth and death of particular human agents. Indeed, the metaphor suggests that we are bound together by something that we make, that needs maintenance, can be torn apart, and is subject to repair. That this fabric of our making is not literally a piece of cloth, not something we can hold in our hands or see on shelves in a shop, does not mean that it is not a product of human labor.

Baldwin and Rollins have brought to our attention a social construction (a metaphor with which we began) that—as attested to by the different historical and interpersonal contexts of which they write—continues to be part of the social fabric of U.S. society: the idea that there are distinct "races"— they have focused on white and black—and that one is by its very nature superior to the other as a specimen of humanity. Indeed, in the works of W. E. B. Du Bois, David Roediger, Noel Ignatiev, and others, we can see how the alleged intrinsic superiority of being white has promised a refuge against the ravages of indignity brought on by attenuation of political freedom or the loss of acceptable work: whiteness attests to a kind of superiority as a human being that is impervious to the contingency of changes in economic, social, or political status.[6] At the same time, this superiority seems desperately in need of affirmation; in particular, as suggested by Baldwin's claim that "the power of the white world is threatened whenever a black man refuses to accept the white world's definition" (*The Fire Next Time*, 95), it requires affirmation from the allegedly inferior group. What kind of work does it take to keep this piece of the U.S. social fabric from being rent?

It is important here to distinguish this question from the questions broached in the rich literature on the distribution of jobs along racial lines. As is well known, one of the many functions of the notion of race has been to lubricate the conflation of the division of labor and the segmentation of the workforce: as job distribution in the United States and most elsewhere continues to show, the idea that there are different kinds of work matches up ever so nicely with the idea that there are different kinds of people and that they ought to do different kinds of work. For example, in the 1990s, white men are twice as likely as black men to be employed in managerial, administrative, or professional jobs, whereas black men are twice as likely as white men to be found in the service sector (William O'Hare et al., "African Americans in the 1990's," 52). Indeed, among the lessons from Judith Rollins's book is the continued push toward racial earmarking of domestic labor.

The focus of this essay, however, is not the distribution of labor along racial lines, but rather the labor it takes to sustain a certain version of racial difference. What shall we call the labor it takes to construct, reproduce, and maintain the idea of distinct white and black racial identities and the natural superiority of one to the other?

One promising resource for spelling out the nature of such work comes from the growing body of literature on several forms of labor closely related to the kind in question. I am thinking in particular about the provision of services, about what has come to be called *shadow work*, and about the complex labor of social reproduction.

It is a commonplace in the 1990s to point to the expanding proportion of paid jobs around the globe that are not in agriculture, government, or the production of goods, but in the service sector—"jobs in which face-to-face or voice-to-voice interaction is a fundamental element of the work" (Cameron Lynne Macdonald and Carmen Sirianni, "The Service Society and the Changing Experience of Work," 3). Familiar examples are order takers at fast-food restaurants, managers in delivery companies, secretaries, telemarketers—where the labor in question "no longer entails the assembly of a product but the creation and maintenance of a relationship" (MacDonald and Sirianni, "The Service Society," 5). Though such service is not palpable or tangible in the same way the production of goods is, it is recognized as work.

The term *shadow work* appears to have been coined by Ivan Illich in a book by that name to refer to work that is not recognized as being part of the economy, even thought it is necessary to that economy (housework is his prime example). The term has come to be used more generally to designate work of any kind in any sector that is unpaid and usually invisible in part because of the terminology used in the labor market and the ways in which productivity is measured.[7] There are shadow aspects to many forms of service work. For example, as Rollins and others have pointed out, domestic workers often are expected to look and act in ways that prop up the ego and identity of their employers. Highly visible secretaries typically have to perform the not-so-visible (i.e., not-to-be-noted) functions of buffers and general smoother-overs. (see Susan Eaton, "'The Customer Is Always Interesting': Unionized Harvard Clericals Renegotiate Work Relationships"). Like so much of the shadow work done at home, shadow work at the workplace is most noticeable when it is absent, even though when present it is not acknowledged as a recognizable part of the economy. Workers are not paid for it, but evaluations of their suitability for the job are likely to be highly influenced by judgments about how well they perform such functions.[8]

The work of social reproduction is "the creation and recreation of people as cultural and social, as well as physical, beings" (Evelyn Nakano Glenn, "From Servitude to Service Work: Historical Communities in the Racial Division of Paid Reproductive Labor," 117). It includes labor such as making sure food is on the table, providing and taking care of clothing and shelter, bringing up children, acculturating them, keeping relationships going (indeed, the love Baldwin says whites need from blacks is a kind of social reproductive work). It isn't necessarily work that is invisible and unpaid— food preparation can be waged or unwaged work in the household or waged work in a restaurant—though often it is, as for example in the socialization of children by adults or in the maintenance of ties with neighbors or merchants. Some aspects of social reproductive labor having to do with creating and maintaining relationships (and teaching others how to have them) are coming out of the shadows both at home and at the workplace.

Most of the literature about service, shadow, and reproductive labor focuses on the workplace and the home. Although the social fabric of which Baldwin and Rollins speak is woven into both workplace and home, it is not confined to those locations. The social fabric woven to guarantee innate white superiority is stronger than the microfabrics within the world of work or of home: even if one's superiority is not attested to in those places, one can somehow find refuge in one's whiteness. That is, the labor necessary for keeping afloat the notions of innate white superiority and black inferiority is also done, has to be done, outside what ordinarily counts as the workplace or the home. At the same time, Rollins describes the kind of shadow work within the workplace that helps to keep the larger social fabric from being rent. To the extent that the domestic worker is supposed to perform certain tasks and equally if not more importantly to "shore up her employer's sense of superiority by not reminding her of her reliance upon the worker," [9] what she is doing not only happens to be, but must also remain invisible (Cameron Lynne Macdonald, "Shadow Mothers: Nannies, Au Pairs, and Invisible Work," 250). It would defeat the purpose of attesting to the superiority of the employer were it an acknowledged and officially paid for part of the employee's job to provide such affirmation. Black domestic workers are not paid for making sure this piece of the social fabric is not rent, but they are not paid unless they do the work of making sure it is not.

The kind of labor it takes to sustain the idea of innate white superiority appears to be like service work in several ways: it involves maintenance of relationships, not the production of objects; the relationships in question are not friendships or marriages or even formal contracts, but they proceed in accordance with certain protocols developed by one party to be followed by the other. However, unlike service work, this labor is unpaid and typically is exacted of people as a condition of paid labor in the service or other sectors.

This labor of racial identity also has elements of social reproductive work: it canindeed, mustbe found outside the workplace as well as inside it; what it reproduces is not bodies but ways of coding bodies as embodiments of natural types of humans: those superior by nature and those inferior by nature.

It is by its very nature shadow work: this work cannot be recognized as such, for the notion of innate white superiority cannot be sustained by a relationship if it is acknowledged that the point of the relationship is to create and maintain the notion.

So we can describe the work exacted of blacks to shore up the notion of innate white superiority as a kind of social reproductive shadow work.[10]

III

I have suggested a couple of approaches to making the case that we should regard what it takes to sustain the notion of innate white superiority and black inferiority as a kind of work. The first flows from thinking through the implications of the powerful metaphors of social fabric and social construction: the ideas and values in terms of which people are related are themselves the work of human creation, maintenance and repair (and thus also subject to resistance and destruction). The second approach relies on taxonomies of work detailed in recent nuanced studies of labor suggest that the work that goes into keeping afloat the idea of innate white superiority is a form of social reproductive shadow labor. I want now to suggest a third way of trying to capture and articulate the nature of such work.

Let's imagine for a moment what a job description would look like for the kind of work required of blacks to keep the notion of innate white superiority from being rent. The analyses of Baldwin and Rollins lead to a description along these lines:

NEEDED: Dark-skinned people to be identified as belonging to a group basically different from and innately inferior as human beings to white-skinned people. Must be willing to affirm or at least not deny such differences and to do so often enough to prevent any possible cracks in the picture of innate white superiority. Invisible menders especially welcome (i.e., those individuals who fix the rips that do appear in the racialized social fabric so that it looks as if they never had needed repair—indeed, as if they are not the kinds of things that are reparable or irreparable).[11] This is a high maintenance relationship.[12] Location: everywhere. Pay: no pay for this work, but doing it a prerequisite for other jobs. Special qualifications: when answering this ad, make sure you act as if you never saw it.

(One way to compare demands implicitly made on blacks with those made on Latinos, Chicanos, Chinese Americans and others is to imagine the details of such job descriptions for each group.)

What has stood in the way of being able to describe the notion of innate white superiority as the product of a kind of labor, and what is to be gained by doing so?

Several reasons why this labor would not immediately be noted as such have to do with the notion of social construction. The very familiarity of the phrase may make us disinclined to think about how much social constructions share in common with physical constructions, which we know need work: they are built, are subject to decay, and typically need maintenance and repair. A tendency to focus on the power and authority of scientific and legal institutions to define the meaning of the term *race* may keep us from looking at what is exacted of those conscripted to live out and give everyday content to such meanings. And the concept of shadow work may be a much needed reminder that in many contexts, social constructionsespecially those having to do with senses of individual or group identitywill collapse under their own weight if they are acknowledged as such.

Finally, what is to be gained by thinking about the idea of innate white superiority as something that requires labor?

(a) First of all, it invites us to ask what the investment might be in obscuring the need for and functioning of such labor. The recent literature on shadow work is quite instructive in this regard: it encourages us, for example, to wonder who gains from making it difficult to understand and appropriately value certain dimensions of clerical work [13] or to ask who gains from ignoring the function of housework in an economy that doesn't formally recognize it as work (Illich, *Shadow Work*, 1). So, too, we can ask: who has what to gain from the failure to recognize or acknowledge the complex work of construction, maintenance, and repair required for that part of the social fabric into which the notion of innate white superiority is so tightly woven?

(b) In the hands of writers such as Baldwin and Rollins, we get to see the scaffolding that props up the never fully secured house of innate white superiority and the perverse ludicrousness of the construction. Having a sense of what it takes to sustain such scaffolding also offers a horrifying reminder of the burdens placed on those doing the work: the idea of innate white superiority and black inferiority is demeaning and degrading to blacks.[14] But the toll such an idea takes begins to show in fuller dimension when we see that it requires a kind of work on the part of blacks to sustain it: the house of innate white superiority threatens to topple in the absence of apparent black affirmation of it. That blacks are supposed to do work necessary to the maintenance and repair of innate white superiority is underscored by the massive resentment of and resistance to such demands. To exact such labor is like requiring someone to provide the kind of self-incriminating evidence that it is the business of the Fifth Amendment of the U.S. Constitution to prohibit.

(c) If maintaining the idea of innate white superiority and black inferiority is work, is there an accompanying economy in which it functions? Yes, a racial economy. In such an economy, there are different racial denominations, the values of which depend upon and always are relative to the values of the others (i.e., none has any value except relatively to the others). Some of the currency is white, and some of it is black.[15] To be white is to be the bearer of white currency, which by definition, by denomination, is worth more than black currency. (Because this racial economy exists in order to provide meaning for being white, to be black in its terms is to be the bearer of the devalued black currency; this racial economy has room for black identity only as a foil for white identity, not as anything that might be created more independently of the notion of higher-valued whiteness). You cannot use the social tender of white currency if you are black, for that would destroy the value of white currency. That is why it is so important for there to be—or rather for there to be thought to be—strict distinctions between the races: knowing which denomination is being used depends on knowing who is using it. That is also why under long-standing and still current political and social conditions, whites are born with a kind of racial capital blacks cannot possibly accumulate. As Cheryl Harris has argued, whiteness is something the ownership of which would become worthless were anyone able to acquire it ("Whiteness as Property").[16]

White highjackings of black currency fuel many dimensions of the economy in the larger sense—for example, in the entertainment and advertising industries—but black highjackings of white currency are rare. Indeed, the examples provided by Baldwin and Rollins point precisely to ways in which erosions of the distinction between white and black currency are prevented: whites do everything they can to keep the distinction between white and black clear and well defined.[17] But that is not quite accurate, for whites are also careful to ensure there's a difference between white highjackings of black currency and the dissolution of the distinction between white currency and black currency. Lucrative appropriations of black identity by whites are always partial in the sense that they count on audiences knowing that what is being offered is not black people or black experience, but a white version of something identified as black (an interesting reverse twist on treating blacks as black versions of white). In short, if Elvis had been black, he wouldn't have been Elvis, and his success depended on his audience's recognition of that fact.

Baldwin and Rollins provide rich descriptions of the rather desperate need of whites to have their whiteness and thereby their innate superiority affirmed. When we think about the workings of the racial economy we can see that such desperation expresses not only a psychological need to feel superior to others in order to have a sense of one's own identity and worth, but a desire to make sure one's racial endowment does not lose its value—not an irrational desire in those wishing to maximize the return on their investment in being white. It is not enough to have an economy in the ordinary sense and a workplace in the ordinary sense reflect and reinforce the notion of white superiority. The very meaning of being white or being black has to incorporate the idea of white superiority and black inferiority, for the currency must have value in every exchange in order to have value in any exchange: How valuable can it be if you are white in all situations, but it counts only in some? And—thinking about the power of James Baldwin's mockery of what he finds whites have to believe about blacks—how valuable can being white be if those you deem your natural inferiors don't want to be white and, in fact, come to pity people so desperate and deluded as to treat their whiteness as proof of innate superiority?

In the context of the kind of racial economy described by Baldwin and Rollins, whiteness is an *investment*—both in the archaic sense of a garment or outer layer and in the sense of something that promises returns. Indeed, putting the two senses together, whiteness is an investment in an investment. Investments (in the nonarchaic sense) depend upon goods maintaining or increasing in value. There is no point in being white unless in being tendered in the racial economy it can be recognized and bring rewards, including the refuge it promises when otherwise the chips are down. Blacks cannot benefit from this economy but are conscripted to do the work central to it both by embodying an identity necessary to the creation and meaning of white identity and by being in relationships with whites that are constructed to carry out the Sisyphean task of affirming innate white superiority (quite literally a form of affirmative action, the action of affirmation). What Du Bois and most recently David Roediger have called the *wages of whiteness*—the privileges of being white or what I have referred to above as *white currency*—are the product of a highly exploitative form of social reproductive shadow work exacted of blacks.

To the extent that the racial economy prevails, the bearer of white currency has a built-in advantage over the bearer of black currency. So one way to gauge how thoroughly woven the racial economy is into the social fabric at any given time is to ask the following questions: Are blacks mistaken in thinking that (in the context of the larger society) if being black can't be made to count positively, it will count negatively? Are whites who wish to benefit from the sheer fact of their whiteness being illogical if they fear that (in the larger society) unless being black continues to count negatively, being white cannot continue to count positively? Careful answers to such questions have to be part of any assessment of affirmative action initiatives and hate speech regulations.

Finally and even more briefly: I have suggested that there is nothing more to white identity than the currency it has, the currency it *is*, in the racial economy.[18] As mentioned earlier, this does not of course mean that all there could possibly be to black identity is its denominational value in the racial economy. How struggles or debates among blacks over the meaning of black identity turn out will have profound implications for the question of whether any denominalization by "race" entails the kind of currency that constitutes what I have called the racial economy. If white identity in the context of racial economy requires labor of a deeply exploitative and degrading kind from blacks, then perhaps one test of any claim to "racial" identity is whether it, too, requires such labor from other "racial" groups.[19]

I I *Dominant Identities and Settled Expectations*

SUE CAMPBELL

What theories of the self and what kinds of self-understandings are necessary to ground and sustain practices that require deep self and social change? In this essay, I test the adequacy of contemporary views of personal identity and personal transformation in addressing the moral necessity that white people become antiracist. Many contemporary theorists have claimed that to engage in liberatory political practices and theory, we must give up a view of the self as unified and celebrate the transformative possibilities of viewing the self as shifting, multiple, and capable of liminal perspectives. I am cautious of how well models of a multiple self apply to those privileged by current social arrangements. I believe that we need models of change that also extend explicitly to the important place of settled expectations in the constitution of socially dominant identities.[1]

Although expectations are rarely explicitly theorized in philosophical psychology, our expectations order our experience. Prejudice has been characterized as a "'stabilized deception of perception' that selectively edits out differences threatening to one's identity" (Patricia Huntington, "Fragmentation, Race and Gender: Building Solidarity in the Postmodern Era," 201). I argue that expectations guide this editing and contribute toward the often uniform and restricted perspectives of the socially dominant. Moreover, the need to forefront the expectations of dominant identities especially depends very much on the nature of expectations that, when easily met, become psychic habits that are unselfconscious and thus protected from self-scrutiny.

In the first section, I critically examine contemporary models of identity change, particularly models of multiple self offered by Sandra Harding and Maria Lugones. In the second section, I elaborate an account of settled expectations as deeply important to an understanding of a socially dominant self. Expectations explain what it is to have a perceptual standpoint. They ground emergence of norms and, when frustrated, lead to emotional responses antithetical to change. In the third section, I examine the writing of southern author and activist Minnie Bruce Pratt in order to display her self-conscious confrontation with her own settled expectations in her struggle to become antiracist.

Models of Identity Change

In post-Lockean writings on personal identity by philosophers such as Derek Parfit, David Lewis, and a host of others, the self is typically presented as individuated independently of its social context. Personal identity theorists approach notions of psychological continuity and change through questions about what makes a person one and the same person over time.[2] In the absence of attention to a person's environment and relations, these theorists propose that a person's self-continuity and psychological stability reside mainly in the degree to which her present psychological states resemble her past psychological states. What makes me the same person over time is the sameness of my perception—the continuance of beliefs, desires, values, and traits of character—but primarily the resemblance of my memories to each other and to my past experience.

The reidentification framework used by personal identity theorists is typically conservative on questions of how much a self can change. Questions of one's relation to one's future self are difficult to articulate in this theoretical tradition because no current psychological resemblances exist to ground an association between a present and future self. I am thus asked to imagine a particular future self and to judge if it resembles me sufficiently to guarantee continuity of identity. Radical psychological change, presented through experiments involving "brainwashing, brain transplant, journey by matter transmitter, purported reincarnation or resurrection, fission into twins, fusion with someone else, or what not," is a threat to the self: "Change should be gradual rather than sudden and (at least in some respects) there should not be too much change overall" (David Lewis, "Survival and Identity," 17). If there are important philosophical and ethical issues about how to regard our obligation toward future change, they are being blocked from consideration by mainstream philosophical views of the self that purport to explicitly address issues of self-continuity and change.

Recent and more explicitly politicized views of the self emphasize the situatedness of people and the ways in which we are constituted or constructed through a variety of social relations. The responses of others to us and their interpretations of our behavior ground certain properties of the self and certain self conceptions, and these properties and conceptions may change with shifting social contexts. Many contemporary authors also theorize identities as importantly ethical/epistemological, sometimes calling on those of us who are privileged to undertake identity shifts or transformations in order to attain a less distorted perspective on ourselves and on a world structured through racial, sexual, and class dominance. These views claim that we are socially constituted knowers and through changing the ways in which we relate or are related to our environment, we can know things differently, which is to become different selves. Radical self change is represented as a positive political responsibility. Sandra Bartky describes it as a "knowing that transforms the self who knows, a knowing that brings into being new sympathies, new affects as well as new cognitions and new forms of intersubjectivity" ("Sympathy and Solidarity: On a Tightrope with Scheler," 179).

I am particularly interested in whether and how these more recent politicized identity models are available to those with dominant social identities, and in the rest of this section, I examine two such models. Sandra Harding and Maria Lugones are among the contemporary theorists who present identity transformation as positive and as something that members of dominant groups can and should undertake.[3] Neither theorist addresses important asymmetries between those whose identities are pressed into change as they move through and attempt to survive in dominant social contexts, and those who must motivate self-change that is not driven by these necessities.

In "Who Knows? Identities and Feminist Epistemologies," Harding develops Patricia Hill Collins's notion of the outsider within, a person who epistemically exploits the dissonance between understandings available to her from the perspective of her own history and activities and those understandings available from within that part of the dominant culture she also negotiates ("Learning from the Outside Within: the Sociological Significance of Black Feminist Thought"). Acting on Collins's advice that anyone uncomfortable with the unquestioned assumptions of insiderism have much to learn from the outsider-within status, Harding argues that those with dominant identities can pervert them in the service of libratory political agendas. We can "attract center identities to the opportunities for libratory knowledge and politics originally generated on the margin" (110). Men, for example, can become feminists and white feminists can become antiracists. Such men and such feminists adopt "perverse identities" through wilfully refusing their insider status, refusing "to do what the culture of the center expects them to do" (107). Men can add to our knowledge of sexism. With the help of feminist insights, they can critically reflect from the perspectives offered by their own experiences on sexuality, work, dominance, and so on. They can add crucial critical perspectives to feminist knowledge—perspectives that only the socially advantaged can provide.

For Harding, perverse identities are centrally epistemic. She refers to individuals who would undertake such identities as "identity knowers" and characterizes the project itself as one of studying and learning (101). As a white person who wishes to be an antiracist, "I have to educate myself about people of colour, their struggles and their cultures. I have to study my own ignorance as well. . . . I have to study white exploitation, domination, oppression, and privilege. I have to generate the kinds of explanations of these conditions that I expect men, for example, to generate of theirs" (109). It is useful to see how a "knowing which transforms the self who knows" is grounded in the outsider-within model that Harding adapts.

Collins discusses the experience of black women who enter academic disciplines and master disciplinary paradigms while remaining "rooted in their own experience as Black women" ("Learning," 59). She follows Kuhn's understanding of a paradigm as a community practice where practitioners come to share values and behaviors; to become a practitioner thus requires a long socialization period. Typically, insiders to a discipline "have undergone similar experiences, possess a common history and share the assumptions about knowledge" that characterize "thinking as usual" (54). To maintain the status of an outsider within is to undergo the process of socialization while resisting or being denied the full conversion to insider status. An outsider within continues to theorize partly from the perspective of her history and activities, using the paradigm to critically reflect on her own experience and using her experience to challenge exclusions and distortions licensed and promoted by the paradigm. Nevertheless, outsiders within are changed by their assimilation of the paradigm. They become different people through the socialization necessary to understand the "fine grained meanings of behavior, feelings and values" that characterize the discipline (Robert K. Merton, "Insiders and Outsiders: A Chapter in the Sociology of Knowledge," 29; quoted in Collins, "Learning," 54).

Collins links identity change—even a change to the complex identity of outsider within—to immersion in a community. Immersion is necessary for a person to internalize the new ways of thinking and acting that help constitute the dual perspective necessary to outsider-within status. It is not obvious that the same possibilities for *immersion* exist for someone who wishes to move from the center. Someone with a dominant identity may be attracted to the margin in the sense that he or she may want to use insights and theory generated by outsiders and by outsiders within to reflect critically on his or her own experience. But communities marginalized by a dominant culture have little reason to trust members of the dominant culture or to allow them to become socialized into their communities. Moreover, outsiders within have dual perspectives in creative tension through enforced participation within a dominant culture, a culture that they must learn to negotiate but in which there is almost never the possibility of full insider status. This is not a type of experience available to someone who wishes to move to the margins.

There is thus an asymmetry in Harding's development of Collins's model. The idea of identity change is undermotivated by the learning agendas for perverse identities that Harding endorses. Important though knowledge is, a call for identity change suggests that we who have dominant identities should change some of the many ways in which we live in the world and in which our daily behaviors express and entrench unearned advantage and dominance over others. Although knowledge is necessary for such transformation, it is not an adequate account of that in which the transformation consists.

Harding, I believe, builds the girding for an identity shift into her appeal for perverse identities by pointing out that nearly all feminists—as feminist philosophers, black sociologists, and lesbian literary critics—are already outsiders within who know how to act out of multiple identities. In calling on white feminists to undertake identity shifts toward antiracism, she implies that as multiples we have the resources within ourselves for effecting identity shifts. It's not at all clear, however, in Harding's account how what is multiple or fragmented in a white feminist's identity is meant to facilitate a very particular kind of political shift to an antiracist practice, whereas in Collins's account it's perfectly clear why black women inside the disciplines make profound contributions to the understanding of their lives. Harding's appeal to a previous multiplicity in the self seems simply to mark the absence of an account of how the dominant undergo an identity shift.

In "Playfulness, 'World'-Traveling, and Loving Perception," Maria Lugones describes a certain process of identity shifting that characterizes the experiences of " 'outsiders' to the mainstream of . . . white/Anglo organization of life in the U.S." (275). Although she is primarily recommending that women of color regard this identity shifting as creative and positive and undertake it in certain ways more wilfully, she also believes that "world" traveling is available "to those who are at ease in the mainstream" (275). *To travel* in Lugones's sense is to acquire flexibility in adapting to social contexts in which one is variously and differently constructed. If we want to truly love other women, we are directed by Lugones to travel to their worlds, coming to understand *"what it is to be them and what it is to be ourselves in their eyes"* (289; emphasis in original).

The idea of an identity shift seems more grounded in Lugones than in Harding because of Lugones's explicit commitment to a constructivist view of identity. We are differently constructed in different worlds. Concretely, for example, our properties can change as we shift contexts. Lugones, herself, can be playful only in some worlds. It is not possible to be playful in a world where everything one says or does is taken as an expression of political seriousness and cultural intensity, where as an outsider one is ill at ease and where things really are politically serious most of the time. In such contexts, as Lugones pointedly and painfully notes, one can have the playfulness constructed right out of one.

Moreover, Lugones adds to our understanding of how to develop an antiracist practice through her insistence that we travel to other people's worlds, learning both how they view themselves and how they view us in situations where our perspective is not ideologically dominant. Lugones's view has an obvious focus on face-to-face encounters, which Harding's account does not have. I doubt, however, that such encounters could constitute opportunities for immersion sufficient to disrupt the assumptions of a dominant identity through the particular strategy of developing a different identity held in creative tension with it.

Lugones's view, in fact, endorses an alternative and seemingly anti-immersion strategy. She recognizes that one can associate with others arrogantly or self-protectively. Moreover, those at ease in a dominant culture may have considerable choice not only about which worlds they inhabit, but also about how they attempt to cross racial, cultural, and class barriers. Thus Lugones identifies a necessary nonself-protective attitude, *playfulness*, which is precisely meant to reconfigure possibilities for intersubjectivity and thus to be personally and politically transformative: "Positively, the playful attitude involves openness to surprise, openness to being a fool, openness to self-construction or reconstruction and to construction or reconstruction of the 'worlds' we inhabit playfully. Negatively, playfulness is characterized by uncertainty, lack of self-importance, absence of rules or a not taking rules as sacred, a not worrying about competence, and a lack of abandonment to a particular construction of oneself, others, and one's relation to them" ("Playfulness," 288).

Lugones's account of "world" travel has had resonance for many theorists who share experiences of fragmentation and multiplicity, and it has played an important role for some feminist philosophers in defining an obligation to examine their own identities for tensions that suggest possibilities for radical political change. There has been little analysis, though, of the attitude of playfulness, which is crucial to the account, and I have found it difficult to understand her model of playfulness in thinking of how to shift from the perspectives that constitute dominant identities. There are two aspects to the model that bother me.

Like Harding, Lugones depends on a prior multiplicity in the self—modeled this time on the experiences of bicultural people subject to ethnocentric racism—to prompt our understanding and endorsement of the possibility of self-change.[5] This is evident in an example she gives of the positive dimension to playfulness: outsiders to the mainstream can intentionally animate stereotypes of themselves in funny and "survival rich" ways unnoticed by those who dominate them. Constructed in an Anglo world as stereotypically intense, a Latino can animate the stereotype by being stereotypically intense or by really being intense, thus taking "hold of a double meaning" (285). Outsiders can become the double-edged tricksters or fools who are "significant characters in many non-dominant or outsider cultures" (285). But the trickster is already a traveler. Her knowledge of how she is seen is an opportunity for playfulness. It is not as though through playfulness she shifts from a dominant identity by coming to understand how she is seen.

Moreover, Lugones's account of playfulness as an absence of rules or as not taking rules seriously posits a separation between the norms that construct identities and the identities constructed that those dominant should reject as an account of their own relation to norms. Rules may encode norms, but they do not explain their emergence. Those with dominant identities first need to take responsibility for the psychic structures that explain the emergence of norms.

I believe that to think of dominant identities in terms of identity transformation is politically useful. The idea of transformation binds self to world without implying the fixity of either. To undergo a transformation is to understand the world very differently, which supposes it can be understood very differently. As well, transformation captures the insight that serious social change has a necessary psychic dimension. I also believe that Lugones's stress on the identity attitude we bring to activities and encounters is essential to understand how those with dominant identities can change so as to become antiracist. In what follows, however, I shall reread the notion of playfulness as unsettling the expectations that structure attention and action in racist ways. Unsettling expectations helps deconstruct the unquestioned normativity of dominance. Moreover, settled expectations are such an important part of dominant identities that their unsettling is not (like playfulness) a change in attitude prior to the shift in self, but helps to constitute the shift.

The Nature of Expectation

I am nearly always expectant. That we can have expectations seems fundamental to our knowing how to go on. We could not plan what to do, even in small ways, without beliefs and attitudes about the future, about what effects our actions might have, and also about what we might undergo. According to Bernard Williams, expectations involve the active thought or contemplation of what the future will be like in terms of a determinate range of possibilities based on our present knowledge, as well as a range of emotions or attitudes directed on the determination of those possibilities. In "The Self and the Future," Williams writes, "central to the expectation of S is the thought of what it will be like when it happens—thought which may be indeterminate, range over alternatives, and so forth (59). This active thinking of what the future will be like, however, need involve little self-awareness that what one is doing is expecting. We often recognize our expectations only in their frustration.

A way to understand how expectation can involve an active contemplation of the future and yet involve little awareness that what we are doing is expecting is to note the role of expectation in complexly structuring attention from *now* till *then*. My expectation of seeing you at lunch will structure my attention in a number of ways. I may pay attention to those features of my environment that are relevant to whether my expectation is met. If my expectation is indeterminate, if I expect either that I will see you at lunch or that you will stay working in your office, I may pay attention to signs that you either will or won't be there. If I am looking very forward to seeing you at lunch, I may attend to what happens in my morning that I think will entertain you, and I may fail to notice things that would normally irritate me. The expectation of seeing you is a perceptual path through my morning that determines what I ignore as well as what I attend to. Finally, how time passes for me and how events seem related, whether I am paying attention to what is said in order to repeat it to you, will depend on my expectation. And all of this may happen with little consciousness that my expectation is at work in structuring my morning. So expectation gives a powerful ordering to experience by selecting what is and is not attended to and by structuring the relation of these perceptions to each other. These activities of selective attending are what give expectation its character.

Augustine, one of the few philosophers to discuss expectation, noticed that the ordering of perception made possible through expectation, in turn structures and orders memory. The mind "expects, attends, remembers: what it expects passes, by way of what it attends to, into what it remembers" (*The Confessions of St. Augustine*, 229). Memories and expectations are reciprocally structuring and not always helpfully so. Expectation orders memory, and habit memory, triggered by familiar circumstances, gives rise to expectation and thus helps me order perception. I may expect to see you in a certain place because I have seen you there many times before. If my expectations are not met, however, if you are not where I expected, it is natural for me to turn to memory, reviewing how I came to think you would be there in the first place. If my relevant memories are of your reliable presence, I will not find the resources in my past to adapt to change. I take from Augustine that we do not understand how we remember without a reciprocal view of how we expect. Theories of personal identity that focus on continuity of memory but pay no attention to how the dynamics of memory are shaped in relation to expectations fail in a fundamental way to capture the temporal dimensions of psychic life and thus are deficient accounts of self-continuity and change.

I develop expectations in an unsorted and unself-conscious way as I move through environments and am affected by them. I may also develop expectations through what I have been taught to expect and through following and imitating what others attend to. Some of my expectations will have normative force—they determine what I think I or others ought to do—because they are overtly about moral matters. I may, for example, expect to be treated justly. However, any of my expectations can gain normative force in being met. Frequently met expectations may come to form the map of the world that I depend on and take as stable, however changeable that world may in fact be.

Thus, a final important point about expectations is that even seemingly trivial ones can have normative force, which is perhaps most obvious in responses to their no longer being met. I expect to see you at lunch only because you have been there before, not because you promised me you would be there. However, if I don't see you at lunch and am disappointed by this, I may feel as if you ought to have been there. I am dependent on your presence though you have done nothing to license this dependency. My response to the frustration of my expectation may lead me to engage critically with my expectation, to identify and assess it. On the other hand, perhaps the experience of disappointment and the feeling that you ought to have been at lunch will prevent me from critically engaging my expectation that you ought to have been there. I may even challenge your absence and call on you to account for it.

Expectations, then, can give rise to creeping dependencies that the world be a certain way and can impose obligations on others that must be coped with, even when the expectations are unreasonable or fix the world unsuccessfully. Many white people who move in mostly white environments, for example, have the expectation that the light-skinned people they meet within these environments are also white. In "Passing for White, Passing for Black," Adrian Piper describes the "hostile reactions" when these expectations are frustrated and her attendant though groundless shame:

> This was the shame caused by people who conveyed to me that I was underhanded or manipulative, trying to hide something, pretending to be something that I was not by not telling them I was black—like the art critic in the early 1970's who had treated me with the respect she gave emerging white women artists in the early days of second-wave feminism until my work turned to issues of racial identity; then she called me to verify that I was black, reproached me for not telling her and finally disappeared from my professional life altogether. (257–58)

In disappearing herself, the art critic removes Piper from her frame of attention rather than reconfiguring her expectations about what women are now making what kind of important political art.

The kind of expectations most frequently mentioned in moral psychology are the expectations others have of our behavior that are either internalized as norms or whose internalization needs to be resisted. Anita Allen, for example, writes that "we are responsible people who deserve self-esteem and the esteem of others, not because we have blindly adhered to communal norms but, rather, because we have chosen to regulate our conduct in accordance with reasonable social expectations" ("Forgetting Yourself," 107). Philosophers recognize the importance of social expectations as the grounding of norms, and the mention of expectation occurs frequently in work that, like Allen's, is concerned with oppressive expectations that should not be internalized, but the focus has been on the norms and their internalization rather than on expectations as the intrapsychic structures that give rise to norms.

If expectations give rise to norms and figure in oppression, we need to understand how they function intrapsychically as well as interpersonally. This understanding is important because expectations are ubiquitously involved in structuring our attention and our responses and may be unselfconscious and difficult to bring to critical attention. Moreover, though expectations may be reasonable or unreasonable and may require response from others, they are often not assessed for reasonability as they are adopted. As well, positive expectations create a negative perceptual space of what is unnoticed, ignored, excluded, or dismissed as unimportant in ways that are themselves missed because only the encoding of expectations as norms is being attended to.

Finally, because expectations structure attention and memory, are interwoven with emotion, and give rise to norms, they are central structures in the constitution of selves and are a way of understanding and ordering the world perceptually, emotionally, and normatively. To be able to reorder the world through reforming expectations can be a deep change in the self. And indeed, the role of intrapsychic expectation often has an important but unmarked place in political activists' and theorists' analyses of the conditions of self and social change.

Expectation and Antiracism

In "Identity: Skin Blood Heart," Minnie Bruce Pratt asks, "How do we begin to change, keep going, and act on this in the world" (19). As Pratt, a white Christian southern lesbian, narrates her struggle against anti-Semitism and racism, she addresses her own questions about change through a profound understanding of the role of expectation in structuring the self and of the relation of expectation to self-stability and racist perception. I use Pratt's narrative to display the importance of a self-conscious engagement, not just with particular expectations, but with the role of settled expectation in the structuring of dominant identities.

The settled nature of expectation is first expressed through Pratt's use of home as both the concrete grounds and the symbol of the structuring of attention through expectation. The shift in home is the unsettling of expectation and the attempt to reform it, leaving Pratt, near the beginning of the essay but chronological end of the narrative,"at the edge between my fear and outside, on the edge of my skin listening, asking what new thing I will hear" (18).

In the course of the narrative, Pratt shifts geographical home four times and in her growing political activism attempts to build community in some of these locations. The linking of expectation to identity through the idea of home is explicit in her description of the southern town in which she was raised: "I was shaped by my relation to those buildings and to the people in those buildings, by ideas of who should be working in the Board of Education, of who should be in the bank handling money, of who should have the guns and the keys to the jail, of who should be *in* the jail; and I was shaped by what I didn't see, or didn't notice, on those streets" (17, emphasis in original). The expectations Pratt presents as significant to her identity are expectations about who belongs in what place, who does what work, who should teach others, who can handle responsibility, who is responsible for judgment and punishment, who is bad and deserves to be punished. All these expectations imply the specific exclusions of who does not belong in that place and determine in general what is unimportant and not worth noticing. Pratt understands expectations as deeply constitutive of the self. They contribute to personal identity and self-stability via the continuity of a perceptual position: "we act out the present against a backdrop of the past, with a frame of perception that is so familiar, so safe that it is terrifying to risk changing it" (17).

Moreover, the view of the town that her father takes her to the bell tower to see is the view of her father and his father, the judge, before him. Pratt's narrative identifies a way of ordering the world as a southern white with expectations that are shared and aligned with social power. The normative force of these expectations, emphasized by Pratt's "should," contribute toward racist understandings and actions, partly through repeatedly not taking into account the lives of people that are not within her frame of perception:

> I was in a discussion of the Women's Pentagon Action with several women, four of us Christian-raised, one Jewish. In describing the march through Arlington cemetery, one of the four mentioned the rows of crosses. . . . No, said the Jewish women, they were headstones with crosses or stars-of-David engraved above the names. We four objected; we had all seen crosses. The Jewish women had some photographs . . . laid them on the table. We saw rows and rows and rows of rectangular gravestones and in the foreground, clearly visible, one inscribed with a name and a star-of-David. (17)

Pratt expects to see Christian graves in a military cemetery, and this expectation determines what is perceptually salient. Exclusions become apparent to Pratt through her political associations, but they are persistent nevertheless: "I say carelessly to my Jewish lover that there were no Jews where I grew up, and she begins to ask me: how do I know? do I hear what I'm saying? and I get afraid; . . . I feel my racing heart, breath, the tightening of my skin around me, literally defences to protect my narrow circle" (18).

The unconscious and settled nature of Pratt's expectations becomes additionally and strikingly apparent when, coming out as a lesbian, she finds herself suddenly excluded from the place she had expected to occupy by right. Her husband threatens court proceedings to gain custody of their sons, and her mother acts as a character witness for him. Her time with her children is restricted and finally they are taken hundreds of miles away. Pratt says: "I was no longer 'the best of women': what did I expect? But I *had* expected that protected circle to be marked off for me by the men of my kind as my 'home': I had expected to have that place with my children. I had expected it as my *right*. . . . the extent of my surprise revealed to me the degree of my protection" (27, emphasis in original).

As Pratt moves into an apartment with her books and her cats, home becomes the problematic symbol of expectations that have been violated, while remaining the ground of a self with a set of expectations that can no longer be met. The shift, however, is also the loss both of a concrete material/geographical/social place with her children and of her identity status as "the best of all women." It is her loss of a right to these things. Thus, finally, Pratt's use of home as a symbol of settled expectations and her understanding of home as both identity and geography engage the relation of settled expectations to property.

In "Whiteness as Property," Cheryl Harris gives Jeremy Bentham's definition of property as "an established expectation, in the persuasion of being able to draw such and such advantage from the thing possessed" (quoted in Harris, 1729). Harris argues that although not all settled expectations constitute property rights, "the relation between expectations and property remains highly significant. . . . [T]hose expectations in tangible or intangible things that are valued or protected by law are property" (1729). Harris is concerned with the relation of race to property in U.S. law. She argues that "the set of assumptions, privileges, and benefits that accompany the status of being white have become a valuable asset that whites have sought to protect. . . . Whites have come to expect and rely on these benefits, and over time these expectations have been affirmed, legitimated and protected by law. . . . [I]n protecting settled expectations based on white privilege, American law has recognized a property interest in whiteness" (1713). She traces whiteness as the basis for the acquisition of land ("a prerequisite to the exercise of enforceable property rights" [1724]), whiteness as protected reputation and status, and the protected expectations of white privilege that have influenced the legal history of affirmative action decision in the United States, where "appropriate remedies [have not been] dictated by the scope of the injury to the subjugated, but by extent of the infringement on settled expectations of whites" (1768).[6]

Harris's masterful account of settled expectations is an additional and compelling reason for those of us with dominant social identities to think about the nature of expectation. In Pratt's text, the loss of her identity status and her home because of her lesbianism is part of the complex recognition of the acts of appropriation and dismissal that originally secured her home and identity through the exclusion of others. Pratt comes to learn that her family owned slaves and that the family land was bountied to her grandfather for driving the Seminoles from their homes. She comes to recognize that her own job at a black college has been gotten with a "segregated-university education" ("Identity," 35). I return later to the importance of these realizations.

Pratt identifies expectations of how the world is socially ordered as settled, racist, and deeply constitutive of the self, thus making change urgent. She says that her love of a particular woman led her "in a complicated way, to work against racism and anti-Semitism" (19). Her commitment to building community with other women ("I needed desperately to have a place that was mine with other women, where I felt hopeful" [30]) is motivation for change, but does not fully account for the psychic possibility of change. If we understand structures of racist perception as partly governed by settled expectations, we can identify at least three challenges to possibilities for change.

First, the expectations of those with dominant identities are often unself-conscious attitudes; they are likely to be more so as they accord with dominant normative perspectives and as they are met, conditions that typically obtain together. Dominant racist and classist perspectives about who is or is not trustworthy make it easy for white middle-class people to cash checks and obtain credit. My expectation that I can cash a check where I want is likely to be wholly unself-conscious, whereas the social structures that make it easy for me to cash checks or obtain credit are likely very obvious to those for whom these things are made difficult. Many writers have thus emphasized the need "for a category of interaction as a necessary condition . . . [of] a critical epistemology" (Huntington, "Fragmentation," 200). Pratt's narrative emphasizes face-to-face encounters and challenges, but settled expectations challenge us to account for how such encounters can be effective.

As Pratt reminds us, "each of us carries around those growing up places, these institutions, a sort of back-drop, a stage-set" ("Identity," 17). Expectations form a framework of interpretation that we bring to our encounters. They structure our responses to perceived similarities so that we may be insensitive to the particular differences that would challenge these same expectations. In the "Speaking Out" column of *Ebony* magazine, Laurence Thomas declares, "In My Next Life I'll Be White." His text illustrates vividly how white women's expectations that black men are a threat are insensitive to the particular features of an encounter that clearly indicate there is no threat. Thomas reports the following encounters: "I was recently walking down a supermarket aisle with hand-baskets full of groceries, one in each hand. A White woman saw me and rushed for her pocketbook, which she had put in the cart. I would have had to put my own groceries down in order to take her pocketbook. No doubt she thought to herself: 'He won't fool me with that old basket-in-each-hand trick.' . . . It would not occur to any-one to think that a 6-foot-tall, 150-pound well-groomed White male in tra-ditional academic attire—tweed jacket and tie—with briefcase in hand was actually seeking to break into a University office simply because he was read-ing a bulletin board outside of the conference hall. . . . What on earth was I reported as?" (84).

In a third example, Thomas simply had to ask a white woman who leapt for her pocketbook in a Middle East hotel, "Do you really think I travelled nearly 6000 miles in order to steal your purse when it is obvious that you are not much better off than I am since we're staying in the same hotel?" (84).

Thomas frequently encounters whites who take home with them wherever they go. They carry the expectation of who should be in jail as a deep per-spective that gives gender and skin color an overriding perceptual salience. There is little reason to be optimistic that the woman in the Middle East-ern hotel critically engaged her expectations when Thomas confronted her. Those with dominant identities have considerable power to order environ-ments through what they attend to; thus, their environments do not impinge on them or change them. This fact should give us reasonable caution about appeals to fragmentation and multiplicity in the self as aids to the political transformations that those with dominant social identities need to under-take. Those with dominant identities must take responsibility for the often racist patterns of interpretation through which they understand the world. To regard one's identity as multiple and as providing diverse standpoints can turn attention away from the responsibility of identifying how systematically distorted one's perspective of others is.

Finally, although our expectations can become apparent to us when they are not met, disruption may lead neither to their critical engagement nor to their reformulation, but rather to emotional responses that are antitheti-cal to change. Affirmative action programs have disrupted the expectations of many whites about how employment and educational opportunities are structured. The reminder that white men have been affirmatively hired is meant to challenge white men to critically engage their expectations, to see the ways that social structures advantage some, disadvantage others, and to notice the ways that expectations retrench norms and rights that contribute to systemic patterns of injustice. But the anger consequent on a sense of vio-lation of entitlement has often prevented this critical engagement and has led to the thwarting of these programs. Unmet expectations can also cause deep anxiety and an inability to know how to negotiate now unfamiliar environ-ments. For a time, Pratt has such a response to the loss of her home and chil-dren: "I felt that I had no place, that, as I moved through my days, I was falling through space" ("Identity," 27).

I cannot give an account of all the strategies one might use to critically en-gage settled expectation. Pratt's engagement is fueled through motivation—

a commitment to her lover and to new communities of interaction—and through political goodwill, as well as through desperation, optimism, and the need to cope with loss. I focus here on how she understands the difficulty and necessity of widening her frame of attention, drawing on Biddy Martin's and Chandra Talpade Mohanty's excellent study of Pratt's work in "Feminist Politics: What's Home Got to Do with It?" Pratt's strategy returns us to the crucial relation between memory and expectation and to a consideration of how her identity is and is not unified.

Once Pratt becomes political and lesbian, her expectations for a safe life are no longer met. The failure of expectation leads back to memory as its ground. But expectation and memory are mutually supportive, and memory may be of no help in reconfiguring expectation, in indicating what new route our attention should take. Pratt recognizes that her expectations of safety are founded on memories of safety, but she also realizes that her memories of safety are the reciprocal effect not only of her own expectations, but also of the settled expectations of others. "My memory and my experience of a safe place to be was based on places secured by omission, exclusion, or violence" ("Identity, 26). Because Pratt comes to understand the settled expectations of white southerners as both identity and as entitlement and property, she is able to destabilize the relation between memory and expectation by coming to learn of those excluded and then, in each place where she lives, re-remembering her own past in the context of understanding the history of those excluded from that place.

For example, the experience of home gives to expectations of how one responds to others and how they will respond, the crucial familiarities that give one a sense of belonging. In the H corridor of Washington, D.C., where Pratt comes to live, she no longer has the security of these expectations: "If you and I met today, reader, on Maryland Avenue, would we speak? I don't know what barriers of gender, color, culture, sexuality might rise between us when we saw each other" (14). The familiar quality of the voices in her neighbourhood and the uncertainty of how she can speak and how others will respond to her speaking move Pratt into memory: " I am grateful . . . to hear a joking that reminds me, with a startled pain, of my father, putting on his tales for his friends, the white men gathered at the drug store. . . . I just want to feel at home where people know me" (12). But Mr. Boone the janitor of her building doesn't raise his eye to Pratt when she speaks: "He is a dark red-brown man from the Yemassee in South Carolina—that swampy land of Indian resistance and armed communities of fugitive slaves, that marshy land at the headwaters of the Combahee, once the site of enormous rice plantations and the location of Harriet Tubman's successful military action that freed many slaves" (12).

In knowing this history and in re-remembering home in the failure of her own expectations for comfortable speech with others, Pratt now remembers "that home was a place of forced subservience," and she knows that her wish to feel at home "is that of an adult wanting to stay a child: to be known by others but to know nothing, to feel no responsibility" (12). To resituate her memory is to move from an understanding of her identity as formed through personal memory, through an understanding that these memories were made possible only by the suppression of other histories, to an understanding and experience of her identity as formed through these exclusions.

I thus agree with Martin and Mohanty ("Feminist Politics") that to understand change we need to see how Pratt challenges her identity as coherent and historically continuous. Pratt's strategy is not, I think, to look for multiplicity or fragmentation within herself, but to find a notion of identity in community where communities are understood not as groups with which she begins to share behaviors, feelings, and values through immersion, but as material and historical locations where some groups have dominated others. In these communities, Pratt's identity shifts because the significance of her past changes as her memories come to have new meanings. At the same time, this past can no longer form the ground of settled expectations that frame and limit her perception with an unquestioned normativity, which also marks a deep shift in the self. The change is not one, however, of giving up the old set of expectations for a new set, but of bringing expectations to consciousness and living with the uncertainties of their no longer being met. It is also not a change that Pratt identifies as the failure or disruption of self-continuity. It is a political change that she identifies with "learning how to live in *this* world" (13; emphasis in original).

To understand Pratt, then, we must first give up a traditional commitment to a unified self where continuity and sense of responsibility are dependent on the conservation of static memory. Pratt finds resources in her past for challenging expectations only insofar as her past is critically re-remembered and reunderstood. Mainstream accounts of the self that locate personal continuity in static remembering are deeply conservative regarding a political status quo. Moreover, we should be concerned by the complete neglect of expectation in theories of personhood in a historical context where whiteness as status can be substantially analyzed in terms of settled expectations. These theories both reflect and support the constitution of the white self as a self that is never aware of the expectations that constitute her identity as privilege and dominance.

Second, the intent of Pratt's narrative is to make explicit the complex nature of expectations as habits of attending that structure her environment through exclusions effected by not taking others into account and as the rights and properties of those like her who have structured this same environment through the power to have their exclusions enforced. I have agreed with Lugones that change requires a metaphysical attitude that is positive toward uncertainty. This agreement returns me to the question of how unsettling expectations—described by Pratt as being at the edge of her skin listening for what new things she will hear—may be importantly different from playfulness.

Lugones gives a provocative figurative depiction of playfulness as two people on a river who begin to break stones and are entranced by the new colors inside. Their attitude of openness to surprise turns the activity into play. It is a metaphysical attitude "that does not expect the world to be neatly packaged, ruly" ("Playfulness," 288). Lugones's prose places us in a limen, a place between social structures.[7] She suggests that I can, in imagination only perhaps, move some distance from the norms and rules that constitute my world and adopt an attitude toward these rules. But if I have a dominant social identity, my lack of openness to surprise and my immunity from reconstruction by others is not primarily overattentiveness to norms and rules external to me; these norms and rules are my expectations embodied in social space.

In "White Privilege and Male Privilege: A Personal Account of Coming to See Correspondences through Work in Women's Studies," Peggy McIntosh lists forty-six daily ways in which she experiences white skin privilege— from "If I should need to move, I can be pretty sure of renting or purchasing housing in an area which I can afford and in which I would want to live" (32) to "I can easily find academic courses and institutions that give attention only to people of my race" (34). Her account resonates with expectations that have historically constituted the daily protection of whiteness as property, and she says she repeatedly forgot each of the forty-six realizations until she wrote them down. She also describes "these special circumstances and conditions" as ones she was made to feel were hers "by birth, by citizenship, and by virtue of being a conscientious, law-abiding 'normal' person of goodwill" (32).

McIntosh lists expectations that are *settled* in two senses: they are so chronically met that they are sedimented—difficult to bring to attention and remember—and they are what she automatically takes to be her public due. She unsettles them in the first sense bringing them to consciousness and writing them down in order to unsettle them in the second sense by providing a finer-grained analysis of which "privileges" are unearned dominance over others. Moreover, unsettling them in the second sense—becoming responsible for unearned dominance—is necessary to sustain unsettling them in the first sense.

Pratt describes her expectations as a backdrop or stage set and thus "takes apart privilege by situating herself again and again in the social, by constantly referring to the materiality of the situation in which she finds herself" ("Feminist Politics," 194). McIntosh describes her expectations as "an invisible weightless knapsack of special provisions, assurances, tools, maps, guides, codebooks, passports, visas, clothes, compass, emergency gear and blank checks" ("White Privilege," 31). I cannot leave the rules of one world or exist playfully in a limen between worlds if I carry these rules and norms psychically and unself-consciously.

Unsettled Expectation

I have given a number of reasons for counting settled expectations as deeply important to an understanding of a socially dominant self that can change and become more antiracist. Expectations explain what it is to have a perceptual standpoint. They engage a complex account of the self as rememberer, and they explain many emotional responses antithetical to change. As habits of attending that are aligned with social power, settled expectations give rise to norms and are the psychic dimension of the settled exclusions often legally recognized as property. Understanding settled expectations gives insight into the intrapsychic complexities of change and offers a model for transformation.

I would argue, finally, that if we unsettle expectations by attending to them theoretically, we can contribute to and learn from a growing body of work in moral psychology concerned with how distinctive kinds and degrees of self-consciousness are the result of social identities that shape a sense of self.[8] This work rejects the mainstream philosophical presupposition of a uniform and universal kind of self-consciousness. It resists the tendency to transmute a particular kind of experience into an overall account of psychic structure and thus yields more adequate understandings of the very different social selves that we are.

If we were to generalize an account of expectation from the settled expectations of dominant identities, we might worry that expectations are always inherently conservative psychic structures and that their existence makes dismal the prospects for change. I would hope that attending to how activist-theorists such as Pratt and McIntosh engage their own expectations in order to gain a grip on their privilege illustrates the necessity and the potentially radical consequences of engaging with expectations. It is also important to see how the settled expectations of those with dominant social identities might contrast to the expectations of those excluded or marginalized by them.

Pratt's use of home as a symbol of settled expectations exposes many dimensions of dominant identities, but as Martin and Mohanty's provocative subtitle ("What's Home Got to Do with It?") implies, this fruitful symbolizing of expectation is only apt for describing someone whose expectations have been at some point settled and secure, someone who has had a home in the senses Pratt invokes. The role of expectations in Pratt's identity is quite different than their role in the identities of those whose social memory includes ancestors violently removed from their homes and transported into slavery[9] and in the identities of those whose homes have been violently and permanently appropriated and resettled. It would be a mistake to think of all types of social identity as significantly constituted by settled expectations that are potentially unsettled.

In "Social Disappointment and the Black Sense of Self," Bill Lawson writes about quite a different experience of expectation than Pratt's: "Most blacks would claim that overall life in the U.S. as citizens has been replete with experiences of social disappointment. The experience of disappointment has come from a failure of the government to live up to their expectation about their treatment as citizens" (151). Part of Lawson's intent is to contribute toward antiessentialist accounts of black subjectivities by arguing that there is no one response to this experience of social disappointment, but that responses vary with the many diverse life experiences of blacks (just as the response to settled expectations no longer being met can differ in the lives of whites). Although many writers have put forth theories about the response of blacks to the experience of social disappointment, arguing, for example, that disappointment causes nihilism or resentment, Lawson illustrates a number of different responses, including utilizing the experience of disappointment as an impetus for activism and change.

Although the responses to the disappointment of expectations vary for blacks in the United States, one general variable that stays the same is that these expectations are not settled, either in being sedimented and difficult to bring to attention or in being met. They are not met. They are highly self-conscious, and how to cope with their continual disappointment is a matter of heated public debate among blacks. As structures of attending, expectations need not be sedimented habits, and they can direct attention to possibilities of radical change.

For those of us with privileged identities, particular expectations are the psychic representation of the facts about the world that we confidently rely on. Many of these facts are political facts. Our more general philosophical understanding of expectation must also be sensitive to the political formation of personal identities. In Pratt's writing, expectation is understood as deep habit that must be unsettled. In Lawson's account, to maintain expectation is itself a challenge, and maintaining expectation often requires determined political commitment.[10]

12 *Moral Risk and Dark Waters*

SUSAN E. BABBITT

In *The Unnatural Lottery: Character and Moral Luck*, Claudia Card introduces the concept of moral risk to describe what is involved in taking responsibility for one's identity when one is defined negatively by social norms and values. Considering arguments for *moral luck*—that is, whether or not one can be good depends upon factors beyond our control— Card argues that taking responsibility for oneself is sometimes a matter of imposing meaning. But because social meanings require uptake and cannot be imposed by individuals alone, there is a moral risk involved for some people in taking responsibility for themselves: For if social validation is not forthcoming, one can fail to receive the recognition upon which one's commitment to one's relations and oneself depends.

In this essay, I consider the implications of the sort of moral risk Card describes for the nature of moral deliberation in general in situations of systemic injustice—in particular, the implications for personal development. I consider Miriam Tlali's novel *Between Two Worlds*, a story about understanding racism in apartheid South Africa. I argue that acquiring understanding of systemic injustice is sometimes personally threatening in a way probably avoided in the acquisition of other kinds of understanding, and that it raises certain questions about human freedom. I argue that investigating systemic injustice requires in the first instance the imaginative capacity to make specific personal commitments, often to a sort of identity or to the loss of it, and I propose as partial explanation of such commitment Lenin's metaphor of human development as a passage through dark waters—a metaphor that helps illustrate the metaphysical challenge of moral understanding in important cases.

Moral Risk

In *The Unnatural Lottery*, Claudia Card is interested in what it means to take responsibility given that the "Pasts we inherit affect who we can become" (49). In other words, she is concerned with what it means to take responsibility, given that how good we can be depends upon factors beyond our control—upbringing, social and class position, and so on. In Card's view, though, it is not enough to talk about the "natural lottery" from which we may acquire assets and capacities. We must also look at the "*unnatural* lottery created by networks of unjust institutions and histories that bequeath to us further inequities in our starting positions and that violate principles that would have addressed, if not redressed, inequities of nature" (20).

Card's question is: How is it possible for oppressed peoples to liberate themselves from the damage (41–42). In thinking about this, one can apply strategies for the liberation of oppressed groups to oppressed individuals: what is needed first of all is a kind of internal unity, integrity. Taking responsibility, Card argues, involves consciously developing integrity that might not have developed spontaneously. In becoming liberated, we become "truer" selves; we have to discover the value of honor and cease to identify with those who put us down. Liberation cannot come simply from outside (41).

Card's particular concern is with lesbian identity. Taking responsibility is a source of self-respect, but the moral luck involved in the case of lesbian identity consists in traditions of homophobia and misogyny according to which homosexuality is deviant, perverse. Taking responsibility for one's identity in this case means standing behind one's identity *as* lesbian. Taking responsibility, Card suggests, is expressed by metaphors of standing behind, maintaining, preserving, protecting, developing: "Taking responsibility here requires *successfully imposing upon rituals and relationships meanings that we can stand behind*" (149, emphasis in original).

But one's ability to be good depends also upon the capacity of others to recognize one's goodness. Social meaningfulness depends upon social cooperation: "I do not manage to identify myself to others in a particular way if they fail to or refuse to recognize me in that way. The need for social uptake in changing meanings suggests a certain moral problem in which the existing meanings of 'lesbian' are deeply negative" (150). Card is not talking about political risk here. The political risk in standing behind something can involve consequences for one's position of power within society. Standing behind one's identity as a lesbian may for instance undermine possibilities for work or for voice. The moral risk, though, is that one may fail to be able to continue to see oneself as good, as fully human, as worthy of respect. Card says that taking responsibility involves the distribution of social control. It involves taking control of what it is possible to identify or to claim as meaningful or to take for granted. If, according to social institutions, one's identity is deviant from what is normal for human beings, then others have no expectations of the particular meaningfulness upon which one's development as a human being depends, and it will be difficult to provide evidence of that development.

If, as Card suggests, one is to effectively resist definition in negative terms, one has to impose new meaning, and imposing new meaning involves coming up with alternative explanations—which, in important cases, are necessary as a matter of survival. If there is no expectation of meaningfulness of a certain sort, then the individual whose life plans and aspirations express such meaningfulness is in the position of always having to explain how it is that her choices can be of the sort that she takes them to be—namely, appropriately meaningful ones. Or if expectations are of a negative sort, if one is already expected to be deviant, then one is required to explain how what is expected is not really the case. If one commits oneself to moral risk, as Card describes it—if, that is, one commits oneself to imposing new meaning—one also commits oneself to *not* explaining what must be explained given a certain accepted set of meanings and values, and moreover to finding a specific, appropriate way to explain to oneself why one does not explain.

Miriam Tlali's novel *Between Two Worlds* is a story about, among other things, the burden of explanation. Muriel, a black woman in apartheid South Africa with a relatively good job in a radio store, comes to realize that the expectations people have of and for her as a black woman constitute an ever-present burden that makes it impossible for her to be understood as a morally respectable person. She is perceived to be dishonest, and it is up to her to explain how what she is doing can be construed otherwise. The expectation is that she is morally deviant and the burden is on her to provide an alternative explanation in each case, that, for instance, she did not finish the job because the boss had prevented her from doing it: "What gnawed at me most was having to explain to the boss about one thing or another. Time and again—no matter how much I tried to avoid it—I would find myself standing before him to explain. Where would it all end?" (63). When she finally tries to quit, she knows that she cannot explain, that they will not understand: "How could I tell him I was leaving because I did not want to make tea and be sent around to the cafés to buy refreshments for the white staff? None of them could understand it" (120).

I am interested in particular in some of the practical implications of such an explanatory burden. As a white graduate student, I remember being surprised once when a fellow graduate student, a black woman, told me that a certain professor was surprised at her good philosophical work. What surprised *me* was, first, that she encountered surprise at her good work, but second and more important, that his surprise was surprising. I had not expected that he would be surprised at her good work but, more important, I had not expected that his surprise would be important in the way that it was. I had not expected, that is, that the expectations that explained his surprise could constitute a particular sort of extra burden for an individual. The professor's surprise indicated that the expectations that he had for her work were different from the expectations he had for my own, but also that such expectations placed upon my friend a burden of explanation that she had to bear and I did not—namely, the burden of explaining how it is that she could do good philosophical work. She might have explained to him how this was, but of course she did not. Even if she did not explain to him, his demand for an explanation and the existence of the expectation that explained his demand required that she explain to herself why she did not explain. And so she explained this also to me.

As Miriam Tlali indicates so powerfully, one cannot simply *not* respond to the general demand for explanation, even if one does not respond to a particular demand, for the demand for explanation *is* the existence of expectations which determine what one can and cannot be understood to be doing. Moreover, to the extent that expectations determine what can be understood by others and by oneself, they also impose important limitations upon what one can do.

I consider the situation of moral risk—of discovering and committing oneself to more adequate meaningfulness—as an explanatory burden generated by commitment in action to a specific self-conception or to expectations about one's own significance. As a result of particular commitments, one comes to identify certain needs for explanation, and to the extent that one pursues explanations, which one must do if one is to maintain the commitments that motivated such explanations in the first place, one becomes committed irreversibly to a certain self-conception—that is, one passes a point of no return in a certain direction of development. To the extent that human freedom consists, at least in part, in the capacity to understand one's situation and control it, human freedom may seem to require in such situations that one undertake personal risk by making commitments that specifically narrow one's life options.

Metaphors and Theory Change

Consider further the story of Muriel in *Between Two Worlds*. Muriel lives, as the title says, between two worlds: "The Republic of South Africa is a country divided into two worlds. The one, a white world—rich, comfortable, for all practical purposes organized—a world in fear, armed to the teeth. The other, a black world; poor, pathetically neglected and disorganized—voiceless, oppressed, restless, confused, and unarmed—a world in transition, irrevocably weaned from all tribal ties" (11). The story is about understanding. At the beginning of the story, Muriel says, "I had thought I had seen everything there is to see, heard everything there is to hear, in my experiences with people, black, white and brown, in this Republic of South Africa. But I was to learn that I had so far seen and heard very little of this beloved land of ours, especially as far as relations between the different races are concerned" (10).

Now, it is not clear that Muriel gains further propositional understanding of racism. It is not clear, for instance, that she learns any new facts about the harms done to black people by the apartheid system, or if she does, it is not clear that learning these new facts is what constitutes the gain of understanding to which she refers at the beginning of the novel. She knows when she arrives at Metropolitan Radio that she should not expect to be able to use the indoor toilet, the one used by the white people. She is not surprised when her boss tells her that the white women object to her using the same toilet. At her last job, she had used the same toilet as the boss and the white women, but no one had objected. Muriel knows the laws of the country, however, and knows that she cannot carry too far the idea of being accepted (22–23).

What Muriel learns that she did not know before is not well explained by her acquiring more information; rather, it is explained by her acquiring a different orientation toward that information, a different sense of what is important and how. For instance, when she first decides to quit her job, Muriel is persuaded to remain by the kindnesses she receives from her fellow workers: "I shook my head. It was no good. The additional crumbs he was now prepared to hand over to me would never be able to keep me happy. In any case, I was not leaving because of the inadequacy of my salary. I had seen what happened to all the other blacks. I had seen them standing there, on this side of the iron bars, looking hopefully toward the boss on pay day. . . . When it was tea-time, Mrs. Kuhn ordered tea from Gants and—here came a shock—an extra cup for me. Imagine! This was to be the procedure in future whenever Johannes was not in the shop at tea-time. Thoughtfully I poured my cup into my own private cup and sipped it from there." (121)

But by the time she quits at the end of the story, she does not see these same acts as kindnesses in the same way. When Muriel finally does quit her job, it is not because of any new awareness of the kinds of wrongs done to her under apartheid—the acquisition of any new information—but rather because of a recognition of what these wrongs mean and their importance:

> These damnable laws that dictate to you where, and next to whom, you shall walk, sit, stand and lie . . . This whole abominable nauseating business of toilets and "separate but equal facilities" . . . What is one to do anyway? One is forever in a trap from which there is no way to escape . . . except suicide. . . . Back at my desk, I made up my mind. I was no longer trembling and hesitant. I took a blank sheet of paper from my desk, and I scribbled my formal letter of resignation. . . . I remembered the resignation note I had once written, after so many false starts, wavering, uncertain, and compared it to that final one. My

handwriting had never looked so beautiful. I had at last decided to free myself
from the shackles which had bound not only my hands, but also my soul. . . .
I did not care. I had no regrets. All I knew was that I could not continue to be
part of the web that has been woven to entangle a people whom I love and am
part of. (189–90)

It is not that what Muriel saw previously as kindnesses she now sees as
something else. She may still think the bringing of the tea is a kindness, for
it is, but that kindness itself comes to acquire different significance. It is an
act of kindness but at the same time it is also part of a trap. What adds to
her understanding is a judgment about the kind of situation she is in when
she experiences the bringing of the tea as a kindness, the kind of situation
in which it acquires that particular significance. Over time, Muriel realizes
that "everything is a mockery," that "life is not what it should be" (126).
The bringing of the tea is still a kindness from a certain perspective, but it is
also an obstacle, and its being so is not just a *different* way of seeing things;
it is also a judgment about the initial perspective according to which the
bringing of the tea is *primarily* a kindness.

In his autobiography of his early years, *The Motion of Light in Water: Sex
and Science Fiction Writing in the East Village, 1960–1965*, Samuel Delaney
suggests that the possession of truths is not as important as what he calls the
"totality"—the story that gives those truths relevance. Delaney's "totality"
is in fact more than a story; it is more like a life. A "totality" generates criteria of relevance because it constitutes actual movement or development in
a certain direction; what becomes important does so relative to that purpose.
Delaney notices that he was never able to remember some incidences of his
life until he began to tell a story of a certain sort, motivated by a commitment to a direction of thought and action (442–43). He claims that he had
to develop a certain orientation, in theory and practice, in order to understand some things about his life that were actually part of his conscious
memories and experience. They were things that he remembered and knew
that he had experienced, but to which he could not give appropriate significance. For instance, he tells the story of how when he was hitchhiking
from New York to Texas, he had finally decided to spend six or seven dol-
lars on a hotel room. Feeling guilty about the decision because his friend Bob
had told him that "in true hustler fashion, when he hitchhiked . . . he never
stayed in hotels or motels unless someone else put him up," Delaney resolved
not to mention it to him (443). As a result, the memory was cut out "of my
own repertoire of things to say about the trip" and became an "unanchored
fragment."

Delaney suggests that he does not remember the decision to stay in the hotel because in the story of a "true hustler," the incident was meaningless—
that is, irrelevant to his understanding and developing of his life *as a* hustler.
In his interpretations of his life *as* a hustler, the incident does not fit. It does

not play a role in the achievement of relevant direction and understanding. Yet Delaney says that he does remember the incident. He remembers that it happened; it is just that it becomes cut off "from language and history" (443). Part of the point of his autobiography is that stories should not aim to reproduce; rather, they should aim to create: writing "creates an experience that is . . . forged and fashioned wholly from [the writer's] knowledge, of [the writer's] memories, by [the writer's] ideology and sensitivity" (491). Moreover, such a creation, he says, "is not a representation of the writer's world but a model of the writer's purport" (491). The writing and creating of a self-narrative is, Delaney suggests, the representation of a "purport." The creation—forged and fashioned from knowledge and memories, by ideology and sensitivity—is the creation of a way of being, an orientation. And it is within the context of such a "purport" that events gain meaning and significance.[1]

This is not a statement of perspectivism. The point is not that one sees things differently depending upon what stories one tells oneself or what concepts one assumes—the "now it's a duck, now it's a rabbit" observation. It is not that the writer *constructs* reality by constructing meanings, but rather, more interestingly, that what is constructed through good writing is explained by the reality out of which it emerges—that the possibility of a certain kind of story requires one to be engaged with that reality in a particular interested way. Now, Delaney's story of the hotel incident may indicate that in some sense what constitutes one's reality depends upon the story, for the hotel incident is not part of his remembered reality until he tells a different story. But the idea is not that the story creates reality or that the story makes real what was not real before. Delaney knew that he had stayed in a hotel at some point. Rather, the incident suggests that the story one does tell will determine what one can identify as being important and relevant aspects of one's reality and will also provide the context for interpreting those aspects.

Delaney claims that writing emerges not as representation, but as creation—creation of "purport." Moreover, the purport is explained, he says, by the complexity of the writer's life, by his existence in a certain way in a particular set of circumstances, as well as by his interest in that existence; it takes place within a process of action or of development. The struggle to see oneself as a *kind* of person involves a struggle for just such a totality—not a totality that reproduces a set of experiences or desires, but one that constitutes the possibility of unifying events in one way rather than in another. Delaney's story as a hustler is such a story: it leaves out what is not relevant to being a hustler. Some other story, depending upon its purpose, importantly leaves out other events. Delaney's purport is a kind of orientation toward the world, an orientation according to which some events and impressions are relevant to that orientation's constituting a story, a unifying "totality," but others are not.

Taking responsibility, as Card says, is not just taking a stand at some point—for instance, declaring for the sake of relevant others that one is committed in certain ways. It is engaging in the broader pursuit of standing behind something that can be meaningful in the right way. "Standing behind" in such cases is a commitment not just to a way of viewing the world, but to a way of existing that makes such a view necessary and that demands explanations of a certain sort.

Yet, as Card notes, if one is to undertake moral risk, one must have some measure of one's success. One must have some reason to think one's commitment worthwhile and some reason to think that one is undertaking risk for some good purpose. As Card also points out, the measure of one's success cannot be simple consequences. It cannot be some particular result because no single success or achievement by itself can constitute vindication of a commitment of this sort and no single set of consequences can constitute evidence of the success of one's way of viewing an entire world and who one is within that world. What one needs to be able to vindicate is the perspective or the orientation according to which a particular success *is* a success in the first place.

Richard Boyd argues that perspective change in science is at least partly explained by the indication through metaphors of similarities that are probable but still to be discovered and by the commitment and success that allows them to be articulated. In "Metaphor and Theory Change: What is 'Metaphor' a Metaphor For?" Boyd points out that a particular kind of theory-constitutive metaphor plays an important role in theory change in young sciences. I draw on Boyd's paper here to make some suggestions about measuring success in the kinds of cases Card describes. I refer to Boyd's discussion in the philosophy of science to show that images, unifying images, are not necessarily arbitrary and to make some remarks about what that implies for measuring the success of storytelling in the case of individual lives. I then refer back to Delaney to try to identify the special and complex features of *self* understanding that are not involved in understanding the physical world.

Boyd describes two kinds of metaphors: literary and scientific. In neither case is there a specific comparison, but rather a kind of open-endedness. Unlike literary metaphors, however, scientific metaphors involve an eventual articulation of cognitive content. In relatively mature sciences, metaphors play a role as catachresis—that is, in introducing terminology where none previously existed. The open-endedness does not distinguish these terms from other scientific terms, which are always open-ended and subject to revision on the basis of empirical investigation. Nor does it mean there is no explication. Explication is a result of successful, scientific research (349).

Consider, for instance, the use of metaphors in cognitive science. The brain is commonly considered a sort of computer, and thought is considered a sort of information processing. There is plenty of controversy about what exactly it means to say that the brain is a computer, but the metaphor is used nonetheless by members of the cognitive science community and used successfully to ground further investigations. Similarly, the notion of "black holes" is an example of terminology introduced where there existed none previously and for which there existed no commonly accepted, noncontroversial explication.

Boyd suggests that the role of metaphor in science indicates the objective, public and programmatic character of much of the tacit basis of scientific work. He has pointed out elsewhere that some scientific knowledge is tacit—that, for instance, some scientific practices are based upon true beliefs that have not yet been articulated ("How to Be a Moral Realist"). But the fact that scientists sometimes know things they don't know they know does not mean that the development of that knowledge is not constrained in precise ways within socially coordinated research programs. Metaphors, for instance, are introduced into scientific discourse with only an intuitive sense of their usefulness, but they provide a basis for future research strategies and become the property of an intellectual community. Scientists cannot know in advance which metaphors will be successful in guiding research, but the introduction of terminology does require some tentative or preliminary indication of the properties of the presumed kinds in question (Boyd, "How to Be a Moral Realist," 371). The introduction of computer terminology, for instance, makes it possible to refer to computer-like aspects of intelligence, which can then be objects of investigation. Of course, it may turn out that such a metaphor does not become capable of articulation. In such cases, it would be abandoned, and the research community would conclude that the proposed respects of analogy did not in fact exist: "The function of such metaphors [e.g., as the brain as computer] is to put us on the track of these respects of similarity or analogy; indeed, the metaphorical terms in such metaphors may best be understood as referring to features of the world delineated in terms of those—perhaps as yet undiscovered—similarities and analogies" (363).

The prevalence of metaphors in science is significant because of what it indicates about the nature of scientific language and theory development: when we cannot assume respects of difference—that is, when we cannot take for granted assumptions about how things and experiences are unified—there's a question about how we come to acquire a more adequate perspective. The role of metaphors in theory change and in the development of new and more adequate perspectives suggests that whether or not our use of language in fact leads us to discover the world is not a question about the relationship between language and specific phenomena or entities, but rather a question about the general increase of understanding—in particular, of the capacity of new ways of representing phenomena and entities to generate more fruitful problems and strategies. Thus, in programs of investigation and discovery in general, we are engaged in processes in which our language and worldview become more adequate for the ongoing development and pursuit of understanding in particular directions.

Now, to return to Muriel: Muriel says she comes to understand something about the nature of racism in her country that she had not understood before. And partly on the basis of what she has understood, she decides to quit her job, a relatively good job for a black woman in South Africa, with no guarantee for her future. She makes a choice about her life based upon the understanding she has acquired, and it would appear that this understanding is explained by her acquisition of a perspective that defines, among other things, relevant similarities and differences within a direction of development.

Muriel doesn't just come to see things differently as a result of her experience at the radio store. Instead, she comes to see differently which differences are more important than others and to see similarities that she had not before recognized as relevant ones. If it were just a *different* view that she acquires, it would be hard to justify the risk to the economic well-being of herself, her husband, and her small daughter. Instead, Muriel begins to use her change of perspective to measure whatever value she perceived previously. The "crumbs" the boss offered her in terms of salary are no longer crumbs or not just crumbs; they are crumbs that constitute part of a deathly trap which must be escaped. It is not that from one perspective her boss offers crumbs and from another, she sees a trap; rather, because she recognizes a trap, she sees differently what was accepted as and are still, in a sense, crumbs.

What Muriel has acquired by the end of the story is a way of seeing things that is more adequate for her commitment to go on in a certain way. In the end and as a result of her struggle, Muriel knows that "I could not continue to be part of the web that has been woven to entangle a people that I love and am part of" (190). What Muriel understands, then, is that there are similarities between her life and a trap and that these similarities are significant to what she wants to do—which is, in some sense, to be free.

The notion of the web here is a constitutive metaphor in Boyd's sense. The image suggests similarities that are probable but for which full articulation is not possible. Just any other image could not replace this image. Boyd says that in the case of science, metaphors are introduced when there is some reason to expect that there might be some similarity between the object of investigation and a more familiar phenomenon. In Muriel's case, there are reasons for the introduction of the web metaphor—namely, her specific difficulties in being understood, the failure of her own expectations within her workplace, and the burdens of explanation.

For Muriel, the picture of a web expresses a connection between her own situation and something more familiar, a connection that itself motivates her claim : "I would never again place myself in a position in which I had to ask for 'pass-books' or be 'loyal to the firm' at my own people's expense" (190).

The difference between Muriel at the end of the book and Muriel at the beginning is not just that "the web" implies that things are not as they seem, that what might seem like kindness and respect, for instance, are not really kindness and respect. Muriel knew this early in the book. She knew, for instance, that what is offered and what might look like respect can really be a "slap in the face" (62). Instead, Muriel's perspective at the end is that things are not as they seem *and* that the explanation of their seeming to be a certain way is a trap of a certain nature, an ensnaring trap.

Boyd's discussion of metaphors in science is useful in understanding the nature and implications of the sort of moral deliberation that Muriel undertakes. First, metaphors are important in science when scientists need to be able to refer to aspects of a phenomenon that are likely to exist, but for which the full theoretical explication is not yet available. That is, they are important when scientists are in the process of discovering a more adequate theoretical perspective, but language and concepts are inadequate for their investigation or for what they are investigating. People encounter entities and phenomena in the world that are not readily identifiable; as a result, they must reexamine relevant systems of classification. In the same way, there are experiences of a more personal, emotional sort that leave people confused: we can know that such experiences are significant, but not know how, and if we cannot attribute appropriate significance, it is difficult to know how to proceed, so such experiences can be debilitating. In situations of moral risk—situations in which our expectations are such that what we are committed to, perhaps a certain expression of human flourishing, is not recognized by others as such—what is required is also theoretical perspective, a way of unifying events. We may well be committed to something good, something morally significant, but unless we are able to bring about or discover the appropriate sorts of stories to tell about that commitment, we cannot *know* that it is morally significant because we have no evidence, even for ourselves, on which to base our knowledge. That is, we may not possess the theoretical, explanatory resources that make our commitment credible *as* a commitment of a certain sort and that can then indicate how best to proceed with such a commitment. We may in some cases act on probable similarities, as Boyd suggests, precisely in order to be in a position eventually to give theoretical content to our perception of such similarities.

Stories and images—in art and in personal experience—often show us events and phenomena as something other than what they are expected to be, and to the extent that we appropriate such a proposed similarity as probable, we commit ourselves to certain possibilities, even if not explicitly. Toni Morrison's powerful novel, *Beloved*, tells the story of a woman who tries to kill her children to protect them from slavery. Morrison portrays the act *as* an act of love. If someone can try to kill her children out of love, if it is plausible that an act can be at the same time one of intentionally depriving children of life and also of loving those children, then we need to ask further questions about either loving or killing children, which we expect to be distinct. One way in which killing and loving acts are of the same sort is in the context in which life as a slave, even for small children, is worse than death.

There is an alternative to this latter view, of course. Another way to make sense of Sethe's both loving and killing her children is to see Sethe's commitment of love as inadequate. We could think, perhaps, that she *thinks* she loves her children but that she is mistaken. This view would be easier, and there would still be an interesting story to tell. Morrison's novel is powerful and disturbing, but not just because it tells a story about a woman who loves her children and tries to kill them. It is powerful because, given what we know about Sethe, we have to look for a particular sort of explanation for this event. Because we have come to know Sethe in a certain way, we must look for an explanation not only that explains how an act can be both a loving act and a killing act, but also that allows us to maintain a commitment to Sethe as a certain kind of person. We have to find an explanation that not only resolves incongruities, but also resolves the incongruities in such a way that we can preserve our admiration for Sethe as a person.

What Delaney calls "purport" is important here because for any set of incongruities, there are plenty of ways to find an explanatory framework that can resolve those incongruities. The story of Sethe makes a particular explanation compelling because of the relationship created between the reader and Sethe. That the mother tries to kill her children because she loves them demands explanation, but as a result of the story in which we are already involved, only a certain sort of explanation is plausible and consistent with a sort of moral evaluation, a commitment to a certain example of humanness we have already recognized in Sethe. We need an explanation that makes sense of what we expect from and of Sethe.

As readers of *Beloved*, we rely upon the author to create the relationship that generates our expectations for Sethe. We know Sethe in a certain way because of the story Morrison tells, and because of the sort of person that Sethe is, we look for a specific sort of explanation for that which needs to be explained—namely, her killing her children. The force and beauty of Toni Morrison's story is that the author generates for us, through art, expectations of importance that require particular explanations of us. We look for an explanation for her choice that also is consistent with her morality and with her real love for her children and for others. If we think of Sethe's situation, though, or the situation of any individual in a position like Sethe's, the story Sethe tells herself about herself that allows her to see herself as worthy, as not crazy in the way others might think, depends in the first instance upon her own expectations that she is this sort of person. Individuals who take responsibility for themselves need not only to explain what needs explaining in their lives—to tell stories about the significance of events—but also to commit themselves to certain judgments of their own importance in order to be able to explain at all.

The theoretical story depends, according to Delaney, upon the purport of a way of being. The suggestion is that to generate a story about a life, someone already has to commit themselves to certain expectations about that life. Someone has to have certain expectations about what is important to that life in order to judge that some available stories better explain that life than do others. There is, then, an added dimension in the case of constitutive metaphors in moral deliberation. Metaphors, like the notion of the brain as computer, are theory constitutive in that they are commitments to strategies of investigation. The philosophy of science has developed the idea of the epistemic gamble. Philip Kitcher points out that Darwin had to gamble on his theory about evolution: like any new and fruitful theory, Darwin's theory raised many unanswered questions—questions, for instance, about how variation occurs (*Abusing Science: The Case Against Creationism*, 50–54). The gamble was that in the application of the theory and the investigations to which it gave rise, not only would such questions be answered, but the questions generated by those answers would also eventually be answered. And indeed, Darwin's theory still raises questions that are still being answered.

In deliberation about self and society, however, the gamble has to do directly with who one is and can be. The issue here is not one of difference, at least not of difference as it is emphasized in much recent theory about identity. Some theorists, for instance, write about how the world looks different depending upon whether a person takes one or another aspect of her identity to be important—say, her white part or her Latin part, and so on.[2] They talk about "border crossing," of seeing things from one perspective one day and from another the next, depending upon who is listening and what the context is. But in appropriating a *constitutive* metaphor, one commits oneself to developing one way of viewing the importance of things and of making sense of one's expectations according to that view instead of according to other views. Moreover, one understands the other possibilities in light of this one view. One takes a certain purport, so to speak, as criterial— that is, as providing the grounds for determining that some explanations are better than others—and one commits oneself therefore to excluding or to ruling out possibilities. Purport, it turns out, is importantly explanatorily exclusionary.

The role of identity in Muriel's deliberations does not involve "border crossing." Muriel's story in *Between Two Worlds* is about understanding, not about how things look different from different perspectives. The role of identity in *moral* risk is not most interestingly about perception and variation. There is no risk in perception and variation: if one doesn't like the results, one can look at things again the other way. Moreover, there is nothing particularly *morally* interesting about how one sees oneself or about how one sees others as a result of how one sees oneself. In moral risk, one commits oneself to the pursuit of a "truer self," as Card says, and one does so out of moral obligation. One pursues a *more adequate* way of conceiving of oneself as a person for the specific purpose of moral understanding—of understanding moral meaningfulness more adequately. What made working at Metropolitan Radio impossible for Muriel in the long term was that she would have to "gobble up [her] conscience"; the suggestion is that she could not be her (one) true self, not that she could not be some self.

The added dimension in any deliberation involving self- and social understanding is that the gamble taken in committing oneself to strategies of investigation is a gamble that undermines certain life possibilities without any assurance that they will be replaced by meaningful possibilities for life. They may turn out to be options for a certain kind of eccentricity or marginality. To the extent, however, that some things cannot be seen at all or at least cannot be seen as important without a more adequate perspective, not taking such a risk is not only risking not knowing, but also, and more important, risking not knowing that one does not know that there are further human possibilities of a relevant sort.

The metaphor discussion also helps resolve a puzzle about the sort of recognition required for motivation in situations of moral risk. Claudia Card says that moral risk has to do with the fact that if recognition is not forthcoming, one risks not being able to maintain one's commitments (*Unnatural Lottery*, 149–50). Recognition, though, is not always useful or desirable. Or, if there is recognition, it is not always appropriate to engage with it. Some writers, for instance, say that they could not continue to write if they were to engage with the ways in which their writing is received. We might think, for instance, that the kind of recognition required to develop or discover a certain sort of moral understanding would be constrained by one's long-term goals. For instance, Sethe's struggle to think of herself as a human being might be guided most effectively by the recognition accorded by members of her community who share her desire for and commitment to human status for blacks. In the novel, though, Sethe is not guided by those who share these long-term goals. She is in fact isolated from what we might think to be her community. The members of that community don't understand what she did in trying to kill her children, and they reject her. Instead, Sethe interacts most centrally with a ghost. We might say, roughly following Boyd, that the epistemic significance of recognition depends upon the role such recognition can play in the development of the story, the "totality" that makes possible the understanding of relevant moral meaningfulness. In the sorts of moral risk situations Card refers to, a process of understanding cannot be constrained primarily by goals or consequences, for it will not be clear what can constitute the realization of goals or the right sorts of consequences. Certainly, in Sethe's case, it is not clear what it would mean in her circumstances to be recognized as fully human. The relevant recognition, it would seem, is recognition defined by her direction and purpose and by the story required for their continued pursuit.

Boyd's notion of the socially coordinated epistemic access afforded by metaphors helps explain how a certain kind of recognition—not just any recognition, though—can constitute some justification or the measure of success. When Boyd says that metaphors make it possible to refer to aspects of a situation that are probable, but not easily articulatable, but that can become articulatable if the metaphor is successful, he does not mean that it becomes possible to tell *some* story about, say, brains as computers, but rather that it becomes possible to tell a story that allows us to increase our understanding in relevant ways. We want to be able to tell a story that allows us to investigate further that which needs to be understood. Boyd suggests that the question to be asked about the success of a metaphor is not about particular results, but rather about what sort of understanding is accessed by our use of the metaphor *within* the process of investigation ("Metaphor and Theory Change," 382).

Dark Waters

In Muriel's case, the web metaphor plays a constitutive role relative to her expectation for survival as a certain kind of person and to the understanding required to act upon that expectation. Muriel could have expected that for people like her, there is only a kind of living death, the kind she sees in Adam:

> I looked at Adam as he moved away. . . . He slowly slouched back to his post, the soles of his unlaced worn shoes hardly leaving the surface of the floor, but rubbing over it with every step. He gave me one more knowing look and shook his head slowly, perhaps regretting my apparent state of utter ignorance and stubbornness. He sat, sullen, facing the door, his eyes staring, his lips partially parted. He sat dead still, big and rugged like the sphinx, as if he was part of the furniture, stiff and static. (94)

If Muriel expected to be like Adam, or if she thought that it was reasonable that people like her end up like Adam, she might have dismissed her perception of nauseating intolerability. She could have experienced the apartheid laws as nauseatingly intolerable, but then gotten used to the laws because she expects for herself only the sort of death she describes in Adam. Then, of course, there would not have been a need for an explanation that contributed to her understanding of how to escape: if Muriel had been stiff and static as the furniture, like Adam, or if she expected to be, she would not have wanted to escape or have cared about the possibility of escape or have needed to understand it.

According to Boyd's description of the nature of scientific knowledge and theory change, the role of metaphors is just one of many ways in which scientific language becomes accommodated to the causal structures of the world. Boyd describes a complex process of dialectical engagement in which investigators modify beliefs as a result of empirical results, which then suggest directions for further development. Boyd and others have discussed the ways in which knowers themselves are involved in this process; such "subjective" elements as values, attitudes, interests, and so on can explain rather than inhibit one's possibilities for understanding.[3] When we consider the ways in which such mechanisms for change in moral and social understanding can involve identifying, situating, and committing *oneself* in certain ways, we can see how moral thought and moral development have a peculiar personal character and require a peculiar kind of personal daring. The manner in which some sorts of similarities come to seem probable in cases of moral deliberation is dependent in the most interesting cases upon a person's already committing herself in action to certain imaginative possibilities. Such a commitment involves explanatory work that increasingly rules out other options, just as Muriel's ensnaring web metaphor rules out returning to the radio store.

Italian Marxist philosopher Antonio Gramsci tried to work out some of the implications of a more naturalistic view of how we understand the self.[4] He understood that acquiring knowledge is a process of causal interaction with the world in which selves and beliefs are changed as a result of engagement. Intriguingly, he tried to work out some of the implications of a more materialist view of how we understand ourselves and our relations with others. He did this in particular in his famous discussion of organic intellectuals, but his now popular ideas are sometimes indebted to V. I. Lenin.[5] In fact, in little known passages from Lenin's *Philosophical Notebooks* are suggestions about what it means for the self that as knowers we are causally situated in relation to the objects of investigation. In the dialectic involving self and the world, there is not just the modification of beliefs, but of the self itself. Lenin, as it turns out, thought that the "personal" is political—indeed, that it had to be if we are to discover human truths, for as material beings, we must engage with the world as whole selves, not just as minds, in order to know that world. The challenge of such a view is that it suggests that we make a mistake when we expect the process of acquiring understanding to be one in which we always maintain or ought to maintain control, even of ourselves.

In other words, if we think of ourselves not as minds looking out at the world, but instead as organically situated products of that world, our understanding requires creation and struggle: "Cognition is the eternal, endless approximation of thought to the object. The *reflection* of nature in man's thought must be understood not 'lifelessly,' not 'abstractly,' *not devoid of movement*, not without contradictions, but in the eternal process of movement, the arising of contradictions and their solution." (Lenin, *Philosophi-*

cal Notebooks, 195; emphasis in original). For Lenin, then, the consequence of a dialectical view was that our subjective perceptions—our attitudes, feelings, intuitions, even desires—are sometimes as they are because the world is as it is. When Lenin says mysteriously about Hegel's dialectic, "Very profound and clever! The laws of logic are the reflections of the objective in the subjective consciousness of man," he may have been expressing the now more acceptable idea that we have "subjective" ideas because of causal engagement with the actual (objective) structures of the world.

This notion of the process of understanding, however, has initially disturbing aspects, at least in relation to liberal views of the self. Liberal philosophy suggests that acting autonomously consists roughly in the capacity to live one's life "from the inside"—that is, according to one's settled preferences and interests, with true beliefs. One's autonomy is interfered with, on this view, if one is coerced, psychologically or otherwise, into living according to values that one has not endorsed. The Lenin and Gramsci view of the personal implications of knowledge gathering, however, suggests that to the extent that we acquire knowledge by interacting with the world, we have to be willing also to be acted upon *by* the world. Therefore, whereas, according to Lenin, Hegel thought that "Inorganic nature which is subdued by the living being suffers this because it is *in itself* the same as life is *for itself*" (*Philosophical Notebooks*, 202), Lenin's response is, "Invert it—pure materialism" (202). Dialectics, for Hegel, had to do with subduing nature, whereas Lenin's inversion involves *being subdued* by nature.

Thus, when Lenin talks about Hegel's notion of "the ideal passing into real" as "dark waters" (114) and as "profound" not only for history but also for the "personal life of man" (114), he could be talking about the personal and practical implications of a particular view of knowledge in general, one thoroughly different from the view that has been central in European and U.S. philosophical traditions. To understand the world, we must be acted upon by the world. We must sometimes be controlled and transformed by circumstances and relations without any relevant assurance of what the moral and cognitive consequences may be. This is, in fact, the situation Muriel commits herself to for the sake of understanding. She comes to understand that there are reasons to think that a similarity exists between her situation and a web of unacceptable entanglement. Although she cannot articulate these reasons, they are good enough that she relies upon them to draw conclusions about the rest of her experience and about what she should do.

Having recognized such a connection and relied upon it inductively, Muriel submits herself to certain possibilities and results. Having recognized the web as entangling, she cannot now rely upon that same web to interpret her experiences and observations. The dark waters of moral understanding consist in the fact that in cases in which there is reason to think that more adequate moral meaning needs to be discovered, one cannot expect to possess in advance sufficient assurance that the commitments one makes in order to investigate and discover such meaning will be successful or even understandable. And the risk is that if they are not, one cannot go back to what or who one was before one undertook such commitments.

To be subverted by nature is not just to have one's thoughts and ideas changed as a result of one's interactions with the world; it is also to have one's self "subverted" by circumstances and conditions. We might have thought that understanding—including moral understanding—is a process of deliberate, controlled evaluation of our beliefs in the face of evidence and that the "subversion by nature" can be understood in terms of a willingness to *confront* the evidence, to be immersed in the sorts of situations that can make such evidence available. Although this is sometimes how it is, Lenin seems to be suggesting that understanding is, at least occasionally, what emerges from a process in which one is controlled by circumstances and conditions, including personal and emotional ones. We cannot always expect to be able to identify with sufficient confidence those particular circumstances and events that are relevant to understanding—hence, the situation of personal risk in moral risk.

It is important, though, that the waters are *moral* dark waters. If understanding in general is acquired through engagement and transformation, we cannot discover human possibilities without sometimes taking such personal risk to who we are and can be. The point about metaphors in science is that the use of such metaphors, even without adequate content, provides a way of referring to aspects of a phenomenon that need to be investigated further and that must be acted upon in order to be investigated further. Metaphors are *constitutive*, Boyd suggests, to the extent that the direction of investigation, of future strategies, is determined by the images themselves and their use in making inferences. To the extent that the identification and commitment of oneself to expectations can also be constitutive in somewhat the same way, as it is in Muriel's case, the uncertainty and metaphorical darkness of such situations is morally significant.

This is not to say, though, that it is the *uncertainty* that is most definitive of the kind of commitment Muriel undertakes. There is a popular postmodernist position that advocates the embracing of uncertainty as an ideal.[6] But when Muriel is uncertain about herself and her position, she accepts the toilet segregation and other indignities as things she can do nothing about. In her uncertainty, she relies upon her current expectations and decides there is no point in staging a one-woman protest. In her "openness" she crosses borders, but eventually, to make sense of such borders, she needs a purport, a perspective constituted by the drive to realize some very specific expectations in particular. At the end of the book, Muriel is no longer uncertain about her position and what it means. What is uncertain and perhaps terrifying are the specific consequences of what she is doing, but Muriel is quite certain about the significance of such uncertainty—namely, that it is relevant to and required for her realization of certain specific goals that she knows cannot be realized in the current circumstances.

Dark moral waters consist in the acquisition of a more adequate moral perspective at the price of a certain control of direction but within a definite perception of cognitive need. The metaphorical darkness refers to the fact that one encounters the explanatory necessities that can bring about a more adequate moral perspective only to the extent that one acts upon certain expectations about who one is. And one may well not possess adequate conceptual resources to fully justify such expectations. If one is motivated primarily by opportunities already well understood and expected, there is no interesting explanatory burden that can constitute the conditions for discovering a more adequate moral perspective. Muriel quits her job, cutting off certain options with no guarantee, and she has no regrets. On the one hand, it may look as though Muriel is in a dangerous and uncertain position, but on the other, she seems very much to be in a position of certainty. The commitment to moral risk may then best be explained not by what one is committed to by some particular sort of promise, but rather by the kind of recognition of relevant impossibilities that can motivate a commitment to unrecognized but probable possibilities in another direction.

Some say the motivation for undertaking moral risk is survival as a person.[7] Indeed, for Muriel, moral risk provides her only option for recognition, by herself and others, as a real person. But the suggestion that people undertake such risk as a matter of survival is too simple. It would seem to be true that, as Card suggests, people are compelled to situations of moral risk by issues of survival *(Unnatural Lottery)*, but given that what characterizes moral risk is precisely that one cannot know in advance the full moral value, or even whether there is any such value, of what one will survive as—Muriel, for instance, may end up seeing herself as economically irresponsible—the more important motivation would seem to be recognition of a certain cognitive and moral inadequacy of meaning and identification of the importance of that inadequacy. Moreover, the identification of inadequacy presupposes very definite expectations about one's specific significance. For the explanatory burden which I have identified as characterizing moral risk exists relative to expectations. It would seem, then, that people do not undertake moral risk *in order to* survive or even in order to become "truer selves," but rather that people end up in situations of moral risk and are able to identify their situations as compelling in this way, *because* of their expectation that their survival be of a certain moral sort.

In moral risk, besides "standing behind," one is compelled to move ahead in order to more adequately identify and theoretically develop the significance of relevant events and phenomena. I have suggested that the position of moral risk is primarily a drive for explanatory unity or the attempt to find a story that makes sense of important judgments relevant to one's going ahead. The problem is that in the case of moral perspective, such a drive for unity involves committing oneself to a particular direction of personal development and to rejecting others; as such, it is a sometimes exclusionary, single-minded commitment. Thus, moral risk is not in the first instance about *moral* commitment; rather, it is about the imaginative capacity that allows individuals to recognize the implications of specific cognitive inadequacies so that, as in Muriel's case, they can make definite, personal commitments at the risk of not knowing whether they are in fact morally valuable ones.

Notes

Introduction

1. We would like to thank Jan Sutherland for her thoughtful reading of the essays and her advice on the introduction.

1. "The Racial Polity," by Charles W. Mills

1. See, for example, the following works in, respectively, cultural studies, labor history, U.S. literature, film theory, sociology, philosophy, history of science, gender studies, legal theory: Henry Louis Gates Jr., *"Race," Writing and Difference*; David Roediger, *The Wages of Whiteness: Race and the Making of the American Working Class* and *Towards the Abolition of Whiteness*; Toni Morrison, *Playing in the Dark: Whiteness and the Literary Imagination*; Eric J. Sundquist, *To Wake the Nation: Race in the Making of American Literature*; Daniel Bernardi, ed., *The Birth of Whiteness: Race and the Emergence of Cinema*; Michelle Fine, Lois Weiss, Linda C. Powell, and L. Mun Wong, eds., *Off White: Readings on Race, Power, and Society*; David Theo Goldberg, *Racist Culture· Philosophy and the Politics of Meaning*; Lewis R. Gordon, *Bad Faith and Antiblack Racism*; Lucius Outlaw Jr., *On Race and Philosophy*; Sandra Harding, ed., *The "Racial" Economy of Science: Toward a Democratic Future*; Ruth Frankenberg, *White Women, Race Matters: The Social Construction of Whiteness*; Ian Haney López, *White by Law: The Legal Construction of Race*; Richard Delgado, ed., *Critical Race Theory: The Cutting Edge*; Kimberle Crenshaw, Neil Gotanda, Gary Peller, and Kendall Thomas, eds., *Critical Race Theory: The Key Writings that Formed the Movement*.

2. Demographically, only 1 percent of philosophers in North American universities are black—slightly more than one hundred people—and arguably this underrepresentation also helps to sustain a conceptual "whiteness" of the discipline.

3. But note that the same could be said about feminist theory. "Feminism, like most broad-based philosophical perspectives, accommodates several species under its genus" (Rosemarie Tong, *Feminist Thought: A Comprehensive Introduction*, 1).

4. See Delgado, *Critical Race Theory*, and Crenshaw et al., *Critical Race Theory*. Some years ago, the African American philosopher Lucius Outlaw Jr. called for a "criti-

cal theory" of race ("Toward a Critical Theory of 'Race,'" 58–82). The *critical* in *critical race theory* has more than one meaning, signifying both the scare-quotes (i.e., nonbiological) sense in which *race* is used and also (as in Outlaw) the general notion of a critical theory of society that seeks both to understand and transform it. *Critical white studies* can be seen as an offshoot of critical race theory that focuses specifically on whiteness.

5. In their introduction, the Blackwell editors state, "Nationalism—still less racism, sexism or ageism—does not figure [here], on the grounds that it hardly counts as a principled way of thinking about things" (*Companion*, 3). But the oppositional nationalism of subordinated groups and nations surely needs to be distinguished from the characteristically chauvinistic nationalism of hegemonic powers.

6. For some overviews and discussions, see: Lorenne M. G. Clark and Lynda Lange, eds., *The Sexism of Social and Political Theory: Women and Reproduction from Plato to Nietzsche*; Susan Moller Okin, *Women in Western Political Thought* and *Justice, Gender, and the Family*; Alison Jaggar, *Feminist Politics and Human Nature*; and Diana H. Coole, *Women in Political Theory: From Ancient Misogyny to Contemporary Feminism*.

7. See, for example, Cornel West, "A Genealogy of Modern Racism," 47–65; Goldberg, *Racist Culture*; Lucius T. Outlaw Jr., "The Future of 'Philosophy' in America," 183–204.

8. See, for example, Mary Briody Mahowald, *Philosophy of Women: An Anthology of Classic and Contemporary Concepts*; and L. Bell, *Visions of Women*. An important start has been made with Emmanuel Eze, who points out that "whereas feminist critics have extensively examined the gender-inflected nature of eighteenth-century science and philosophy, a similar critical engagement is lacking in the area of race" (*Race and the Enlightenment*, 8).

9. See Eric Williams, *Capitalism and Slavery*; and E. L. Jones, *The European Miracle*. For a defense of this "Third Worldist" perspective, see J. M. Blaut et al., *1492: The Debate on Colonialism, Eurocentrism, and History*, and J. M. Blaut et al., *Colonizer's Model of the World: Geographical Diffusionism and Eurocentric History*.

10. David Hume, footnote added in the 1753–54 edition of his essay "Of National Characters," first published in 1748, cited in Eze, *Race and the Enlightenment*, 33.

11. It is through Martin Bernal's *Black Athena: The Afroasiatic Roots of Classical Civilization* that the challenge to conventional histories of Greek civilization first became known to a mass white readership, but the claim is much older in the oppositional ("vindicationist") black tradition—going back, in fact, to the nineteenth century. See, for example, Cheikh Anta Diop, *The African Origin of Civilization: Myth or Reality*.

12. For an elaboration of this argument, see Charles W. Mills, *The Racial Contract*, 63–72.

13. For critiques of mainstream sociology, see, for example, Robert Blauner, *Racial Oppression in America*; David T. Wellman, *Portraits of White Racism*; and Stephen Steinberg, *Turning Back: The Retreat from Racial Justice and American Thought and Policy*.

14. Hartz speaks of "the fragments of Europe" in the New World (*The Founding of New Societies: Studies in the Histories of the United States, Latin America, South Africa, Canada, and Australia*).

15. See Francis Jennings, *The Invasion of America: Indians, Colonialism, and the Cant of Conquest*; Theodore W. Allen, *The Invention of the White Race*; Pierre L. van den Berghe, *Race and Racism: A Comparative Perspective*; Alexander Saxton, *The Rise and Fall of the White Republic*; James Oakes, *The Ruling Race: A History of American Slaveholders*; Roediger, *Wages of Whiteness* (the phrase originally comes from Du Bois's *Black Reconstruction*); Andrew Hacker, *Two Nations*; and Cheryl I. Harris, "Whiteness as Property."

16. See Jennifer L. Hochschild, *The New American Dilemma: Liberal Democracy and School Desegregation*; Stokely Carmichael and Charles V. Hamilton, *Black Power: The Politics of Liberation in America*.

17. The fact that (perceived) group interests rather than individual interests are the main determinants of white and black attitudes is one of the central and most important findings of Donald R. Kinder and Lynn M. Sanders in *Divided by Color: Racial Oppression and Democratic Ideals*.

18. See Noel Ignatiev, *How the Irish Became White*; Elaine K. Ginsberg, *Passing and the Fictions of Identity*; Adrian Piper, "Passing for White, Passing for Black," 234–69.

19. See Toni Morrison, *Playing in the Dark*; Sundquist, *To Wake the Nation*; and Bernardi, ed., *The Birth of Whiteness*.

20. For a discussion, see Charles W. Mills, "Revisionist Ontologies: Theorizing White Supremacy," 105–34.

21. Derrick Bell, "Property Rights in Whiteness: Their Legal Legacy, Their Economic Costs"; Harris, "Whiteness as Property"; and George Lipsitz, "The Possessive Investment in Whiteness: Racialized Social Democracy and the 'White' Problem in American Studies."

22. For details, see, for example, Melvin Oliver and Thomas M. Shapiro, *Black Wealth/White Health: A New Perspective on Racial Inequality*; Douglas S. Massey and Nancy A. Denton, *American Apartheid: Segregation and the Making of the Underclass*; and Hacker, *Two Nations*.

23. Obviously, there is a greatly differentiated class and gender benefit. A full treatment, which is beyond the scope of this chapter, would require the analysis of these differentials within the white population and of the possible opening they offer for progressive social change.

24. See Mary Frances Berry, *Black Resistance, White Law: A History of Constitutional Racism in America*; Marx, *Making Race and Nation*; and Desmond King, *Separate and Unequal: Black Americans and the U.S. Federal Government*.

25. Lynn C. Curtis and Fred Harris, *The Millenium Breach* (an update of the 1967 Kerner Commission Report); see also Massey and Denton, *American Apartheid*; Hacker, *Two Nations*; Steinberg, *Turning Back*; Kinder and Sanders, *Divided by Color*.

2. "Fanon, Philosophy, and Racism," by Lewis R. Gordon

This essay emerges from my discussion of Fanon and philosophy in my book, *Her Majesty's Other Children: Sketches of Racism from a Neocolonial Age*.

1. Think of the contrast between Western philosophical conception of its modern icons and its philosophical underside's conception: in most Western philosophy curricula, modernism is constituted by the thought of Descartes, Hobbes, Spinoza, Leibniz, Locke, Smith, Hume, and Rousseau. For Enrique Dussel, European modernism is marked by the deeds of Columbus, Cortés, and Pizarro. He writes, "Modernity was born in 1492 with the 'centrality' of Europe[;] eurocentrism originated when Europe was able to dominate the Arab world, which had been the center of the [European] known world up to the 15th century. The 'I,' which begins with the 'I conquer' of Hernán Cortés or Pizarro, which in fact precedes the Cartesian *ego cogito* by about a century, produces Indian genocide, African slavery, and Asian colonial wars. The majority of today's humanity (the South) is the other face of modernity" (Dussel, *The Underside of Modernity: Apel, Ricoeur, Rorty, and Taylor and the Philosophy of Liberation*, 20).

2. Culture in Africa literally was defined as non-African. Thus, *black Africa* called for

a search for culture that was uniquely African. But because culture itself was defined as European or Asiatic, black Africa was considered and to some extent is still considered a cultureless place. The black contributions to northern African society (which isn't called *white Africa*) is thus glossed over in the designation. North Africa, although spoken of in terms of European and Asiatic cultures, is given a racial identity of whiteness.

3. For discussion, see William Preston's "Nietzsche on Blacks" and his *Nietzsche as Anti-Socialist: Prophet of Bourgeois Ennoblement*.

4. For a discussion on Manichaeism, see R. Wilson, "Mani and Manichaeism," 149–50.

5. All translations of Fanon's work throughout this chaper are mine except where otherwise noted.

6. For Rousseau's view, see *Du contrat social*. Many English translations are available under the title *The Social Contract*.

7. The most popular biographical accounts are David Caute, *Frantz Fanon*, and Irene Gendzier, *Frantz Fanon: A Critical Study*. The film version is Isaac Julien, *Frantz Fanon: "Black Skin, White Mask"* (1995), a film that, when screened at the Black Harvest Film Festival (Art Institute of Chicago, 1996), was described by an audience member as "covering up more than uncovering Fanon." For "uncovering" Fanon, I recommend Hussein Bulhan, *Frantz Fanon and the Psychology of Oppression*; Lewis R. Gordon, Denean Sharpley-Whiting, and Renée T. White, eds., *Fanon: A Critical Reader*; and Denean Sharpley-Whiting, *Fanon and Feminism: Theory, Thought, Praxis*.

8. This essay is Sartre's famous preface, "Orphé noir," to Léopold Sédar Senghor's edited collection of black poets, *Anthologie de la nouvelle poésie Nègre et malgache*, which was originally published in Paris by Présence Africaine in 1948.

9. For a recent survey, see the bibliography in Gordon, Sharpley-Whiting, and White, eds., *Fanon*.

10. For discussion of some of these views, as well as the postcolonial view discussed below, see Lewis R. Gordon, *Fanon and the Crisis of European Man*, chap. 5.

11. See C. L. R. James's short pamphlet, "From Du Bois to Fanon"; Pietro Clemente, *Frantz Fanon, tra esistenzialist e rivoluzion*; Ato Sekyi-Otu's "Form and Metaphor in Fanon's Critique of Racial and Colonial Domination"; and Emmanuel Hansen, *Frantz Fanon: Social and Political Thought*.

12. For examples of these interpretations, see Gwen Bergner, "The Role of Gender in Fanon's *Black Skin, White Masks*"; Mary Ann Doane, "Dark Continents: Epistemologies of Racial and Sexual Difference in Psychoanalysis and the Cinema"; Clarisse Zimra, "Right the Calabash: Writing History in the Female Francophone Narrative"; and Marie-Aimée Helie-Lucas, "Women, Nationalism and Religion in the Algerian Liberation Struggle." There are many more. See Sharpley-Whiting for a full bibliography and response. Sharpley-Whiting, *Fanon and Feminisms*, points out not only that many of these writers misrepresent Fanon's thought, but also that they often extol white male writers who have been influenced by Fanon as "feminist," in spite of those writers' often clearly misogynist declarations. Jean Genet, for instance, used many of Fanon's ideas and was much admired and respected by Euro-feminists and gay theorists, although he declared that what was positive about Fanon was his having only passed through a woman by the necessity of birth. See discussion in Sharpley-Whiting's text and also Edmund White's award-winning biography, *Genet: A Biography*. Think also of the Euro-feminist use of the thought of Kant, Nietzsche, Heidegger, Foucault, or Derrida, without apologies. In the end, the question is unavoidable: Why is Fanon's thought on women misogynist but Angela Davis's and Genet's feminist when they argue the same case, with the same conclusions? The visceral response to Fanon on the part of Euro-feminists is ultimately black male phobic: Fanon was a black man and, as such, was being rebuked for speaking be-

yond his "place." The racist conclusion is that the discourse on women is reserved for white women, white men, and women of color. Finally, we should observe the politics here. The attack on Fanon is also linked to an attack on liberation theorists. If revolutionary politics of the left is rewritten as intrinsically misogynist and homophobic, what kind of politics remain as acceptable political alternatives? For discussion of the political significance of these criticisms, see Joy Ann James, *Transcending the Talented Tenth: Black Leaders and American Intellectualism*, and for more on the context of this discussion, see Denean Sharpley-Whiting and Renée White, eds., *Spoils of War: Women of Color*.

13. Sylvia Wynter's articles are many, but "Is 'Development' a Purely Empirical Concept or Also Teleological? A Perspective from 'We the Underdeveloped'" is representative. Paget Henry's articles are also many, but see especially: "CLR James, African and Afro-Caribbean Philosophy," "African and Afro-Caribbean Existential Philosophy," and "Fanon, African, and Afro-Caribbean Philosophy." See also Paget Henry and Paul Buhle, "Caliban as Deconstructionist: C. L. R. James and Post-Colonial Discourse," which, although focusing on James, contextualizes Fanon's contribution as well.

14. Sharpley-Whiting reports, by way of bell hooks, that there was hostility toward hooks's presentation of Fanon's work in a spring cultural studies conference on Fanon's work in England. The Euro-feminists at that conference attacked hooks for engaging Fanon's ideas instead of "working him over." See Sharpley-Whiting's discussion of Fanon's influence on bell hooks's thought in her final chapter of *Fanon and Feminisms*.

15. For a review of some of the books published during this period, see Anthony C. Alessandrini's "Whose Fanon?"

16. *Philosopher* here means something more than a person with a doctorate in philosophy. I regard many individuals with that title to be scholars of or on philosophy instead of philosophers. Philosophers are individuals who make original contributions to the development of philosophical thought, to the world of ideas. Such thinkers are people whom scholars study. It is no accident that philosophers in this sense are few in number and that many of them did not have doctorates in philosophy—for example, René Descartes, David Hume, Søren Kierkegaard, William James, Edmund Husserl, Karl Jaspers, Jean-Paul Sartre, Simone de Beauvoir, and Alfred Schutz.

17. The secondary literature on Marx and Sartre is dotted with excursions into theoretical discussions of race. For a bibliography, see Lewis R. Gordon, *Bad Faith and Antiblack Racism*.

18. Cornel West is another philosopher who may come to mind. Yet, in spite of his being well- rooted in discussions of race, West's major contribution in the end may be his effort to forge a genealogy of modern scientific racism in *Prophesy, Deliverance!: An Afro-American Revolutionary Christianity*. For discussion of West, see our discussion of black academic intellectuals in part 2 of *Her Majesty's Other Children: Sketches of Racism from a Neocolonial Age*. See also James's discussion of postmodern black intellectuals in *Transcending the Talented Tenth*. A problem with West's account is that it tells us less about what racism is than about its evolution in a particular form of discourse. The problem is that black inferiority was a part of European discourse before the emergence of modern science, and even if it were concomitant with modern science, there is still the need to explain its existence among populations who were not even aware of natural scientific developments and assertions. Did slave traders read Buffon, Gobineau, and Kant? Maybe some did, but that hardly explains whether the texts were cause or ideological rationalization (effect).

19. See also Douglas's discussion of his recognition of the similarity between his condition and the ox in his later narrative, *My Bondage and My Freedom*, chap. 15.

20. See Gordon, *Bad Faith and Antiblack Racism*, 95–96.

21. See Gordon, *Her Majesty's Other Children*, chap. 4, for a developed discussion of these dynamics.

22. The title of this fifth chapter has been translated in the Grove edition by Charles Lamm Markmann as "The Fact of Blackness," which has generated a slew of misinterpretations of Fanon's thought in the English language. The French, "L'expérience vécue du noir," is rooted in a phenomenology of lived experience *(expérience vécue)* with a drama of its own. For discussion, see Ronald A. T. Judy, "Fanon's Body of Black Experience."

23. Craig Kilborn of the Comedy Central television station's *Daily Show* made the following remark about the Republican primary convention, at which reportedly one out of five delegates was a millionaire and more than 90 percent of the delegates were white male: "This is a party for everyone. We don't care if you are a rich white man from Palm Springs, Florida, or a rich white man from Palm Beach, California. This party has a place for you." In a different context, the cry against so-called reverse discrimination manifests this ideology. Whites have been racialized as a discriminated-against group by virtue of an egalitarian positioning with blacks. See Robert Westley's essay, "The Rhetoric of Equal Protection," for a development of this argument.

24. See W. V. O. Quine's *From a Logical Point of View*.

25. A classic example is Sartre's *L'être et le néant: essay d'ontologie phénoménologique*. For an existential phenomenological discussion of Quine's view of ontology, see Gordon, *Bad Faith and Antiblack Racism*, 81–82.

3. "On Race and Philosophy," by Lucius T. Outlaw Jr.

This essay is a revision of the introductory essay of Lucius T. Outlaw Jr. *On Race and Philosophy*, 1–21.

1. For an argument denying that races exist see David R. Roediger, "Introduction: From the Social Construction of Race to the Abolition of Whiteness," in his *Towards the Abolition of Whiteness*.

2. The review is taken from Lucius T. Outlaw Jr., "The Future of 'Philosophy' in America," in *On Race and Philosophy*, pp. 192–196.

3. "*Homo sapiens* was presented as a species divided into a number of races of different capacity and temperament. Human affairs could be understood only if individuals were seen as representatives of races for it was there that the driving forces of human history resided" (Michael Banton and Jonathan Harwood, *The Race Concept*, 30).

4. 5 For a particularly focused discussion of the difficult problem of articulating such a political philosophy, see John Rawls, *Political Liberalism*.

5. For an engaging reconstruction and critical discussion of the historical emergence and recent forms of political struggles over identity, see Charles Taylor, "The Politics of Recognition."

6. "Talk of 'race' is particularly distressing for those of us who take culture seriously. For, where race works—in places where 'gross differences' of morphology are correlated with 'subtle differences' of temperament, belief, and intention—it works as an attempt at metonym for culture, and it does so only at the price of biologizing what *is* culture, ideology. . . . What exists 'out there' in the world—communities of meaning, shading variously into each other in the rich structure of the social world—is the province not of biology but of the human sciences" (Kwame Anthony Appiah, *In My Father's House: Africa and the Philosophy of Culture*, 45).

7. Shipman (166) attributes the characterization of proposals to substitute another term for the troublesome *race* as "lexical surgery" (Stanley M. Garn, "Race," 115).

8. For this sketch I rely heavily on Berger and Luckmann's *The Social Construction of Reality*.

9. In our historical accounts of philosophizing, we philosophers have tended to provide narrations that legitimate us as those, and only those, capable of fulfilling such crucial functions as being the producers and guardians of the knowledges vital to surviving and living well. Of course, we have had competitors. Centuries ago we won out over the women-witches with the assistance of priests and preachers, but later had to strike a deal with our former allies to share the job. For nearly three thousand years of Western history, a powerful minority of persons in various peoples among the variety of still changing populations, collectivities, and geopolitical configurations we call "Europe" have convinced themselves (and others) that they alone—or they primarily—have the most well-developed capacity for knowing than anyone else, than non-Europeans especially, and that they thus have produced or can produce the knowledges needed to provide the ordering necessary for survival and well-being of their natal or adopted communities, some even claim for the entire world, a few even claim for the known and unknown universe ("true for all possible worlds," as some philosophers require of our justifications. . .). But this is a story of racism at work in fields of the intellect in which rationalizations of white supremacy have been constructed. I say more about these matters in *On Race and Philosophy*. For the moment I'm supposed to be pursuing the third path, between racist and anti-racist endeavors.

10. A number of thinkers have wrestled with this problem. For example, in *Liberalism, Community, and Culture* Will Kymlicka makes a valiant effort to revise political liberalism to accommodate the "cultural rights" of certain kinds of groups.

4. "Moral Asymmetries in Racism," by Lawrence Blum

1. My argument employs a concept of a *racial group*. I want to make it clear that I join the current consensus in regarding *race* as a scientifically invalid concept, and one that is misleading in ordinary discourse because it tends to imply the validity of some scientific notion of *race*. However, the notion of a racial group is meant to denote a group whose historical and social experience is/has been shaped by being regarded as a "race" and treated as such. This definition confers a certain social and historical reality on the notion of *race*, but makes it clear that such a concept can be understood only as a socially constructed one, not a biologically authentic one.

2. For excellent discussions of the concept of *institutional racism* and its history, see Robert C. Smith, *Racism in the Post-Civil Rights Era: Now You See It, Now You Don't*, chaps. 2, 4; and Robert Miles, *Racism*, 50–61.

3. *Institutional* and *individual* are not the only forms of racism. Usefully distinguished from both is *cultural* racism, which refers to culturally pervasive racist images and stereotypes.

4. How one draws the line between what is racism and what is not (yet that might be blameworthy and related to race) is a complex issue beyond the scope of this paper, and is not necessary to the argument herein.

5. Although the racism in question is perpetrated by an individual (this is what makes it what I call *individual racism*), it is *as* a member of a specific ("racial") group that the person indulges in racism. I am indebted to Sue Campbell for this point.

6. I am influenced in the distinction between two forms of racism by Laurence Thomas's discussion of the different forms of prejudice involved in anti-black and anti-Jewish racism. See "The Evolution of Anti-Semitism" and "Characterizing the Evil of American Slavery and the Holocaust." Ultimately, one would want some account of why

the two forms of racism carry the moral opprobrium that they do; and I would trace both historically to systems of racial oppression, such as slavery, colonialism, Nazism, segregation, apartheid. Our modern sense of *racism* is deeply affected by racism's enmeshment in these historical phenomena, different instances of which have involved inferiority-based and hatred-based racisms (again, cf. L. Thomas). At the same time, I would argue that the term no longer requires the presence of these or other actual institutional forms of racism, which is part of the reason why groups that have suffered from racism in its institutionalized forms can themselves *be* racist, even against members of their racial oppressor group.

7. Other examples of this view: *(a)* Paula Rothenberg, a philosopher and the author of a widely used collection on race and gender, says, "[R]acism involves the subordination of people of color by white people. Blacks can be prejudiced, but racism means, at least, prejudice plus power" (*Racism and Sexism: An Integrated Study*, 6). *(b)* Spike Lee: "Black people can't be racist. Racism is an institution. Black people don't have the power to keep hundreds of people from getting jobs or the vote. . . . Now black people can be prejudiced. Shit, everybody's prejudiced about something. I don't think there will ever be an end to prejudice. But racism, that's a different thing entirely" ("Interview"). *(c)* Joseph Barndt, "Racism is the power to back up one's [racial] prejudices" (*Dismantling Racism: The Continuing Challenge to White America*, 28). (d) Andrew Hacker cites Coleman Young, the mayor of Detroit, as arguing that blacks within the United States "cannot be called racists, for the simple reason that they are an oppressed people. Racism, he has said, should be attributed only to those who have the power to cause suffering. . . . Racism takes its full form only when it has an impact on the real world" (*Two Nations*, 33).

8. It is, of course, not racist to point out that blacks score lower on certain kinds of tests than whites or Asians. What is racist is Herrnstein and Murray's implication that some inherent, race-based, deficiency can be inferred from this type of fact.

9. Another example within Japan is the *burakumin*, a group that is more distinctly thought of by Japanese as "racially" distinct from Japanese, even though Westerners cannot distinguish the two groups. Japanese tend to regard burakumin as inferior and discriminate against them. Consider also the case of the Japanese government official who confessed to racist sentiments toward blacks. He said that although he knew that these sentiments were wrong, he could not help but feel dirtied by contact with a black person. Surely, this is a case of racism, of a racist feeling. The perpetrator is not a white person, but he is a person in power. On Japanese racial attitudes, see Dorinne Kondo, *Crafting Selves*, 11.

10. "Racialized" ethnicity can apply even to groups defined partly in terms of religion, even though one's religion is usually considered a matter of personal choice. For example, in the eyes of Serbs, the Muslim aspect of Bosnian ethnicity is part of a semiheritable status that Bosnians are born into, which is what makes Serbian hatred of Bosnians close enough to a full-bodied racism to count as racism for the purposes of this essay. Jews are another group once thought of almost entirely as a *religious* group, but since the nineteenth century or so have come more and more to be seen as a racialized ethnic group. The Nazi view of Jews was, of course, a fully and unequivocally racialized one.

11. This example is adapted from V. Ooka Pang, "Ethnic Prejudice: Still Alive and Hurtful." Her example is of first graders, whose attitudes may not be sufficiently congealed into truly racist ones, even if they engage in an act of "racist exclusion." (I am indebted to Sue Campbell for insightful comments on the Ooka Pang example.)

12. I argue in detail later that the power dynamic discussed here affects the harm, the moral wrong, and the blameworthiness of racism, but not whether the phenomenon *is* racism. Also, although in a sense any racist action that harms another individual—for example, making a hurtful racist remark—involves an exercise of "power," the forms of

power at stake in my disagreement with Feagin and Vera have some institutional or systemic structure.

13. I am indebted in my discussion of power and dominance to the work of Jorge Garcia, especially "The Heart of Racism."

14. Garcia emphasizes the point that there are vice-based forms of racism in the absence of "racialist" or "scientific racist" ideologies and beliefs about racism ("The Heart of Racism").

15. Strikingly, Spike Lee's portrayal of racism in his superb film *Do the Right Thing* (1987) belies his cavalier remarks about individual racial prejudice on the part of persons of color. In one powerful montage scene Lee has five characters—a Korean, an African American, an Italian, a Jew, and a Latino—spit out racial epithets at one of the other groups. The audience is clearly meant to react to this scene not as a universal condition of innocuous prejudice, but rather as a disturbing, widespread manifestation of racism, which the film implies is in some form responsible for the serious racial divisions explored in the film.

16. Perhaps sometimes the term *racist* is used in a way that may seem to imply that using a racial slur or holding the belief that one group is intellectually inferior to another puts one on the same moral plane as Heinrich Himmler and the Ku Klux Klan. Such a sloppy use of the term *racism* does pay tribute to one important truth about it as a term of moral assessment—namely, that it embraces a territory marked by moral seriousness. This is why it is misleading to categorize as "racist" the *less* serious forms of racial ignorance or insensitivity discussed earlier.

17. I am here shifting from the term *victim* to the more antiseptic term *target* to refer to the person to whom or against whom a racist action is directed. The current discourse saddles the former term with a larger political ideology, but the term itself also misleadingly implies a uniformly deeply damaging effect of the racist action on its recipient.

18. Although I am arguing for a moral asymmetry between white-against-black racism and black-against-white racism, my view does not mean, for example, that it is worse for a white person to kill a black person than for a black person to kill a white person. The moral evil of the act independent of its racial character may be so great as to dwarf the moral asymmetry effects. But perhaps we should not in any case think that the moral evil of the asymmetry effects is or is always commensurable with the other dimensions of moral assessment of the act. We might not be able to "sum up" the different moral dimensions into one overall measure of the action's moral disvalue. Thus, even though it would be absurd to say that it is worse for a white to kill a black than for a black to kill a white, it would still be true to say that the two types of killing may raise somewhat different issues and that, in some regard, more damage is caused by one than the other. For example, lynching an individual black man in the U.S. South took no more lives than killing a white man, but the former killing served to and was intended to reinforce a system of racial subordination, whereas the latter did not.

19. The manner in which this asymmetric psychic damage to the target affects our moral assessment of the perpetrator of the act is, however, a complex one. For instance, some young persons may display a swastika as a sign of rebellion—aware that it is strongly disapproved of by the despised "establishment" but unaware or insufficiently aware of the reasons for this mainstream disapproval. It is important to recognize that racism generally causes psychic harms whether it is intentional or not. Although people who have engaged in unintentional racist insults or other racist actions sometimes believe that they have absolved themselves of all responsibility for those actions by sincerely disavowing their prior awareness of the racist character of what they have said or done, this attempted exculpation fails. They are responsible for harm that should have been anticipated, even

if it was unintended, and this idea applies pro tanto to racism. Still, blameworthiness for racism is to some extent affected by its intentionality; moreover, the harm caused by racism is affected by the target's beliefs regarding the intentionality of the racism. (However, the effect is not a simple one. For example, it cannot be said that the target is always harmed less by unintentional than intentional racism.)

20. In "What's Wrong with Bitterness?" Lynne McFall argues that bitterness may be rational and appropriate, even if in some sense "counterproductive" to seeking the most practicable way to deal with one's situation. The argument being considered here is not that the descendants of members of victimized groups are necessarily bitter, but only that their dwelling on their historical victimization is unhelpful. McFall's argument could perhaps be extended to say that even if such a response were in some way unhelpful, it is still a rational and appropriate response to one's victimization.

21. Resistance to the historical legacy argument may come from a general U.S. American reluctance to acknowledge this truth—to acknowledge that one is, in part, one's history. Students' resistance to this truth may stem from an additional source: that the status of student may involve a sense of making oneself anew, of open possibilities, of self-creation, not easily reconciled with a full acknowledgment of the historical sources of one's identity.

22. Although the racism being discussed here involves a strong tendency to cause harm to self-worth, it should not be assumed that psychic harm is an inevitable result of racist acts. Racist attacks on self-worth can be withstood and countered from other quarters—a rich cultural tradition that supports the self-esteem of its inheritors, a strong antiracist dimension to one's moral and political culture or to personal beliefs that resists the implication of inferiority. The moral evil of the particular dimension of racism being discussed here stems from its attack on self-worth, not from the guaranteed success of that attack. A respected and growing literature challenges the ready assumption of an earlier era—legitimized most famously in the use of the argument that racial segregation results in lower black self-esteem in the *Brown v. Board of Education* case in 1954—that blacks have lower self-esteem because they are devalued by whites. See William E. Cross Jr., *Shades of Black: Diversity in African-American Identity*, and Daryl Michael Scott, *Contempt and Pity: Social Policy and the Image of the Damaged*.

23. Epithets such as "white trash" and "redneck" carry a racial connotation and are more derogatory than the epithets mentioned in the text; but they are not simply racial epithets. Both are epithets for white people seen as "lower class"; hence, they partake of an inferiority-based dimension that is itself analogous to that of race.

24. I believe that I owe the general line of thought regarding the significance of patterns of racism to Debra Satz of Stanford University.

25. During the Gulf War, such an incident of anti-Arab persecution took place in Chelsea, Massachusetts, where an Arab American family was driven from its home. Although active, actional anti-Arab racism was most prominent during that period, the widely held stereotypes of Arabs and Arab Americans (the distinction is not clearly made in the popular mind in the United States) as terrorists and cutthroats are in some ways among the most objectionable ethnic and racial stereotypes of any group in the United States.

26. There is also the unfortunate but familiar matter of intragroup racism—people being racist against members of their own group. (Discrimination by blacks against darker-skinned blacks is an example.) Probably some version of the three effects would apply here as well, though the fact that the perpetrator is a member of the target's own group certainly has an impact on the psychic dynamic and thus the character of those effects.

27. I would like to thank the various audiences before whom earlier versions of this es-

say were read: Northwestern University (especially Connie Rosati), College of William and Mary, Suffolk University, Oberlin Colloquium in Philosophy (especially Marilyn Friedman for her acute commentary on my presentation), Bryn Mawr College, and members of a reading group (David Wong, K. Anthony Appiah, David Wilkins, Manisha Sinha, Martha Minow), who have discussed it with me. I would also like to thank Susan Babbitt and Sue Campbell for excellent suggestions on the penultimate version.

5. "Racism: Paradigms and Moral Appraisal (A Response to Blum)," by Marilyn Friedman

1. I do not in fact challenge this view because I agree with it. Rather, I suggest that one of its underlying presumptions be revised, and I consider a question prompted by Blum's view that he himself does not raise.

2. A paradigm is a definitive example of something. It shapes thinking about that something by providing a pattern or template for recognizing and understanding other potential instances of the thing. I share the view of many contemporary philosophers that moral thinking is shaped importantly by moral paradigms—of wrongful acts, of human virtues, and so on.

3. I am assuming that anti-Scandinavian sentiment in the United States was not historically long-lived or substantial.

4. Blum suggests that it is arguable that "any incident of racism . . . strengthens *racism in general*" (chapter 4 in this volume). He himself provides no argument for this point, however. One possibility is that acts of race-based hatred or scorn, even when directed against someone whose race has not been the target of significant racism, have the potential to reinforce the idea that race *as such* is an appropriate reason for hating or scorning someone. This idea in turn can make people feel entitled to act in a racist manner toward those with a significant history of racism.

This suggestion is plausible, but it does not clearly show that acts of race-based hatred lacking a social pattern are bad *in themselves* in virtue of their racial basis. The racist wrong that they exhibit is a feature of their potential consequences, and the race-based wrong of those consequences might only materialize when the number of such acts reaches a critical mass.

Being insulted once on the basis of the color of one's eyes, when eye color is not a basis for significant social patterns of hatred, seems no more wrong than any act of unjustified hatred or scorn, whatever its basis. There is nothing about the eye-color basis, as such, that makes the act more or differently wrong.

5. See note 1.

6. At the end of this essay, however, I suggest that the concept of reactive racism might indeed apply to acts that become so widespread as to constitute a significant racist pattern. Such acts would then become more paradigmatic in nature.

7. It is possible to imagine racism that is a reaction to such racism that was itself a reaction to primary racism, and perhaps on and on. Thus, the concept of reactive racism admits of a perhaps indeterminate number of orders or levels. My discussion in this essay concentrates mainly on what can be termed, in unaesthetic philosophical jargon, *first-order reactive racism*.

8. Racism by black African Americans against, for example, white *Jewish* Americans is, at present, a heated topic. The battle over whether or not Jews played a substantial role in the historic slave trade of black Africans seems to be, in part, a battle to decide the nature of the relational background between black African Americans and white Jewish

Americans. The assumption seems to be that if Jews did significantly trade black African slaves, then reactive hatred or scorn by African Americans against Jewish Americans today might be less wrong than otherwise, perhaps even positively all right, all things considered.

9. Physical violence against someone's person is, in my view, a paradigm of prima facie wrongness. As such, it is more difficult to justify by counterbalancing considerations than are other sorts of prima facie wrongs.

10. This attitude involves a desire for revenge. Both philosophers and ordinary folk have questioned the moral value of revenge. Yet revenge is still likely to be gratifying to someone who has suffered badly at another's hands. In the same way that any human satisfaction not yet proven unjustifiable should be regarded as a prima facie moral plus, on utilitarian grounds at least, this gratification counts as a prima facie moral value until we have positive reason to think otherwise.

11. I am not suggesting that reactively racist acts are the *only* means by which victims of primary racism can regain self-respect. They may, however, provide *one* means.

12. See, for example, *R.A.V. v City of St. Paul* 112 S. Ct. 2538 (1992).

13. Some white women may also believe that they have been the targets of unjustified reverse (racial) discrimination, but this viewpoint is far less evident in public debate, probably because programs such as affirmative action have also tended to protect the interests of white women.

14. My apologies (again) to Larry Blum for having finished an earlier version of this essay at the last minute for the Oberlin Colloquium of 21 April 1995, at which I commented on his fine paper. As well, my thanks to Susan Babbitt and Sue Campbell for helpful editorial suggestions on my essay.

6. "Contempt and Ordinary Inequality," by David Haekwon Kim

1. To qualify my description of contempt, I want to allow that one can have contempt merely for some aspect of the other. As long as the standard of evaluation is relatively unimportant, contempt remains localized. However, contempt, like disgust, seems to have a dispersive staining effect. It is often difficult to contain contempt to only one aspect of a target.

2. My understanding of the emotions has been deeply influenced by many, most notably the following: Ronald deSousa, *The Rationality of Emotion*; Michael Stocker (with Elizabeth Hegeman), *Valuing Emotions*; Laurence Thomas, *Living Morally* and "Rationality and Affectivity: The Metaphysics of the Moral Self"; Amélie Rorty, "Explaining Emotions"; Martha Nussbaum, "The Discernment of Perception"; Nancy Sherman, *The Fabric of Character*; Lawrence Blum, *Friendship, Altruism, and Morality*; Stephen R. Leighton, "Aristotle and the Emotions"; Lynne McFall, "What's Wrong with Bitterness?"; Daniel Haggerty, "Shame," and "White Shame"; Raul Vargas, "Cognitive Rage."

3. I thank Michael Stocker for clarification here.

4. See also, Adrian Piper, "Higher Order Discrimination."

5. Sue Campbell has pressed me to clarify my take on racist fear, and Daniel Haggerty my take on other racist emotions. I have tried, perhaps with less success than either they or I would have liked.

6. On the ontology and politics of racial identity and white identity in particular, I have learned a great deal from Linda Martin Alcoff's *Philosophy and Racial Identity* and "What Should White People Do?"

7. I thank Laurence Mordekhai Thomas for drawing my attention to this passage and insightful discussion of it.

8. Unsurprisingly, the motif of purity in sexual relations and national membership looms large in white supremacist discourse. Raphael Ezekial's *The Racist Mind* and Jesse Daniels's *White Lies* are especially illuminating.

9. Concerning another form of racist shame, one connected with a condescending benefactor role, I have learned from Daniel Haggerty's "White Shame."

10. I thank Sue Campbell for suggesting stylistic integration here.

11. I thank Laurence Thomas for many discussions on the connection between race and paternalism and for so much else. His letter in *Proceedings and Addresses of the APA* 70, no. 2 (1996): 156–59, has been very helpful.

12. A potential exception is racially closed subcultures in which whites are represented as intrinsically evil, a representation that is not mere rhetorical hyperbole. Even here, however, there is a crucial asymmetry. The demonization of whites is coherent only against the backdrop of a long history of white terrorism. For a moving account of this asymmetry, see bell hooks, *Killing Rage*, 31–50.

13. For extensive editorial help, not to mention substantive critical recommendations, I am indebted to Sue Campbell. I also thank Susan Babbitt for pressing me to clarify my discussion of the emotions, at an oral presentation of a condensed version of this essay at the Fourteenth Annual Social Philosophy Conference at Queen's University in Kingston Ontario. In connection with this conference, I would like to thank my audience for thoughtful questions and recommendations for further exploration. For patient, insightful, and sometimes hilarious responses to the essay, I thank Heather Battaly, John Draeger, Daniel Haggerty, Jaejin Kim, Linda Martin Alcoff, Eric Parkinson, Michael Stocker, Laurence Thomas, and Raul Vargas. My deepest gratitude is to Laurence Mordekhai Thomas and Jaejin Kim.

7. "Colonial Racism," by Nkiru Nzegwu

1. Tommy Lott, "Du Bois on the Invention of Race," *Philosophical Forum* 24, no. 1–3 (fall–spring 1992–93): 166–187; Victor O. Okafor, "An Afrocentric Critique of Appiah's *In My Father's House*," *Journal of Black Studies* 24, no. 2 (December 1993): 196–212; Lewis R. Gordon, "Race, Pan-Africanism, and Identity: Antiblack Philosophy in Kwame Anthony Appiah's *In My Father's House*"; Cleaver Headley, "Alain Locke's Sociocultural Conception of Race," *APA Newsletter* 96, no. 2 (spring 1997): 8–12.

2. For a review of West African intellectuals who reshaped Pan-Africanism see J. Ayodele Langley, *Pan-Africanism and Nationalism in West Africa: 1900–1945*. For Langley's analysis of Sekyi's Pan-Africanist views, see pages 98–103.

3. Rina Okonkwo, *Heroes of West Africa Nationalism*, 112. He brilliantly argues for the substitution of culture for race and calls to question the Africanness of Negroes by calling them black white men. Furthermore, Langley's analysis reveals that the crux of Sekyi's opposition to African Americans assuming a leadership position in Africa was advanced on cultural grounds that totally repudiates the legitimacy of the biological argument of kinship even though he concedes the ancestral connection. In his view, melanin is irrelevant because the Americanization process has made African Americans more "American" in ideal than African. For them, Africa is an abstract romantic illusion (*Pan-Africanism*, 99).

4. Blyden, as Appiah describes him, "was a native of the New World and a Liberian

by adoption; like Crummell, he was a priest and a founder of the tradition of Pan Africanism" (*In My Father's House*, 21). Appiah recognizes Blyden as a "polyglot scholar: his essays include quotations in the original languages from Dante, Virgil and Saint-Hilaire; he studied Arabic" (21), was a professor at Liberia College, and was the Liberian ambassador to Queen Victoria's court.

5. Here, I have centered Africa, and I am looking at history and the world from that perspective. In my view, the problem with many theoretical works is that they rely too heavily on the text (the colonial book of lies) to understand Africa and Africans.

6. I am aware that the liberal move is propelled by the urge to safeguard the notion of agency and individual responsibility. For liberals, the idea that treating racism as a institutional phenomenon may absolve the individual from personal accountability. The problem with such fears is that they sacrifice the phenomenon for the individual. In the attempt to rescue the idea of individual agency, the entrenched nature of racism and the structural relation of power are diluted and insufficiently taken into account. As a result, the racialized is placed unfairly on the same level as the racist, who benefits immeasurably from the structural relationship, and both are held accountable in the same way.

7. E. A. Ayandele presents interesting information on Ijebu attitudes to Europeans. See "Ijebuland 1800–1891: Era of Splendid Isolation."

8. Based on the hospitality they received in Africa, whites have often argued that they were treated with awe and reverence. What they always neglect is to say in what ways the treatment given to them is reserved exclusively for whites and never extended to visitors. Because whites may treat guests shabbily, and have no idea about Africans' respect for visitors, they mistake hospitality for reverence. Some West Africans have also argued that the whites are routinely treated with deference in Africa. Again, this observation must be qualified by putting it in proper context. To what extent is the respect accorded to whites tied to the exalted offices they hold in multinational corporations in parts of the region? The issue is that the class position of whites in Africa today must be factored into analysis before any expansive claims can be made.

9. Interestingly, this element of the ludicrous remains even though there are Lebanese and Indian citizens of Nigeria. The automatic assumption is that they are not Nigerians because historically Lebanese and Indians resisted integration, defined themselves as foreigners, and refused to become citizens. Those who were born in Nigeria and have defined themselves as Nigerians are treated as "locals."

10. It is important to state that these racist tirades were not exclusively about bodies, they were also about cultures and different cultural formations.

11. An example from the 1820s would be the *Royal Gold Coast Gazette and Commercial Intelligencer* established by Sir Charles MacCarthy, governor of Sierra Leone and in charge of the British trading establishments on the Gold Coast. Ivor Wilks notes that MacCarthy had developed "a pathological, a truly obsessional, hatred for Asante, and launched an extraordinary campaign (of disinformation) to destabilize its authority on the Gold Coast" (*One Nation, Many Histories: Ghana Past and Present*, 47).

12. Saburi O. Biobaku, *Egba and Their Neighbours 1842–1872*; Ayandele, "Ijebuland," 88–107; and Omoniyi Adewoye, *The Judicial System in Southern Nigeria 1854–1954*.

13. Quotation was culled from Crummell's "Our National Mistakes and the Remedy for Them" (1870).

14. The situation is different in East Africa and South Africa, which had large white settler communities and where Africans were discriminated against both culturally and

bodily. This situation differs from the situation in the United States where the target is the body, given that blacks lacked a distinct culture.

15. This policy was often flouted. Besides, interracial unions that did not involve officials were outside the jurisdiction of this policy. Ordinary social contact was, however, allowed between members of the same sex.

16. Although what ultimately determines which culture is to be devalued is the coloration of the people, the emphasis of colonial racists in West Africa is not so much the skin of the people as the issue of cultural inferiority.

17. Unlike the Japanese, the Asante failed because they never paid close attention to the cultural factor and, in my view, failed to set clear technological goals.

18. In a review of the journal, *Transition*, Michael Echeruo questioned the scholarly objectives of the editors on precisely this issue. See "From Transition to Transition," *Research in African Literature* 22, no. 4 (1991): 135–45. Oyekan Owomoyela, "With Friends Like These . . . A Critique of Pervasive Anti-Africanisms in Current African Studies Epistemology and Methodology," *African Studies Review* 37, no. 3 (1994): 77–101. Paul Tiyambe Zeleza's recent book is fully devoted to this problem: *Manufacturing African Studies and Crises*.

19. Even if Appiah wants to observe Crummell and Americo-Liberians' "metamorphosis from position of underlings to one of mastery, with a vast population of degraded subjects around" (Langley, "Introduction," 32) this does not justify the exclusion of local perception and the indigenous cognitive schemes and traditions.

20. For this section, I am relying on Agnes Aidoo's historical research, which she completed in 1975, the same year that Ivor Wilks's history of the Asante was published. My preference for Aidoo is dictated by the following factors: Wilks's account shows a considerable lack of awareness of the constitutional importance and implication of the Asantehemaa's role as the royal genealogist. In his accounts of the nomination of prospective Asantehenes, Wilks totally obscures the Asantehemaa's role and makes it seem as if the affair is entirely managed by men. This completely writes out of significance the importance of these female figures. The effect of this distortion finds reflection in his evaluation of the reigns of Afua Kobi's sons, Kofi Kakari and Mensa Bonsu, and of Yaa Akyaa's two sons, who became Asantehene. That Wilks's narrative minimizes the significance of the two Asantehemaa political manuverings and contradicts Asante oral history, which preserves a much more vibrant image of these two women. Because I am focusing on the speech of Asantehemaa Afua Kobi, it makes more sense to rely on Aidoo's more nuanced historical work because it attends to the significance of the Asantehemaa's status in court life.

21. G. K. Nukunya states that although Omanhenes may appear autocratic, in reality their "powers are very much limited"; they have to run all their decisions by the National Mpanyimfo and the Asantehene (*Tradition and Change in Ghana: An Introduction to Sociology*, 70).

22. Persistent military attacks and political insurgency of a pro-British coalition of states in the Volta region, the eastern border of Asante empire, led to the Krepi expedition of 1869–1871. Under Genderal Adu Bofo, the Asante army defeated the pro-British coalition of Akyem, Akuapem, Ga, Ada, and Krepi in a three-year military campaign. The defeat resulted in the capture of the three Europeans living in the Volta region (Aidoo, "Political Crisis," 200–202).

23. Agnes Akosua Aidoo deals with these issues in "Asante Queen Mothers in Government and Politics in the Nineteenth Century" (65–77).

24. Awareness of this phenomenon is crucial to avoid the mistake of automatically accepting any analysis as correct simply because the individual is African born. As intellec-

tuals such as Sekyi pointed out decades ago, there is more to Africanness than skin pigmentation. Nigerians are discursively clear on this point. They have been known to derisively dismiss as white or foreigner any native born who lacks the cultural knowledge that is the marker of identity.

25. Appiah was born in England. He went to primary school in Ghana and secondary school in England. His undergraduate and graduate education were at Cambridge University. His period of residency in Ghana and the secluded circumstances under which his family lived definitely differ from the sort of culturally informative experiences that Joe Appiah had as a child.

26. For those who wish to take issue with this claim, see Martin Bernal's *Black Athena: The Afroasiatic Roots of Classical Civilization*; and the essays in Sandra Harding's *The "Racial" Economy of Science: Toward a Democratic Future.*

27. Eve Kosofsky Sedgewick: in which social bonds between persons of the same sex—that is, men—are privileged (*Between Men: English Literature and Male Homosexual Desire*, 1).

28. Interestingly, although Appiah is duly sensitive to the complexities of his father's Asante, Ghanaian, African, Christian, and Methodist multiple identities, which he also wants us to accommodate, he lacks a similar sensitivity to African women, who are clearly not represented in his book.

29. See Nzegwu, "Questions of Identity and Inheritance."

30. It is for this reason that Appiah's two comments—"Never confuse a martilineal [*sic*] society with a society where women are in public control" and "Never assume that individual women cannot gain power under patriarchy" (184)—confuse gender with biology. Even when the opanin is male, one cannot arrive at the complexity of gender relations in a matrilineal society by arguing from anatomy.

31. See Joe Appiah's biography for his construction of things.

32. The fortune would thus have been passed on to Joe Appiah's children who are completely outside the lineage and cannot legitimately inherit its wealth, which the lineage had made available to him as its custodian, nor could he appropriate the assets for them.

33. The attempt to use a codicil to "reform" funeral obsequies is dictatorial because it attempts to curb discussion on an important cultural change. All his life, Joe Appiah knew the stipulations of the tradition, and if reform was his objective, he should have accomplished it while he was still alive.

34. It must be remembered that Appiah's father never relinquished his role as the head of matriclan; hence, one cannot reasonably expect the abusua to abide by the tenets of a codicil that "speaks" after his death. As Joe Appiah himself put it after his appointment to the head of the Akroma Ampim abusua: "Now every word of mine was an edict—never to be challenged so long as I breathed the breath of life" (*Joe Appiah*, 183). Aware that his word would no longer carry the force of an edict once he was dead and that the issue he desired to enforce would be objectionable to the abusua, he utilized an Anglo-Saxon legal instrument to secure his will. He counted on the fact that the British-derived legal code of modern-day Ghana would supercede the Akan legal process for instituting change. Thus, the production of a codicil by the conjugal family at the death of the head of the matriclan is aimed at subverting consensus rather than encouraging it.

35. See the flap jacket of the 1992 edition of the book.

36. This essay has benefited tremendously from the many discussions I had with Rifaat Abou-El-Haj on the issue of recolonization and neocolonialism in which nationals and descendants of nationals of formerly colonized regions of the world are the agents of colonialism. Also, I wish to acknowledge the residency I received from the Institute for the

Study of Gender in Africa of the James Coleman African Studies Center, UCLA. The residency has provided me with the similar opportunity and resources to complete a number of projects that I have been engaged with for quite awhile.

8. "Reading the Colonizer's Mind," by Olufemi Taiwo

1. See Albert Memmi, *The Colonizer and the Colonized*; Aime Cesaire, *Discourse on Colonialism*; Frantz Fanon, *The Wretched of the Earth*.

2. I do not argue for this assumption here. I have done so elsewhere. See Olufemi Taiwo, "Running Aground on Native Shores: The Saga of Colonialism and Modernity." This assumption is not without ground. G. W. F. Hegel identifies colonialism this way. See *Philosophy of Right*.

3. See Taiwo, "Running Aground."

4. For an account of phases of evangelization, see Lamin Sanneh, *West African Christianity: The Religious Impact*.

5. See Sanneh, *West African Christianity*, chap. 6; Ajayi, *Christian Missions*; E. A. Ayandele, *The Missionary Impact on Modern Nigeria, 1842–1914*.

6. See Olufemi Taiwo, "Colonialism and Its Aftermath: The Crisis of Knowledge Production."

7. Christianity of the second wave. The earlier wave evangelized rulers.

8. My concern here is not with the evaluation of the activities of the missionaries. Although it may appear that I applaud their revolutionary goals, I do not wish to suggest that revolution is essentially good or that all revolutionary movements are good. My limited purpose here is to contrast their attitude with that of their administrator colleagues.

9. Although Lugard did not indicate the nature of his illness, his biographer, Margery Perham, had no reticence disclosing it. He had been jilted in love, which had led to illness. His mental illness puts in context his claim that what he needed was "active hard work—rather than rest." See Perham, "Introduction" in *The Diaries of Lord Lugard*, vol. 1, 18.

10. In "Running Aground," I have discussed fully these issues concerning the tension between missionaries and colonial administrators such as Lugard and how the latter aborted the project of modernity in the colonies.

11. Of course, what I just pointed out presupposes that the option of creating a modern bureaucracy was available. I have argued elsewhere that at least in some parts of southern Nigeria at the time Lugard was putting in place the policy of indirect rule, there were bodies of modern trained individuals who could have been pressed into service with minimal training as civil servants. See "Running Aground."

12. See Omoniyi Adewoye, *The Judicial System in Southern Nigeria, 1854–1954*.

13. Lugard contended, "The procedure of the Supreme Court is too elaborate, the rules by which it is bound are too rigid, for adaptation to a society such as exists among the primitive tribes" of the interior of Nigeria. Quoted in Adewoye, *The Judicial System in Southern Nigeria*, 141.

14. Adewoye, *The Judicial System in Southern Nigeria*, especially chap. 5: "The judicial reorganization was thus in the nature of a response to what was considered a serious political or administrative problem: how to curtail the influence of the African lawyer" (137).

15. See Taiwo, "Colonialism and Its Aftermath."

16. The research for this essay was facilitated by a research leave granted by Loyola University, Chicago, in the spring of 1995 and a travel grant from the American Philo-

sophical Society, Philadelphia, in the summer of 1996. My gratitude goes to both organizations. Neither organization may be held responsible for any views contained in the essay.

9. "Split-Level Equality: Mixing Love and Equality," by Laurence M. Thomas

1. Recent work in what is known as chaos theory is most instructive here. The mental complexity of any and every kind of human being is vastly superior to any and every other kind of earthly creature. The complex dependence patterns of infant human beings upon adult human beings simply could not obtain between infants and adults of other species. Correspondence with Gregory T. Stevens has been helpful here. See Thomas S. Smith and Gregory T. Steven, "Emergence, Self-Organization, and Social Interaction: Arousal-Dependent Structure in Social Systems."

2. In writing this essay, I have benefited from the comments of the editors and discussions with Nasri Abdel-Aziz, David Kim, Gregory Koch, and Michael Stocker. A version of this essay was presented at the University of Cape Town (South Africa) as one of my 1997 Kovler Lectures.

10. "'Race' and the Labor of Identity," by Elizabeth V. Spelman

1. In a remark he soon regretted having made, historian Kenneth Stampp expressed his belief that "innately Negroes *are*, after all, only white men with black skins, nothing more, nothing less" (*The Peculiar Institution: Slavery in the Ante-Bellum South*, vii–viii).

2. Baldwin has no doubt about the tremendous political, social, and economic power whites in the United States yield. His analysis seems geared to showing how contrary to their own best self-interest the acquisition and deployment of such power is.

3. See, for example, Cameron Lynne Macdonald and Carmen Sirianni, eds. *Working in the Service Society*.

4. In this connection, students of Aristotle may recall his wish that visible characteristics of human beings reveal their given natures—it would be so much easier to pick out those who were meant "by nature" to be slaves (*Politics*, 1254b34–1255a2).

5. Cose *(The Rage of a Privileged Class)* recounts the endless occasions on which black professionals—many of whom are at the top of their professions—come up against the assumption on the part of their white coworkers (at every level in their organizations) that blacks really aren't, really can't be, the equal of whites. It is painfully clear to the blacks Cose interviewed what the consequences for them would be were they to bring attention to that assumption or try to do anything to undermine it. True, unlike the domestic workers Rollins got to know, black professionals aren't expected to wear clothing or engage in obvious forms of deferential behavior attesting to the natural superiority of whites (though their attire may need to be geared to combating the presumption that they aren't as professional as their white coworkers). But the implicit sanctions against disturbing the presumption of white superiority are so heavy that the price of securing and keeping one's job typically includes not getting angry at the daily expressions of disbelief that blacks could have such jobs, let alone do them well. It is as if whites know that the presumption of white superiority sewn into the social fabric is always vulnerable to rending and ripping and so they constantly reinforce the threads by means of what otherwise may appear to be gratuitous expressions of the assumptions that blacks couldn't possibly really belong there. They appear to count on blacks feeling caught in a double bind: if

blacks don't complain about such treatment, there can't really be anything wrong with the social fabric (no matter that it is likely to include the assumption that what blacks want is to be the same as whites, in the sense Baldwin so richly derided, or the certainty that the corporation has no problem with racism). And if blacks do complain, their job—or certainly their enjoyment of many of its possible benefits—is likely to be on the line.

6. See W. E. B. DuBois, *Black Reconstruction in America, 1860–1880*, 17–31 and *passim*; David Roediger, *The Wages of Whiteness: Race and the Making of the American Working Class*, 12–13, and *passim*; Noel Ignatiev, *How the Irish Became White*, 96 and *passim*.

7. See Macdonald, "Shadow Mothers," 248; and Eaton, "The Customer," 306.

8. Some workers—for example, flight attendants—are explicitly employed to do what Arlie Russell Hochschild calls "emotional labor," producing emotions in themselves and in their customers that are deemed essential to the success of the enterprise (*The Managed Heart: Commercialization of Human Feeling*, 7 ff.).

9. This reminds us, as does Rollins's own analysis, that it is not only racial identity that requires labor.

10. For an enlightening discussion of some of the work whites are trained to do, see Lillian Smith, *Killers of the Dream*.

11. Invisible mending is offered by tailors for those who don't want their garments to show even the slightest sign of having been patched up.

12. This not uncommon expression has recently been elevated to the status of a book title: *High Maintenance Relationships: How to Handle Impossible People* by Les Parrott III.

13. See, for example, Eaton, "The Customer," 297.

14. This idea is also, according to Baldwin, a sure sign of pitiful white self-delusion.

15. The racial economy is another place at which comparisons amongst African Americans, Japanese Americans, Chicanos, and others might fruitfully be explored.

16. For a review of some of the legal standards historically used to establish whiteness, see Harris, "Whiteness as Property." Naomi Zack has suggested that the formula for establishing whiteness amounts to this: white skin and no nonwhite forbears ("Race and Philosophic Meaning," 33). Or, as Ian F. Haney López puts it, whites are "those who are not non-white" (Haney López, *White By Law: The Legal Construction of Race*, 28).

17. As Ian Haney López has pointed out, many of the legal definitions of whiteness have involved anxious attempts to exclude people from parts of Japan, India, and Mexico (among other places) from naturalization and citizenship—another reason why full exploration of the meaning of whiteness must include more than a history of white/black relationships. See *White By Law*, esp. 1–18, 49–77.

18. Hence, I would join Ian Haney López and others in wondering whether there could be any point to trying to redeem or look for the "positive" aspects of white identity. See Haney López, *White By Law*, esp. 30–33, 183 ff.

19. Many thanks to Martha Minow, Larry Blum, Frances Smith Foster, Susan Babbitt, and Sue Campbell for very helpful criticism and comments.

11. "Dominant Identities and Settled Expectations," by Sue Campbell

1. Dominant identities are those identities most affirmed by current social structures. I recognize that many persons are affirmed in one dimension of their identities—through having white skin privilege, for example—while not being affirmed in other dimensions of their identity. However, particularly because of the power of racial categorizations, I do

not think that the reality of different dimensions to one's identity always leads to a multiple or fragmented self or undermines the argument about settled expectations that follows. Like Peggy McIntosh, I find the connotations of the word *privileged* both too passive and too positive to describe certain social identities and so prefer the word *dominant* ("White Privilege and Male Privilege: A Personal Account of Coming to See Correspondences through Work in Women's Studies," 31).

2. As well as Derek Parfit, *Reasons and Persons*, and David Lewis, "Survival and Identity," see most of the selections in Amélie Rorty, ed., The *Identities of Persons*, and in Daniel Kolak and Raymond Martin, eds., *Self and Identity: Contemporary Philosophical Issues*.

3. I have been persuaded of the importance of thinking about transformation experiences by Susan Babbitt's *Impossible Dreams: Rationality, Integrity and Moral Imagination*.

4. See Naomi Scheman's "Queering the Center by Centering the Queer: Reflections on Transsexuals and Secular Jews" for a important engagement with Lugones.

5. Lugones's commitment to multiplicity in the self is explicit in "Structure/Antistructure and Agency under Oppression": "I am giving up the claim that the subject is unified. Instead I am understanding each person as many" (503).

6. Harris herself draws on work by Margaret Radin on property and personhood to link the settled expectations of white privilege to the personal identities of whites. She argues that white privilege is bound up in the anticipation whites have of their future selves, and thus the realization of these expectations is necessary to their identities ("Whiteness as Property," 1730).

7. See Lugones, "Structure/Antistructure," 505.

8. For example, Anita Allen's recent discussion of temporarily forgetting one's race as a case of forgetting oneself highlights that certain norms govern kinds and degrees of self-consciousness—African Americans are obligated to be "alive to being black" ("Forgetting Yourself," 120) in social transactions—and these norms may be essential for sustaining self-esteem. In the same volume of essays (*Feminists Rethink the Self*, edited by Diana Tietjen Meyers), Naomi Scheman attempts to performatively deconstruct the norm of integrity that encourages those privileged to think of themselves as a "block of unclouded substance" ("Queering the Center," 125). In a recent talk at Dalhousie University, "Philosophy and Race: The Whiteness (Apparently Not So Unbearable) of Being," Charles Mills juxtaposed the opening paragraphs of Ralph Ellison's *Invisible Man* to the Cartesian self to point out how alien the "cogito" consciousness would be for a black man such as Ellison. See also the contributions to Lewis R. Gordon, ed., *Existence in Black: An Anthology of Black Existential Philosophy*.

9. In "Of Property: On 'Captive' 'Bodies,' Hidden 'Flesh,' and Colonization," G. M. James Gonzalez speaks of slavery as "a continuing colonial infectious disease" and of the slave as "a captive being . . . severed and removed from its roots, its habitat" (130–31). He says, "But where is home? In a fragmented state, home is a mythic place to which there is no return" (133). For an understanding of "homeplace" as resistance, see bell hooks, "Homeplace: A Site of Resistance," in *Yearning: Race, Gender, and Cultural Politics*.

10. There are many influences on this paper: work by Nathan Brett and by Jan Sutherland on habit and agency, by Ronald de Sousa on emotional salience, and by Genevieve Lloyd on the temporality of the self. I am grateful to Jan Sutherland, Duncan MacIntosh, and Rockney Jacobsen for discussions about expectation, to Charles Mills for a timely campus visit that helped me focus my concerns, and to Susan Babbitt for persuading me I had something to say on the topic.

12. "Moral Risk and Dark Waters," by Susan E. Babbitt

1. I have benefited in thinking about Delaney's notion of purport from discussions with Chris Beeman.

2. See, for example, Naomi Zack, ed., *American Mixed Race: The Culture of Microdiversity*, part 5. This is not to criticize such discussions but to draw a distinction between what is being proposed here and what has become a popular concern.

3. See, for example, Richard Boyd, "Scientific Realism and Naturalistic Epistemology"; Peter Railton, "Marx and the Objectivity of Science"; and Philip Kitcher, "The Naturalists Return."

4. See, for example, "The Intellectuals" in *Selections from the Prison Notebooks of Antonio Gramsci*, edited by Q. Hoare and G. Nowell-Smith, 3–14.

5. V. I. Lenin, *Philosophical Notebooks*, vol. 38 of *Collected Works*. References in the text are to this edition.

6. See, for example, Michael Roemer, *Telling Stories: Postmodernism and the Invalidation of Traditional Narrative*.

7. For example, Sarah Hoagland said this in conversation at the Engendering Rationalities conference, 18–20 April 1997, University of Oregon, Eugene.

Bibliography

Adewoye, Omoniyi. *The Judicial System in Southern Nigeria, 1854–1954*. Atlantic Highlands: Humanities, 1977.

Afriyie, Afua. "Afua Afriyie: The Personal Queen of Otumfuo Opku Ware II." *Around Ghana: A Magazine of Events and Places*, souvenir issue (1995): 33–42.

Aidoo, Agnes Akosua. "Asante Queen Mothers in Governments and Politics in the Nineteenth Century." In *Black Women Cross-Culturally*, edited by Filomena Chioma Steady. Cambridge, Mass.: Schenkman, 1981.

———. "Political Crisis and Social Change in Asante Kingdom, 1867–1901." Ph.D. diss., University of California, Los Angeles, 1975.

Ajayi, J. F. Ade. *Christian Missions in Nigeria, 1841–1891: The Making of a New Elite*. Ibadan, Nigeria: University of Ibadan Press, 1965.

Alcoff, Linda Martín. "Philosophy and Racial Identity." *Philosophy Today* 41, no. 1 (spring 1997): 67–76.

———. "What Should White People Do?" Manuscript.

Alessandrini, Anthony C. "Whose Fanon?" *The C. L. R. James Journal* 5, no. 1 (1997).

Allen, Anita. "Forgetting Yourself." In Meyers 1997.

Allen, Theodore W. *The Invention of the White Race*, vol. 1: *Racial Oppression and Social Control*. New York: Verso, 1994.

Anthias, Floya, and Nira Yuval-Davis. "The Concept of 'Race' and the Racialization of Social Divisions." In *Racialized Boundaries: Race, Nation, Gender, Colour and Class and the Anti-racist Struggle*. New York: Routledge, 1993.

Apollon, Willy. "Four Seasons in Femininity or *Four Men in a Woman's Life*." *Topoi* 12, no. 2 (September 1993): 101–15.

Appiah, Joseph. *Joe Appiah: The Autobiography of an African Patriot*. New York: Praeger, 1990.

Appiah, Kwame Anthony. *In My Father's House: Africa in the Philosphy of Culture*. New York: Oxford University Press, 1992.

Aristotle. *Politics*. Translated by Benjamin Jowett. New York: Modern Library.

———. *Rhetoric*. In *The Complete Works of Aristotle*, edited by Jonathan Barnes, vol. 2. Princeton: Princeton University Press, 1984.

Augustine. *The Confessions of St. Augustine*. Translated by F. J.Sheed. London: Sheed and Ward, 1945.

Ayandele, E. A. "Ijebuland, 1800–1891: Era of Splendid Isolation." In *Studies of Yoruba History and Culture*, edited by G. O. Olusanya. Ibadan, Nigeria: University of Ibadan Press, 1983.

———. *The Missionary Impact on Modern Nigeria, 1842–1914*. London: Longman, 1966.

Babbitt, Susan E. *Impossible Dreams: Rationality, Integrity, and Moral Imagination*. Boulder, Colo.: Westview Press, 1996.

Baldwin, James. *The Fire Next Time*. New York: Dell, 1963.

Banton, Michael, and Jonathan Harwood. *The Race Concept*. New York: Praeger, 1975.

Barndt, Joseph. *Dismantling Racism: The Continuing Challenge to White America*. Minneapolis: Augsburg, 1991.

Bartky, Sandra. "Sympathy and Solidarity: On a Tightrope with Scheler." In Meyers 1997.

Beauvoir, Simone de. *The Second Sex*. 1949. Edited and translated by H. M. Parshley. New York: Knopf, 1953.

Bell, Derrick. *Faces at the Bottom of the Well: The Permanence of Racism*. New York: Basic Books, 1992.

———. "Property Rights in Whiteness: Their Legal Legacy, Their Economic Costs." In Delgado 1995.

Bell, Linda. *Visions of Women*. Clifton, N.J.: Humana, 1983.

Berger, Peter L., and Thomas Luckmann. *The Social Construction of Reality*. New York: Doubleday, 1966.

Berghe, Pierre L. van den. *Race and Racism: A Comparative Perspective*. 2d ed. New York: Wiley, 1978.

Bergner, Gwen. "Who Is That Masked Woman, or the Role of Gender in Fanon's *Black Skin, White Masks*." *Publications of the Modern Language Association of America* 110, no. 1 (January 1995): 75–88.

Bernal, Martin. *Black Athena: The Afroasiatic Roots of Classical Civilization*. Vol. 1 of *The Fabrication of Ancient Greece, 1785–1985*. New Brunswick, N.J.: Rutgers University Press, 1987.

Bernardi, Daniel, ed. *The Birth of Whiteness: Race and the Emergence of Cinema*. New Brunswick, N.J.: Rutgers University Press, 1996.

Berry, Mary Frances. *Black Resistance, White Law: A History of Constitutional Racism in America*. 1971. New York: Allen Lane, 1994.

Biobaku, Saburi. *Egba and Their Neighbors 1842–1872*. Ibadan, Nigeria: University of Ibadan Press, 1991.

Blauner, Robert. *Racial Oppression in America*. New York: Harper & Row, 1972.

———. "Talking Past Each Other: Black and White Languages of Race." *American Prospect* 10 (spring 1992): 55–64.

Blaut, J. M., with contributions by Andre Gurder Frank, Samir Amin, Robert A. Dodgshon, and Rohen Palan. *1492: The Debate on Colonialism, Eurocentrism, and History*. Trenton, N.J.: Africa World Press, 1992.

———. *The Colonizer's Model of the World: Geographical Diffusionism and Eurocentric History*. New York: Guilford, 1993.

Blum, Lawrence. *Friendship, Altruism, and Morality*. Boston: Routledge and Kegan Paul, 1980.

Blumer, Herbert. "Race Prejudice as a Sense of Group Position." *Pacific Sociological Review* 1, no. 1 (spring 1958): 3–4.

Boyd, R. N. "How to Be a Moral Realist." In *Essays on Moral Realism*, edited by Geoffrey Sayre-McCord. Ithaca: Cornell University Press, 1988.

———. "Metaphor and Theory Change: What Is 'Metaphor' a Metaphor for?" In *Metaphor and Thought*, edited by A. Ortony. Cambridge: Cambridge University Press, 1980.

———. "Scientific Realism and Naturalistic Epistemology." *PSA* 2 (1980): 613–62.

Bulhan, Hussein. *Frantz Fanon and the Psychology of Oppression*. New York: Plenum, 1985.

Busia, K. A. "The Political Heritage." In *Ideologies of Liberation in Black Africa, 1856–1970*, edited by J. Ayo Langley. London: Rex Collings, 1979.

Buxton, Sir Thomas Fowell. *The African Slave Trade and Its Remedy*. 1840. 2d ed. Cass, 1967.

Card, Claudia. *The Unnatural Lottery: Character and Moral Luck*. Philadelphia: Temple University Press, 1996.

Carmichael, Stokely, and Charles V. Hamilton. *Black Power: The Politics of Liberation in America*. New York: Vintage, 1967.

Caute, David. *Frantz Fanon*. New York: Viking, 1970.

Césaire, Aimé. *Discourse on Colonialism*. New York: Monthly Review Press, 1972.

Clark, Lorenne M. G., and Lynda Lange, eds. *The Sexism of Social and Political Theory: Women and Reproduction from Plato to Nietzsche*. Toronto: University of Toronto Press, 1979.

Clemente, Pietro. *Frantz Fanon, tra esistenzialism e rivoluzione*. Bari, Italy: Casa Editrice Guis, 1971.

Collins, Patricia Hill. "Learning from the Outsider Within: The Social Significance of Black Feminist Thought." In Hartmann and Messer-Davidow, 1991.

Coole, Diana H. *Women in Political Theory: From Ancient Misogyny to Contemporary Feminism*. Boulder, Colo.: Lynne Rienner, 1988.

Coon, Carelton S. *The Origin of Races*. New York: Alfred A. Knopf, 1962.

Cose, Ellis. *The Rage of a Privileged Class*. New York: Harper Collins, 1995.

Crenshaw, Kimberle, Neil Gotanda, Gary Peller, and Kendall Thomas, eds., *Critical Race Theory: The Key Writings That Formed the Movement*. New York: New Press, 1995.

Cross, William E., Jr. *Shades of Black: Diversity in African-American Identity*. Philadelphia: Temple University Press, 1991.

Curtis, Lynn C., and Fred Harris. *The Millennium Breach*. Washington, D.C.: Milton S. Eisenhower Foundation, 1998.

Daniels, Jesse. *White Lies*. New York: Routledge, 1997.

Dawson, Michael C., and Ernest J. Wilson III. "Paradigms and Paradoxes: Political Science and African-American Politics." In *Political Science: Looking to the Future*, edited by William Crotty. Vol. 1: *The Theory and Practice of Political Science*. Evanston, Ill.: Northwestern University Press, 1991.

Delaney, Samuel. *The Motion of Light in Water: Sex and Science Fiction Writing in the East Village, 1960–1965*. New York: Richard Kasak Books, 1993.

Delgado, Richard, ed. *Critical Race Theory: The Cutting Edge*. Philadelphia: Temple University Press, 1995.

Diop, Cheikh Anta. *The African Origin of Civilization: Myth or Reality*. 1955. Edited and translated by Mercer Cook. Westport, Conn.: Lawrence Hill, 1974.

Doane, Mary Ann. "Dark Continents: Epistemologies of Racial and Sexual Difference in Psychoanalysis and the Cinema." In *Femmes Fatales*. New York: Routledge, 1991.

Douglass, Frederick. *My Bondage and My Freedom*. Edited by William L. Andrews. Urbana: University of Illinois Press, 1987.

———. *Narrative of the Life of Frederick Douglass, an American Slave, Written by Himself*. 1845. New York: New American Library, 1968.

Drake, St. Clair, and Horace R. Cayton. *Black Metropolis: A Study of Negro Life in a Northern City*. 1945. Chicago: University of Chicago Press, 1993.

Du Bois, W. E. B. *The Autobiography of W. E. B. Du Bois: A Soliloquy on Viewing My Life from the Last Decade of Its First Century*. New York: International Publishers, 1968.

———. *Black Reconstruction in America, 1860–1880*. 1935. New York: Atheneum, 1992.

———. "The Conservation of Races." In *The Seventh Son*, vol. 1. Edited by Julius Lester. New York: Random House, 1971.

———. *The Souls of Black Folk*. New York: Washington Square Press, 1970.

Dussel, Enrique. *The Underside of Modernity: Apel, Ricoeur, Rorty, and Taylor and the Philosophy of Liberation*. Translated by Eduardo Mendieta. Atlantic Highlands, N.J.: Humanities Press, 1996.

Eaton, Susan. "'The Customer Is Always Interesting': Unionized Harvard Clericals Renegotiate Work Relationships." In Macdonald and Sirianni 1996.

Echeruo, Michael. "From Transition to Transition." *Research in African Literature* 22, no. 4 (1991): 135–45.

———. *Victorian Lagos: Aspects of Nineteenth Century Lagos Life*. London: Macmillan, 1977.

Eze, Emmanuel Chukwudi, ed. *Race and the Enlightenment: A Reader*. Cambridge, Mass.: Blackwell, 1997.

Ezekiel, Raphael. *The Racist Mind*. New York: Penguin Books, 1995.

Fanon, Frantz. *Les Damnés de la terre*. Préface de Jean-Paul Sartre, présentation de Gérard Chaliand. 1961. Paris: François Maspero éditeur S.A.R.L.; Paris: Éditions Gallimard, 1991.

———. *Peau noire, masques blancs*. Paris: Editions de Seuil, 1952

———. *The Wretched of the Earth*. 1961. Translated by Constance Farrington. New York: Grove Press, 1968.

Feagin, Joe, and Hernan Vera. *White Racism*. New York: Routledge, 1995

Fine, Michelle, Lois Weis, Linda C. Powell, and L. Mun Wong, eds. *Off White: Readings on Race, Power, and Society*. New York: Routledge, 1997.

Fishman, Joshua. "Ethnicity as Being, Doing, and Knowing." In *Ethnicity*, edited by John Hutchinson and Anthony D. Smith. New York: Oxford University Press, 1996.

Frankenberg, Ruth. *White Women, Race Matters: The Social Construction of Whiteness*. Minneapolis: University of Minnesota Press, 1993.

Fredrickson, George M. *Black Liberation: A Comparative History of Black Ideologies in the United States and South Africa*. New York: Oxford University Press, 1995.

———. *White Supremacy: A Comparative Study in American and South African History*. New York: Oxford University Press, 1981.

Garcia, Jorge. "The Heart of Racism." *Journal of Social Philosophy* 27 (1996): 5–45.

Garn, Stanley, M. "Race," *Man* 200 (1951): 115.

Gates, Henry Louis, Jr. "Critical Fanonism." *Critical Inquiry* 17 (1991): 457–78.

———, ed. *"Race," Writing, and Difference*. Chicago: University of Chicago Press, 1986.

Geismar, Peter. *Frantz Fanon*. New York: Dial Press, 1971.

Geiss, Imanuel. *The Pan-African Movement: A History of Pan-Africanism in America, Europe, and Africa*. 1968. Translated by Ann Keep. New York: Africana, 1974.

Gendzier, Irene. *Frantz Fanon: A Critical Study*. New York: Pantheon Books, 1973.

Gibeson, Nigel, "Beyond Manicheanism: A Critical Study of Frantz Fanon's Dialectic of Liberation." Dissertation Abstracts International. Ann Arbor, Mich., 1996.

———, ed. *Rethinking Fanon*. Atlantic Highlands, N.J.: Humanities Press, forthcoming.

Gilroy, Paul. *The Black Atlantic: Modernity and Double Consciousness*. Cambridge, Mass.: Harvard University Press, 1993.

Ginsberg, Elaine K., ed. *Passing and the Fictions of Identity*. Durham, N.C.: Duke University Press, 1996.

Glazer, Nathan, and Daniel P. Moynihan, eds. *Ethnicity: Theory and Experience*. Cambridge, Mass.: Harvard University Press, 1975.

Glenn, Evelyn Nakano. "From Servitude to Service Work: Historical Continuities in the Racial Division of Paid Reproductive Labor." In Macdonald and Sirianni 1996.

Goldberg, David Theo. *Racist Culture: Philosophy and the Politics of Meaning*. Cambridge, Mass.: Blackwell, 1993.

Gonzalez, G. M. James. "Of Property: On 'Captive' 'Bodies,' Hidden 'Flesh,' and Colonization." In Gordon 1997.

Goodin, Robert E., and Philip Pettit, eds. *A Companion to Contemporary Political Philosophy*. Cambridge: Basil Blackwell, 1993.

Gordon, Lewis R. *Bad Faith and Antiblack Racism*. Atlantic Highlands, N.J.: Humanities Press, 1995.

———. *Fanon and the Crisis of European Man: An Essay on Philosophy and the Human Sciences*. New York: Routledge, 1995.

———. *Her Majesty's Other Children: Sketches of Racism from a Neocolonial Age*. Lanham, Md.: Rowman & Littlefield, 1997.

———. "Race, Pan-Africanism, and Identity: Antiblack Philosophy in Kwame Anthony Appiah's *In My Father's House*." Paper delivered at the Thirty-Eighth Annual African Studies Association Meeting, November 1995, University of Central Florida, Orlando.

———, ed. *Existence in Black: An Anthology of Black Existential Philosophy*. New York: Routledge, 1997.

Gordon, Lewis R., Denean Sharpley-Whiting, and Renée T. White, eds. *Fanon: A Critical Reader*. Oxford: Blackwell, 1996.

Gouges, Olympe de. "Declaration of the Rights of Woman and Citizen." In *European Women: A Documentary History, 1789–1945*, edited by Eleanor S. Riemer and John C. Font. New York: Schocken, 1980.

Gramsci, Antonio. "The Intellectuals." In *Selections from the Prison Notebooks of Antonio Gramsci*, edited by Q. Hoare G. Nowell-Smith. 1971. New York: International Publishers, 1983.

Hacker, Andrew. *Two Nations*. New York: Ballantine Books, 1995.

Haggerty, Daniel. "Shame." Unpublished manuscript.

———. "White Shame." Paper delivered at the Fourteenth Annual International Social Philosophy Conference, 19 July 1997, Queen's University, Kingston, Ontario.

Hampton, Jean Hampton. *Political Philosophy*. Boulder, Colo.: Westview, 1997.

Haney López, Ian F. "The Social Construction of Race." In Delgado 1995.

———. "White by Law." In Delgado 1995.

———. *White by Law: The Legal Construction of Race*. New York: New York University Press, 1996.

Hannaford, Ivan. *Race: The History of an Idea in the West*. Washington, D.C.: Woodrow Wilson Center Press, 1996.

Hansen, Emmanuel. *Frantz Fanon: Social and Political Thought*. Columbus: Ohio State University Press, 1977.

Harding, Sandra. "Who Knows? Identities and Feminist Epistemologies." In Hartmann and Messer-Davidow 1991.

———, ed. *The "Racial" Economy of Science: Toward a Democratic Future*. Bloomington: Indiana University Press, 1993.

Harris, Cheryl I. "Whiteness as Property." *Harvard Law Review* 106 (1993): 1709–91.

Hartmann, Joan E., and Ellen Messer-Davidow. *(En)Gendering Knowledge: Feminists in Academe*. Knoxville: University of Tennessee Press, 1991.

Hartz, Louis, with contributions by Kenneth D. McRae, Richard M. Morse, Richard N. Rosencrance, and Leonard M. Thompson. *The Founding of New Societies: Studies in the History of the United States, Latin America, South Africa, Canada, and Australia*. New York: Harcourt, Brace & World, 1964.

Hegel, Georg Wilhelm Friedrich. *The Philosophy of History*. Translated by John Sibree. New York: Dover, 1956.

———. *The Philosophy of Right*. Translated by T. M. Knox. Oxford: Oxford University Press, 1952.

Helie-Lucas, Marie-Aimée. "Women, Nationalism, and Religion in the Algerian Liberation Struggle." In *Opening the Gates: A Century of Arab Feminist Writing*, edited by Margo Badran and Miriam Cooke. Bloomington: Indiana University Press, 1990.

Henry, Paget. "African and Afro-Caribbean Existential Philosophy." In Gordon 1997.

——. "CLR James, African and Afro-Caribbean Philosophy." *CLR James Journal* 4, no. 1 (winter 1993):

——. "Fanon, African, and Afro-Caribbean Philosophy." In Gordon, Sharpley-Whiting, and White 1996.

Henry, Paget, and Paul Buhle. "Caliban as Deconstructionist: C.L.R. James and Post-Colonial Discourse." In *C.L.R. James's Caribbean*, edited by Paget Henry and Paul Buhle. Durham, N.C.: Duke University Press, 1992.

Herrnstein, Richard, and Charles Murray. *The Bell Curve: Intelligence and Class Structure in American Life*. New York: Free Press, 1994.

Hersch, Jeanne. "The Concept of Race." *Diogenes* 59 (fall 1967): 114–33.

Hochschild, Arlie Russell. *The Managed Heart: Commercialization of Human Feeling*. Berkeley: University of California Press, 1984.

Hochschild, Jennifer L. *The New American Dilemma: Liberal Democracy and School Desegregation*. New Haven: Yale University Press, 1984.

hooks, bell. "Homeplace: A Site of Resistance." In *Yearning: Race, Gender, and Cultural Politics*. Toronto: Between the Lines Press, 1990.

——. *Killing Rage*. New York: Henry Holt & Co., 1995.

Huntington, Patricia. "Fragmentation, Race and Gender: Building Solidarity in the Postmodern Era." In Gordon 1997.

Ignatiev, Noel. *How the Irish Became White*. New York: Routledge, 1995.

Illich, Ivan. *Shadow Work*. Boston: M. Boyars, 1981.

Jaggar, Alison. *Feminist Politics and Human Nature*. Totowa, N.J.: Rowman & Allanheld, 1983.

James, C. L. R. *The Black Jacobins: Toussaint L'Ouverture and the San Domingo Revolution*. 1938. New York: Vintage, 1963.

——. "From Du Bois to Fanon." East Lansing, Michigan 48823: PLSI East Lansing, n.d.

James, Joy Ann. *Transcending the Talented Tenth: Black Leaders and American Intellectualism*. New York: Routledge, 1997.

Jennings, Francis. *The Invasion of America: Indians, Colonialism, and the Cant of Conquest*. New York: Norton, 1976.

Jinadu, Adele L. *Fanon: In Search of the African Revolution*. London: KPI, Routledge & Kegan Paul, 1986.

Jones, E. L. *The European Miracle*. New York: Cambridge University Press, 1981.

Judy, Ronald A. T. "Fanon's Body of Black Experience." In Gordon, Sharpley-Whiting, and White 1996.

Kinder, Donald R., and Lynn M. Sanders. *Divided by Color: Racial Politics and Democratic Ideals*. Chicago: University of Chicago Press, 1996.

King, Desmond. *Separate and Unequal: Black Americans and the U.S. Federal Government*. Oxford: Clarendon, 1995.

King, Martin Luther, Jr. *Where Do We Go from Here?* Boston: Beacon Press, 1967.

Kirk-Greene, A. H. M. "New Introduction." In Lugard 1970.

Kitcher, Philip. *Abusing Science: The Case against Creationism*. Cambridge, Mass.: MIT Press, 1984.

——. "The Naturalists' Return." *Philosophical Review* 101, no. 1 (January 1992): 53–114.

Kolak, Daniel, and Raymond Martin, eds. *Self and Identity: Contemporary Philosophical Issues*. New York: Macmillan, 1991.

Kondo, Dorinne. *Crafting Selves*. Chicago: University of Chicago Press, 1990.

Kymlicka, Will. *Liberalism, Community, and Culture*. Oxford: Oxford University Press, 1989.

Langley, J. Ayodele. *Pan-Africanism and Nationalism in West Africa: 1900–1945*. Oxford: Clarendon, 1973

——, ed. *Ideologies of Liberation in Black Africa 1856–1970*. London: Rex Collings, 1972.

Lawson, Bill E. "Social Disappointment and the Black Sense of Self." In Gordon 1996.

Lee, Spike. "Interview." *Playboy* 38 (July 1991): 51–68.

Leighton, Stephen R. "Aristotle and the Emotions." In *Aristotle's Rhetoric*, edited by Amélie Rorty. Berkeley: University of California Press, 1996.

Lenin, V. I. *Philosophical Notebooks*. Vol. 38 of *Collected Works*. Edited by Stewart Smith and translated by Clemens Dutt. Moscow: Foreign Languages Publishing House, 1961.

Lewis, David. "Survival and Identity." In *The Identities of Persons*, edited by Amélie Rorty. Berkeley: University of California Press, 1976.

Lewis, Helen Block. *Shame and Guilt in Neurosis*. New York: International Universities Press, 1971.

Lipsitz, George. "The Possessive Investment in Whiteness: Racialized Social Democracy and the 'White' Problem in American Studies." *American Quarterly* 47 (1995): 369–87.

Little, K. L. "U.N.E.S.C.O. on Race." *Man* 31 (1951): 17.

Lovejoy, Arthur. *The Great Chain of Being: A Study of the History of an Idea*. 1936. Cambridge, Mass, Mass.: Harvard University Press, 1964.

Lugard, Frederick D. *The Dual Mandate in British Tropical Africa*. Edinburgh: William Blackwood and Sons, 1922.

——. *Political Memoranda, Revision of Instructions to Political Officers on Subjects Chiefly Political and Administrative, 1913–1918*. 3d ed. London: Cass, 1970.

——. *The Rise of Our East African Empire*. 2 vols. London: Frank Cass & Co., 1968.

Lugones, Maria. "Playfulness, 'World'-Travelling, and Loving Perception." In *Women, Knowledge, and Reality: Explorations in Feminist Philosophy*, edited by Marilyn Pearsall and Ann Garry. Boston: Unwin Hyman, 1989.

——. "Structure/Antistructure and Agency under Oppression." *Journal of Philosophy* 87 (1990): 500–507.

Macdonald, Cameron Lynne. "Shadow Mothers: Nannies, *Au Pairs*, and Invisible Work." In Macdonald and Sirianni 1996.

Macdonald, Cameron Lynne, and Carmen Sirianni. "The Service Society and the Changing Experience of Work." In Macdonald and Sirianni 1996.

——, eds. *Working in the Service Society*. Philadelphia: Temple University Press, 1996.

Mahowald, Mary Briody, ed. *Philosophy of Woman: An Anthology of Classic and Current Concepts*. 1978. 2d ed. Indianapolis: Hackett, 1983.

Mandt, A. J. "The Inevitability of Pluralism: Philosophical Practice and Philosophical Excellence." In *The Institution of Philosophy: A Discipline in Crisis*, edited by Avner Cohen and Marcelo Dascal. La Salle, Ill.: Open Court, 1989.

Mansbridge, Jane, and Susan Moller Okin. "Feminism." In Goodin and Pettit 1993.

Maran, René. *Un homme pareil aux autres*. Translated by Charles Lamm Markmann. Paris: Editions Arc-en-Ciel, 1947.

Martin, Biddy, and Chandra Talpade Mohanty. "Feminist Politics: What's Home Got to Do with It?" In *Feminist Studies/Critical Studies*, edited by Teresa de Lauretis. Bloomington: Indiana University Press, 1986.

Massey, Douglas S., and Nancy A. Denton. *American Apartheid: Segregation and the Making of the Underclass*. Cambridge, Mass.: Harvard University Press, 1993.

McFall, Lynne. "What's Wrong with Bitterness?" In *Feminist Ethics*, edited by Claudia Card. Lawrence: University Press of Kansas, 1991.

McIntosh, Peggy. "White Privilege and Male Privilege: A Personal Account of Coming to See Correspondences through Work in Women's Studies." In *Gender Basic: Feminist Perspectives on Women and Men*, edited by Anne Minas. Belmont, Calif.: Wadsworth, 1993.

Memmi, Albert. *The Colonizer and the Colonized*. Boston: Beacon Press, 1972.

Merleau-Ponty, Maurice. *The Visible and the Invisible: Followed by Working Notes*. Edited by Claude Lefort and translated by Alphonso Lingis. Evanston, Ill.: Northwestern University Press, 1968.

Merton, Robert K. "Insiders and Outsiders: A Chapter in the Sociology of Knowledge." *American Journal of Sociology* 78 (1972): 9–47.

Meyers, Diana Tietjens, ed. *Feminists Rethink the Self*. Boulder, Colo.: Westview Press, 1997.

Miles, Robert. *Racism*. London: Routledge, 1989.

Mill, John Stuart. *On Liberty; with The Subjection of Women; and Chapters on Socialism*. 1869. Edited by Stefan Collini. New York: Cambridge University Press, 1989.

Miller, Alice. *The Drama of the Gifted Child*. New York: Basic Books, 1981.

Mills, Charles W. "Non-Cartesian Sums: Philosophy and the African-American Experience." *Teaching Philosophy* 17, no. 3 (October 1994): 223–43.

——. "Philosophy and Race: The Whiteness (Apparently Not So Unbearable) of Being." Paper delivered as an Austin-Hempel lecture, November 1997, Dalhousie University, Halifax, Nova Scotia.

——. *The Racial Contract*. Ithaca: Cornell University Press, 1997

——. "Revisionist Ontologies: Theorizing White Supremacy" *Social and Economic Studies* 43 (September 1994): 105–34.

Mohanty, Chandra. "Under Western Eyes: Feminist Scholarship and Colonial Discourses." In *Third World Women and the Politics of Feminism*, edited by Chandra Mohanty, Ann Russo, and Lourdes Torres. Bloomington: Indiana University Press, 1991.

Morrison, Toni. *Beloved*. New York: Penguin Books, 1988.

——. *The Bluest Eye*. New York: Washington Square Press, 1970.

——. "Home." In *The House that Race Built: Black Americans, U.S. Terrain*. Edited by Wahneema Lubiano. New York: Pantheon, 1997.

——. *Playing in the Dark: Whiteness and the Literary Imagination*. Cambridge, Mass.: Harvard University Press, 1992.

Murphy, Jeffrie. "Forgiveness and Resentment." In *Forgiveness and Mercy*, edited by Jeffrie Murphy and Jean Hampton. Cambridge: Cambridge University Press, 1988.

Nozick, Robert. *Anarchy, State, and Utopia*. New York: Basic Books, 1974.

Nukunya, G. K. *Tradition and Change in Ghana: An Introduction to Sociology*. Acera: Ghana Universities Press, 1992.

Nussbaum, Martha. "The Discernment of Perception." In *Love's Knowledge*. New York: Oxford University Press, 1990.

Nzegwu, Nkiru. "Questions of Identity and Inheritance: A Critical Review of Kwame Anthony Appiah's *In My Father's House*." *Hypatia* 11, no. 1 (winter 1996): 175–201.

Oakes, James. *The Ruling Race: A History of American Slaveholders*. New York: Vintage Books, 1983.

O'Hare, William P., Kelvin M. Pollard, Taynia L. Monn, and Mary M. Kent. "African Americans in the 1990s," *Population Bulletin* 46, no. 1 (July 1991): 2–4. Qtd. in Stephan Small, *Racialized Barriers: The Black Experience in the United States and England in the 1980's*. London: Routledge, 1994.

Okihiro, Gary Y. *Margins and Mainstreams: Asians in American History and Culture*. Seattle: University of Washington Press, 1994.

Okin, Susan Moller. *Justice, Gender, and the Family*. New York: Basic Books, 1989.

——. *Women in Western Political Thought*. Princeton: Princeton University Press, 1979.

Okonkwo, Rina. *Heroes of West Africa Nationalism*. Enugu: Delta Publications of Nigeria, 1985.

Oliver, Melvin L., and Thomas M. Shapiro. *Black Wealth/White Wealth: A New Perspective on Racial Inequality*. New York: Routledge, 1995.

Ooka Pang, V. "Ethnic Prejudice: Still Alive and Hurtful." In *Facing Racism in Education*, edited by N. Hidalgo, C. McDowell, and E. Siddle. Cambridge, Mass.: Harvard Education Review, 1990.

Outlaw, Lucius T., Jr. *On Race and Philosophy*. New York: Routledge, 1996.

——. "Toward a Critical Theory of 'Race.'" In *Anatomy of Racism*, edited by David Theo Goldberg. Minneapolis: University of Minnesota Press, 1990.

Owomoyela, Oyekan. "With Friends Like These . . . A Critique of Pervasive Anti-Africanisms in Current African Studies Epistemology and Methodology." *African Studies Review* 37, no. 3 (1994): 77–101.

Parfit, Derek. *Reasons and Persons*. Oxford: Clarendon Press, 1984.

Parrott, Les, III. *High Maintenance Relationships: How to Handle Impossible People*. Wheaton, Ill.: Tyndale, 1996.

Perham, Margery. Introduction to *The Diaries of Lord Lugard*, edited by Margery Perham. 4 vols. Evanston, Ill.: Northwestern University Press, 1959.

Piper, Adrian. "Higher Order Discrimination." In *Identity, Character, and Morality*, edited by Amélie Rorty and Owen Flanagan. Cambridge, Mass.: MIT Press, 1994.

——. "Passing for White, Passing for Black." In *Passing and the Fictions of Identity*. Edited by Ellen K. Ginsberg. Durham, N.C.: Duke University Press, 1996.

——. "Xenophobia and Kantian Rationalism." *The Philosophical Forum* 24, nos. 1–3 (fall–spring 1992–93): 209–14.

Pittman, John P. "Introduction." *Philosophical Forum* 24, nos. 1–3 (fall–spring 1992–93): 3–10.

Pratt, Minnie Bruce. "Identity: Skin Blood Heart." In *Yours in Struggle: Three Feminist Perspectives on Anti-Semitism and Racism*, by Ellen Bulkin, Minnie Bruce Pratt, and Barbara Smith. Brooklyn, N.Y.: Long Haul Press, 1984.

Preston, William. *Nietzsche as Anti-Socialist: Prophet of Bourgeois Ennoblement*. Atlantic Highlands, N.J.: Humanities Press, 1998.

——. "Nietzsche on Blacks." In Gordon 1997.

Puzzo, Dante A. "Racism and the Western Tradition," *Journal of the History of Ideas* 25 (1964): 579–86.

Quine, W. V. O. *From a Logical Point of View*. Cambridge, Mass.: Harvard University Press, 1953.

R.A.V. v City of St. Paul, 112 S. Ct. 2538 (1992).

Railton, Peter. "Marx and the Objectivity of Science." *PSA* 2 (1984): 813–25.

Rawls, John. *Political Liberalism*. New York: Columbia University Press, 1993.

——. *A Theory of Justice*. Cambridge, Mass.: Harvard University Press, 1971.

Read, Alan, ed. *The Fact of Blackness: Frantz Fanon and Visual Representation*. Seattle: Bay Press, 1996.

Roediger, David R. *Towards the Abolition of Whiteness*. London: Verso, 1994.

——. *The Wages of Whiteness: Race and the Making of the American Working Class*. New York: Verso, 1991

Roemer, Michael. *Telling Stories: Postmodernism and the Invalidation of Traditional Narrative*. Lanham, Md.: Rowman & Littlefield, 1995.

Rollins, Judith. *Between Women: Domestics and Their Employers*. Philadelphia: Temple University Press, 1985.

Rorty, Amélie. "Explaining Emotions." In *Explaining Emotions*, edited by Amélie Rorty. Berkeley : University of California Press, 1980.

Rothenberg, Paula. *Racism and Sexism: An Integrated Study*. New York: St Martin's, 1988.

Rousseau, Jean-Jacques. *Du contrat social*. Chronologie et intro. par Pierre Burgelin. Paris: Garnier-Flammarion, 1966.

Rozin, Paul. "Disgust, Contagion, and Preadaptation." Paper delivered at the Twenty-third Annual Society for Philosophy and Psychology Conference at the New School for Social Research, 6 June 1997, New York, New York.

Rozin, Paul, Jonathan Haidt, and Clark McCauley. "Disgust." In *Handbook of Emotions*, edited by Michael Lewis and Jeannette Haviland. New York: Guilford Press, 1993.

Russell, Jennifer M. "The Race/Class Conundrum and the Pursuit of Individualism in the Making of Social Polity." *Hastings Law Journal* 46, no. 5 (July 1995): 1353–1455.

Said, Edward W. *Culture and Imperialism*. New York: Knopf, 1993.

Sanneh, Lamin. *West African Christianity: The Religious Impact*. London: C. Hurst, 1983.

Sartre, Jean-Paul. *Anti-Semite and Jew*. New York: Schocken Books Inc, 1995.

———. "Black Orpheus." Translated by John MacCombie. In *"What Is Literature?" and Other Essays*, edited by Steven Unger. Cambridge, Mass.: Harvard University Press, 1988.

———. *L'être et le néant: essai d'ontologie phénoménologique*. Paris: Gallimard, 1945. Translated by Hazel Barnes as *Being and Nothingness: A Phenomenological Essay on Ontology*. New York: Philosophical Library and Washington Square Press, 1956.

Saxton, Alexander. *The Rise and Fall of the White Republic*. New York: Verso, 1990.

Scheman, Naomi. "Queering the Center by Centering the Queer: Reflections on Transsexuals and Secular Jews." In Meyers 1997.

Schutz, Alfred. *Phenomenology of the Social World*. Translated by George Walsh and Frederick Lehnhert. Evanston, Ill.: Northwestern University Press, 1967.

Scott, Daryl Michael. *Contempt and Pity: Social Policy and the Image of the Damaged Black Psyche: 1880–1996*. Chapel Hill: University of North Carolina Press, 1997.

Sedgwick, Eve Kosofsky. *Between Men: English Literature and Male Homosexual Desire*. New York: Columbia University Press, 1985.

Sekyi, Kobina. "The Future of Subject Peoples." In *Ideologies of Liberation in Black Africa, 1856–1970*, edited by J. Ayodele Langley. London: Rex Collings, 1979.

Sekyi-Otu, Ato. *Fanon's Dialectic of Experience*. Cambridge, Mass.: Harvard University Press, 1996.

———. "Form and Metaphor in Fanon's Critique of Racial and Colonial Domination." In *Domination*, edited by Alkis Kontos. Toronto: University of Toronto Press, 1975.

Serequeberhan, Tsenay. *The Hermeneutics of African Philosophy: Horizon and Discourse*. New York: Routledge, 1994.

Shapiro, David. *Neurotic Styles*. New York: Basic Books, 1965.

Sharpley-Whiting, T. Denean. *Fanon and Feminisms: Theory, Thought, Praxis*. Lanham, Md.: Rowman & Littlefield, 1997.

Sharpley-Whiting, T. Denean, and Renée T. White, eds. *Spoils of War: Women of Color, Cultures, and Revolutions*. Lanham, Md.: Rowman & Littlefield, forthcoming.

Sherman, Nancy. *The Fabric of Character*. New York: Oxford University Press, 1989.

Shipman, Pat. *The Evolution of Racism: Human Differences and the Use and Abuse of Science*. New York: Simon and Schuster, 1994.

———. "Facing Racial Differences—Together." *Chronicle of Higher Education*, 3 August 1994, B1–3.

Shklar, Judith. *Ordinary Vices*. Cambridge, Mass.: Harvard University Press, 1984.

Smith, Lillian. *Killers of the Dream*. New York: Norton, 1949.

Smith, Robert C. *Racism in the Post-Civil Rights Era: Now You See It, Now You Don't*. Albany: State University of New York Press, 1995.

Smith, Rogers M. "Beyond Tocqueville, Myrdal, and Hartz: The Multiple Traditions in America." *American Political Science Review* 87 (1993): 549–66.

Smith, Thomas S., and Gregory T. Steven. "Emergence, Self-Organization, and Social Interaction: Arousal-Dependent Structure in Social Systems." *Social Theory* 14 (1996): 131–53.

Sousa, Ronald de. *The Rationality of Emotion.* Cambridge, Mass.: MIT Press, 1991.

Stampp, Kenneth. *The Peculiar Institution: Slavery in the Ante-Bellum South.* New York: Knopf, 1956.

Steinberg, Stephen. *Turning Back: The Retreat from Racial Justice in American Thought and Policy.* Boston: Beacon, 1995.

Stocker, Michael (with Elizabeth Hegeman). *Valuing Emotions.* New York: Cambridge University Press, 1996.

Sullivan, Harry Stack. "Clinical Studies in Psychiatry." In *Clinical Studies in Psychiatry,* edited by Helen S. Perry, Mary L. Gawel, and Martha Gibbon. New York: W. W. Norton, 1956.

Sundquist, Eric J. *To Wake the Nations: Race in the Making of American Literature.* Cambridge, Mass.: Harvard University Press, Belknap Press, 1993.

Taiwo, Olufemi. "Colonialism and Its Aftermath: The Crisis of Knowledge Production." *Callaloo: A Journal of African American and African Arts and Letters* 16, no. 4 (1993): 891–908.

———. "Running Aground on Native Shores: The Saga of Colonialism and Modernity." Unpublished manuscript.

Taylor, Charles. "The Politics of Recognition." In *Multiculturalism: Examining the Politics of Recognition,* edited by Amy Gutman. Princeton: Princeton University Press, 1994.

Taylor, Henry Louis, Jr. "The Hidden Face of Racism." *American Quarterly* 47 (1995): 397.

Thomas, Laurence. "Characterizing the Evil of American Slavery and the Holocaust." In *Jewish Identity,* edited by David Theo Goldberg and Michael Krausz. Philadelphia: Temple University Press, 1993.

———. "The Evolution of Anti-Semitism." *Transition* 57 (1992): 94–108.

———. "In My Next Life I'll Be White." *Ebony* 46, no. 2 (December 1990): 84.

———. *Living Morally.* Philadelphia: Temple University Press, 1989.

———. "Rationality and Affectivity: The Metaphysics of the Moral Self." *Social Philosophy and Policy* 5 (1988): 154–72.

Tlali, Miriam. *Between Two Worlds (Muriel at Metropolitan).* Mississauga, Ontario: Copp Clark Longman, 1987.

Tocqueville, Alexis de. *Democracy in America.* Vol. 1. New York: Alfred A. Knopf, 1945.

Tong, Rosemarie. *Feminist Thought: A Comprehensive Introduction.* Boulder, Colo.: Westview, 1989.

Tully, James. *Strange Multiplicity: Constitutionalism in an Age of Diversity.* New York: Cambridge University Press, 1995.

Vargas, Raul. "Cognitive Rage." Unpublished manuscript.

Washington, Booker T. *Up from Slavery: An Autobiography.* New York: Bantam, 1970.

Wellman, David T. *Portraits of White Racism.* 2d ed. New York: Cambridge University Press, 1993.

West, Cornel. *Prophesy Deliverance!: An Afro-American Revolutionary Christianity.* Philadelphia: Westminster, 1982.

Westley, Robert. "The Rhetoric of Equal Protection." In Gordon 1997.

White, Edmund. *Genet: A Biography.* New York: Vintage, 1994.

Wilks, Ivor. *Asante in the Nineteenth Century.* London: Cambridge University Press, 1975.

———. *One Nation, Many Histories: Ghana Past and Present.* Accra, Ghana: Anansesem Publications, 1996.

Williams, Bernard. "The Self and the Future." In *Problems of the Self: Philosophical Papers, 1956–72.* Cambridge: Cambridge University Press, 1973.

Williams, Eric. *Capitalism and Slavery.* 1944. New York: Capricorn, 1966.

Wilson, R. McL. "Mani and Manichaeism." In *The Encyclopedia of Philosophy*. Vol. 5. Edited by Paul Edwards. New York: Macmillan and Free Press, 1967.

Winant, Howard. *Racial Conditions: Politics, Theory, Comparisons*. Minneapolis: University of Minnesota Press, 1994.

Wollstonecraft, Mary. *A Vindication of the Rights of Men; with A Vindication of the Rights of Woman and Hints*. 1792. Edited by Sylvana Tomaselli. New York: Cambridge University Press, 1995.

Wynter, Sylvia. "Is 'Development' a Purely Empirical Concept or Also Teleological? A Perspective from 'We the Underdeveloped.'" In *Propects for Recovery and Sustainable Development in Africa*, edited by Aguibou Y. Yasane. Westport, Conn.: Greenwood, 1996.

Zack, Naomi. "Race and Philosophic Meaning." In *Race/Sex*, edited by Naomi Zack. New York: Routledge, 1997.

——, ed. *American Mixed Race: The Culture of Microdiversity*. Lanham, Md.: Rowman and Littlefield, 1995.

Zeleza, Paul Tiyambe. *Manufacturing African Studies and Crises*. Dakar, Senegal: Codesria Book Series, 1997.

Zimra, Clarisse. "Right the Calabash: Writing History in the Female Francophone Narrative." In *Out of the Kumbla: Caribbean Women and Literature*. Trenton, N.J.: Africa World Press, 1990.

Contributors

Susan E. Babbitt teaches philosophy at Queen's University at Kingston, Ontario. She is the author of *Impossible Dreams: Rationality, Integrity and Moral Imagination* (1996) and a number of articles in moral psychology and moral epistemology.

Lawrence Blum is professor of philosophy and Distinguished Professor of Liberal Arts and Education at the University of Massachusetts, Boston. He is the author of *Friendship, Altruism, and Morality* (1980), *A Truer Liberty: Simone Weil and Marxism* (coauthor: V. J. Seidler; 1989), and *Moral Perception and Particularity* (1994), as well as many articles on race, culture, and multicultural education.

Sue Campbell teaches philosophy and women's studies at Dalhousie University, Halifax, Nova Scotia. She is the author of *Interpreting the Personal: Expression and the Formation of Feelings* (1997) and writes on the political dimensions of emotion and memory experience.

Marilyn Friedman teaches philosophy at Washington University in St. Louis. She is the author of *What Are Friends For? Feminist Perspectives on Personal Relationships and Moral Theory* (1993), the coauthor of *Political Correctness: For and Against* (1995), and the coeditor of two books, *Feminism and Community* (1995) and *Mind and Morals: Essays on Ethics and Cognitive Science* (1996).

Lewis R. Gordon teaches Afro-American studies and philosophy of religion at Brown University. He is the author of *Bad Faith and Anti-Black Racism* (1995), *Fanon and the Crisis of European Man: An Essay on Philosophy and the Human Sciences* (1995), and *Her Majesty's Other Children: Philo-*

sophical Sketches from a Neocolonial Age (1997). He is also editor of *Existence in Black: An Anthology of Black Existential Philosophy* (1997) and coeditor of *Fanon: A Critical Reader* (1996) and *Black Texts and Textuality: Constructing and De-Constructing Blackness* (1998).

David Haekwon Kim is a Ph.D. candidate at Syracuse University and the James Irvine Scholar in Philosophy at the University of San Francisco. His dissertation analyzes the role of emotion and political ecology in agent evaluation, with special attention paid to race relations and racial feelings.

Charles W. Mills is associate professor of philosophy at the University of Illinois at Chicago. His main area of interest is oppositional political theory, particularly around issues of class, gender, and race. He is the author of *The Racial Contract* (1997) and *Blackness Visible: Essays on Philosophy and Race* (1998).

Nkiru Nzegwu is an associate professor in the departments of Africana studies, art history, and philosophy at Binghamton University. She is the recipient of numerous awards and has published widely on gender issues as well as on African, African American, and African Canadian art and culture. In addition to curating major shows on African and African Diaspora art, she has recently edited two anthologies on African art: *Issues in Contemporary African Art* (1998) and *Contemporary Textures: Multidimensionality in Nigerian Art* (forthcoming).

Lucius T. Outlaw Jr. is the T. Wistar Brown Professor of Philosophy at Haverford College. His areas of specialization and research include African philosophy, African American philosophy, continental philosophy, and social and political philosophy. Several of his essays are collected in *On Race and Philosophy* (1996).

Elizabeth V. Spelman is professor of philosophy at Smith College. The author of *Inessential Woman: Problems of Exclusion in Feminist Thought* (1988) and *Fruits of Sorrow: Framing Our Attention to Suffering* (1997), she is presently at work on a book about the nature of repair.

Olufemi Taiwo is associate professor of philosophy at Loyola University. He is the author of *Legal Naturalism: A Marxist Theory of Law* (1996). He is currently working on a collaborative project, funded by the Getty Foundation, on Yoruba art and aesthetics.

Laurence M. Thomas, a regular member of the CRÉA seminar in Paris, is professor in the departments of philosophy and political science at Syracuse University, where he is also a member of the Jewish Studies Program.

Index